GUNFIGHT

GUNFIGHT

*The Battle over the Right to
Bear Arms in America*

ADAM WINKLER

W. W. NORTON & COMPANY
NEW YORK   LONDON

For information about permission to reproduce selections from this book,
write to Permissions, W. W. Norton & Company, Inc.,
500 Fifth Avenue, New York, NY 10110

For information about special discounts for bulk purchases, please contact
W. W. Norton Special Sales at specialsales@wwnorton.com or 800-233-4830

Manufacturing by Courier Westford
Book design by Lovedog Studio
Production manager: Anna Oler

Library of Congress Cataloging-in-Publication Data

Winkler, Adam.
Gunfight : the battle over the right to bear arms
in america / Adam Winkler.
p. cm.
Includes bibliographical references and index.
ISBN 978-0-393-07741-4 (hardcover)
1. Firearms—Law and legislation—United States—History.
2. Gun control—United States. 3. United States. Constitution.
2nd Amendment. I. Title.
KF3941.W56 2011
344.7305'33—dc22
2011014429

W. W. Norton & Company, Inc.
500 Fifth Avenue, New York, N.Y. 10110
www.wwnorton.com

W. W. Norton & Company Ltd.
Castle House, 75/76 Wells Street, London W1T 3QT

1 2 3 4 5 6 7 8 9 0

To Melissa, for her enduring inspiration;
and to Danny, for her smile.

Contents

PREFACE

WHEN PEOPLE HEARD I WAS WRITING A BOOK ABOUT GUNS, THEIR first question was always the same: "Is it pro-gun or anti-gun?" The goal of *Gunfight*, however, is to move beyond the stark, black-or-white, all-or-nothing arguments that have marked the gun debate in America over the past forty years or so. This book shows that we can have both an individual right to have guns for self-defense and, at the same time, laws designed to improve gun safety. The two ideas—the right to bear arms and gun control—are not mutually exclusive propositions. In fact, America has always had both.

The founding fathers enshrined the right to bear arms in the Second Amendment of the U.S. Constitution, but they also supported gun control laws so extensive that few Americans would today support them. They barred large portions of the population from possessing firearms, required many gun owners to register their weapons, and even conditioned the right on a person's political leanings. The Wild West, which occupies the very heart of America's gun culture, was filled with firearms; yet frontier towns, where the civilized folks lived, had the most restrictive and vigorously enforced gun laws in the nation. Gun control is as much a part of the history of guns in America as the Second Amendment.

The longstanding effort to balance gun rights with gun control was just one of many surprising discoveries I made while researching this book. I also found that race and racism have played a central role in the evolution of gun law. America's founders strictly prohibited slaves and even free blacks from owning guns, lest they use them for the same purpose the colonists did in 1776: to revolt against tyranny. America's most notorious racists, the Ku Klux Klan, which was formed after the Civil War, made their first objective the confiscation of all guns from newly freed blacks, who gained access to guns in service to the Union Army. In the twentieth century, gun control laws were often enacted after blacks with guns came to be perceived as a threat to whites. Ironically, it was conservatives like Ronald Reagan—still a hero to the members of the National Rifle Association—who promoted new restrictions on guns.

Indeed, the gun rights movement so familiar to modern-day Americans is a relatively new phenomenon, even though the ability of individuals to bear arms is one of our oldest constitutional rights. For much of its history, the NRA, which was founded in 1871 by a former reporter for a newspaper not known for its sympathy for gun rights, the *New York Times*, supported rather extensive gun control laws. When a wave of laws requiring a license to carry a concealed weapon swept the nation in the 1920s and 1930s, leaders of the NRA were closely involved with the drafting of the bills, which they then lobbied state governments to adopt. It wasn't until the 1970s that the NRA became the political powerhouse committed to a more extreme view of gun rights we know today.

What I learned about the Second Amendment was unexpected too. For all the attention paid to whether that ambiguously worded provision guarantees individuals a right to own guns or just protects states' right to form militias, the right to bear arms has never rested primarily on the U.S. Constitution. The vast majority of states—forty-three as of this printing—protect the right of individuals to bear arms in their own state constitutions, meaning most Americans would enjoy the right regardless of the Second Amendment. And while my research led me to conclude that the NRA was correct in reading the

Second Amendment to guarantee an individual right to bear arms, I was startled to discover that it was only recently that the NRA made the Second Amendment the heart of its mission. Although long a supporter of law-abiding individuals' access to firearms, the NRA for most of its history ignored the Second Amendment.

It was my desire to share these discoveries, which shatter so many of the myths of America's gun culture, that led me to write *Gunfight*.

PART I

CHAPTER 1

BIG GUNS AND LITTLE GUNS AT THE SUPREME COURT

JASON MCCRORY AND DAN MOTT WERE THE FIRST IN line. It was early Sunday evening, and McCrory pulled his rabbit fur hat tight around his ears to protect himself from the frigid March wind whipping down First Street in Washington, D.C. A security guard told the two men, both in their early twenties, where on the sidewalk to wait. They were soon joined by two men from Phoenix, who had come straight from the airport. Then three more people arrived, with heavy winter coats, thick scarves, woolen caps, and sleeping bags—everything they'd need to sleep on the street for two nights, waiting for Tuesday morning. McCrory and Mott curled up in blankets to get some sleep, but the weather made that all but impossible. It "was cold, cold, cold," McCrory recalled. "After about four am, it was too cold to sleep." Despite the chill, people kept arriving and joining the queue in front of the United States Supreme Court.[1]

The reason scores of people were willing to camp out on the street in front of the Supreme Court like groupies at a rock concert is captured in a single word: "guns." The justices were scheduled to hear a case about one of the most heated, polarizing issues in America. Pro-gun and anti-gun forces debate each other with passionate intensity. One side views guns as essential to personal freedom, while the other insists they are instruments of mayhem and violence. Guns are lightning rods of American culture, and in such a charged atmosphere common ground is hard to find. Every gun control proposal is an occasion for pitched battle, with the stakes portrayed as nothing less than the future of life, liberty, and justice.

When the sun rose behind the Supreme Court Building on Tuesday morning, the culture war over guns would move into the serene and sanctified halls of the nation's highest court. The justices were going to rule on a question that, incredibly, the Court had never before squarely addressed. Did the Second Amendment to the Constitution guarantee individuals the right to own guns?

The Second Amendment is maddeningly ambiguous. It provides, "A well regulated Militia, being necessary to the security of a free State, the right of the people to keep and bear Arms, shall not be infringed." Yet to many of those sleeping outside the Supreme Court Building, the words couldn't be more clear. Gun rights supporters unquestionably believed that the Second Amendment guaranteed individuals the right to own guns and imposed strict limits on gun control. Gun control advocates believed that the only guarantee the Second Amendment offered was a state's right to have a militia, like the National Guard, with no restrictions on gun control. For decades, the federal courts had sided with the gun control advocates, taking their cue from an ambiguous 1939 Supreme Court decision. Since then, America's highest court had stubbornly refused to weigh in on the meaning of the Second Amendment.

The morning of the hearing, scores of protesters, reporters, and camera crews joined the street sleepers in front of the famous marble staircase of the Supreme Court. The gathering was anything but tranquil, as both sides in the gun debate were determined to be heard. They "turned the steps and sidewalk in front of the ornate building into a theater of lively debate on citizens' rights to own firearms," reported the *Washington Post*. Some carried signs declaring "GUN CONTROL KILLS," "MILITIAS, NOT MURDER," and the ever popular "GUNS DON'T KILL PEOPLE, PEOPLE DO." Well-intentioned law students in the crowd tried to mediate the chaos with thoughtful discussions about the original meaning of the Second Amendment, but the chants of a gun rights supporter with a bullhorn drowned them out. "More guns!" the man bellowed. "Less crime!" a group of fellow gun enthusiasts shouted back. "More guns!" "Less crime!"

Gun control proponents in the crowd tried to break up the rhythm. They whispered something to one another and then waited for the man with the bullhorn to repeat his chant. "More guns!" he yelled, prompting the anti-gun people to scream out in unison, "More death!" Yet, as in gun politics generally, their voices were no match for the better-coordinated, more-intense voices on the pro-gun side, which simply hollered even louder.

It was March 18, 2008, and everyone was certain the case on that day's docket, *District of Columbia v. Heller*, would be a landmark. Usually the spectator seats in the Supreme Court sit empty, but Jason McCrory and Dan Mott knew that this was no ordinary case. The Court makes seats available to the public on a first-come, first-served basis, and the many people who camped out on the street didn't want to miss out. The first fifty in line would be awarded seats. By the morning of the hearing, however, hundreds of people were lined up around the block—so many that the Court mercifully decided to allow them all to come in and watch for three minutes each. Anyone who had braved the elements deserved to witness at least some of this historic event.

Wearing a helmet over his silver hair and a puffy down parka on top of his dark blue suit, Walter Dellinger pedaled his titanium

Litespeed bicycle past the crowd, his tie dangling loosely from his neck. The sixty-six-year-old Dellinger was a former solicitor general of the United States—the federal government's chief advocate before the Supreme Court—and he currently headed the appellate division of one of the nation's premier law firms, O'Melveny and Myers. When it came to Supreme Court lawyers, Dellinger was among the very best. He had taught constitutional law for over forty years and argued twenty cases in the nation's highest court. In 2008 alone, Dellinger had three cases before the justices. *Heller* was one of them.

Dellinger parked his bike on the empty rack at the north side of the Supreme Court Building. Although the team of lawyers Dellinger worked with on the *Heller* case came to the Court by more prosaic means, Dellinger preferred to ride. It cleared his mind and sharpened his focus. He could practice his argument in his head while he rode, without being distracted by the telephone ringing or an urgent email. On his ride this morning, he rehearsed his argument that the Second Amendment did not protect an individual right to bear arms outside of the militia. Dellinger's client was the District of Columbia, whose gun control laws were being challenged in the *Heller* case. D.C. outlawed handgun ownership and required that all long guns—rifles and shotguns—be kept disassembled or secured with a trigger lock. The District had the strictest gun control laws in the nation, and it was Dellinger's job to keep them in place.[2]

Arguing the other side was Alan Gura, a Georgetown Law School graduate in his midthirties whose task would be to convince the justices that the Second Amendment guaranteed the right of individuals to own guns. He wasn't a constitutional law expert like Dellinger, however, nor was he a partner at a big-name law firm. Gura practiced law out of a small, one-person office in Alexandria, Virginia, not far from his home. He had no paralegals or even a secretary to help him. His practice was remarkable mainly for being exactly what one wouldn't expect of a lawyer arguing a landmark constitutional law case in the Supreme Court. He spent most of his time suing police officers for abuse and handled copyright and trademark cases on the side. He had never before argued a case at the U.S. Supreme Court.

Gura arrived at the Court on foot, having spent the preceding night in a Hyatt hotel a few blocks away. Although he lived with his wife and young son less than ten miles from the Supreme Court, Gura didn't want to take any chances with his commute. He couldn't afford to show up late for what would certainly be one of the most important days of his career. Not when the weight of the gun rights movement was resting on his shoulders.[3]

The National Rifle Association wasn't happy that Alan Gura was carrying that burden. In fact, the NRA never wanted this case to be brought at all. In 2002, when rumors first circulated that a lawsuit might be filed against the D.C. gun laws, the NRA did everything it could to try to stop it. When Gura refused to quit, the NRA tried to hijack his case and replace him with its own, more-experienced lawyers. When that failed, the NRA lobbied Congress to pass a law overturning the D.C. gun laws, which would have rendered Gura's case moot. The NRA wasn't just trying to protect its turf. The nation's leading gun rights organization was dead set against a Supreme Court ruling on the meaning of the Second Amendment.

The leaders of the NRA thought Gura's lawsuit was too risky. They dreaded the prospect of losing, of having the Supreme Court declare in no uncertain terms that the Constitution didn't protect an individual's right to bear arms. Such a ruling would be especially devastating from *this* Supreme Court, which was politically conservative and had a strong majority of justices, seven of nine, appointed by Republican presidents. Gura speculated that the NRA was also worried he might win. The NRA's most effective fund-raising strategy was to threaten gun owners that the government was coming to get their guns. *The gun grabbers are out to destroy the Second Amendment. Your donation will enable us to fight them off. Contribute now, or your right to bear arms will be nothing more than a distant memory.* That strategy helped make the NRA one of the most influential interest groups in America. Gura suspected the NRA was fearful its fund-raising machine might grind to a halt if the Supreme Court held that the Second Amendment guaranteed an individual's right to own guns.

Gura walked around the north side of the building, past the bike rack and to the separate entrance reserved for special visitors. Only parties appearing before the Court, accredited journalists, members of the Supreme Court bar, and invited guests of the justices were permitted to use this door. Security was still tight, even for special guests. Gura took off his overcoat, placed his briefcase on the X-ray machine's conveyor belt, and emptied his pockets of loose change, keys, and his iPhone. Like everyone else, he too had to pass through a metal detector. This was, after all, the Supreme Court of the United States: no guns allowed.

•   •   •

EMBLAZONED ON the exterior of the former NRA offices at 1600 Rhode Island Avenue in Washington, D.C., was a quotation from the Second Amendment: "THE RIGHT OF THE PEOPLE TO KEEP AND BEAR ARMS SHALL NOT BE INFRINGED." For years, the gun lobby has used the Second Amendment as a rallying cry in its fight against gun control. Portraying themselves as inheritors of our founding fathers' legacy, many in the gun rights community promote a hard-line view of gun rights that casts even modest gun laws as illegitimate, unconstitutional burdens. They oppose nearly every gun control proposal because any law regulating guns threatens to put us on a slippery slope to involuntary disarmament. Pass this law, and eventually all civilian guns will be confiscated. Perhaps this explains why the first clause of the Second Amendment, the part that refers to the necessity of a "well regulated Militia," was omitted from the NRA's display. To the gun lobby, the Second Amendment is all right, with little room for regulation.

The NRA wasn't always a vigorous opponent of gun control. For most of its history, the organization promoted reasonable gun safety laws. In fact, the Second Amendment historically was of little importance to the NRA; that provision was rarely mentioned in the organization's official publications before the 1960s. Inspired by a wave of gun control laws and promoted by the rising conservative movement that would eventually propel Ronald Reagan to the presidency, the

NRA became increasingly militant. After a group of anti–gun control hard-liners staged a coup at the NRA's annual meeting in 1977, the NRA was transformed into a political powerhouse devoted to a rigid view of the Second Amendment.

The gun lobby insists that the right to own a gun, like the right to free speech, should be robust, unfettered, and uninhibited by government regulation. Because every gun law is a step toward total disarmament, the most extreme pro-gun forces oppose widely popular laws such as background checks on gun purchasers and even restrictions on civilian ownership of machine guns. Their distaste for compromise makes effective gun safety laws extremely difficult to get passed. Even after a dozen children are murdered at Columbine High School and a congresswoman is shot at a constituents event in Arizona, many in the gun rights community fight to prevent even modest reforms from being enacted. Almost any gun control infringes the Constitution, in their view, and nearly every law puts us on the inevitable pathway to civilian disarmament.

More worrisome still, an absolutist view of the right to bear arms became an organizing principle for fringe paramilitary groups like the Michigan Militia in the 1990s. Opposition to gun control stirred one radical, Timothy McVeigh, to declare war on the federal government, leading to his bombing of the Murrah Federal Building in Oklahoma City—prior to 9/11, the worst act of domestic terrorism in American history. Of course, gun rights groups bore no responsibility for his treason. The two are linked instead by an unreasonable view of the Second Amendment that casts nearly any gun safety measure as an infringement of the sacred rights of individuals.

The other side of the gun debate is prone to its own brand of extremism. "Gun grabbers," as they are called in certain circles, will support seemingly any form of gun control, no matter how unlikely the law is to taper gun violence. Their ultimate goal is to eliminate all privately owned firearms—or, at least, make the United States more like England, where handguns are illegal and all other guns are rare. This group became vocal in American politics in the late 1960s, reflecting the liberal idealism of the Great Society: government regulation could solve our problems, eliminate poverty, and reduce crime. Gun grabbers deny the existence of the right to bear arms because such a right might interfere with the gun control they believe America so desperately needs. The Second Amendment, they insist, is only about state militias and says nothing about individual gun ownership. For them, the Second Amendment is all regulation and no right.

Despite the utopian dreams of some gun control advocates, guns in America aren't going anywhere. A gun-free America is a profoundly unrealistic goal. There are approximately 280 million guns in the United States, almost one per person. And no matter what laws are passed, many gun owners feel far too strongly about their guns to give them up. The former NRA president and Academy Award–winning actor Charlton Heston was speaking for millions when he famously declared, "From my cold, dead hands!" Disarmament is no more likely to succeed than Prohibition or the War on Drugs—other unsuccessful efforts to eliminate small, easy-to-conceal items that people feel passionate about.[4]

Nevertheless, disarmament was the motive behind the D.C. laws challenged in the *Heller* case. The D.C. city council hoped that its ban on handguns would trigger a nationwide movement to eliminate civilian ownership of guns. The folly of its idealism was highlighted when, a decade or so after enactment of its strict gun laws, the District came to be known as the "murder capital of America." Americans are not likely to adopt effective gun safety laws until they come to grips with the same simple fact the D.C. city council ignored: guns are here to stay. Until that one fact is recognized, the gun debate will continue to spiral outwards toward the extremes.

In the absence of any short-term hope of disarmament, gun control extremists throw their support behind poorly designed and predictably ineffective reforms. The statistics that clearly suggest bans on handguns and assault weapons don't reduce crime—or even the number of handguns and assault weapons in circulation—don't seem to matter. Their taste for any and all flavors of gun control, even ineffectual ones, also breeds further distrust among gun owners who think these laws are really aimed at harassing them. From the perspective of gun lovers, if a gun law doesn't reduce crime or violence, then the true objective must be to make owning guns difficult.

To be sure, many gun owners and many people who support gun control defy these extremes. Yet theirs are not the voices usually heard in the gun debate. Instead, the debate is dominated by more strident groups: one set on getting rid of the guns, the other determined to stop guns from being restricted in even modest ways.

The extremism that marks America's current gun debate reflects a larger polarization of American politics over the past thirty years. From abortion to healthcare, from same-sex marriage to taxes, Americans are so profoundly divided over political issues that the separation is becoming nearly impossible to bridge. Even new technology—and its ability to instantly access more sources of information than ever before—has not helped close the gap. Studies show that people overwhelmingly choose sources that align ideologically with their already established views. Even straightforward factual questions are filtered through political biases; when people are asked whether inflation rose or decreased under a given president, those from the opposition party report far worse inflation than actually occurred. The facts don't matter, only the political points scored. Political discourse has grown so uncivil that one's opponents aren't just mistaken or wrong in their policy choices; they are "fascists" (as the left liked to call George W. Bush) or "socialists" (as the right likes to call Barack Obama) seeking to ruin the county and trash our liberties. It's hard to compromise with someone whose goal is destruction of everything you hold dear.[5]

Despite the political cleave between gun rights proponents and gun controllers, in one sense they share the same view of the right to keep and bear arms. Both pro-gun and anti-gun hard-liners insist that the right to bear arms is fundamentally inconsistent with gun control. Gun rights advocates claim that nearly every gun control infringes on their individual right to bear arms and must therefore be unlawful. Gun control proponents also believe that an individual right to bear arms is inconsistent with gun control. That's why they deny the existence of the right in the first place. Each side in the gun debate reaches different conclusions, but they begin with the same premise: we can't have both an individual right to own guns and gun control. We must choose one or the other.

•   •   •

THE HISTORY and tradition of the right to bear arms in the United States tell a different story. Gun rights and gun control are not only compatible; they have lived together since the birth of America. Despite the controversy over the meaning of the Second Amendment, Americans have always had the right to keep and bear arms as a matter of state constitutional law. Today, nearly every state has such a provision in its own constitution, clearly protecting an individual right unattached to militia service. In fact, it is one of the oldest, most firmly established rights in America—regardless of the Second Amendment.

At the same time, we've also always had gun control. The founding fathers instituted gun control laws so intrusive that no self-respecting member of today's NRA board of directors would support them. Early Americans denied the right to gun ownership even to law-abiding people if they failed a political test of loyalty to the Revolution. The founders also declared that free white men were members of the militia and, as such, were forced to appear with their guns at public "musters" where government officials would inspect the weapons and register them on public rolls. When pressing public necessity demanded it, the founding fathers were also willing to impress guns from law-abiding citizens, even if those citizens were left without guns to defend themselves from a criminal attack.

Unlike the unreasonable right to bear arms promoted by extremists in the gun debate, a reasonable right to bear arms has always been available to Americans—one that balances gun rights with gun control. Although the precise equilibrium has always been in flux, changing in response to the times, the story of guns in America is about regulation and right. We don't have to choose between fully automatic machine guns and water pistols. The history of guns in

America shows that we can take a middle course, recognizing the right to bear arms and the legitimacy of many forms of gun control.

This book shows how generations of Americans have struggled to find the proper balance between gun rights and regulation—and highlights how gun control, not just guns, transformed and shaped the American identity. When seen from this angle, much of what people commonly believe about guns is revealed to be wrong or incomplete. America, it is often said, has a gun culture. We've heard that so many times that it's become a cliché. It is less well recognized, however, that America also has a gun *control* culture. The frontier towns of the Wild West, where Hollywood tells us shootouts were common at high noon, in reality had extensive gun control and little gun violence. Town ordinances in the famous gun havens of the West, places like Tombstone, Arizona, and Dodge City, Kansas, required newcomers to hand their guns over to the sheriff or leave them with their horses at the stables on the outskirts of town. You are certain to see more gunfights in a two-hour movie about the Wild West than you would have seen in a year on the dusty streets of Deadwood, South Dakota.

When the nuanced history of gun rights and gun control is examined, odd contradictions and startling surprises abound. The South, today a bastion of strong gun rights, was the region where some of the earliest, most burdensome gun control laws in American history were first enacted. In many ways, the gun control laws of the South in the nineteenth century were stricter than those of the same states today. Surprisingly, many of those early laws were designed not to keep guns out of the hands of blacks but to reduce violence among white men. To be sure, like so much in America, gun rights and gun control have also been tainted by racism. Few people realize it, but the Ku Klux Klan began as a gun control organization; after the Civil War, the Klan and other violent racist groups sought to reaffirm white supremacy, which required confiscating the guns blacks had obtained for the first time during the conflict. To prevent blacks from fighting back, the night riders set out to achieve complete black disarmament. In the 1960s, race was also central to a new wave of gun control laws, which were backed by liberals and even some conservatives, like Ronald Reagan.

Enacted to disarm politically radical urban blacks, like the Black Panthers, these laws sparked a backlash that became the modern gun rights movement—a movement that, ironically, is largely white, rural, and politically conservative.

The debate over guns is usually portrayed as a cultural battle between urban and rural, with the latter seeing guns as part of their cultural heritage of hunting. In fact, one of the most powerful elements in today's gun rights movement represents urban gun owners: people who value firearms as a last line of defense against criminals. Self-defense, not hunting, is at the core of the right to bear arms; that helps explain why so many people fight so hard for their guns and why Americans' guns could never be successfully confiscated. If it's hard to persuade a hunter to give up the rifle his father gave him for his twelfth birthday, imagine the difficulty of persuading a person to disarm when he thinks his very life is at stake.

The dualism of gun rights and gun control was on clear display the day Alan Gura and Walter Dellinger had their own gunfight at the Supreme Court. They and the nine justices would debate the meaning of the Second Amendment and the history of gun rights in America at the most reasoned, intellectual level. At the same time, security at the Court mandated that no actual guns be brought into the building. Having a gun in the Supreme Court was not the exercise of a fundamental right, but an unwelcome threat of violence. On the day of the Supreme Court hearing, as it has been throughout the American experience, the right to bear arms was balanced by gun regulation.

Gunfight is about that symbiotic relationship between gun rights and gun control in America and the landmark lawsuit that brought the Second Amendment to the Supreme Court for the first time in seventy years.

CHAPTER 2

"GUN GRABBERS"

ON A SUNDAY IN JUNE 1975, TWO MEN BROKE INTO THE back room of the Hechinger Hardware store in Marlow Heights, Maryland, a working-class community just across the southeastern border of Washington, D.C. Before they could loot the safe, however, two uniformed security guards who were making their rounds suddenly appeared. What began as an ordinary robbery quickly spiraled out of control. The robbers pulled out their handguns and shouted "Don't move!" and then started shooting. The unarmed guards ran the other way and shouted warnings to the customers in the store before being chased into the parking lot. As John Hechinger, the owner of the store, recalled, "one of the gunmen climbed on top of a car hood, and with two hands on the pistol fired away at one of the guards until he hit him." The robbers fled the scene but were arrested later that day. One of the two "men" turned out to be a fourteen-year-old boy.[1]

John Hechinger was not only the owner of the hardware store but also the first chairman of the Council of the District of Columbia, the city council of the nation's capital. Two years before the robbery, in December 1973, Congress established home rule for the District of Columbia, giving the city's residents the self-governance they had long sought. It allotted the council and mayor power to pass ordinary laws governing the District, rather than having to rely on Congress to do it for them. At Hechinger's urging, one of the first major laws the council considered was a gun control law: a ban on the civilian possession and sale of handguns in the city.[2]

In hearings over the proposed gun ban, Hechinger recounted the story of the botched robbery to dramatize the need to eliminate guns in D.C. In the early 1970s, the nation's capital was suffering under the weight of violent crime and poverty. Just blocks away from the broad avenues and gleaming marble advertised in postcards and guidebooks were blighted ghettos overwhelmed by guns and crumbling infrastructure. Most American cities were experiencing "white flight" as middle-class whites fled to the suburbs; in D.C., blacks were fleeing too. "I got sick of all those street dudes harassing me, and that school board making all the noise instead of getting my kids a decent education," said David James, an African American postal worker. "So I packed up and moved out." Welfare rolls, venereal disease, and infant mortality rates were all skyrocketing. *Fortune* magazine called D.C. "one of the sickest cities" in America.[3]

Nationwide, the illicit use of guns was soaring. In 1974 alone, there were over 325,000 reported incidents of firearms being used illegally to assault or threaten citizens—more than 890 per day—a disproportionate share of which were in the nation's capital. Too many of those episodes involved handguns; approximately 75 percent of firearm-related murders were committed with a handgun. As one study reported, "These data indicate clearly that firearms, especially handguns, are major instruments of murder, robbery, and aggravated assault." Although no other major city had a ban on handguns, the acute desperation of urban life in D.C. persuaded lawmakers like John Hechinger to take a stand.[4]

Like every other gun control proposal in recent memory, the D.C. gun ban had its vigorous opponents. The National Rifle Association sent out a mass mailing to its members in D.C. calling on them to stop the council. As if a ban on handguns wasn't bad enough, the mailing misrepresented the governing law on handguns in the District; a few days later, an NRA spokesman was forced to apologize for the errors. Douglas Moore, a member of the NRA and the one council member opposed to the ban, warned that the Ku Klux Klan was enjoying a "resurgence" in the neighboring states of Maryland and Virginia. The ban, he said, "will make it difficult for the people of this city—the majority of whom are black—to defend themselves." The other council members, most of whom were black, ridiculed the threat of an imminent Klan invasion.[5]

The law that finally passed in July 1976 banned handguns and required shotguns and rifles to be kept in an inoperable state, either disassembled or secured with a trigger lock. Although long guns could be assembled for specified "recreational" purposes, like hunting, the law banned the use of such firearms for non-recreational purposes, like self-defense. In other words, even if you owned a shotgun, you couldn't use it against a burglar coming through the window. This was obviously too much for the NRA. The same day that the D.C. mayor, Walter Washington, signed the law, the nation's preeminent gun rights organization announced a boycott of the city. Its next annual meeting of the membership, scheduled to take place in D.C. in April 1977, would be moved to Cincinnati.[6]

A young first-term Republican congressman representing southern Texas decided to try to overturn the ban. A doctor before running for elected office, Ron Paul had a deep antipathy to big government—so much so that his medical practice had refused on ideological grounds to accept Medicare payments. His election to Congress in 1976 was an early sign of one of the most important changes in the American political landscape, for he was the first Republican ever elected from his part of Texas, where Democrats had enjoyed one-party rule ever since Lincoln, a Republican, conquered the South. In the years that followed Paul's election, the South would transform into the red-state stronghold of the Republican Party.[7]

Even though D.C. enjoyed self-government, Congress retained

the power to revise the laws of the District. Since 1976 was an election year, many in Congress didn't want to risk touching the volatile issue of gun control. Paul was the exception, and he managed to push through the House a proposal limiting the city council's power to change D.C.'s gun laws. A favorable Senate vote and signature by President Gerald Ford soon followed. Although Paul's intent was to reverse the new D.C. gun laws, the wording of his law was sloppy enough that it could be read to limit only the council's power in the future, rather than apply retroactively. And that's exactly how the lawyers for the District interpreted it. By the time Congress recognized the drafting mistake, the political will for reversing the D.C. gun ban had dissipated.[8]

John Hechinger and the other supporters of D.C.'s gun ban knew that the law would not have much of an impact on gun crime. Criminals could easily cross the border into Maryland and Virginia, where gun laws were far more lenient. A study at the time conducted by the Bureau of Alcohol, Tobacco, and Firearms—the main federal agency charged with enforcing federal gun laws, now called the Bureau of Alcohol, Tobacco, Firearms, and Explosives and known colloquially as ATF—found that 80 percent of guns seized in D.C. crime investigations had been purchased in other states. The District was flooded with out-of-state guns, and the council members knew it. Banning the possession and sale of handguns wasn't going to stop the crime wave devastating D.C. On the day the council voted 12–1 in favor of the handgun ban, council member Marion Barry, a supporter of the ban, made a frank acknowledgment. "What we are doing today will not take one gun out of the hands of one criminal."[9]

So why did the council adopt the gun ban even though everyone knew it would not be effective? Because the idealism of gun control proponents knows few boundaries. The council members thought the D.C. law would spark a nationwide trend to ban all handguns in America—if not all guns period. "My expectation was that this being Washington, it would kind of spread to other places," recalled the council member Nadine Waters. At his press conference the day the bill was signed into law, Mayor Washington said, "We know this bill is not a panacea; it is just the beginning of a long process in this nation." The *Washington Post* editorialized that although the ban wouldn't have much of an effect on crime in D.C., it was "worth every bit of effort that has gone into it" because it would send a "message" to Congress that the time had come for national handgun legislation. Hechinger, who was also on the board of Handgun Control, Inc., a major gun control advocacy organization, stated it simply: "We have to do away with the guns."[10]

•   •   •

GUN CONTROL diehards share John Hechinger's goal. They hope that the United States can eventually become more like the United Kingdom, where all handguns are banned and long guns (shotguns and rifles) are uncommon. "The time has come for us to disarm the individual citizen," said former New York City Police Commissioner Patrick Murphy. In 1991, the Communitarian Network, a nonprofit organization founded by the sociologist Amitai Etzioni and committed to repairing the moral fabric of America, endorsed "domestic disarmament" in its own platform, supported by mainstream public and political figures like Henry Cisneros, who would go on to become President Clinton's secretary of housing and urban development; Newton Minow, former chairman of the Federal Communications Commission; and Albert Shanker, then president of the American Federation of Teachers. Mass disarmament was also becoming popular in the media, and according to Juan Williams, a columnist for the *Washington Post* and later a Fox News commentator, "We should be talking about getting rid of guns in this country."[11]

However nice some might imagine life in a society without any guns to be, disarmament is an unrealistic goal. There are just too many guns and too many gun owners unwilling to give them up. Over four million new guns are bought each year. Gun are in approximately 40 percent of homes and, though more common in rural communities than in urban ones, are found in every city, every town, and every suburb in the country. The United Kingdom, where the gun lobby is almost nonexistent, adopted strict gun control before an unmanageable number of firearms wound up in private hands. Historically, game laws restricted gun ownership by commoners, and, by the late 1930s, any person who wanted to possess a handgun or a rifle had to obtain a license, which would not be issued for reasons of ordinary, personal self-defense. When the U.K. finally banned handguns in the mid-1990s, there were fewer than two hundred thousand gun owners (compared with more than eighty million in America). America's guns are simply too common for a British-style gun ban to be feasible.[12]

Americans, inspired by the folklore of the frontier and ideologically disposed to personal liberty, love their guns too much. In 1989, California passed a law requiring all assault weapons to be registered within a year. By the end of that time, less than 20 percent of the estimated number of assault weapons in the state were registered. In a survey of gun owners in Illinois, 73 percent said they would not comply with a law requiring them to turn in their guns. Taking away those guns by force would also be impractical, because it would require sending out the police to conduct door-to-door searches for weapons. Even those who favor vigorous gun control aren't likely to support such a profound invasion of privacy. Just in case, however, a host of books available on Amazon.com teach how to hide guns in underground caches so that authorities would not be able find them.[13]

Efforts to ban small, easily hidden items that people feel strongly attached to have been tried before. In 1920, the Eighteenth Amendment to the Constitution went into effect, outlawing the manufacture, sale, and transportation of "intoxicating liquors." Prohibition, it was thought, would stop men from beating their wives, reduce street crime, and minimize absenteeism at work. The law, however, fueled the creation of a huge black market for alcohol—a market readily serviced by organized crime—and pushed the consumption of liquor underground into speakeasies. More recently, the War on Drugs has been a failure in getting rid of marijuana, cocaine, and other illegal drugs. All the money spent over the past thirty years on law enforcement and housing drug criminals in prison has left the staggering reality that 41 percent of Americans have tried illegal drugs and that sixteen million Americans use them in a given month. Worse yet, the attempt to rid society of drugs has spurred the growth of gangs, which like the mob in the 1920s, service public demand. There already exists a black market for guns, where felons barred from buying and owning guns can find them. If all guns were outlawed, the black market expansion alone would be so overwhelming that the ban would end up doing more harm than good.[14]

Why are gun owners so unwilling to comply with gun bans? One answer is found in the story of Tom Palmer, an openly gay man who encountered trouble one night in 1982 walking down the street with a friend in San Jose, California. Palmer had the misfortune of passing by a group of men who decided that it would be a good night for some gay bashing. "They stood up, 19 or 20 young guys, followed us," Palmer recalled. The men started shouting anti-gay epithets. "They told us, 'We're going to kill you.' 'They'll never find the bodies.'" Palmer and his friend did what thousands of years of conditioned behavior had taught them to do when faced with overwhelming danger: they started to run. Then Palmer suddenly stopped, remembering what he was toting around. "I turned around and showed them the business end of a pistol." He warned the men that if they took another step, he'd shoot. They didn't take another step. The leader of the hoodlums quickly became a fan of gun control. "Do you have a permit for that?" he asked.

Palmer's confrontation ended with no one getting hurt. "Merely having a gun, being able to display it when I was threatened, saved my life," says Palmer. To many people who don't own firearms, a gun is just a killing machine. To Tom Palmer, a gun is a lifesaver. In San Jose at the time, it was illegal for Palmer to carry that gun without a license, and he didn't have one. Palmer surely doesn't have any regrets about violating the law that night.[15]

Self-defense is one of the main reasons gun owners won't ever give up their guns, but no one knows precisely how often a gun is brandished or fired in self-defense. In academic circles, the statistics are subject to heated debate. Estimates range from 100,000 to 2.5 million "defensive uses" of guns per year. Whatever the actual number, there are clearly a great many incidents in which guns are brandished to save lives or stop crimes. Even the low estimates suggest that guns are actively used for protection hundreds of times per day. In an ideal world, the police would be there to help. If the police aren't around, however, a gun can be a potential victim's last line of defense.[16]

For years, the Democratic Party has misunderstood why guns are so important to gun owners. In 1968 and 1972, the party's platform made no mention of the right to bear arms but called for the passage of strict new gun control laws. The rise of the New Right, however, propelled Richard Nixon to the White House and forced the Democrats to soften their position. Being vehemently anti-gun was increasingly understood to be costly on election day. While still calling for controls on handguns, the 1976 party platform affirmed "the right of sportsmen to possess guns for purely hunting and target-shooting purposes." That didn't resonate with gun owners, many of whom believed guns to be valuable for personal self-defense, not only recreational shooting. Gun owners reasonably suspect that if the right to bear arms is justified merely as a hobby, it won't be protected for long.[17]

According to Abigail Kohn, an academic who has studied America's gun culture, "The probability of getting rid of guns in America is practically zero." So long as there are murderers, rapists, and gay bashers, people will want guns to protect against them. Guns are permanent in America. This fact—perhaps the most important for modern gun policy in the United States—is one the D.C. gun ban supporters failed to grasp.[18]

•   •   •

THE FALSE and exaggerated claims that underlie so much of today's gun debate were highlighted the day in 2001 when Michael Bellesiles, a historian at Emory University, came to the University of California at Irvine to give a lecture on the history of guns in America. Professors are often invited to speak at other universities, but usually the audience for such "talks," as they are known in academic circles, is only a handful of professors and a graduate student or two. Bellesiles, however, drew a large crowd. Humanities Lecture Hall at Irvine was packed and included many people from outside the academy. Even more unusual than the size of the audience were the protesters. Four men, one in a flak jacket, another with a shaved head, stood outside passing out brochures entitled "The Lies of Michael Bellesiles."[19]

For Bellesiles, the protests were nothing new. Ever since the publication of his book *Arming America* the year before, he had given campus lectures all over the country with protesters as a constant presence. Both the invitations and the protests stemmed from the surprising history recounted in Bellesiles's book. *Arming America* argued that guns in early America were rare and that most of the people who owned guns did not keep them in good working order. Early America, Bellesiles concluded, did not have a gun culture.

If Bellesiles's book had been written by a gun control organization, it would have been taken as advocacy. Bellesiles, however, wasn't a staffer at a gun control group. He was an academic, a tenured professor of history, committed to objective research based on data. His view of guns in the decades immediately after the Revolution was backed by a rigorous methodology that yielded hard facts.

Bellesiles conducted an incredibly detailed study of probate records from the late 1700s and early 1800s. When someone dies, his estate goes into "probate," a legal proceeding in which all of that person's property is identified and divvied up among his surviving relatives. Bellesiles dug through piles of old probate records in libraries across the country and discovered that only a fraction, about 15 percent, included guns in the itemized inventories of decedents' property. More than half the guns in probate inventories were listed as damaged or inoperable. Meticulous and painstaking research clearly showed that guns were extremely rare in early America.[20]

The implications of Bellesiles's findings weren't academic. They meant that the NRA's view of the Second Amendment was wrong. Ever since the late 1960s, a debate has raged over the meaning of the Second Amendment to the Constitution. Three in four Americans tell pollsters that, like the NRA, they believe that the Second Amendment was intended to protect the right of individuals to own guns.

Yet federal courts had taken a sharply different view. For over seventy years, the federal courts said that the Second Amendment protected only the right of states to form militias, like the National Guard. In what came to be known as the "militia theory" of the Second Amendment, the courts ruled that the provision was not intended to protect an individual right to bear arms for self-protection.[21]

The reasoning behind the militia theory was that when the Constitution was originally sent to the states for ratification in the late 1780s, many people objected that it would give the federal government too much power. One especially worrisome threat was that the federal government would take over the state militias and disarm them. This was a grave concern since the founding generation did not have standing armies, and states relied primarily on armed citizens organized into militias for military defense. Moreover, the memory was fresh of English kings that had tried to disarm dissenters, who were then unable to fight back against unjust royal decrees. Having themselves just experienced the tyranny of the Crown, the American revolutionaries were not about to allow a president to do the same. The Second Amendment was part of the solution, because it prevented the federal government from disarming the state militias.

The militia theory of the Second Amendment meant that the amendment's right "to keep and bear Arms" belonged to "the people" of the states as a collective body. As a result, it offered no assurances to an individual of access to guns for personal reasons like self-defense. Short of efforts by the federal government to disarm the state militias, the amendment said nothing about gun control. As state militias eventually became irrelevant as means of national defense, so too did the Second Amendment.[22]

The Supreme Court never officially endorsed the militia theory of the Second Amendment, but had inspired it nevertheless. In a 1939 case, *United States v. Miller* (discussed in greater detail later), the Court said that Congress could ban sawed-off shotguns because such weapons bore no relationship to service in state militias. While the opinion in that case never held that individuals don't have a right to own guns or that only militias were protected by the amendment, in the ensuing decades the lower federal courts interpreted the opinion to back the militia theory. The Supreme Court never objected. Despite numerous opportunities after *Miller*, the justices declined for nearly seventy years to rule on any Second Amendment cases. Their inaction gave further credence to the militia theory, which in time was endorsed by nearly all the federal circuits.[23]

At times, individual justices did explicitly support the militia theory. In 1991, former Chief Justice Warren Burger, a conservative Nixon appointee, said in an interview on PBS that the claim of the NRA and other gun rights proponents that the Second Amendment protected an individual right to own guns was "one of the greatest pieces of fraud—I repeat the word 'fraud'—on the American public by special interest groups that I have ever seen in my lifetime." At his Irvine lecture, Michael Bellesiles explained how his book provided empirical support for Chief Justice Burger's charge. Guns were so rare in the founding era that they could not have been valued as a means of individual self-defense.[24]

Thanks to the scientific rigor of Bellesiles's historical study, *Arming America* earned rave reviews. The book's political implications were easily and eagerly recognized. Although historians usually disavow any interest in contemporary problems—a good work of history is sufficiently important for shedding light on the past—the modern-day dispute over the Second Amendment was never far from the surface in reviews of Bellesiles's book. In a glowing assessment in the *New York Review of Books*, Edmund S. Morgan, emeritus professor of history at Yale University, wrote, "Bellesiles will have done us all a service if his book reduces the credibility of the fanatics who endow the Founding Fathers with posthumous membership in what has become the cult of the gun." A review in the *Journal of American History* commended Bellesiles for attacking "the central myth behind the National Rifle Association's interpretation of the Second Amendment."[25]

Gun control proponents were gleeful. Despite the strength of the militia theory in the federal courts, for years gun controllers were confronted with the Second Amendment every time they proposed a new measure to enhance gun safety. "You can't restrict guns," they would be told by pro-gun politicians. "Individuals have a right to bear arms." Because that supposed right was the main obstacle to the enactment of gun control, advocates insisted that individuals did not enjoy that right. Bellesiles's book provided such a sterling piece of evidence that the Second Amendment was not about personal gun ownership that it was impossible to ignore.

When *Arming America* was awarded the prestigious Bancroft Prize, given annually by Columbia University to the most distinguished scholarly works in the field of American history, Handgun Control, Inc., John Hechinger's gun control organization, released a statement celebrating Bellesiles's achievement. "The National Rifle Association and its allies rely on a mythology about guns and the Second Amendment because they have few legitimate, rational arguments. By exposing the truth about gun ownership in early America, Michael Bellesiles has removed one more weapon in the gun lobby's arsenal of fallacies against common-sense gun laws."[26]

There was just one problem with Bellesiles's finding about the rarity of guns in early America. It wasn't true.

•   •   •

WHEN MICHAEL BELLESILES finished his prepared remarks at Irvine, the floor was opened to questions from the audience. The first question came from one of the four protesters who had been handing out leaflets prior to the talk. "You say the probate records show very few guns, and argue that this proves people in early America didn't have guns. But when my father died, there was nothing in his will about his guns—even though he owned four of them. But he had told me he wanted me to have them, and now I do. Are probate records really a good source of evidence on gun ownership?"

"I'm sure you're right about your father's will," Bellesiles replied. "But wills in the eighteenth century were different. People didn't own very many things compared to today, and their wills contained a detailed list of everything they had, down to the knives and forks. There are other problems with probate records—they are biased in many ways. But I'm confident that if an eighteenth-century man owned a gun, it would be in his will. Remember that we're talking here about wills in the 1700s."

Another one of the protesters raised his hand and Bellesiles called on him. "I want to ask about your use of probate records," the second protester said. "You say probate records showed few guns, but my father owned several guns that did not appear in his will when he died. My brother and I divided them up." The members of the audience looked around bewildered. Clearly nothing Bellesiles could say was going to satisfy the gun enthusiasts.[27]

The protesters at Irvine weren't the only ones asking questions. Jim Lindgren, a law professor at Northwestern University, was among the inquiring minds. Lindgren was not a gun guy. He didn't own any guns, and the bit of his scholarship that touched upon guns was pro-gun control. Something about Bellesiles's story intrigued him. Could it really be true that America's longstanding view of its founding fathers was so wrong? Lindgren was a stickler for academic truth, and Bellesiles's findings didn't strike him as realistic.

The foundation of academic research is its ability to be replicated and verified. Scholars at today's research universities understand that they have an obligation to make it known how and where they collected their data. Their work is expected to be properly footnoted so that other scholars can look up the sources themselves, and, if large datasets are used, they are supposed to be made available for others to inspect. Complicated regressions should indicate clearly which formulas were used and what variables were analyzed. Transparency is the norm.

Arming America followed all of these conventions. Almost every other sentence of Bellesiles's book had a footnote. The 442 pages of text were followed by 125 pages of citations. Each of the numerous tables and graphs had long lists of sources used to compile the data. This wasn't advocacy hurriedly put together. It was serious academic scholarship. Anyone with the time and inclination to replicate and verify Bellesiles's findings had all the needed information. Unfortunately for Bellesiles, Jim Lindgren decided to do just that.

Lindgren thought the "data fit together almost too neatly." The variation in the number of guns reported in different regions was, in his view, "suspiciously slight" and "the increases over time were extremely regular." The closer Lindgren and others looked at the data behind Bellesiles's most controversial claim—that guns were rare in early America—the more suspicious they became.[28]

The first sign of something amiss was that Bellesiles's numbers did not match those of other established historians who had previously studied probate records from the founding era. Whereas most historians had reported that anywhere between 40 and 79 percent of probate inventories listed guns, Bellesiles listed only 15 percent. An easily accessible and well-known national database of probate records from 1774 showed that 54 percent of estates included guns. Bellesiles dismissed the 1774 database as incomplete, which it was, and argued that the earlier historians' numbers could only have been estimates. His own research was systematic and comprehensive, and thus more reliable.

However, as Lindgren began to reexamine some of Bellesiles's probate inventories, serious discrepancies emerged. In one set of records from Providence, Rhode Island, Lindgren found that Bellesiles had "misclassified over 60 percent of the inventories." Bellesiles not only erroneously listed guns as broken when the inventories detailed nothing of the sort; he also "counted" wills, Lindgren reported, that simply did not exist. As Lindgren looked into other sets of probate records, the errors compounded. In some counties, Bellesiles had failed to account for numerous estates that listed guns in their inventories. In other instances, he counted all the estates but incorrectly identified inventories as lacking guns when, in fact, they included them. In one group of records relating to gun crime, Lindgren found an error rate of 100 percent.

To Lindgren, the disturbing thing was not that Bellesiles's work had errors—all researchers make mistakes—but that there were so many and that they all seemed to go the same way, toward a finding of fewer guns. "What is unprecedented in such a prominent book," said Lindgren, "is how many errors it contains and how systematically the errors are in the direction of the thesis."

Facts about guns are easily and often erroneously construed by gun controllers. Among gun control advocates, it is a given that widespread gun ownership leads inevitably to high rates of gun crime. Yet that isn't true. Unlike other Western nations, Switzerland has no standing army and relies instead on a citizen militia for national defense. Young men are required to undertake military training and keep a military-style "assault" rifle ready for battle. Although a large number of citizens own firearms, gun crime in Switzerland is almost nonexistent. It is indeed so rare that the Swiss don't even bother to compile annual statistics on guns used in crime.[29]

In the United States, however, guns are associated with enough deaths—approximately thirty thousand annually—to warrant the maintenance of detailed statistics. These deaths, however, don't all involve criminals killing innocent people. More than half of all firearms fatalities each year are suicides, not homicides. People are more likely to kill themselves with a gun than to be killed by someone else with a gun. Depression and other mental health problems cause suicide, not guns, and it's fair to say that most people who die from a purposeful, self-inflicted gunshot wound would likely have tried to kill themselves even if they hadn't had access to a firearm. (Guns do, however, make suicide attempts more successful; nothing is quite as effective at ending your life than a bullet in the temple.)[30]

Of the remaining gun deaths that occur annually in the United States, the vast majority involve criminals shooting other criminals. In urban areas, where gun crime is most common, upwards of 75 percent of gun homicides feature a victim with a prior criminal record. Often, that criminal record is earned in a gang, like the Bloods or the Crips, where shooting someone is a rite of initiation. In Los Angeles County, half of all homicides each year are tied to gang violence: one gangbanger shooting another or a drug deal gone bad. Indeed, a small number of recidivist offenders, most in drug-dealing gangs, commit a large proportion of the violent gun crime. The gun problem in America, in other words, is largely a suicide problem and a gang problem.[31]

Perhaps the most powerful image in the gun control arsenal is of a young child finding her daddy's gun and accidentally shooting herself or her little brother. Even here, however, the statistics show that the problem is far less pervasive than often believed. Less than 3 percent of firearms fatalities are caused by accidents, and only a fraction of those involve pre-adolescent children. Far more young children drown in swimming pools than die of accidental gunshot wounds. That doesn't mean that pools are more dangerous than guns—one hopes that kids are spending more time swimming than fiddling with their parents' guns—but it does suggest that accidental gun deaths aren't quite as common as one might think, given the prominence of childhood accidents in the conversation about guns.[32]

While investigating the surprising and controversial facts Michael Bellesiles relied upon in his book, Jim Lindgren decided to examine a set of probate records from the mid-1800s that Bellesiles claimed to have found in the San Francisco Superior Court. When Lindgren sought out the records, he made a shocking discovery. The court's collection of probate records from the relevant period had all been destroyed in the San Francisco earthquake of 1906 and the catastrophic fire that subsequently engulfed the city. Bellesiles couldn't have used the superior court's records unless he had conducted his research a century ago.

Pressure mounted on Bellesiles to turn over the computer files and spreadsheets that reflected his collected data on probate records. Bellesiles, however, had no computer files or spreadsheets. He claimed that he had compiled mountains of data from 11,170 probates on ordinary yellow pads with penciled "tick marks." While this was a highly unusual way for an academic to record reams of data, even more suspect was the reason why Bellesiles couldn't turn these yellow pads over. He claimed that a flood in his office had turned the pads to pulp. The flood was real; a pipe broke in Bowden Hall one night and inundated the Emory University History Department. Whether the yellow pads ever actually existed remains a mystery.[33]

Arming America was a hefty book and contained much more information about the rise of America's gun culture than just the probate records. Yet it was these records that were the primary evidence for Bellesiles's most important claim, that guns in early America were rare. "Nearly every sentence that Bellesiles wrote about probate records in the original hardback edition of *Arming America* is false," concluded Lindgren.

Emory University set up a panel of distinguished scholars to review Bellesiles's findings. In October 2002, the panel issued a scathing report that "found evidence of falsification" and "serious failures of and carelessness in the gathering and presentation of archival records." His scholarship failed to live up to the norms established "in the American Historical Association's definition of scholarly 'integrity.'" On the day the report was released, Bellesiles resigned from Emory, leaving his tenured position and his academic reputation behind. Soon thereafter, the trustees of Columbia University took the unprecedented step of rescinding the Bancroft Prize awarded to *Arming America*.[34]

Where did Michael Bellesiles go wrong? Not when he took on the gun lovers; they are used to being attacked. Not when he made a surprising discovery about an important facet of life in early America; historians do that all the time. Bellesiles went wrong where so many anti-gun people go wrong: by hoping that appearances are all that matter. Although academic research can be verified, rarely does anyone undertake the effort. Outright fraud is uncommon, so there isn't much incentive for people to parse the footnotes. Bellesiles may have thought that if he made his book look authoritative—if he cited thousands of sources and couched his argument in the form of academic scholarship—he could forever change the gun debate in America.

The D.C. council also elevated appearances over substance. While its members knew a handgun ban was not going to reduce crime or diminish gun violence, they believed that such a symbolic law could send a message that it was time to get rid of the guns once and for all.

•   •   •

WITH THIRTY-NINE seconds left in the 2008 Super Bowl, the New York Giants trailed the undefeated New England Patriots by 4 points. The

Giants had the ball on the Patriots' 8-yard line. Much maligned Giants quarterback Eli Manning took the snap from center and looked for an open man. On the left side of the field, the superstar wide receiver Plaxico Burress made a quick stutter step, skirted around Patriots cornerback Ellis Hobbs, and bolted for the end zone. Manning lobbed the football to the back corner of the end zone, where Burress caught it, sealing one of the most miraculous victories in the history of the sport. The Giants took home the Lombardi Trophy, and Burress, who scored the winning touchdown, was the toast of Manhattan.[35]

It wasn't long, however, before Burress again made headlines. Later in the year, he was out partying at the Latin Quarter nightclub in Manhattan with a couple of his teammates. A few minutes after he arrived, club employees invited him up to the VIP room so that he could get away from the throngs of people surrounding New York's latest hero. As he was walking up the stairs, he missed a step and his .40-caliber Glock semiautomatic pistol, which had been tucked into the waistband of his baggy black jeans, came loose and began to slide down his leg. He instinctively reached to grab the gun. Unfortunately for Burress, he grabbed the trigger, shooting himself in the thigh. One of the legs that had powered the New York Giants to a Super Bowl victory now had a gaping hole, and Burress was rushed to the hospital.[36]

Although Burress's injury was not life threatening, he was in considerable trouble. The Giants suspended him without pay for the coming season. Even worse, because Burress did not have a license to carry a gun on the streets of New York City, he was brought up on criminal charges. When police searched his home, they found additional firearms that Burress was not licensed to have. Burress eventually pled guilty and was sentenced to two years in prison.

The media response to Burress's accident was predictable. John Feinstein, one of the nation's leading sportswriters, wrote that the professional sports leagues "need to do something about their players and their guns." And Feinstein had just the answer. "The owners and players should agree that players can't own handguns," he advised. "Now let's not start screaming about the Second Amendment," wrote Feinstein. "To begin with, the amendment should be abolished."[37]

The Second Amendment isn't going to be abolished anytime soon, but incidents like the one involving Plaxico Burress never fail to expose the most extreme gun control zealots who will do or say anything to eliminate guns in America. Although the fanatical gun right supporters are often referred to as "gun nuts," the gun control side can be just as unreasonable. Like gun nuts, gun grabbers approach questions about firearms with militant ideology rather than common sense. To every crisis, they have the same solution: we must do away with the guns.

Gun control hard-liners vehemently deny that individuals have any right to own firearms. Given the militia theory's prevalence in the federal courts over the past seventy years, they can be forgiven for dismissing the idea that the Second Amendment guarantees such a right. Yet the individual right to bear arms has never depended on that amendment. Each of the fifty states has its own constitution that guarantees the fundamental rights of its citizens. Forty-three of the fifty state constitutions contain language that clearly and unambiguously protects the right of individuals to own guns. Several of these provisions date back to the founding. The right guaranteed by those state constitutions is not a right to serve in the militia. As the state courts have recognized since the early 1800s, such provisions directly protect the right of individuals to own guns for self-defense. Even though many gun controllers insist on denying its existence, the right to bear arms, irrespective of the Second Amendment, is a longstanding, well-established right in American law.[38]

One of the ironies of the militia theory is that most of its supporters are liberals, who usually argue against strictly following the original intent of the founding fathers. When it comes to abortion, gay rights, or the death penalty, these same people insist the Constitution is a living thing that should evolve to reflect contemporary values. Nevertheless, when it comes to the Second Amendment, original meaning is suddenly idolized. The truth is none of our constitutional rights are really restricted to their original meaning. Historians often argue that the First Amendment's guarantee of freedom of the press, for example, was only designed to prevent "prior restraint"—

the idea that government could stop speech before it was published. All mainstream constitutional scholars today (and certainly the Supreme Court justices) believe that the First Amendment protections for speech and the press are broader and prevent government from punishing speech after the fact. The Fourteenth Amendment was designed to protect the freedmen after the Civil War, but today its guarantee of "equal protection of the laws" is enjoyed by everyone, including women, ethnic minorities, gays—even corporations.

David Kopel and Eugene Volokh, two scholars who advocate for gun rights, have shown that a sincere commitment to a living Constitution should lead one to embrace the view that the Second Amendment protects an individual's right to possess firearms for self-defense. By any objective measure, contemporary values support the individual-rights view. Polls show that approximately three in four people agree that the Second Amendment protects individuals, not just state militias. Congress, one important organ of current popular understandings, has echoed that sentiment repeatedly, stating in legislation that the amendment guarantees an individual right. Perhaps an even better reflection of contemporary constitutional values can be found in state constitutions, which evolve quicker than the federal Constitution because of their more malleable structures. As noted above, the vast majority of these already protect the individual's right to possess a firearm. Kopel argues that opponents of the individual-rights view of the Second Amendment can't really be adherents of a living Constitution but must instead believe in a "dead Constitution"—one that allows judges to discard any textual provision they no longer deem socially useful.[39]

Some gun control advocates insist that they don't want to eliminate civilian gun ownership. Yet there are clearly others who do want to rid America of all guns. Newspapers such as the *Chicago Tribune* and online magazines like *Salon* have echoed John Feinstein's call for outright repeal of the Second Amendment. Like those who deny the existence of the right in the first place, these liberal news outlets argue that since we can't have both a right to bear arms and gun control, gun rights must go.[40]

Nelson "Pete" Shields III, one of the founders of Handgun Control, Inc.—later renamed the Brady Center to Prevent Gun Violence—argued for eliminating all handguns. "We're going to have to take this one step at a time. . . . Our ultimate goal—total control of all guns—is going to take time." The "final problem," he insisted, "is to make the possession of all handguns and all handgun ammunition" for ordinary civilians "totally illegal." Sarah Brady, who serves as chair of the Brady Center, argues that "the only reason for guns in civilian hands is for sporting purposes," not self-defense, and supports the creation of a national gun licensing system in which only people with government approval can have a gun. Self-defense, the core reason why many people in America own guns, would not be a proper basis for government approval to be granted.[41]

The desire to eliminate guns was reflected in a wave of lawsuits brought by gun control groups in the 1990s. These suits claimed, among other things, that guns were "defective" products and that manufacturers should be liable for the injuries caused by their firearms. If successful, the suits would have bankrupted America's gun companies and scared foreign companies from selling their guns in the U.S. market. Of course, just because a gun can kill someone doesn't make it a defective product. Unlike the Ford Pinto that exploded into a fireball in a crash, guns are designed to do exactly what the lawsuits complained about: shoot a projectile at high enough speed to kill or seriously wound someone. U.S. Department of Justice statistics show that nearly two thousand people are murdered each year by means of knives, but no one would suggest that knives are defective. In time, most of these gun manufacturer suits were thrown out of court. Yet the damage they did to the cause of gun control remains with us to this day. Gun lovers saw the suits for what they were: an effort to make the sale of guns to civilians so costly that no business would want to do it.[42]

The gun lobby, led by the NRA, is far too powerful to permit repeal of the Second Amendment or allow guns to be eliminated through backdoor channels. No one knows the strength of the NRA better than gun control advocates, who've been stymied so often in their efforts to restrict guns. Used to losing battles over gun control, gun controllers latch onto any proposal popular enough to make it through the legislature—usually right after some school shooting or other tragedy. Whether or not a proposed law will actually curb gun deaths is irrelevant; gun control extremists will stand behind it. John Hechinger and the D.C. city council offer a perfect example. They knew that their gun ban was not going to reduce crime or gun violence, but they supported it anyway in hopes of starting a nationwide trend.[43]

Bad gun laws do start trends—only they might be better termed backlashes. The gun rights community sees ineffective gun laws as proof that gun controllers are less interested in reducing crime than in harassing lawful gun owners and laying the groundwork for eventual disarmament. Liberals dismiss this fear as nonsense, but feel the same way when even minor hurdles are erected to women's ability to choose abortion. There, such restrictions on access are seen only as efforts to bully women and to set a precedent for ultimately outlawing all abortions.

Consider the federal ban on so-called assault weapons, adopted in 1994 during the Clinton administration. The controversy flared up a few years earlier, when Josh Sugarmann, founder of the pro-gun control Violence Policy Center, published a study entitled "Assault Weapons and Accessories in America." Sugarmann called for a ban on guns he termed assault weapons—a name derived from a German World War II–era rifle called the *Sturmgewehr*, or storm rifle. The *Sturmgewehr* was developed as a lightweight military rifle that infantry troops could carry into battle when they stormed an enemy position. In the years since, many gun manufacturers have produced similar-looking rifles, which are now standard issue in most major armies. They've also become popular with gun collectors, hobbyists, and hunters for their dramatic, military appearance.

To someone unfamiliar with guns, a military-style gun is synonymous with a machine gun—that is, a fully automatic firearm capable of repetitive fire with a single pull of the trigger. While the *Sturmgewehr* did have fully automatic fire capability, today's popular assault rifles do not. Machine guns have been heavily regulated in the United States since the 1930s. Sugarmann was referring to semiautomatic rifles that just *looked like* machine guns. A semiautomatic rifle can't spray fire like a machine gun. Instead, when you pull the trigger on a semiautomatic, it fires only one bullet. It's called a semiautomatic because the gun loads another round into the chamber with each trigger pull. Yet that round is not automatically fired, as it is in a machine gun. For the gun to shoot two bullets, the trigger has to be pulled twice. Sugarmann was unusually frank about how public misperception of assault weapons would make banning the sale of them easier. "The weapons' menacing looks, coupled with the public's confusion over fully automatic machine guns versus semiautomatic assault weapons—anything that looks like a machine gun is assumed to be a machine gun—can only increase the chance of public support for restrictions on these weapons."[44]

Public support for banning these weapons was also sought through an alarmist media campaign that suggested only criminals and domestic terrorists owned them. Handgun Control, Inc. took out an advertisement featuring a Klansman holding a Colt AR-15 asking, "Why is the NRA allowing him easy access to assault weapons?" The ad described the guns as those preferred by "white supremacists, Skinheads, the Nationalist Movement, the Order, the Ku Klux Klan and other paramilitary groups." According to the major gun control groups, these guns had no legitimate civilian use. The fact that there are several million assault rifles owned by law-abiding citizens and that such firearms are often used in target-shooting competitions—such as the National Matches at Camp Perry, known as the "World Series of the Shooting Sports"—didn't seem to matter.[45]

Some people oppose assault weapons because they are semiautomatic and don't need to be manually loaded before each shot. That logic, however, would mean that over 70 percent of handguns in America—including the vast majority of sidearms carried by police officers and security guards, and a significant minority of common rifles used for hunting and competition shooting—would need to be confiscated. And many guns that aren't semiautomatic do effectively the same thing. Revolvers are not considered semiautomatic because the trigger pull that fires the first round doesn't lead to a new round being loaded into the chamber. Instead, the trigger pull causes a cylinder to rotate, which in turn chambers a new round. Whether you are shooting an ordinary revolver or a semiautomatic handgun, the result is more or less the same. Pull the trigger, a single bullet fires. Pull it again, another bullet fires. If we really wanted to ban every firearm capable of firing quickly, we'd have to get rid of the great majority of guns in America.

The Clinton administration wasn't willing to go that far. So the federal assault weapon ban enacted in 1994 didn't ban the sale of every gun capable of somewhat rapid fire. Instead, the federal law attempted to ban the sale of any semiautomatic rifle that had the menacing military-style appearance of a machine gun. The law defined assault weapons largely by their visual characteristics, rather than their lethality. For example, semiautomatic rifles were deemed to be assault weapons if they had a detachable ammunition magazine and any combination of a pistol grip, flash suppressor, telescoping stock, or bayonet mount. Nothing about these features makes a gun considerably more dangerous, perhaps with the exception of a bayonet fitting. The last time anyone checked, there wasn't exactly a rash of bayoneting incidents.[46]

Although the law targeted semiautomatic guns with the look of a military-style machine gun, not even this combination really made an assault weapon too dangerous for civilians. At least Congress didn't think so, as revealed by the remarkably large number of exceptions included in the legislation. The law, which banned the sale of only 19 specific guns by name, exempted 661 rifles that lawmakers feared might otherwise be considered assault weapons under the terms of the law. And there was little evidence that the 19 guns explicitly banned were unusually dangerous. "Appearances notwithstanding, 'assault weapons' are functionally indistinguishable from normal looking guns," writes David Kopel, the gun expert who also wrote about how proponents of the living Constitution should read the Second Amendment. "They fire only one bullet with each press of the trigger and the bullets they fire are intermediate-sized and less powerful than bullets from big game rifles."[47]

The assault weapon ban was a little bit like a law designed to reduce dog bites that only outlawed the sale of Doberman pinschers with clipped ears. Those dogs are vicious looking and certainly capable of doing serious harm. Yet this law wouldn't improve public safety, given that other similarly dangerous dogs aren't affected and one could own a Doberman without clipped ears. Such a law, like the D.C. handgun ban and the federal assault weapon ban, would be a triumph of symbolism over substance.

The assault weapon ban's emphasis on appearances also created another problem. Because the law defined the unlawful weapons by their outward appearance and features like bayonet fittings, manufacturers of the specific guns banned by the law were able to make slight changes in the design of their firearms to skirt the ban. The exact same rifle could still be sold without the bayonet fitting or the pistol grip. Sales of such copycat firearms were brisk because gun owners thought they had to buy them before more laws were passed banning these guns too. One of the ironies of gun control is that it often leads to the sale of even more guns.

The backlash from the assault weapon ban was not felt only in gun stores. Congress itself was affected, in a profound way. The Democratic Party had controlled the House of Representatives since 1954, almost half a century as the majority party. The enactment of the assault weapons ban just before the 1994 election, however, gave Republicans an issue that energized the NRA and others in the Republican base intensely committed to gun rights. Led by Newt Gingrich, a Republican congressman from Georgia, the Republicans stormed Capitol Hill, capturing a majority in the House. Only two years in office, President Clinton faced a hostile Congress—one that eventually impeached him. Clinton himself credited the NRA with swinging the 1994 election.[48]

In 2004, the federal assault weapon ban expired, over the angry protests of gun control advocates and many Democrats. After the election of President Barack Obama in 2008, Attorney General Eric

Holder suggested reenacting the law, but Speaker of the House Nancy Pelosi decided not to bring such a bill to a vote. Although Pelosi was a Democrat, she realized that risking future elections for such insignificant public safety gains wasn't worth it.[49]

Such common sense doesn't always prevail in anti-gun circles, where it's popular to echo the views of people like Tom Diaz of the Violence Policy Center, who argues that firearms industry executives "truly are evil, minions of the Satan." New York City once expressed its anti-gun fervor by banning the sale of toy pistols that were black, blue, silver, or aluminum. In more recent years, the mayor of Seattle, following a shooting, announced that he would ban guns on city property, even though (as he himself acknowledged) state law prohibited local officials from enforcing this kind of policy. In New Jersey, school officials suspended four kindergartners for pretending their fingers were guns in a playground game of cops and robbers, while a community college in Texas banned students from wearing empty holsters on campus because other students might be intimidated by the mere possibility of armed students. And in New Orleans after Hurricane Katrina, law enforcement began confiscating guns from law-abiding people even though police protection was nowhere to be found amid the looting and theft. Often, if there's a crisis, the easy solution is to do away with the guns.[50]

Then there are the New York City laws that Plaxico Burress violated that night at the club. Burress didn't have the license to possess a firearm that New York City requires, much less one permitting him to carry a gun in public. The irony is that high-profile figures like Burress are, critics claim, among the few people who can easily obtain a carry license. Under New York City's regulations, you can receive such a license only if you have "proper cause," by which the city means you face "extraordinary personal danger, documented by proof of recurrent threats to life or safety" or the equivalent. Under this standard, regular people who fear for their personal safety aren't awarded permits, whereas celebrities and powerbrokers—who might receive death threats because of their public profiles—can. Carry permits have been granted to real estate mogul Donald Trump, Seagrams founder Edgar

Bronfman Sr., radio personalities Don Imus and Howard Stern, cosmetics titan Ronald Lauder, and actor Robert De Niro but denied to shopkeepers, deliverymen, and real taxi drivers.[51]

It's only slightly easier in New York to obtain a permit to simply keep a gun at home or in one's place of business. The New York City police commissioner has to determine that the applicant has "good moral character"—a highly discretionary standard. That, coupled with the steep fees, lengthy time for processing, and regular renewal requirements, is enough to dissuade most people in New York from applying for a "premises" permit. With a population of over 8.3 million people, the city has fewer than 40,000 premises permits. That's about one-half of one percent of the population that's allowed to keep a firearm even at home for self-defense. It's not a total gun ban, but it's awfully close. People in the public eye like Plaxico Burress and Donald Trump often have reason to worry about being the victims of a violent criminal. Yet so do ordinary citizens. They are the ones, not the rich and famous, who are most often victimized by crime.[52]

●　　●　　●

THE KENTUCKY COURTS public housing project was built with the best of intentions in the 1960s, designed to be a safe, clean, and affordable residence for the working class of southeastern Washington, D.C. By the 1990s, however, the decrepit units, with rotted-out walls, collapsing ceilings, and pigeons infesting the ventilation spaces, had become uninhabitable for everyone but heroin and crack addicts looking to buy drugs and get high—although poor, respectable tenants with no other options continued to live there. A drug gang, known as the Kentucky Courts Crew, operated out of the complex, supplying the neighborhood users. The drugs brought with them shootouts between gangs competing for control over the trade. Residents quickly learned to sleep through the nocturnal gunfire, awaking often to find new bullet holes in their windows and exterior walls. The police were afraid to enter the buildings; when they did, they usually had their guns drawn. The only burst of color came not from a garden but from yellow police tape strung around the body of the latest victim of gang violence. The D.C. government agency that ran Kentucky Courts, the D.C. Department of Public and Assisted Housing, was so ineffective that it eventually was put into court receivership. In 1997, Kentucky Courts was closed and the tenants moved elsewhere. Despite the chain-link fence surrounding them, the buildings remained a haven for drug addicts and dealers, and gunfights in the area continued.[53]

Dick Heller, a white security guard at a federal building in Washington, the Thurgood Marshall Federal Judicial Center, lived across the street from the abandoned housing project. At work, he carried a handgun holstered on his hip to protect the people who worked there. At home, however, D.C. law banned him from possessing a firearm to defend himself from the neighborhood criminals. "You hear strange things in the night and you want to protect yourself if you need to," Heller explained. One night, Heller came home to find an unwelcome surprise: a stray bullet had been fired into his front door.[54]

The neighborhood around the Kentucky Courts was hardly the only part of the nation's capital ravaged by drug dealers and gun crime. No city was more affected by the crack cocaine epidemic of the late 1980s and the tidal wave of street violence it produced. In 1977, the first year of the gun ban, there were 192 homicides in D.C., a rate of 28 per 100,000 residents. In 1991, the peak year of drug-related killings, there were 482 homicides in D.C., a rate of 81 per 100,000 residents. In 1976, firearms were used in 63 percent of homicides in the District. By 1991, that proportion had increased to 80 percent of homicides. Not only did killing become more common after the gun ban, but guns also became a more common way to kill.[55]

While it's impossible to know whether D.C.'s crime data would have been worse had the ban on handguns never been adopted, it was clear that the city's strict gun control laws neither significantly reduced the ability of criminals to obtain handguns nor prevented gun crime from soaring. And, given that Chicago was the only major city to follow D.C.'s lead on banning handguns, the strict gun laws enacted by the District certainly did not spark the nationwide movement to disarm civilians some of its backers had hoped.

Like Dick Heller, Shelly Parker also wished she could own a handgun for self-protection. In 2002, Parker, a former nurse, moved to a neighborhood not far from Capitol Hill where drug dealers sold their goods right out in the open. Horrified, she became a one-woman drug buster, patrolling the streets and telephoning the police whenever she saw drug buys. The drug dealers responded with intimidation: they smashed her car window, stole her security camera, and drove a car into her back fence. One night, a drug dealer stood at her gate and shouted, "Bitch, I'll kill you! I live on this block too!" Parker began to fear that one of the dealers would someday make good on that threat. When she called the police to tell them of the threats, one officer had an ingenious solution: get a gun. The officer undoubtedly knew that owning a handgun was against the law, but how else could she ensure her protection? Parker was an upstanding, law-abiding citizen. Unless she wanted to become a lawbreaker herself, the D.C. gun laws left her defenseless and put her life in danger. "The only thing between me and somebody entering my home are harsh words," Parker said. "That's all I have."[56]

Shelly Parker, Dick Heller, and Tom Palmer—the gay man whose gun saved him one night in San Jose—didn't know each other until 2002, when they were recruited by a pair of libertarian lawyers to become plaintiffs in a lawsuit challenging D.C.'s gun laws as an infringement on their Second Amendment right to keep and bear arms. If the D.C. government wouldn't recognize their right to keep a gun for self-defense, maybe the U.S. Supreme Court would.

CHAPTER 3

"GUN NUTS"

THE IDEA TO BRING A LAWSUIT CHALLENGING THE DIS-
trict of Columbia's gun laws was first thought up at a happy
hour in early 2002. Two young lawyers, Clark Neily III and
Steve Simpson, were winding down after work when their
discussion turned to the right to bear arms. For decades
the federal courts had insisted that the Second Amendment preserved only the right to serve in state-organized
militias. There were, however, important legal and political developments that suggested the time might be ripe to
get the Supreme Court to reconsider that line of cases.[1]

On the eve of the NRA's annual convention, in May
2001, George W. Bush's attorney general, John Ashcroft,
wrote a letter to the gun rights group announcing a major
policy shift. The Justice Department had long endorsed
the militia theory of the Second Amendment, arguing in
the lower courts that the Constitution protected only the
rights of states to form militias. Career prosecutors favored
this reading because their job was to go after criminals,
who often employed guns in committing their crimes. The

War on Drugs, declared during Ronald Reagan's first term in office, made gun crimes especially valuable to the Justice Department. Drug dealers often had guns on them, a fact that prosecutors liked to exploit to increase prison sentences.

The Bush administration, however, decided to take a different view of the Second Amendment—one favored by the NRA, which was one of the biggest backers of Bush's election campaign. During the 2000 race, the NRA spent millions on Bush's behalf, accounting for nearly one of every three dollars spent by outside groups on independent expenditures to help the Bush/Cheney ticket. The NRA also spent lavishly on Republican candidates in numerous high-profile Senate races, helping secure a majority favorable to Bush's platform. As Democrats themselves recognized, the NRA again deserved much of the credit for a strong Republican showing at the polls.[2]

Ashcroft's letter renounced the militia theory of the Second Amendment and endorsed the individual-rights view. The Justice Department now "unequivocally" supported the view that the amendment guaranteed "the private ownership of firearms," the letter said. Soon afterward, Ashcroft sent around a memorandum to all federal prosecutors officially informing them of the administration's new position.[3]

James Jay Baker, the chief lobbyist for the NRA, stood before a raucous crowd at the NRA's convention in Kansas City to tell them about Ashcroft's letter. "One year ago, at our last gathering, I warned that we stood at a crossroads," he began. "I was not exaggerating when I said the 2000 election would determine whether we marched into the 21st century with new hope for our Second Amendment rights— or whether lawful gun ownership in America would slowly be fading to just a faint memory." With "anti-gun" Al Gore defeated, "we now have a President, and a Vice President, in the White House who respect our rights as gun owners, and who honor the Constitution that guarantees those rights." After Baker read an excerpt of the letter, the audience erupted in thunderous applause. "Ladies and gentlemen, fellow gun owners, fellow officers and members of the National Rifle Association, it is indeed a new and better day."[4]

In November of that year, a federal appeals court in Texas took Ashcroft's cue and held that the earlier decisions interpreting the Second Amendment to apply only to state militias had been wrong. The case, *United States v. Emerson*, involved a man who had been brought up on charges of illegally possessing a firearm. Timothy Joe Emerson's wife had previously accused him of threatening her, which led her to obtain a temporary restraining order against him. Under federal law, a person under such an order is prohibited from possessing firearms. Emerson, however, refused to give up his Beretta pistol and was indicted. Emerson argued that under the Second Amendment, he should be able to keep his gun because the Constitution guaranteed him the right to have one for personal self-defense.

The federal appeals court agreed with the broad outlines of Emerson's interpretation of the Second Amendment. The original meaning of the Second Amendment, the court said, was to guarantee individuals, not just militias, the right to bear arms. Nevertheless, because people with a history of violence could be legally barred from possessing guns, the court explained that Emerson had to stand trial anyway. Emerson appealed to the U.S. Supreme Court, but the justices decided not to hear the case. As they had for decades, they avoided weighing in on the Second Amendment controversy. Still, the lower court decision in the *Emerson* case marked a profound shift in the law. For the first time in decades, a federal court had agreed that the Second Amendment guaranteed individuals, at least law-abiding ones, a right to have a gun.[5]

Sipping his drink at happy hour, Clark Neily wondered what Ashcroft's letter to the NRA and the *Emerson* case meant for the future of the Second Amendment. With his square jaw and short cropped black hair, Neily would have looked at home in military garb, but his round, wire-rimmed glasses suggested an occupation in the more traditional professions. His uncanny ability to speak in paragraphs without a stutter or pause gave him away as a well-trained lawyer. And he was notorious around his office for being a fierce and intense litigator. "If there were a black belt in litigation, Clark Neily would own one," said one of his colleagues. "This is one hard-charging, take-no-prisoner, lay-it-on-the-line kind of guy."[6]

Both Neily and Simpson were attorneys at the Institute for Justice, a public interest civil rights law firm in Arlington, Virginia, just across the Potomac from Washington, D.C. The Institute for Justice was founded in 1991 as a conservative version of the NAACP Legal Defense Fund, the civil rights group that brought *Brown v. Board of Education* and other landmark cases that overturned "separate but equal." Like the Legal Defense Fund, the Institute for Justice consisted of a group of lawyers who strategically set out to vindicate the rights of individuals and change the law in the process. The difference between the two organizations was that the Institute for Justice devoted itself to more traditionally conservative causes like private property rights, economic liberty, school choice, and freedom of speech for business interests.[7]

Neily, Simpson, and their colleagues at the Institute for Justice represented a brand of American conservatism that was emerging as a powerful force on the political scene at the turn of the twenty-first century: libertarianism. Libertarians are united by the principles of limited government, free markets, and the maximization of all forms of individual liberty, including property rights. Inspired by the teachings of Friedrich Hayek, Milton Friedman, and Ayn Rand, libertarians aligned themselves with the Republican Party in the 1950s and 1960s in response to the unprecedented growth of the federal government by the Democratic programs of Franklin Roosevelt's New Deal and then Lyndon Johnson's Great Society. Yet libertarians never fit comfortably into the left/right spectrum, especially when social conservatives, guided by the Christian Right, came to dominate the Republican Party and pushed for government intervention to restore traditional family values, oppose abortion, and counter gay rights. The fissures between libertarians and social conservatives would only grow under the presidency of George W. Bush, whose two terms in office witnessed extraordinary growth in the size of the federal government and a new wave of burdens on individual liberty—such as warrantless wiretapping, library snooping, and the expansion of executive power—in pursuit of the War on Terror.[8]

The right to bear arms was one of the rights extolled by libertarians. They believed that government shouldn't have a monopoly on force and that individuals should have the means to protect themselves from criminals and, if need be, a tyrannical and corrupt government. To them, gun control was just another ineffective big-government solution to a social problem. They believed that it was individuals who should be able to decide for themselves how to best protect their homes and families, without overweening government bureaucrats.

Neily thought the Supreme Court might be open to the libertarian view of gun rights if the justices were confronted with a more sympathetic plaintiff than Timothy Joe Emerson. Emerson was a gun owner who had threatened to hurt innocent people and, because of his actions, had a restraining order imposed on him by a court of law. Perhaps one of the reasons the Court had long refused to hear a Second Amendment case was that the type of people who challenged gun control laws were usually criminals or dangerous people whose gun possession merely raised the chances of someone's getting hurt. The Court might be more inclined to hear a case involving a law-abiding person who wanted to own a gun for self-defense.[9]

It's a cliché and somewhat facetious to say, "I'm going to take my case all the way up to the Supreme Court!" In fact, it's a nearly impossible thing to do. The justices hear very few cases. Virtually all appeals to the Supreme Court are discretionary; the justices choose whether to hear them. Especially in recent years, the Court's "docket"—its caseload for a given year—has shrunk. Thirty years ago, the justices heard 150 cases a year. Today, they hear half that number, less than 1 percent of all the cases in which their opinion is sought.[10]

Getting any case to the Supreme Court, Neily knew, would be a long shot. Neily, however, specialized in hopeless cases. One of the Institute for Justice's primary goals was to scale back government licensing schemes; as libertarians, the institute's lawyers thought that licensing was usually just big government meddling with people's decisions about what kind of work they wanted to do. The courts, though, have long upheld government's ability to require a license to practice any number of professions or jobs. On behalf of the institute, Neily regularly brought what many lawyers considered fanciful cases asserting that various kinds of licensing laws were unconstitutional. In one, he challenged a state law banning anyone from holding herself out as an "interior designer" without a license. In another, he argued against a law that barred anyone but a licensed veterinarian from filling the cavities of horses. He even challenged a Louisiana law requiring flower stores to have a licensed florist on staff, saying he hoped the courts would "tear this un-American licensing racket out by its roots."[11]

The city whose gun laws were the most attractive to sue was Washington, D.C. While the justices were not sympathetic to Timothy Joe Emerson's challenge to the federal law that banned people under domestic violence restraining orders from possessing firearms, they might be more inclined to overturn a law where everyone, even law-abiding citizens, was banned from owning a handgun. The District had the most restrictive gun laws in the nation, which even provided that legally owned shotguns and rifles could not be used in self-defense. Besides, the city was just across the river from Neily's office.[12]

Suing the District of Columbia was also attractive because of a quirk in constitutional law. Although most Americans aren't aware of it, the Bill of Rights—the first ten amendments to the Constitution—applies only by its terms to the federal government. These precious individual rights were not meant to apply to state and local governments. Recall that when the Constitution was first proposed to the states for ratification, many people thought it gave too much power to a central government, just as the Crown had too much power over the colonies under English rule. The main opponents of the Constitution, the Anti-Federalists, argued that clear limits on the ability of the federal government to invade individual rights were necessary. The Bill of Rights was James Madison's answer: add to the Constitution a list of individual rights that the federal government couldn't restrict. That is why the First Amendment says, "*Congress* shall make no law" abridging free speech or religious liberty. The Bill of Rights imposed limits on what the federal government could do, not on what the state of Rhode Island or the city of Boston could do.

Today, of course, Rhode Islanders and Bostonians enjoy the same rights of free speech and religious liberty as all Americans. In the early and middle twentieth century, as the economy became increasingly national in scope and two world wars pushed Americans to define themselves as one people, the Supreme Court held that most of the provisions of the Bill of Rights *did* apply to state and local governments. The textual basis for these rulings was the Fourteenth Amendment, one of the landmark provisions adopted right after the Civil War. Yet the Supreme Court had never ruled that all of the Bill of Rights provisions applied to the states, only some. The Second Amendment was one of the few provisions the justices had yet to expand.

The District of Columbia is largely self-governing, with its own legislature (a city council) and its own executive (a mayor). For constitutional purposes, however, it is still considered a federal territory. Because the District is the nation's capital, the Constitution gives Congress ultimate authority over the area. That is why when D.C. passed its strict gun control laws in 1976, Congressman Ron Paul was able to push for federal legislation to overturn the law. And because the District is a federal enclave, it is unquestionably covered by the Second Amendment.

By challenging D.C.'s gun laws—rather than, say, San Francisco's—Neily would only have to persuade the courts that the Second Amendment guaranteed the right of individuals to have guns. That would be a challenge, but certainly less difficult than having to persuade the courts to also rule that the amendment applied to the state and local governments. The latter was a completely separate question and would require considerably more research and effort. Why bite off more than absolutely necessary? Suing D.C. instead of San Francisco would make Neily's case much simpler.

A Second Amendment lawsuit seemed to be a good fit for the Institute for Justice. Not only was the right to bear arms extolled by liber-

tarians, but a Second Amendment case was just the sort of long shot
the institute's lawyers like to pursue. Neily and his colleagues at the
institute saw themselves as revolutionaries, although ones with passion and humor. (Their motto was, "We change the world, and have
fun doing it.")[13]

William "Chip" Mellor, the president and general counsel of the
Institute for Justice, did not, however, want to make the Second
Amendment case part of the institute's agenda. Earlier in his career,
Mellor saw that institutions lose their edge when they allow themselves to become distracted from their core areas of expertise. For
the institute, the Second Amendment was a good fit ideologically,
but not institutionally. The institute had a defined, established mission organized around a handful of identifiable, clear issues like private property rights and school choice. The organization would be
best served in the long run by staying focused on those core areas of
expertise.[14]

Mellor wasn't opposed, though, to Neily's working on the case on
his own time. While he agreed to allow Neily to pursue the case as a
side project, outside of work, Mellor thought it would be too much of
a distraction for Steve Simpson, who was new to the institute and just
learning his way around. Simpson had to drop out of the case.[15]

Neily could have understandably given up at that point. It was
just a happy hour conversation that had taken on a life of its own.
But Neily wasn't able to let the idea go and wanted to make it work
even if the Institute for Justice was not the right vehicle. He figured
he could devote some time to the case on nights and weekends, yet
that wouldn't be enough to develop the case and take it all the way to
the Supreme Court. His day job was already too demanding, he was
engaged to be married, and he had little free time as it was. Another
lawyer would be needed to handle the daily demands of the lawsuit.
Neily also had to find someone to pay that lawyer's fee.

Neily thought of the perfect candidate to finance the case. After
finishing law school, Neily had clerked for a federal judge in D.C.,
Royce C. Lamberth. One of Neily's co-clerks that year was an
unusual—and unusually wealthy—man named Robert A. Levy. Bob

Levy was twenty-six years Neily's senior. He had decided to go to law school at the age of fifty. He had such an air of authority about him that when Levy worked for Judge Lamberth, for months the security guards at the courthouse called him "Your Honor," thinking he must be a newly appointed judge.[16]

Before going to law school, Levy had made his fortune with a financial information and software company he founded, CDA Investment Technologies. In 1986, he sold the firm, which was known for ranking investment funds, for tens of millions of dollars. He wasn't shy about spending the money on things he believed in and gave generously to libertarian causes.[17]

Levy also had a Ph.D. and could have gone to just about any law school in the country. Surprising for a man who made his riches compiling rankings, he ignored the traditional measures of law school quality and chose to attend George Mason University School of Law, at the time a relatively low-profile school in Arlington, Virginia. George Mason appealed to Levy because it had a reputation of being "the Libertarian Law School." As the *National Review* noted approvingly, George Mason's professors "lean decidedly to the right"—unlike the professors at most other law schools. A visitor to Berkeley's law school will likely see in the parking lot bumper stickers for Greenpeace and Obama/Biden. Visit George Mason, and you'll see ones that say, "There's no government like no government."[18]

After clerking together, Neily and Levy remained friends. As Levy recalled, they shared "a political philosophy centering on strictly limited government and expansive individual liberties." Both men were active in the D.C. libertarian community, and both worked for libertarian organizations—Neily at the Institute for Justice and Levy at the Cato Institute, a public policy think tank. When Neily approached Levy about getting involved in the case, Levy was intrigued. Levy wasn't a gun guy, but he had written a white paper for Cato in 2001 that was very critical of gun control. Sounding the NRA's favorite themes, Levy argued that gun control laws "haven't worked and more controls won't help." Restrictions on guns, he wrote, amounted to a "compromise" of the Second Amendment and "a less invasive remedy already exists: enforce existing laws." When Levy agreed to finance the case with his own money, Neily called it the "watershed moment" for his lawsuit.[19]

The newly formed team now had to find a lawyer to handle their case. Levy was a lawyer but, like Neily, he wasn't the right person to take on the job. Although he went to law school, after his clerkship he had gone to work as a public policy analyst and had never litigated an actual case.

An obvious choice to lead the case was a Virginia lawyer named Steve Halbrook, the nation's leading expert on the right to bear arms. He had litigated numerous cases for the NRA and was the author of seminal works on the Second Amendment, including a leading history of gun rights in America, *That Every Man Be Armed: The Evolution of a Constitutional Right*. A tall man with a full head of wavy gray hair and a furry white mustache covering part of his flushed red face, Halbrook was decidedly soft-spoken. In conversation, he would answer whatever question he was asked and say little more. The effect was that whoever Halbrook was talking to was likely to walk away thinking Halbrook agreed with him, whether that was true or not. One thing, however, was never ambiguous with Halbrook: his firm belief in the right of individuals to have guns. He liked to say that the federal courts' embrace of the militia theory was equivalent to stamping "Void Where Prohibited by Law" on the Bill of Rights.[20]

In October 2002, Levy and Neily hired Halbrook to look into the feasibility of a lawsuit against the D.C. gun laws. Halbrook did some preliminary research, and Levy and Neily thought about hiring him to be the lead lawyer in the case. Halbrook was interested, but he was a top-notch lawyer and his standard rate was $400 per hour. That wasn't an outrageous sum for a talented and experienced lawyer. Still, Levy balked. To win what they were after—a Supreme Court ruling—would take thousands of hours. There would be the filing of a lawsuit, potentially a trial, then an appeal to the federal circuit courts, and only after all that, a Supreme Court hearing. All told, the lawsuit could take five, six, maybe seven years of work. At nearly $400 an hour, that would amount to a hefty sum. And, of course,

Levy couldn't really expect to win. The militia theory of the Second Amendment was well established in the federal courts, and the justices of the Supreme Court, as indicated by their refusal to hear the appeal in the *Emerson* case, weren't necessarily eager to take on this controversial issue.[21]

Neily and Levy decided to look elsewhere. They needed someone who wouldn't be so expensive. Levy remembered a young lawyer he met who was active in the Washington libertarian community named Alan Gura. At thirty-one, Gura was a litigator with his own little firm in Alexandria. Raised in Beverly Hills, where he attended Beverly Hills High School with future celebrities like Angelina Jolie and Tori Spelling, Gura was by his own account a "real guns and drugs libertarian"—meaning he thought government had no business banning things like handguns and marijuana, even though he didn't have a strong taste for either. He was not a gun aficionado, although, like many people in Beverly Hills, he did buy his first gun when the Rodney King riots broke out in 1992. Unlike most of his high school classmates, however, he had never tried pot. To Gura, guns and drugs should be legal simply because individuals had the right to choose what to do with their lives without government interference.[22]

Boyish with a thick mop of messy black hair, Gura was born in Israel and moved to L.A. when he was young. He went to Cornell University and then Georgetown for law school. One year in law school, he interned at the Institute for Justice. His first few years after graduating were spent handling civil cases for the state of California. Eventually, he returned to D.C., where he took a job at a big multinational firm, Sidley & Austin. At Sidley, he represented the District of Columbia in civil rights suits brought by prisoners. He left a year later and formed his own firm before joining up with a partner.[23]

In the fall of 2002, Levy called Gura and asked him whether he wanted to work on the gun case. Gura had never worked on a case involving the Second Amendment. Yet Levy wanted to know whether Gura was interested in using the experience he gained as a lawyer defending the District of Columbia to sue the city over its gun laws. Levy warned that the case law was distinctly against them and that the goal—an authoritative interpretation of the Second Amendment by the Supreme Court—would take years of work. For all this, Levy could pay only what he called "subsistence wages."

Whether or not Levy realized it, that sort of challenge merely made it more likely that Gura would accept. Maybe it was the Israeli in him, or perhaps the Beverly Hills upbringing, but whatever the source, Gura was supremely self-confident. He may not have had that much experience; nevertheless, he had a limitless faith in his abilities as a lawyer. Gura considered his legal services worth more than Levy was offering, but the libertarian in him believed in Levy and Neily's mission. "I didn't see it primarily as some moneymaking opportunity," Gura recalled. It was instead a history-making opportunity, both for the Second Amendment and, perhaps, for Alan Gura. If he won this case—and he firmly believed he could win it—he would make a huge name for himself. A high-profile case like this would make headlines and bring in a wealth of new clients, maybe turning him into one of the elite Supreme Court specialists. Victory could even make him part of the enduring lore of the Constitution, the Thurgood Marshall of the Second Amendment.

This case could be Gura's pathway to the top of the legal profession. Still, to make that happen, he needed assurances from Levy that he wouldn't be dropped off the case when the spotlight came. If this case did eventually end up in the Supreme Court, would Levy then hire a big-name Supreme Court advocate to handle the case? Levy told Gura not to worry. Take this case for a reduced rate and, whatever happened, "it would be his baby." Buoyed by that promise, Gura in December 2002 signed on.[24]

• • •

EVEN BEFORE Alan Gura was invited to head up the lawsuit, relations between the libertarian lawyers and the National Rifle Association were strained. Clark Neily and Bob Levy thought the NRA would be a helpful ally in their suit to restore the Second Amendment. They found instead that the nation's leading gun rights organization was firmly opposed to their lawsuit—and would do almost anything to stop it.

In August 2002, Levy was contacted by a professor from his alma mater, George Mason law school. Nelson Lund was the Patrick Henry Professor of Constitutional Law and the Second Amendment—a professorship endowed by the NRA Foundation to advance the cause of the right to bear arms. Lund, Levy said, "was a wonderful teacher and I had him for a couple of courses." Lund, after hearing through the grapevine that Levy was planning to file a Second Amendment case against the D.C. government, wanted to meet with him. Later that month, Lund and Charles "Chuck" Cooper, a lawyer who often worked with the NRA, came to the offices of the Cato Institute in D.C. to dissuade the libertarian lawyers from bringing the lawsuit altogether.[25]

Lund and Cooper insisted that the lawsuit was too risky. In all likelihood, the case would not reach the Supreme Court. And if it did, the Court was probably going to rule against them. Although conservatives dominated the Court—seven of the nine justices were Republican appointees—Lund and Cooper didn't think there were five votes for the individual-rights view. Several of the Court's conservatives, like Chief Justice William Rehnquist and Sandra Day O'Connor, were not libertarians. They were law-and-order conservatives, willing to countenance big government especially when it came to issues relating to crime. They were also generally hostile to expansive readings of individual rights. The NRA would not be well served by a decisive ruling by a conservative Court affirming the militia theory of the Second Amendment.

The lack of sure votes on the Supreme Court was, according to Levy, the NRA's "*stated* concern." The libertarian lawyers thought there was also another, less obvious one. Even a victory for gun owners might have an adverse impact on the NRA as a political organization and lobbying group. The NRA thrived over the years thanks to crisis-driven fund-raising appeals warning members that the government was coming to take their guns. Every time a new gun control law was proposed, the NRA sent out mass mailings telling members that they needed to send money right away to stop the law. If they didn't help out immediately, the NRA threatened, their right to bear arms would be destroyed forever. As one former lobbyist for the NRA admitted, "nothing keeps the fund-raising machine whirring more effectively than convincing the faithful that they're a pro-gun David facing an invincible anti-gun Goliath." If the Supreme Court ruled that the Second Amendment guaranteed the right of people to own guns, then the government would be constitutionally prohibited from civilian disarmament. Although people familiar with the NRA called the idea that the organization was afraid of winning nothing short of absurd, that was exactly what the libertarian lawyers concluded.[26]

Cooper and Lund failed to persuade the libertarian lawyers to drop the case. Levy thought the NRA was far too pessimistic about the Supreme Court. While no one was certain how the current justices felt about the individual right to bear arms, President George W. Bush, who in 2002 was riding a wave of popular support after the 9/11 attacks of the preceding year, would likely appoint one or two new justices in the next few years. He would probably get a chance to replace Justice Sandra Day O'Connor, a moderate who disappointed conservatives by voting to affirm *Roe v. Wade* and permitting affirmative action in higher education. O'Connor had already spoken of retirement. Newspapers reported that when she heard news reports that Democratic presidential nominee Al Gore had won the 2000 election, she told a group of friends at an election night party, "This is terrible." Her husband apparently explained to the partygoers that she wanted to step down and have her replacement appointed by a Republican. The relatively liberal Justice John Paul Stevens, who was eighty-two, might also be nearing retirement. The composition of the Court, Levy predicted, was likely to change in the libertarian lawyers' favor by the time their case reached the justices.[27]

The libertarian lawyers also thought that the Bush administration's adoption of the individual-rights theory and the *Emerson* decision all but guaranteed that a Second Amendment case would eventually be brought to the Supreme Court. Across the country, lawyers for criminal defendants charged with gun crimes were beginning to argue that such laws were unconstitutional infringements of the individual right to bear arms under the Second Amendment—and they were all pointing to Ashcroft's letter to the NRA for support. Bob Levy realized that there was a good chance the next Second Amendment case would be brought by a violent criminal. "You don't want a bank robber or a crackhead up there as a poster boy for the Second Amendment," Levy observed. If a "good case doesn't reach the nine justices, a bad one will." A "good case" was one with sympathetic, law-abiding plaintiffs who had understandable reasons to be armed. Levy wanted the Supreme Court to hear a challenge brought by ordinary people who fear violent criminals.[28]

The NRA's Second Amendment experts told the libertarian lawyers that if they insisted on bringing their lawsuit, they had to include some "trap doors"—additional, extraneous claims that the Court could use to decide the case without having to reach the Second Amendment question. If, as Lund and Cooper believed, the Court was hostile to the individual right to bear arms, the justices might still want to avoid ruling on the issue altogether. The justices were well aware of how strongly many Americans supported the view that the Second Amendment secured their right to have guns. Give those justices an out, Lund and Cooper advised. Don't force them to rule on the Second Amendment if they are going to hold that it protects only the right of state militias to have guns.[29]

This was exactly what the libertarian lawyers didn't want to do. It wasn't merely the D.C. gun laws they were after, and they certainly weren't about to have them overturned on grounds other than the Second Amendment. Their goal was to provoke a Supreme Court ruling affirming the constitutional right to bear arms. Cluttering up the case with extraneous legal claims could defeat the whole purpose of the lawsuit. Levy was putting his own money behind the case because it was a lawsuit that had constitutional significance. He wasn't interested in just striking down D.C.'s handgun ban; he wanted to reinvigorate the Second Amendment.

In February 2003, Alan Gura put the finishing touches on the complaint he would file on behalf of the libertarian lawyers in the U.S.

District Court for the District of Columbia, the federal trial court in Washington. It was straightforward and spare, only a handful of double-spaced pages with no extraneous issues or "trap doors." "At a minimum," Gura's complaint said, "the Second Amendment guarantees individuals a fundamental right to possess a functional, personal firearm, such as a handgun or ordinary long gun (shotgun or rifle) within the home." The D.C. government, by banning handguns and prohibiting the use of other guns in self-defense, was violating the Second Amendment.[30]

For the lead plaintiff—the one whose name would go first on the complaint—Gura chose Shelly Parker, the elderly woman who fought the drug dealers in her Capitol Hill neighborhood. Every time the press wrote a story about *Shelly Parker et al. v. District of Columbia*, her name and story would have to be featured. The battle over the Second Amendment would not take place exclusively in the courts. This was a public relations battle, too, and this poor woman, whose life was repeatedly threatened by thugs, was the perfect person to represent a group of law-abiding citizens who wanted guns for self-defense.

• • •

ALAN GURA knew how opposed the NRA was to this lawsuit, so he was shocked that he hadn't heard anything from the NRA people after filing the complaint. Then, two months later, Gura received an unexpected notice from the U.S. District Court for the District of Columbia, the same court in which he brought his lawsuit. The NRA had filed its own lawsuit challenging the D.C. gun laws, and the lead attorney in *Seegars v. Ashcroft*, the NRA's case, was Steve Halbrook.[31]

The reason for the NRA suit quickly became clear. The NRA's complaint included the trap doors that Lund and Cooper originally asked the libertarian lawyers to include in their lawsuit. At the same time, Halbrook also filed a motion to "consolidate" his case with Gura's. Consolidation is a legal procedure whereby two separate cases are joined together for one trial, before the same judge, because they raise similar issues. By trying to consolidate the two cases, the NRA was trying to hijack Gura's case and force the court to consider the trap door claims. To Gura, it was obvious that the NRA was "frustrated by" his "unwillingness to adopt its recommendations." So the NRA "decided to take matters into its own hands." Bob Levy said it was little more than a "none-too-subtle attempt to take control of the litigation."[32]

A week after the NRA case was filed, a meeting at the Cato Institute offices was arranged with Gura, Levy, Neily, and Halbrook to try to work things out. "It did not go well," Gura recalled. Halbrook explained that the NRA wanted him, not Gura, to argue the case. After all, Halbrook was the leading expert on the Second Amendment and had substantial experience trying gun cases. Gura was a novice. The NRA, Levy recalled, "thought we were neophytes" and wanted to bring in "the big guns." The stakes were too high for the gun rights movement to rely on Gura, a rookie the NRA brass suspected was underqualified, to protect the Second Amendment. Of course, this didn't sit well with Gura, who very much believed he was the best person for the job.[33]

The meeting only hardened the resolve of the libertarian lawyers. Gura filed a motion with the court opposing consolidation of the two cases. Court filings are usually sedate, but Gura's anger was palpable. The NRA's effort was "untimely, ill-conceived and inappropriate," Gura told the court. Not only were the two cases substantively different—the trap door claims wouldn't have to be addressed in Gura's suit—but the NRA's case was really just "sham litigation." Gura's motion said the *Seegars* case was "motivated not by a bona fide desire" to challenge the D.C. gun laws, "but by the improper strategic goals of . . . the National Rifle Association."[34] In July 2003, the district court judge, Emmet G. Sullivan, agreed that the two cases should not be consolidated.

The NRA, of course, was not known for backing down from a fight. It hadn't become a political powerhouse by accepting "no" for an answer. If the NRA couldn't kill Gura's lawsuit in court, it would simply move the clash to a battlefield where the NRA had a long track

record of success: Capitol Hill. A week after Judge Sullivan decided
not to join together the two cases, the NRA had Senator Orrin Hatch,
one of its staunchest allies in Washington, introduce a bill in Congress designed to render the Gura lawsuit moot. Dubbed the "District
of Columbia Personal Protection Act," Hatch's bill would overturn
the D.C. gun laws and permit District residents to possess handguns.
If passed, Gura's case would be thrown out of court, and there would
be no Supreme Court ruling on the Second Amendment.[35]

The libertarian lawyers were furious. "All the facts point to an
NRA effort to frustrate" their lawsuit, said Bob Levy. "Essentially,
the NRA is saying, 'If we can't control the litigation, there won't be
any litigation.'" In Levy's view, Hatch's proposal was a bad idea on
the merits. While it would give D.C. residents access to firearms for
self-defense, the law could be reversed by a more liberal Congress in
future years. A ruling by the Supreme Court was more durable.[36]

While the Hatch bill percolated on Capitol Hill, the two competing
lawsuits carried on in the U.S. District Court, each before a different
judge. In neither case was a full-blown trial necessary. Trials are used
when the parties to a case disagree about the basic facts underlying
the lawsuit, like whether a criminal defendant was at the scene of the
crime or a truck driver was sleeping at the wheel when he crashed
into a bus. If the parties agree on all the facts and only disagree about
what the law is, judges generally decide the case without a jury trial,
on the basis of the arguments of the two sides. In both the *Parker*
and the *Seegars* cases, there weren't any factual issues in dispute. The
questions were essentially ones of law: did the Second Amendment
protect an individual right to own a gun? Did the D.C. gun laws violate that right?

In March 2004, Judge Sullivan ruled that *United States v. Miller*—
the old Supreme Court case that suggested somewhat ambiguously
that the Second Amendment applied only to state militias—required
the dismissal of Gura's lawsuit. "Because this Court rejects the notion
that there is an individual right to bear arms separate and apart from
service in the Militia," Sullivan explained, Gura's suit presented "no
viable claim under the Second Amendment of the United States Con-

stitution." Although Gura's motions "extol many thought-provoking and historically interesting arguments for finding an individual right, this Court would be in error to overlook sixty-five years of unchanged Supreme Court precedent and the deluge of circuit case law rejecting an individual right to bear arms not in conjunction with service in the Militia."[37]

Alan Gura expected Judge Sullivan's ruling. He knew a trial court was not likely to rule in his favor given the prevailing case law on the Second Amendment. And Sullivan's dismissal was hardly the end of the case. Now he could file an appeal to the U.S. Court of Appeals for the D.C. Circuit, the court just below the Supreme Court. Only after that court ruled would he be able to file a motion for review by the Supreme Court itself. In effect, Sullivan's ruling opened the door for him to proceed to the next battleground in the war to save the Second Amendment.

The biggest problem with Sullivan's ruling wasn't the decision itself, but that it took so long for him to issue it. In the meantime, the judge handling the NRA's case, *Seegars*, had issued a ruling dismissing that lawsuit. This meant that Steve Halbrook had the chance to file an appeal before Alan Gura did. When Gura filed his appeal, the D.C. Circuit Court ruled that Gura's case would be put on hold pending resolution of the appeal in the *Seegars* case. In other words, Halbrook would get to argue his case before a panel of appellate judges and Gura wouldn't. The NRA was now effectively in control of the litigation over the D.C. gun laws.

• • •

WHEN WILLIAM C. CHURCH and George W. Wingate founded the National Rifle Association in 1871, it wasn't to lobby against gun control. Church, a former reporter for the *New York Times*, said the goal was to "promote and encourage rifle shooting on a scientific basis." Church and Wingate had fought for the North in the Civil War and were shocked by the poor marksmanship of Union soldiers, many of whom hailed from cities and whose inexperience with firearms allowed the vastly outnumbered Confederate soldiers, who knew more about guns, to extend the war. The two men thought that if young soldiers were better trained to shoot, the American military would be a more effective fighting force. Their military goals were reflected in their choice to be the NRA's first president: General Ambrose Burnside, the Civil War leader whose remarkably thick facial hair gave rise to the term "sideburns."[38]

The NRA's primary activity was holding target-shooting competitions, not lobbying against gun control. The organization famous today for what one commentator called its "fierce government-is-the-enemy rhetoric" matured with the assistance of generous government subsidies. In 1872, the New York State Assembly gave the group $25,000—the equivalent of nearly $500,000 in 2010—to purchase land on Long Island for a rifle range. Thirty years later, the U.S. Army began both giving away surplus firearms and ammunition to NRA-affiliated clubs and lending soldiers to help run NRA shooting competitions—all free of charge. After World War I, the military sold 200,000 decommissioned rifles at cost exclusively to NRA members. For decades, the U.S. government paid for an annual NRA-sponsored marksmanship competition at Ohio's Camp Perry.[39]

Historically, the leadership of the NRA was more open-minded about gun control than someone familiar with the modern NRA might imagine. In the 1920s and 1930s, NRA leaders wrote and lobbied states to enact landmark gun control legislation. The resulting Uniform Firearms Act was a model law that banned anyone without a permit and a "proper reason" from carrying a concealed gun in public. The law also imposed a waiting period on handgun purchases and required sellers of handguns to be licensed. The NRA eventually supported enactment of the first significant modern-day gun control laws adopted by Congress, the National Firearms Act of 1934 and the Federal Firearms Act of 1938. These laws taxed certain firearms heavily, required some gun owners to register their weapons, and created a licensing system for dealers sending guns across state lines. The NRA wasn't a blind supporter of any and all gun control, but the leaders of the organization were willing to compromise with lawmakers to enhance public safety.[40]

According to one scholar who studied the NRA's signature publication, *American Rifleman*, the "Second Amendment was glaringly absent before the early 1960s." In other words, the Second Amendment was not nearly as central to the NRA's identity for most of the organization's history. Indeed, when the NRA moved into a new headquarters in 1957, the major thrust of the organization's mission was reflected in the motto displayed next to the main entrance: FIREARMS SAFETY EDUCATION, MARKSMANSHIP TRAINING, SHOOTING FOR RECREATION. Even in 1975, when the NRA put out an "NRA Fact Book on Firearms Control," leaders still believed that the Second Amendment was "of limited practical utility" as an argument against gun laws.[41]

In the 1960s, the NRA's membership began to change. As a result of rising crime rates, an increasing proportion of members were buying guns for self-protection. The leadership of the NRA didn't understand the importance of this shift and decided that the organization should recommit itself to hunting and recreational shooting. In 1976, Maxwell Rich, the NRA's executive vice president and effective head of the organization, announced that the NRA would sell its building in Washington, D.C., and relocate its headquarters to Colorado Springs. The NRA would retreat from political lobbying and expand its outdoorsman activities and environmental awareness programs.[42]

Rich's plan sparked outrage among a growing body of staunch, hard-line gun rights advocates within the ranks. These dissidents were led by a blue-eyed, bald-headed bulldog of a man named Harlon Carter. Carter was born in Granbury, Texas, a small town of a few thousand people known as the onetime home of Davy Crockett. Like the "King of the Wild Frontier" himself, Carter loved guns from childhood. He was an excellent shot and would go on to win two national shooting titles and set forty-four national shooting records during his lifetime. His most infamous shot, however, came at the age of seventeen when, in defense of his mother, he unloaded a shotgun into the chest of a knife-wielding Mexican teenager.[43]

For years, Carter tried to keep the story secret, even affirmatively denying he was the same "Harlon Carter" involved in the shooting. He needn't have worried. The dissidents who supported Carter were the vanguard of the gun rights movement, and their view of guns was decidedly different from that of Maxwell Rich and the NRA's old guard. Rich's proposal to relocate to Colorado Springs reflected his view that guns were primarily about sport: they were a coveted part of a rural American subculture of hunting and marksmanship. The dissidents, however—and the gun rights movement that would follow in their wake—valued guns as a means of self-defense. Guns weren't just tools that facilitated a traditional means of bonding between father and son; they were protectors of personal liberty. With crime on the rise in urban areas, guns were precious because they enabled a victim to fight back. When Carter's story came out years later, the hard-liners in the NRA loved it. Who better to lead them than a man who really understood the value of a gun for protection?[44]

In 1976, Carter was the head of the NRA's Institute for Legislative Action, the gun group's lobbying arm. The ILA had been established only the year before at the advice of allies in Congress. Its mission was to fight off the increasingly strict gun control proposals coming from state and federal lawmakers. Yet Maxwell Rich and the leadership of the NRA treated the ILA like an unwanted stepchild, with a skimpy budget and numerous restrictions on its operation. Carter, by contrast, thought the future of the NRA lay in its nascent political mission as a protector of the Second Amendment. He subscribed to what he termed the "Potato Chip" theory of gun control: lawmakers take "a little nibble first, and I'll bet you can't eat just one." The NRA, in Carter's view, was the only organization that could stop civilian disarmament of Americans, yet the current leadership couldn't be trusted to do it.[45]

Rich and the old guard decided to take decisive action to quell the growing insurrection in the ILA. In what became known as the "Weekend Massacre," on a Saturday in November 1976, they fired or pushed out eighty employees associated with Carter's new guard, including the entire staff of the ILA.[46]

Carter and the dissident hard-liners decided to fight back. They quietly formed the "Federation of the NRA" and began plotting revenge. They got their chance on May 21, 1977, when the NRA opened its annual meeting in Cincinnati—the meeting that had been moved out of D.C. in protest of that city's strict new gun laws.[47]

As two thousand NRA members filed into the Cincinnati Convention-Exposition Center that spring day, Maxwell Rich had no idea what was coming. Carter and his lieutenant Neal Knox had a carefully thought-out plan. Knox was perhaps even more extreme than Carter. He didn't only want to stop new gun laws from being passed; he wanted to roll back the existing ones, too, like longstanding rules discouraging civilian ownership of machine guns. Knox was so suspicious of government that he speculated the assassinations of Martin Luther King Jr. and John and Bobby Kennedy were part of a plot to advance gun control. Vehemently opposed to compromise when it came to guns, Knox had disparaged one NRA leader as the Monty Hall of the gun movement. "He's the guy that plays 'Let's Make a Deal.'"[48]

Carter and Knox's plan took advantage of a provision in the NRA bylaws that required full consideration of any motion made by a member from the floor. Aided by walkie-talkies, the Federation of the NRA launched a coordinated attack on the existing leadership. It proposed changes to how the board was elected and how the top leaders of the organization were chosen. The federation also moved to revise the bylaws to recommit the NRA to fight gun control and increase funding of the ILA. The contentious meeting lasted until four the next morning. When the sun rose, Rich and the old guard were out. Harlon Carter was the new executive vice president of the NRA.

Under Carter's leadership, the NRA, now committed to a more rigid approach to gun control, became one of the most powerful forces in American politics. Guns, in the new NRA's view, were about self-defense, not just hunting. Armed with a new philosophy, the organization's membership tripled, its fund-raising multiplied, and its influence soared. The NRA's new attitude was reflected in the revised motto displayed at the NRA's headquarters: THE RIGHT OF THE PEOPLE TO KEEP AND BEAR ARMS SHALL NOT BE INFRINGED.[49]

●   ●   ●

IT WAS no accident that the first clause of the Second Amendment— the part that refers to "A well-regulated Militia, being necessary to the security of a free State"—wasn't bolted to the exterior of the NRA's building. Harlon Carter and his most important successor, Wayne LaPierre Jr., were strongly opposed to nearly all proposals to regulate guns and those who own them.[50]

In some ways, LaPierre, who became executive vice president in 1991, was an unlikely choice to head the NRA. Unlike Carter, LaPierre was not a skilled shooter and certainly didn't look like your stereotypical gun guy. With his perfectly coiffed hair, wire-rimmed glasses, and three-piece suits, he looked like a corporate executive. When it came to gun rights, however, LaPierre was proud to be viewed as an extremist. "To me, 'hard-liner' just means protecting the right of Americans to own firearms in this country," he said.[51]

LaPierre was the perfect spokesman for the new NRA. Like many in the gun lobby, he worried that every gun law marked a certain step down the slippery slope to eventual confiscation—or, in his words, a move to "eliminate private firearm ownership completely and forever."[52]

Politicians vying for the support of the gun lobby knew exactly what to say. After Republicans took control of Congress in 1994, Newt Gingrich announced, "As long as I am Speaker of this House, no gun control legislation is going to move." In the 2008 Republican primary season, John McCain, who was known to support a variety of gun laws, was in dire need of the NRA's support for his presidential bid. To win it, he declared, "I strongly support the Second Amendment and I believe the Second Amendment ought to be preserved— which means no gun control." Gingrich and McCain didn't say they would support only effective gun control or gun control that limited only criminal misuse of guns. Their statements were unambiguous: *no gun control.*[53]

• • •

ON MARCH 30, 1981, a young man named John Hinckley Jr. stood in the light rain outside the Hilton Washington Hotel. Inside, President Ronald Reagan was giving a speech to the Building and Construction Tradesmen convention. Hinckley waited on the street, hiding a .22-caliber RG 14 Röhm revolver he had purchased for twenty-nine dollars at Rocky's Pawn Shop in Dallas. Hinckley wasn't a rabid Democrat opposed to Reagan's conservative policies. He was mentally ill and madly in love with the actress Jodie Foster, whom he had seen in the movie *Taxi Driver*—a film in which the lead character, played by Robert De Niro, attempts to kill a presidential candidate. Hinckley thought that if he killed Reagan, Foster would be impressed and fall in love with him. When the president emerged from the building, Hinckley fired six shots in three seconds. Reagan and three others, including his press secretary, James Brady, were hit. No one died, but Brady, who was shot in the head, was left permanently paralyzed.[54]

A longtime Republican, Brady's wife, Sarah, became an activist for new gun laws that would do more to keep mentally ill people like Hinckley from obtaining weapons. She joined the board of directors of Handgun Control, Inc.—the gun control group that John Hechinger was involved with—which eventually changed its name to the Brady Center to Prevent Gun Violence. Sarah Brady's signature proposal was for a law that came to be known as the Brady bill, which would require a gun purchaser to wait several days before receiving a purchased gun. During that waiting period, law enforcement would undertake a background check on the buyer to be sure that he was legally allowed to own firearms.[55]

Although federal law already banned felons and the mentally ill from having guns, the law was not easily enforced. So-called prohibited purchasers simply lied to gun dealers when asked about their background. Even if the dealer was, as most are, conscientious and law-abiding, there was often no way to verify the information. A few states required background checks, but most didn't. The Brady bill would require background checks nationwide and minimize "lie and buy."[56]

The old NRA had long supported waiting periods. The Uniform Firearms Act, written and promoted by the NRA's leaders in the 1920s, included a forty-eight-hour delay on the delivery of handguns. In the 1960s, the NRA endorsed a proposed federal law that would have required a seven-day waiting period to enable background checks on handgun purchasers. An NRA pamphlet from the 1970s noted, "A waiting period could help in reducing crimes of passion in preventing people with criminal records or dangerous mental illness from acquiring guns." NRA Secretary Frank C. Daniel once recognized that waiting periods have "not proved to be an undue burden on the shooter and the sportsman." Such a law, he argued, "adequately protects citizens of good character."[57]

Only twenty years later, Wayne LaPierre's NRA was vehemently against this sort of compromise. LaPierre strongly opposed waiting periods and believed that preventing law-abiding people from getting a gun right away was an infringement of their constitutional rights. He also thought Sarah Brady's law was "nothing more than the first step toward more stringent 'gun control' measures. Some people call it 'the camel's nose under the tent,' some call it 'the slippery slope,' some call it a 'foot in the door,' but regardless of what you call it, it's still the same—the first step." A waiting period put us on the inevitable path to complete disarmament of civilians.[58]

Sarah Brady was an incredibly sympathetic character, and LaPierre knew that tackling her head-on was a recipe for a public relations disaster. So he pushed the NRA's allies in Congress to add to the Brady bill a provision that critics said would render the law ineffective. LaPierre's amendment would mandate instantaneous computerized background checks and a waiting period no longer than twenty-four hours. According to critics, this reasonable sounding proposal had one major flaw: it was not yet technologically feasible.

Gun control groups pointed out that the software hadn't been created yet and that most of the states hadn't even centralized their records of convictions and adjudications of mental incompetence. The gun lobby insisted that the law would create incentives for the government to set up an effective system quickly, but in a rare loss for the NRA, lawmakers voted down LaPierre's amendment.[59]

Support for the Brady bill was so strong that many leading Republicans supported it. Former President Ronald Reagan, whose staunch pro-gun views had led the NRA to make him the first presidential candidate ever endorsed by the organization, now disappointed the gun group. "You do know that I'm a member of the NRA and my position on the right to bear arms is well known," Reagan said. "But I want you to know something else, and I am going to say it in clear, unmistakable language: I support the Brady Bill and I urge the Congress to enact it without further delay." He was joined by Richard Nixon and Gerald Ford. Of course, none of the former Republican presidents had to face LaPierre's wrath at the next election.[60]

The Brady law that was enacted in 1993 mandated a five-day waiting period for handgun purchases. The NRA's idea of instant checks was also incorporated into the bill, but in a feasible way. The federal government had five years to establish a computerized national database that gun dealers could use to verify that buyers weren't prohibited purchasers—known as the National Instant Criminal Background Check System, or NICS. The instant-check provisions applied more broadly than the waiting period, covering all firearms, not just handguns. Today, every time someone purchases a firearm from a federally licensed gun dealer, the dealer has to conduct a NICS background check, which ordinarily takes less than a minute to perform.[61]

To the gun lobby, even the revised Brady bill went too far. In communications to its members, the NRA made clear its opposition. "When Bill Clinton signed the Brady Bill into law on November 30, a drop of blood dripped from the finger of the sovereign American citizen," read an NRA statement in *American Rifleman*. Soon rogue government agents will start to "go house to house, kicking in the law-abiding gun owners' doors." Gun owners who relied on the NRA for information about political developments had to be scared.[62]

Having failed to stop passage of the Brady bill, the NRA went to court and argued that the law was unconstitutional—but not on Second Amendment grounds. Instead, the NRA claimed the law was an invalid federal infringement on states' rights. Although LaPierre had endorsed the idea of instant checks, in court the NRA argued, "the whole Statute must be voided," including the NICS. The case made it to the Supreme Court as *Printz v. United States*. The Court didn't rule on the constitutionality of background checks but did hold that state officials could not be forced to conduct them. Although the Court had long held that the federal government can offer incentives to the states to encourage their officials to do something—like provide highway funds in exchange for lowering the speed limit to fifty-five miles per hour—in *Printz* the Court said that the federal government could not "commandeer" or force state officials to act if they didn't wish to.[63]

The law was also suboptimal because states weren't required to turn over mental health records to the NICS. According to one study, nearly 90 percent of all disqualifying mental health records were omitted from the system—a problem highlighted in 2007 when Seung-Hui Cho, a twenty-three-year-old who had been diagnosed with various mental disorders, passed a background check and bought two guns from a dealer and used them to kill thirty-two people in a rampage at Virginia Tech University. It's not clear that even more complete reporting would have stopped Cho from obtaining his guns, but the incident spurred Congress to enact a law providing more encouragement to states to report mental health adjudications.[64]

Although an NRA lawyer claimed that the Brady bill wouldn't work, because criminals "do not, to any appreciable degree, buy handguns from federally licensed firearms dealers," more than 1.5 million illegal gun purchases were rejected because of background checks in the decade or so after the law was enacted. Some of those buyers undoubtedly found other ways to get their hands on guns. Yet the easiest way—at a gun store, where there was the greatest variety at the most competitive prices—had been shut down.[65]

• • •

ERIC HARRIS and Dylan Klebold wanted to get their hands on guns, but because of their age—both were seventeen at the time—no dealer was allowed to sell them one. As minors, they were "prohibited purchasers" under federal law. Undeterred, they turned to Dylan's girlfriend, eighteen-year-old Robyn Anderson, who, like far too many other friends of prohibited purchasers, was willing to make a "straw purchase." She would pretend to buy the guns for herself and then, after securing the weapons, turn them over to Eric and Dylan. When Anderson went to a gun store, she balked after being asked to fill out the required NICS form. After all, she knew that it was illegal for her to buy Harris and Klebold guns and didn't want to leave a paper trail. So Harris, Klebold, and Anderson decided to take advantage of another loophole in the Brady background check system. They went to the Tanner Gun Show in Adams County, Colorado, and Anderson bought guns for the boys there.[66]

The "gun show loophole" is a misleading name. Gun sales at gun shows have to follow the same rules as gun sales anywhere else. Any federally licensed gun dealer who sells guns at a gun show has to comply with the Brady requirements just as if he were selling the guns at his store. Someone who is not federally licensed, however, can sell guns at a gun show or anywhere else without having to conduct a background check. This latter type of transaction is called a "private sale," and the loophole in federal law that allows this to happen creates many more problems than a loophole for just gun shows would.[67]

The gun lobby opposed making people other than federally licensed dealers conduct background checks. The argument was that any person regularly in the business of selling guns was required by law to have a federal license and that the type of people who sold guns without a license were one-timers, like a son who inherited a gun from his dad. For such irregular sellers, it would be a hassle to fill out the paperwork and run a background check, and making them do so was another example of onerous, unnecessary restrictions on law-abiding gun owners. Congress agreed, and private sellers were exempted from the obligation to conduct background checks.

Today, however, 40 percent of all gun purchases occur through private sales at gun shows, at flea markets, through classified advertisements, or among friends with no background check. In addition to the son selling his dad's gun, many people buy and sell guns as a hobby or side business but don't obtain a federal license—an option especially attractive to the fringe of the gun community that opposes the very idea of federal regulation of gun sales. Doing this could get them arrested, but the gun lobby has fought for years to keep the funding for the Bureau of Alcohol, Tobacco, Firearms, and Explosives low; as a result, ATF can't possibly keep up with the four million gun transactions that occur each year.[68]

The worry about gun shows is really a concern about private sellers and their attractiveness to criminal purchasers. Gun shows are by their very nature good gathering places for buyers looking for private sellers who won't have to conduct a background check. At gun shows, private sellers parade around with signs that say, "Gun for Sale. No Background Check Required." An investigation of gun shows in three states found that 63 percent of private sellers sold guns to purchasers who had told the sellers they "probably couldn't pass a background check."[69]

Anderson went to the Tanner Gun Show because that's where she could find numerous people selling guns who weren't licensed and didn't have to conduct a background check. She recalled, "Eric and Dylan were walking around the floor asking sellers if they were private or licensed. They wanted to buy their guns from someone who was private, so there would be no paperwork or background check." The sellers at the gun show didn't seem to care who the gun was for so long as Anderson was the one officially making the purchase. "I think it was clear to the sellers that the guns were for both Eric and Dylan. They were the ones asking the questions and handling the guns." When they found a gun the boys liked, Anderson said, "Klebold was the one who paid the cash and accepted the gun."[70]

According to ATF, the effect of the private gun sale loophole "has often been to frustrate the prosecution of unlicensed dealers masquerading as collectors or hobbyists but who are really trafficking firearms to felons or other prohibited persons." Meanwhile, the gun lobby decried the Brady law as ineffective because criminals could still find a way to get guns. Of course, we don't rescind laws banning murder or speeding even though people still kill and speed. No law is perfect, and no law is effective if by that one means it is never violated. The Brady law would certainly have been more effective if the gun lobby–backed loophole that permits 40 percent of gun sales to go through private, unlicensed sellers didn't exist. Dennis Henigan, a gun control advocate, calls the loophole an example of the "gun control catch-22." "The NRA and its allies claim gun control laws don't work. When comprehensive controls are proposed, the NRA then works to ensure that they will be as weak as possible. Then the NRA argues, once again, that gun control laws don't work."[71]

A potential fix to the private gun sale loophole would require all gun purchases to be transacted through a federally licensed dealer, who would conduct a background check. An unlicensed seller could find a buyer, and then the two could go to a neighborhood gun store to conduct the background check on behalf of the private seller. This is perfectly feasible; indeed, it's the law in California and four other states. If every gun sale had to go through a background check, that would be one more barrier for prohibited purchasers to overcome in their search for guns. Unfortunately, Robyn Anderson didn't have to give her personal information to the private, unlicensed sellers she met at the Tanner Gun Show.

Harris and Klebold used the guns they bought there to open fire on students and teachers at Columbine High School in Littleton, Colorado, in April 1999. Twelve students and one teacher were killed and more than twenty others wounded before the two teens turned the guns on themselves. It was, at the time, the second-worst gun mas-

sacre at a school in U.S. history. And it might have been avoided had
Anderson been required to submit to a background check. "I would
not have bought a gun for Eric or Dylan if I had had to give any personal information or submit to any kind of check at all," Anderson
later said ruefully. "It was too easy. I wish it had been more difficult.
Then I would never have helped them buy those guns." Even after
Columbine, the gun lobby still opposed legislation to close the private sale loophole.[72]

•   •   •

GUN RIGHTS absolutists have an answer for America's crime problem: more guns. If only the teachers at Columbine High and the
students at Virginia Tech had been armed, the casualties could have
been avoided, they say. The problem wasn't the loopholes in the background check system. It was the school policy that banned guns on
campus. If teachers or students had been armed, they could have shot
Harris and Klebold right when the trouble began and defended themselves. Indeed, if the killers had known that other people on campus
were armed, they might never have opened fire in the first place. Crazies target "gun free zones" because that's where they know they can
do the most damage.

This notion was captured in the title of a book by John Lott Jr., a
scholar who became a favorite son of the gun rights extremists: *More
Guns, Less Crime*. The central argument of Lott's book was that states
that eased restrictions on concealed carry of firearms saw crime rates
drop. (The debate over that part of Lott's research is discussed later,
in chapter 6.) One of Lott's claims was that having more guns was
valuable because they don't even have to be fired to stop the criminals. Ninety-eight percent of the time people just brandished a gun,
Lott said, and scared the attacker away. Lott's claimed source for this
information was "national surveys," which he later specified as polls
"by the *Los Angeles Times*, Gallup and Peter Hart Research Associ-
ates." It turned out that none of the polls he cited directly supported
his claim.[73]

Jim Lindgren, the Northwestern professor who helped uncover Michael Bellesiles's misconduct, now turned his attention to Lott. Initially, Lott said that he was misunderstood and that the "national surveys" he mentioned were really one survey—which he performed himself. With the help of research assistants, Lott said he had conducted a telephone survey of almost 2,500 people. Lindgren asked Lott to provide him with that data so that he could verify Lott's claim. Lott said he couldn't do that. He had lost all the data in a computer crash. Lindgren then requested any evidence of the survey: the identity of the funding source, the names of any research assistants who made calls, phone records, the survey questions, the coding instrument, anything. Echoing Bellesiles, Lott said he had no such evidence.[74]

Meanwhile, a former student of Lott's, Mary Rosh, came to his defense. She wrote glowing reviews of Lott's book on Amazon.com and in comments posted to websites. She dismissed the controversy over the alleged survey and insisted that Lott was "a meticulous researcher" who was "not driven by the ideology of the left or the right." "I have to say that he was the best professor I ever had," she gushed in one online forum. Mary Rosh, however, turned out to be a fiction. There was no such person. Her postings were written by John Lott.[75]

None of this was enough to dissuade the gun rights diehards. Nor are they dissuaded by the fact that the United States has one of the highest murder rates and more guns per capita than any Western industrialized nation. Here, more guns have not led to a low crime rate. The extreme of the gun rights community is nonetheless committed to the idea that guns reduce crime. In response to growing gun control elsewhere, the Georgia town of Kennesaw, population 21,000, passed a city ordinance that *required* households to have a gun and ammunition. The mayor requested that other cities send him any confiscated weapons "so that we may issue them to our indigent citizens." In Harrold, Texas, a small rural community, the lessons of Columbine and Virginia Tech were not lost. The town announced that, from now on, its teachers were permitted to bring loaded weapons into school. Of course, if the school had a history of gun violence it could have hired an armed guard instead, someone with training in security. The school, however, didn't have any track record of gun problems. The new rule was based not on history but on ideology: more guns, less crime.[76]

Driven by this belief, Arizona lawmakers in 2010 decided to loosen the rules for people to carry concealed firearms. While most states allow concealed carry for people who first obtain a permit, Arizona's legislators decided to eliminate the permit requirement altogether. If law-abiding gun owners didn't have to jump through any hoops, they would be more likely to carry their guns in public—and potential killers, knowing that fact, would be less likely to attempt their crimes. The threat of being shot by others, however, didn't discourage Jared Loughner, a mentally unstable twenty-two-year-old, from going to a constituents meeting for U.S. Representative Gabrielle Giffords and unloading his Glock 19 pistol on the congresswoman and other bystanders. Giffords was shot in the head, six people were killed, including a federal judge attending the event, and fourteen others wounded. Mass murderers like Loughner aren't easily deterred by other people's guns.

•   •   •

THE EXTREME version of the right to bear arms promoted by the gun lobby has hurt the longstanding relationship between the NRA and one of its more important allies, law enforcement. Police officers tend to be sympathetic to gun rights; no one knows better than they how a firearm can protect against criminals. For decades, police organizations supported the NRA for its tough law-and-order positions and out of gratitude for the numerous annual shooting competitions the NRA organized for police officers. The police even relied on the NRA for training. "The NRA and police were tight," recalled one officer. "If you asked someone, 'Where do I go to learn first aid?' they'd send you to the Red Cross. There's no place else. If you asked somebody, 'Where do I go to learn how to shoot?' there was just no other place: It was the NRA."[77]

While police officers shared the NRA's respect and appreciation for guns, they didn't agree with the approach of gun rights hard-liners. The rift became clear when, in the early 1980s, Mario Biaggi, a Democratic congressman from New York, proposed a bill to ban what became known as cop-killer bullets. This type of ammunition was invented years earlier to provide police officers with stronger bullets to use in shootouts with criminals, who sometimes took cover behind metal car doors that ordinary handgun bullets couldn't penetrate. Most bullets are made of lead, a soft metal that spreads out when it hits something hard. By contrast, the bullets Biaggi wanted to ban, officially named KTWs, were made with harder metals that reduced the ability to spread on contact, making penetration of hard targets easier. Nonetheless, the innovation never caught on with police departments. The bullets were too strong: they could penetrate a car door and keep on going, endangering innocent bystanders, or ricochet wildly.[78]

In 1981, NBC ran a news story on how the KTW bullets were capable of penetrating the Kevlar vests that police officers usually wore for protection. There hadn't been any reported incidents of criminals using the KTW bullets to shoot policemen wearing body armor, but the story made headlines anyway. Soon after the segment was aired, the New York City Policemen's Benevolent Union contacted Representative Biaggi to ask for his help in banning the KTW bullets. Biaggi understood the dangers confronting police. Before his election to Congress, he had been a New York City police officer. During his twenty years of service, he had been shot several times.

While the gun lobby correctly observed that shots from many rifles are also capable of penetrating body armor, that was only a distraction; police are usually threatened by handgun fire, not rifle fire. Ordinary handgun bullets don't penetrate protective vests. The more central argument of the gun lobby was that the ban had to be opposed because it was, like all gun control laws, the first step to total gun confiscation. The NRA called the proposed ban "a Trojan Horse waiting outside the gun owners' doors." Biaggi's proposal wasn't a well-meaning attempt to eliminate a specific dangerous bullet, it was an all-out assault on the Second Amendment by "anti-gun forces" who "will go to any lengths to void your right to keep and bear arms." When supporters of Biaggi's proposal reached out to the NRA to work out a deal, the NRA refused. No compromise was possible.[79]

Law enforcement organizations didn't appreciate the NRA's stubbornness on what some officers saw as a life-or-death issue. Police chiefs took to the airwaves to denounce the extremist position of the NRA's leaders. "They'll say anything," Chief of Police Neil Behan of Baltimore remarked. Even many NRA supporters were unhappy; Jerry Kenney of the New York *Daily News*, a gun rights advocate, wrote, "But the stand the N.R.A. is taking in the name of its many millions of members to allow the production and sale of ammunition that has no logical use except to penetrate armor and bullet-proof vests is an outrage." Eventually, a ban on the sale of KTWs was enacted.[80]

The gun lobby predictably responded by attacking those who advocated for gun control. Prominent police chiefs and heads of police officer associations were targeted for public condemnation, expanding the rift. "As a consequence, nearly every established police organization has broken with the NRA," notes the political scientist Robert Spitzer, including the International Association of Chiefs of Police, the International Brotherhood of Police Officers, the Law Enforcement Officers Association, the National Sheriffs Association, and the National Association of Police Organizations. While the NRA insisted that the split was only with police chiefs, and that the rank-and-file remained firmly opposed to gun control, the nation's largest association of officers, the Fraternal Order of Police, also distanced itself from the NRA.[81]

The NRA exacerbated the problem by demonizing one group of law enforcement officers in particular, those from the federal Bureau of Alcohol, Tobacco, Firearms, and Explosives. "If I were to select a jack-booted group of fascists who were perhaps as large a danger to American society as I could pick today, I would pick BATF," said board member John Dingell. Many police officers objected to the

NRA picking on one of their own. Wayne LaPierre's rhetoric often strayed beyond the bureau to include law enforcement officers more generally. LaPierre, objecting to what he saw as the increasing militarization and aggressiveness of law enforcement under President Clinton, wrote, "if you have a badge, you have the government's go-ahead to harass, intimidate, even murder law-abiding citizens." The men and women in blue may have shared the NRA's love of firearms, but they couldn't help being offended by LaPierre's overheated accusations.[82]

Today, police chiefs are among the strongest supporters of reasonable gun control. Given their natural affinity for guns, however, they lament the transformation of the nation's leading gun rights organization. "I've been in law enforcement for 36 years," says Joe Casey, chief of the Nashville police and president of the International Association of Chiefs of Police. "I can remember when the NRA was a hunting and gun safety organization. Clearly the 'new' NRA has abandoned its traditions and is putting gun industry profits ahead of the public welfare."[83]

The gun lobby likes to say that we don't need new gun laws, that we just need to vigorously enforce the ones we already have. Yet, in practice, the gun lobby sometimes seems uninterested in supporting the nation's gun laws. The NRA's board of directors included a rogue gun dealer named Sandy Abrams, whose Valley Gun in Baltimore was determined by federal officials, after more than nine hundred offenses, to be a "serial violator" of federal gun laws. Abrams's guns had a suspicious way of disappearing. At one point, he could not account for 27 percent of his inventory. These guns didn't appear to have been stolen. Abrams never filed a police report about a theft or filed an insurance claim—that is, he didn't do what you'd expect a businessman to do when a huge chunk of his inventory disappears without a trace. Abrams just didn't have the guns anymore. Federal law enforcement agents suspected that the guns were sold illegally without the required background checks, and they traced numerous homicides, assaults, and other crimes to guns that were once part of

Abrams's inventory. ATF eventually revoked Abrams's federal license to sell firearms. Nevertheless, Abrams was reelected to serve on the NRA's board.[84]

• • •

WHILE THE NRA says we need better enforcement of our current gun laws, the explicit agenda of even more-radical pro-gun groups is to eliminate gun control entirely. The Second Amendment Foundation sells stickers with the words "Gun Control" encircled in red and a diagonal line through it, signaling its view that gun control itself should be prohibited. Gun Owners of America, a vocal gun organization that boasts 130,000 members, differentiates itself from the NRA by claiming to be even more opposed to gun control. Gun Owners of America touts itself as "The Only No-Compromise Gun Lobby in Washington," a description of the organization bestowed by Ron Paul, the congressman who tried to overturn the District of Columbia's handgun ban right after it was adopted in 1976. Larry Pratt, Gun Owners of America's executive director, writes, "Gun control has no place in a free society."[85]

A few minutes perusing Gun Owners of America's website reveals its objective, laid out in articles that call for—with all capital letters to make sure the message gets across—"ALL existing gun control laws to be immediately REPEALED." According to Pratt, "the Constitution gives Congress no authority to enact gun control legislation," and any person without a criminal conviction, even minors, should be allowed to have fully automatic machine guns. The only compromise Gun Owners of America is willing to make is to bar felons from having guns. By this, they mean someone actually serving in prison; an op-ed posted on the site argues that any person who's served his sentence should have unrestricted access to guns, regardless of the crime.[86]

Aaron Zelman, the deceased founder of Jews for the Preservation of Firearms Ownership, agreed that gun control was inherently unconstitutional. "Our main goal is to destroy gun control," he said,

apparently rejecting even commonsense laws that ban gun possession by felons or restrict fifteen-year-old gangbangers from having
access to machine guns. In its "Blueprint for Ending Gun Control,"
the organization implies that seemingly reasonable gun control laws
are the first steps not only to civilian disarmament but to genocide,
pointing to what happened in Nazi Germany, where the Jews were
left unable to fight back. Americans must "acknowledge that not
one of the 25,000 gun laws in America is legal under the Second
Amendment."[87]

This radical wing of the gun rights movement focuses less on the
value of guns for self-defense against criminals than on their value
for fighting tyranny. They argue that guns are the last line of defense
against our government, which is determined to deprive Americans
of their rights. The Second Amendment, in this view, gives Americans the right to rise up and revolt against the government. It guarantees, in other words, not only a right to bear arms but a right of
insurrection.[88]

For people like Zelman and Pratt, the battle over guns is spiritual.
Pratt maintains that Scripture demands that people possess firearms.
Zelman didn't share Pratt's Christianity but recognized, as religions
have for ages, that success depends on shaping the hearts and minds
of the young. For that, his organization created a product it called
"Goody Guns," cookie cutters to help kids make homemade treats in
the shape of handguns. The idea was to inculcate the belief that guns
are good before kids end up in public schools, where they'll be left, in
Zelman's words, in "the clutches of the gun prohibitionists."[89]

In the skewed worldview of the gun rights hard-liners, guns don't
kill people; gun control does. After 9/11, Pratt and others blamed the
disaster on the fact that airplanes were "gun free zones." Had it not
been for the law banning guns on airlines, someone could have shot
the hijackers before the planes crashed into the World Trade Center
and the Pentagon. They didn't just advocate for pilots to carry firearms for self-defense in the secured cockpit; they thought that all passengers should be allowed to carry them on board too. The question
of whether more guns would lead to increased hijackings, or what the

devastating effect of a gunfight's crossfire could be on innocent passengers, was dismissed as the paranoia of the anti-gun crowd.[90]

In 2008, this radical sentiment even made an appearance on the presidential campaign trail. That year, one of the candidates for the Republican Party nomination was Ron Paul. Laws banning guns on airplanes, Paul said, created "an opening for people who wanted to do us harm." Blame for the terrorist attack didn't belong just to the terrorists; gun control advocates shared responsibility. "I think it was the lack of respect for the Second Amendment," Paul said, "that contributed a whole lot to the disaster of 9/11."[91]

•   •   •

IN THE early 1990s, the unreasonable version of the right to bear arms promoted by the gun lobby began to attract the wrong kind of people. Sharing this one-sided vision of the Second Amendment were the informal paramilitary groups, calling themselves "militias," that sprouted up across the country. Groups of men—and they were mostly men—were organizing themselves to fight off what they saw as an increasingly tyrannical federal government and what they imagined was the inevitable invasion of the United States by the United Nations. Militias stockpiled firearms, conducted training exercises, and on occasion distributed racist screeds at gun shows, where they sought sympathetic ears.

Experts on the militia movement say the groups were united by an uncompromising understanding of the right to bear arms and a conspiratorial view of government. To militias, the Second Amendment meant that any and all gun control was unconstitutional. "Undoubtedly, the most important tenet of the modern militia movement is that American citizens must be permitted to purchase and possess any firearm or amount of firearms they desire," noted Robert L. Snow, a retired police captain who studied the private armies. As one militia in Pennsylvania claimed, "every gun 'law' in Pennsylvania and these United States is inherently and unquestionably unconstitutional."[92]

The roots of the modern-day militia movement are sometimes

traced back to Larry Pratt, of Gun Owners of America. Pratt promoted the formation of such groups in the early 1990s as a response
to two horrible incidents involving federal law enforcement. In 1992,
federal agents raided the home of a white supremacist and surviv-
alist named Randy Weaver in Ruby Ridge, Idaho. Weaver had been
indicted on federal charges of selling illegal firearms but refused to
appear in court. When federal agents came to arrest him, a shootout
and standoff ensued in which FBI snipers shot and killed Weaver's
wife—while she was holding their ten-month-old daughter. Weaver
eventually surrendered, and the federal government ended up pay-
ing out over $3 million in a civil settlement with the Weaver family.
Then in 1993, federal agents found themselves in a gun battle with
members of the Branch Davidians, a religious sect in Waco, Texas.
The FBI laid siege to the Branch Davidians' compound for almost
two months. When agents finally tried to move in, a fire engulfed the
compound and seventy-six people, including more than twenty children, were killed. To some in America's heartland, it seemed that the
federal government was declaring war on the people.

Ruby Ridge and Waco supplied kindling for the early militia
groups, but the movement exploded after November 1993, when
Congress passed the Brady bill. To some on the fringe, this gun control law was proof that the government was determined to deprive
Americans of their constitutional rights. Within three years, there
were 858 known militia groups.[93]

Prone to conspiracy theories, militia members were convinced
that the United Nations was secretly coming to take away Americans' guns. "Whether American citizens support the idea, damn the
concept or deny its existence, the new world order conspiracy has
been upon us for a long time," argued Richard Mack, an Arizona
sheriff who started his own militia. Wayne LaPierre concurred:
"The U.N. is the most lethal threat ever to our Second Amendment
rights." The "U.N. wants to impose on the U.S." nothing less than
"total gun prohibition," wrote LaPierre. First comes disarmament,
then genocide. "How long until a U.N.-declared official date of hate
is celebrated with governments actually killing people?" he asked.

Perhaps, he worried, sounding more and more like Aaron Zelman of Jews for the Preservation of Firearms Ownership, the "day has already come."[94]

LaPierre's intemperate words might surprise some, given that he is the leading spokesman for one of the nation's most powerful and popular interest groups. Yet on pro-gun websites such views are commonplace. The notion that the United States is going to be completely disarmed by the United Nations "now permeates gun culture in the United States," writes Joan Burbick, the professor who studied the NRA's *American Rifleman*. That may be hyperbole, and, of course, most gun owners reject the United Nations conspiracy theory as nonsense. The deeper one delves into the extreme gun rights discourse, however, the more shocking it becomes. Mark Koernke, the gun-loving host of a shortwave radio program and member of the Michigan Militia, warned that Americans would soon be disarmed by a secret police force made up of National Guardsmen, gang members, and Nepalese Gurkhas. He claimed that in salt mines underneath Detroit, bivouacked Russian troops await their orders from the United Nations to come out and take the country by force.[95]

The vast majority of militias were harmless. Yet one very dangerous man was attracted to their conspiracy theories and extreme hard-line opposition to gun control. Timothy McVeigh, a U.S. Army veteran, attended a few militia meetings but was reportedly asked to leave because of his aggressive promotion of violent revolution. McVeigh "felt strongly about the right to bear arms and protecting the Second Amendment—he was fanatical about that," said his friend Kerry Kling. Indeed, McVeigh liked to stamp his letters with the logo "I'm the NRA." Eventually, however, McVeigh concluded that the NRA was not making a strong enough stand against gun control and decided to make his own. On April 19, 1995, he detonated a bomb outside the Alfred P. Murrah Federal Building in Oklahoma City, killing 168 people. It was the worst act of terrorism on U.S. soil prior to 9/11. McVeigh chose the Murrah building because it housed a regional office of the Bureau of Alcohol, Tobacco, and Firearms; on the day of the bombing, McVeigh had in his possession pamphlets critical of the federal agency.[96]

Just weeks after the Oklahoma City bombing, the NRA held its annual convention in Phoenix. The organization adopted a resolution stating that the organization "vehemently disavows" those who seek to make war on the government in the name of the Second Amendment. Neither the NRA leadership nor its members supported violent revolution, and they wanted to make clear that, contrary to the stamps on McVeigh's letters, he absolutely was not the NRA. Critics, however, weren't satisfied with the resolution, which continued, "Although the NRA has not been involved in the formation of any citizen militia units, neither has the NRA discouraged nor would the NRA contemplate discouraging exercise of any constitutional rights." Critics thought the NRA should do more to distance itself from the militia movement. Instead, later that year the NRA reelected to its board T. J. Johnston, the "commander" of a thousand-member militia in Orange County, California, and gave an award to Richard Mack, the Arizona sheriff who had organized a militia of his own and warned of the New World Order.[97]

The hallmarks of unreason betrayed by the fringe of the modern gun rights movement aren't characteristic of the vast majority of gun owners in America. Most gun owners are, as the gun lobby rightly notes, law-abiding citizens. Most gun owners have no trouble supporting efforts to do more to keep terrorists and other criminals from obtaining guns. "Gun owners come in all colors and stripes," observed gun culture expert Abigail Kohn. "They are police officers, soldiers, farmers and ranchers, doctors and lawyers, hunters, sport shooters, gun collectors, feminists, gay activists, black civil rights leaders." Unlike some in the gun lobby, strong majorities of gun owners favor compromise when it comes to gun control. According to a recent study by the National Opinion Research Center, 72 percent of gun owners support background checks and a five-day waiting period for gun purchases; 66 percent support extending background checks to private sales (closing the "gun show loophole"); 79 percent support mandating gun-safety courses for gun buyers. The vast majority of gun owners don't believe that more guns are always the answer; 84 percent believe, for instance, that guns should still be banned on college campuses. Most gun owners, in other words, are not gun nuts.[98]

•   •   •

WHEN THE NRA decided to wrest control over the D.C. gun lawsuit from Alan Gura in 2003, the organization's leaders made a mistake similar to the one they made in the early 1990s: they made the federal government their enemy. Gura had sued only the D.C. government, but Steve Halbrook, the NRA's lawyer, sued both the D.C. government and John Ashcroft, the attorney general of the United States. As head of the Department of Justice, Ashcroft wasn't a completely inappropriate party to sue. D.C. was a federal enclave, so the Justice Department played a role in enforcing D.C.'s gun laws. Although the D.C. city attorney prosecuted misdemeanor violations of the gun laws, the Justice Department often added gun charges to its prosecution of drug dealers and other serious felons in the District.

Gura thought adding Ashcroft and the federal government as defendants was foolish. The Department of Justice had some of the finest lawyers in the country. Although the pay wasn't great, the prestige of working on the president of the United States' team attracted brilliant, hardworking attorneys from the best law schools in the county. The District of Columbia city government didn't offer the same luster. "Why sue a defendant that is very sharp and very skilled," asked Gura, when you don't have to? "The city has lots of turnover in lawyers." The District, Gura observed, simply doesn't "bring the same resources to a case the federal DOJ brings, and you just don't pick fights with unnecessary defendants."[99]

When Halbrook met with Gura and the other libertarian lawyers at the offices of the Cato Institute to discuss the controversy over whether their two cases should be consolidated for trial, Halbrook explained his reasoning. Ashcroft had clearly endorsed the individual-rights theory of the Second Amendment in his letter to the NRA. An administration committed to the right to bear arms, Halbrook argued, could never support D.C.'s draconian gun laws, which obviously went too far. Halbrook thought Ashcroft was likely to concede that the D.C. gun laws were unconstitutional. In a sense, Halbrook wouldn't have to win his case; Ashcroft would simply throw up his hands in surrender.[100]

Gura thought Halbrook's theory was, in a word, "crazy." Ashcroft had clearly stated that the Justice Department "will continue to defend vigorously the constitutionality, under the Second Amendment, of all existing federal firearms laws." Even after Aschroft's letter was circulated, the Justice Department continued to prosecute criminals under the D.C. laws too. The Bush administration supported the right of individuals to have guns, but Gura was certain that bringing its highly skilled lawyers into the case was a serious blunder.[101]

Within months, Gura was proven right. In the NRA's lawsuit, the Department of Justice lawyers raised an issue that hadn't been raised by D.C.'s lawyers. The DOJ argued that the plaintiffs in the NRA's case lacked "standing" to sue. Standing is a legal doctrine that requires a plaintiff to show that he has suffered some real, actual harm as a precondition to challenging a law. Anyone can say she doesn't like the law. Standing means that only someone who has been affected personally by the law can seek relief in court. None of the NRA's plaintiffs could show any personal harm from the handgun ban. None of them had tried to register a handgun, and none had been arrested for having a handgun. The harm to the plaintiffs was purely speculative and hypothetical—or so the federal judge overseeing the NRA's case held. The NRA's lawsuit was dismissed.[102]

When Gura heard about the court's ruling, he didn't know whether to laugh or cry. He was thrilled the competing NRA lawsuit had been thrown out and no longer posed a threat to his own case. The NRA would now have to go back to square one and find new plaintiffs, bring a new lawsuit, obtain a ruling from the lower court—and only then could it bring an appeal.

Although Gura was back in control of the D.C. gun litigation, he faced the same standing problem that doomed the NRA's case. The libertarian lawyers had worked hard to recruit just the right plaintiffs, and beginning in the summer of 2002, they undertook an exhaustive search for people they thought would be ideal. They wanted a diverse group of men and women, blacks and whites, rich and poor, all united by compelling stories about why they needed guns for self-protection. "No Looney Tunes" was their motto. "You know, you don't want the guy who just signed up for the militia," Bob Levy, who financed the litigation, said. "And no criminal records. You want law-abiding citizens." They also needed to be sympathetic people everyone could relate to. "Virtually all the decisions that addressed the Second Amendment were styled *United States v. Somebody*," said Gura. "'Somebody' was a crack dealer, a bank robber—some low-life who had made a spurious Second Amendment claim as part of a package of desperate appeals."[103]

To find just the right people, the lawyers searched gun websites, wrote op-eds encouraging people to contact them, and looked for news stories about people who might be attractive for their case. They considered dozens of potential plaintiffs, interviewing them by phone or in person. "We talked to a lot and we rejected a lot," Levy recalled.

Finding sympathetic plaintiffs was strategic. Good ones might make the courts more open to a Second Amendment argument—and would also help with public relations. "We knew that the case would unfold not only in the courtroom but in the court of public opinion," said Levy. "Accordingly, we needed plaintiffs who would project favorably and be able to communicate with the media and the public."

In shopping for plaintiffs, the lawyers took their cue from the civil rights movement. In the 1940s and 1950s, Thurgood Marshall and the NAACP Legal Defense Fund perfected the art of finding attractive plaintiffs in suits challenging "separate but equal." Marshall and his team of lawyers didn't just wait for a case to come to them. They set a goal, devised a legal strategy to achieve it, and went and recruited plaintiffs who presented the case in the best possible light. Like "the strategy that Thurgood Marshall and the NAACP had pursued with great success in the civil rights arena," Levy said, the strategy in his own case "required sympathetic clients, a media-savvy approach, and strategic lawyering."[104]

The six plaintiffs selected were both diverse and sympathetic. They included Shelly Parker, the black woman who fought the drug dealers; Tom Palmer, the gay white man who used a gun to fight off homophobic attackers; and Dick Heller, the white security guard whose house was shot up. They were accompanied by Gillian St. Lawrence, a wealthy blond woman who lived in Georgetown; Tracey Ambeau, another black woman living in a bad neighborhood; and George Lyon, a white man whose neighbor had been murdered by home intruders several years earlier. Gura described them as "six average, normal people who come from all walks of life." Parker, whose story about the threats on her life was by far the most gripping, was chosen to be the lead plaintiff—the one whose name would be first in the title of the case.[105]

Despite all the effort expended on finding the right plaintiffs, no one had thought standing was going to be an issue. They were all D.C. residents, and the harm they suffered was the fear of being arrested if they went out and bought a handgun. The only person who foresaw the standing problem in the beginning was someone with no formal role in the lawsuit. Dane von Breichenruchardt, a large man with a looming presence and a thick, white handlebar mustache, was an active libertarian in the D.C. area and friends with both Dick Heller and Bob Levy. It was von Breichenruchardt who first introduced Levy to Heller. Years earlier, he had been a plaintiff in a lawsuit that was thrown out of federal court for lack of standing. When Heller was considering joining the lawsuit against D.C.'s gun laws, von Breichenruchardt therefore advised him to try to register one of the handguns that Heller owned and kept in storage outside of the city. In July 2002, Heller did just that. He filled out the necessary forms and brought them down to the appropriate office of the District city government. Heller's registration was denied, but the police officer on duty knew the purpose of Heller's visit. Before he left, the officer said, "Good luck with your case, Mr. Heller."[106]

Heller's seemingly futile act saved Alan Gura's case. When the lawyers for the District took the hint from the Justice Department and questioned the standing of Gura's plaintiffs, the court ruled that none of the challengers had standing—none, that is, except Dick Heller. He had suffered an actual injury. He had tried to register a handgun and been turned away. Shelly Parker and the others were all dismissed from the lawsuit, but Dick Heller could continue on.[107]

Unfortunately, the libertarian lawyers designed the case to be tried in both a court of law and the court of public opinion, and Dick Heller wasn't the best person to go before the news cameras. Shelly Parker's story was so sympathetic that even a devoted pacifist might hand her a gun after all she had been through. Heller, in contrast, was an antigovernment ideologue. He liked to say people needed guns not to fight off criminals but to revolt against the U.S. government, which, in his view, was becoming more like Moscow every day. He wanted a gun to fight "the insanity of it, the overreach of government relegating all of us to second-class citizenship." The lawyers instructed him to keep a lid on the antigovernment stuff and stay on message. "They almost wrote it down for me: 'I just want to defend my own life in my own home.'" He wasn't the ideal plaintiff, but now he was all they had.[108]

With the NRA's competing case dismissed, Bob Levy recalled, the libertarian lawyers "hoped that would be the end of our problems with the NRA. Unfortunately, it was not." The NRA's lawsuit was over, but another arrow remained in its quiver. It could still push its allies in Congress to pass the District of Columbia Personal Protection Act, the proposed law that would overturn D.C.'s gun laws. The NRA was still dead set against Gura's bringing his Second Amendment case to the Supreme Court, and the flameout of its own lawsuit would hardly be enough to stop one of the most powerful interest groups in America. In the new NRA, compromise was not an option.[109]

PART II

CHAPTER 4

GUNS OF
OUR FATHERS

FOR DECADES LEGAL SCHOLARS SHOWED LITTLE INTEREST
in the Second Amendment. Before 1959, there were only
a handful of articles on the amendment in law reviews,
the main forum for legal scholarship. The theory that
the amendment was merely about protecting state militias from being disarmed by the federal government was
widely accepted. None of the articles argued that it protected an individual right to own guns for personal self-
defense. In the 1960s, at the time the NRA's *American
Rifleman* began featuring the Second Amendment promi-
nently, legal scholars started to give the individual-rights
view a bit more attention—but only a bit. Three law review
articles supporting the individual right to bear arms were
published that decade, still a distinct minority compared
with an additional eleven written in support of the militia
theory. Yet a flood of individual-rights scholarship soon
followed. Between 1980 and 1999, there appeared 125 law
review articles on the Second Amendment, the vast majority of which argued that the amendment was about indi-

vidual rights. It was this body of scholarship that Alan Gura would draw upon to support his case in the D.C. Circuit Court of Appeals.[1]

The shift was so dramatic that individual-rights scholars started calling theirs the "standard model" of the Second Amendment. The terminology was borrowed from the sciences to refer to a theory so well proven that no credible expert in the field disagrees with it. Darwinian natural selection, for example, is the standard model of human evolution. The consensus on the Second Amendment was not nearly as great as the consensus among scientists about evolution; some of the most distinguished historians in the nation still maintained that the Second Amendment was only about protecting state militias from being disarmed by the federal government. Nevertheless, the terminology stuck.[2]

The rise of the new scholarly "consensus" dates back to 1965. Every year, the American Bar Association (ABA) sponsors an essay competition on constitutional law issues. The winning essay is published in the *ABA Journal*, the most widely circulated periodical for lawyers. That year, the question was "What does the Second Amendment, guaranteeing 'the right of the people to keep and bear arms,' mean? Does the guarantee extend to the keeping and bearing of arms for private purposes not connected with a militia?" The winning essay was written by Robert Sprecher, a Chicago lawyer who not long afterward was nominated to the federal bench by Richard Nixon. Sprecher argued that the original meaning of the Second Amendment had been "lost." The founding fathers, he claimed, sought to secure "the right to arm a state militia and also the right of the individual to keep and bear arms" for personal self-protection.[3]

Sprecher's essay was the first of what would be an explosion of pro-individual-rights scholarship. In 1995, Glenn Harlan Reynolds, the law professor who coined the standard-model terminology for the Second Amendment, wrote, "for whatever reason, the past five years or so have undoubtedly seen more academic research concerning the Second Amendment than did the previous two hundred."[4]

One reason for the increase was money from the NRA and other gun rights groups to support academic research favoring the individual-rights theory. Most of the early individual-rights scholarship was written by lawyers employed by gun rights organizations, such as Steve Halbrook, Robert Dowlut, and Richard Gardiner—all of whom worked at one time or another as lawyers representing the NRA. The NRA later helped finance "Academics for the Second Amendment," devoted to promoting the individual-rights view through conferences and seminars. Over time, the writing of pro-individual-rights articles would extend well beyond people with financing from gun groups. Even so, seed money from the NRA and others helped transform the once barren field of individual-rights scholarship.[5]

This strategic effort to nurture new ideas about the Second Amendment was part of a larger movement by conservatives to reclaim the Constitution. In the 1950s and 1960s, the judicial activism of the liberal Warren Court in the fields of race discrimination, sexual privacy, separation of church and state, and criminal defendants' rights sparked a backlash. The so-called New Right that eventually lifted Ronald Reagan to the presidency began to coalesce around social issues like busing, abortion, school prayer, and "law and order." The NRA's Cincinnati revolt was timed perfectly. A vigorous defense of the individual right to bear arms became a central plank in the emerging platform of the New Right.[6]

The new legal movement rejected the older conservative buzzwords of "judicial restraint" and "strict construction." It wasn't enough to try to dismantle the rulings of the Warren Court. Conservatives needed "counterrights" of their own to be protected by the courts: the right to life, the right to religious expression, victims' rights, and property rights. Think tanks like the Heritage Foundation (1973), the Cato Institute (1977), and, in the context of guns, the Second Amendment Foundation (1974) were formed to help devise strategies to make these counterrights a reality.[7]

These rights were portrayed as part of the "original intent" of the Constitution's framers. Although Supreme Court Justice Robert Jackson once remarked, "Just what our forefathers did envision, or would have envisioned had they foreseen modern conditions, must be divined from materials almost as enigmatic as the dreams Joseph was called upon to interpret for Pharaoh," adherents of originalism claimed to know what the framers intended to protect: private property, prayer in school, abortion restrictions, and the death penalty.[8]

No one was more important to this movement than a young University of Chicago law professor named Antonin Scalia, the most vocal proponent of originalism. Prior to joining the Chicago faculty, Scalia had served in the Ford administration in the Office of Legal Counsel (OLC), whose primary function is to provide expert and objective legal advice to the attorney general. Scalia's appointment to OLC was approved by the Senate in August 1974—two weeks after the resignation of President Richard Nixon. Scalia's first task at OLC was to prepare a legal opinion analyzing whether Nixon was obligated to turn over the Watergate tapes. In what would be the first in a long line of legal opinions favoring political conservatives, Scalia concluded that the tapes belonged to Nixon personally and that the former president did not have to give them to Congress.[9]

At the University of Chicago, Scalia sought to advance the conservative cause by helping a group of his students to form the Federalist Society in 1982. A network of law students and lawyers dedicated to redefining the terms of legal debate, the Federalist Society sought to recapture the law from the dominant liberal orthodoxy. Through its events and conferences, it "facilitated the orderly development of conservative legal ideas and their injection into the legal mainstream," writes Steven Teles, the author of a sympathetic and authoritative account of the rise of the conservative legal movement. Conservatives credited the Federalist Society with "helping to 'turn the tide' against liberal control of the legal profession, the law schools, and the courts." Scalia played a formative role. He put groups of conservative students at various law schools in touch with each other, served as a faculty adviser to the Chicago students, and was a featured speaker at the first Federalist Society conference. He helped with fund-raising and even allowed student members from other schools to stay at his home when they came to Chicago for Federalist Society events.[10]

To bring their counterrights to life, conservatives mimicked the left and created public interest law firms, like the Institute for Justice and the Pacific Legal Foundation. Clint Bolick, who founded the Institute for Justice with Chip Mellor, advised that "public interest litigators should represent the most disadvantaged individuals and should try whenever possible to find a plaintiff whose plight outrages people." Gaining protection for counterrights meant strategic litigation: pursue only the best cases, establish precedents in piecemeal fashion, and remain committed to a small number of causes. Staying focused on the core mission meant rejecting cases to which they might nonetheless be sympathetic. That may be why years later Mellor would not invite Clark Neily, who conjured up the idea of a lawsuit against the District of Columbia during happy hour, to put the D.C. gun case under the umbrella of the Institute for Justice. The institute had a well thought-out, set agenda and stuck to it.[11]

In the 1980s, President Reagan's attorney general Ed Meese brought the new legal conservatives into the highest levels of government. Meese sought out judicial nominees who shared his philosophy of originalism and were committed to the rights that conservatives favored. His effort was coordinated with the conservative think tanks and the Federalist Society. During two terms, President Reagan appointed half of the federal judges in America, along with three Supreme Court justices. The most consequential Reagan appointee was that young University of Chicago law professor, Antonin Scalia.[12]

With originalism on the rise, scholars and gun advocates turned their attention to the original meaning of the Second Amendment. The NRA was becoming a key player in the conservative coalition, promoting the idea that the Second Amendment guaranteed individuals the ability to have and use guns for self-defense. Those who looked into the history of the Second Amendment discovered that the right to bear arms was a lot older than most Americans ever imagined.

•   •   •

FEW SCHOOLCHILDREN ever study what happened on December 16, 1689, but it was one of the most important dates in American history—even though the events of that day happened an ocean away.

To appreciate why that day was so significant, we must go back a few years earlier, to 1685, when James II became king of England, Scotland, and Ireland. James was a Roman Catholic, a situation the Protestants, who included most of the powerful people in English society, such as most members of Parliament, didn't like. The Protestant elite thought Catholics were agents for the pope, whom they suspected of still trying to regain the influence over the English empire lost during the reign of the divorce-happy Henry VIII a century and half earlier. Hostility to Catholics was such that English law barred them both from public offices and from commanding forces in the military. Despite discomfort with his religion, James was the only recognized heir to the throne after the death of his brother, Charles II. James's ascension was made more palatable by the fact that he had no sons. His two grown daughters, Mary and Anne, were both Protestants, so his ascension did not threaten to reestablish a Catholic dynasty.[13]

Soon after James became king, he revealed another belief, even more worrisome than his Catholicism. He thought kings had absolute and unlimited power. England had had many powerful rulers over the centuries, but ever since the Magna Carta in 1215, its monarchs recognized that they were bound to act in accordance with the laws passed by Parliament. James thought he was answerable only to God.[14]

Within months of James's ascension, two rebellions were launched to topple him from the throne. James was able to suppress them easily, but the experience led him to conclude he needed a sizable standing army to protect him from future attacks—contrary to the tradition that a monarch would have only a small personal security force in times of peace. He also thought that he would be better served by an army that included some friendly Catholics. Even though it was against the law, he appointed Catholics to positions of authority within the military. The archbishop of Canterbury, one of the most important people in England, petitioned James to reconsider some of his policies. James responded by imprisoning the archbishop in the Tower of London. When lawmakers objected to James's conduct, the king suspended Parliament for the rest of his reign. King James was within his recognized authority to do that, but the controversial move inspired his opponents to see to it that his reign ended quickly.

To lower the risk of a rebellion, James decided to take advantage of laws passed before his reign to confiscate as many guns from potential dissidents as he could. The Militia Act of 1664 authorized the king's deputies to seize the weapons of anyone deemed to be "dangerous to the Peace of the Kingdom." To James, the 98 percent of the population that was Protestant fit this description, and he set out to disarm many of them. He ordered gunsmiths to deliver up lists of all gun purchasers and used the Game Act of 1671, which, in the name of protecting wild animals from overhunting, barred gun possession by anyone "not having Lands and Tenements of clear yearly value of one hundred pounds," to disarm commoners.[15]

In 1688, James's wife gave birth to a son, alarming Protestants. Since a son would be heir to the throne, the threat of a Catholic dynasty was suddenly real. James's twenty-six-year-old daughter, Mary, was among those who suspected that the newborn was not even James's child. Her husband, William of Orange, who was Dutch, shared her suspicions and personally aspired to the English throne. A group of eminent English noblemen determined that James had to be removed from power and invited William to form an army to help them. With Dutch soldiers, William launched an attack, and James, who lacked solid support from either the people of England or even his own army, was forced to abandon the throne. With barely a fight, James fled to France. In early 1689, the Parliament anointed William and Mary joint sovereigns. They ruled as king and queen together.

To scholars of English history, the toppling of James II became known as the Glorious Revolution. What made the revolution so glorious was not just that James was forced to flee and Protestants returned to power without much bloodshed. As a condition to taking the throne, William and Mary agreed to abide by the laws of Parliament and exercise only limited, rather than absolute, power. They also promised to respect the individual rights of Englishmen—rights that were codified on December 16, 1689, in what was called the English Bill of Rights.

The bill set forth that James had violated "the Laws and Liberties of this Kingdom." By imprisoning people like the archbishop for merely complaining about the king's edicts, James had trampled on the right of Englishmen to petition the government for redress of their grievances. By arresting people for no lawful reason, he had violated the rights of Englishmen to due process of law. "By causing several good Subjects, being Protestants, to be disarmed," he had ignored "true, ancient and indubitable rights." The English Bill of Rights reaffirmed the importance of these rights, including a provision on personal weapons. "Subjects which are Protestants may have Arms for their Defence suitable to their Conditions and as allowed by Law."

In the years after the Glorious Revolution, the right of English Protestants to have guns was recognized as an individual right—not a right belonging only to those serving in militias. William Blackstone, the eighteenth-century jurist whose *Commentaries on the Laws of England* are still cited today as the authoritative account of old English law, described the English Bill of Rights as recognizing "the right of having and using guns for self-preservation and defense." The right to have arms, he said, was an "auxiliary" right necessary to preserve the basic rights of man: "personal security, personal liberty, and private property." English court cases from the 1700s were in accord. Judges, like those in the 1744 case of *Malloch v. Eastly*, repeatedly recognized that it was "settled and determined" law that "a man may keep a gun for the defense of his house and family."[16]

A century after the Glorious Revolution, Americans ratified their own Bill of Rights as the first ten amendments to the newly formed Constitution. The founding fathers borrowed liberally from the English Bill of Rights, including the right to petition government in the First Amendment, the sanctity of due process in the Fifth Amendment, and the right to keep and bear arms in the Second.

These were the rights that they enjoyed as Englishmen and that they intended to maintain in their new nation.

• • •

THE BRITISH CROWN once again sought to disarm political opponents in the 1770s, only this time in the American colonies. Colonists were becoming increasingly rowdy and rebellious, angered by, among other things, their lack of voice in Parliament back in London. The Crown responded to the hostility by imposing ever harsher measures to maintain its authority.

One of those measures was confiscation of colonists' guns. In 1774, King George III ordered the cessation of all exports of firearms and ammunition to the colonies. The next year, he ordered British commanders to disarm certain provinces, especially in the north; the effort in Massachusetts, the most unruly colony, led Samuel Adams to complain that the Crown had "told us we shall have no more guns, no powder to use." The British military conducted arbitrary searches of ships and carriages to find firearms. Eventually, Boston was put under military occupation. People seeking to leave had to hand over their guns on the way out. Complete disarmament of the colonists appeared inevitable. In 1775, the *Virginia Gazette* reported, "The inhabitants of this country, my Lord, could not be strangers to the many attempts in the northern colonies to disarm the people, and thereby deprive them of the only means of defending their lives and property. We know, from good authority, that the like measures were generally recommended by the Ministry" to the king.[17]

The American colonists had no standing army of their own, but had for decades formed militias composed of ordinary men to fight the Indians. These militias relied on the privately owned guns of the men called out to serve, in addition to stockpiled guns and gunpowder put away for times of need. The British began seizing those stockpiles to make it harder for the colonies to rebel—a move that only inspired the colonists to see to it that George III's reign over them ended quickly.

The founding fathers were fond of guns. George Washington owned fifty of them. As a general, he appreciated their effectiveness as instruments of warfare. Yet the founders thought guns were useful for more than just fighting wars. John Adams, a lawyer, regarded guns as a means of protection against criminal attack. In his 1787 book *A Defense of the Constitutions of the Government of the United States of America*, Adams argued that "arms in the hand of citizens" could be used effectively for "private self-defense."[18]

Thomas Jefferson received his first gun at the age of ten, and his papers are filled with notations about his many firearms. A tinkerer and scientist, he marveled at the mechanical properties of guns and what he saw as shooting's positive effect on discipline. In a 1785 letter to his fifteen-year-old nephew, Jefferson prescribed a detailed regimen for self-improvement: "A strong body makes the mind strong. As to the species of exercise, I advise the gun. While this gives a moderate exercise to the body, it gives boldness, enterprize and independance to the mind. Games played with the ball and others of that nature, are too violent for the body and stamp no character on the mind. Let your gun therefore be the constant companion on your walks. Never think of taking a book with you."[19]

After rebellious colonists, led by a silversmith named Paul Revere, dumped English tea into Boston Harbor in 1773, the British ordered General Thomas Gage and his troops to occupy Boston. Gage, commander in chief of all British forces in the New World, was the most powerful man in America. When he learned the following spring that the rebels were secretly stockpiling guns and ammunition in an arsenal in nearby Concord, Gage ordered seven hundred troops to seize the weapons. The night before the British raid, Revere set out on his famous midnight ride to warn the people of the countryside. Contrary to legend, however, he didn't cry out as he rode, and he was not alone. The outskirts of Boston were filled with Loyalists and British patrols, so Revere and the dozens of other midnight riders whispered their warning instead, and only to trusted friends. Still, the message was the same: the British are coming, the British are coming. And the reason they were coming was to take away the colonists' guns.

The existence of other riders was fortunate because Revere himself was captured by Redcoats. Eventually he was released, but the British confiscated his horse, forcing him to finish his mission less glamorously on foot. Nevertheless, by the time the Redcoats arrived in Lexington on their way to Concord, scores of armed minutemen—so called because they could quit their daily routines, grab their own guns, and be ready to fight in a minute's time—had heard the warning and come out to make a stand. The Redcoats and the colonists stood face to face in Lexington Green on the morning of April 19. Someone fired the first shot, though who it was and even what side he was on has been lost to history. Nevertheless, that pull of the trigger produced what Ralph Waldo Emerson called "the shot heard 'round the world." It was the start of the American Revolution—a war ignited by a government effort to seize the people's firearms.[20]

•   •   •

NEARLY TWO hundred years later, on a humid evening in the summer of 1963, Don Kates, with an M1 Carbine and a Smith & Wesson Chief's Special revolver in his hands, stood guard outside the home of a local civil rights activist in eastern North Carolina. This was Ku Klux Klan country, and the woman whom Kates was defending, a plaintiff in a civil rights suit, had received a serious death threat. Ordinarily, someone fearing for her life might call the police, but the police in these parts tended to side with the racists. She needed someone else to protect her, even if Don Kates wasn't the obvious choice.[21]

Born and raised in the San Francisco Bay Area, Kates was only twenty-two years old and had just finished his first year as a student at Yale Law School. That summer, he was in North Carolina volunteering as a law clerk to work on civil rights cases. He may not have had much legal experience, but he had brought guns with him to the volatile South, and the teacher needed those guns more than anything else that night. Kates and a handful of others stood armed guard in case anyone decided to carry out the death threat. Even though the night ended without incident, the experience taught Kates a valuable lesson. For oppressed people who can't rely on the police, having a gun is sometimes the only means of protection. Guided by that insight, Kates would become the most influential proponent of the view that the founding fathers intended the Second Amendment to guarantee the right of individuals to own guns.

Kates was not a political conservative and even called himself a "John F. Kennedy liberal." He went to the progressive Reed College in Portland, Oregon, and during law school worked for the famously radical William Kunstler, a leftist lawyer who represented clients like the Weather Underground and the Black Panthers. After graduating from Yale, Kates returned to California, where he worked at Legal Services for the Poor and the San Mateo Legal Aid Society. For a few years, he was a law professor at St. Louis University Law School. He left when his contract was not renewed—retribution by the Catholic school, he said, for his pro-choice bumper sticker. His pet parrot was named Che after the Argentine Marxist revolutionary Che Guevara.[22]

It was the radical in Kates that fed his interest in firearms. Government oppression of the people, he believed, is possible only if government has a monopoly on the use of force. Where citizens have the ability to fight back, oppressors hesitate to go. Perhaps the reason why the Klan didn't attack that night in North Carolina was that, thanks to Kates and others, the civil rights activist had the ability to return fire. In the late 1970s, Kates, then in private practice, began to represent clients in gun cases, leading him to research the history of the Second Amendment. Eventually, he published a series of articles in legal magazines and journals on gun rights, one of which appeared in the *Michigan Law Review*. His was the first article ever to appear in a law review from a top ten law school arguing that the Second Amendment protected an individual right to keep guns for self-defense. It would prove to be a groundbreaking work that revolutionized Second Amendment scholarship. When the wave of individual-rights scholarship eventually came, it followed the channel Kates had carved out.[23]

Kates's research showed that few ideas were as frequently and consistently endorsed by Americans of the Revolutionary period as the right of ordinary citizens to possess guns. Immediately after the

Revolutionary War erupted, the individual colonies began to propose constitutions of their own to establish their independent sovereignties. These proposals invariably referred to what the Declaration of Independence called man's "inalienable rights." Jefferson, the author of the Declaration, proposed that Virginia's constitution include a provision that said, "No freeman shall be debarred of the use of arms." In Pennsylvania in 1776 and Vermont in 1777, revolutionaries suggested that their own declarations of rights recognize that "the people have a right to bear arms for the defence of themselves and the state." These statements did not say anything about limiting that right to people serving in state militias.[24]

After independence from Britain was gained and America's first constitution—the improvidently named Articles of Confederation and Perpetual Union—had proven unworkable, the framers came together to propose a new charter. The document, written largely by James Madison and Gouverneur Morris, sparked immediate controversy when it was submitted to the states for ratification in 1787. Madison, who thought that the Articles of Confederation failed because states had too much autonomy, envisioned a more powerful, centralized federal government, whose laws would bind all the states. What worried many opponents of ratification, however, was that the federal government could use its newfound power to trample on the rights of individuals that were supposed to be inalienable. Known as Anti-Federalists, the opponents of the Constitution pointed out that this was exactly what had happened under English rule when power was centralized in London.[25]

One especially controversial aspect of the Constitution was its grant of authority to Congress to "provide for organizing, arming, and disciplining, the Militia" of the individual states. The framers were fearful of a regularly employed force of soldiers that potentially could be used to suppress the people, as James II had tried to do. Instead, the framers preferred America's army to be the common people, who could be organized into local militias to fight off enemies when necessary, just as the revolutionaries did in the 1770s. The Constitution's "militia clauses" were designed to give Congress the power to call up the state's militias should England, France, or any other country try to invade. Anti-Federalists, however, worried that the federal government would use the militia clauses to disarm the citizenry and that the president would assert military control over the county.[26]

New Hampshire recommended that a Bill of Rights similar to the one in England be added to the text. It should provide that "Congress shall never disarm any citizen, unless such as are or have been in actual rebellion." The New York, Virginia, Rhode Island, and Massachusetts ratifying conventions agreed. Pennsylvania ratified the Constitution unconditionally, but not without a strong "Minority Report" that suggested additional protections for free speech, due process, and the right to bear arms: "That the people have a right to bear arms for the defense of themselves and their own State or the United States, or for the purpose of killing game; and no law shall be passed for disarming the people or any of them unless for crimes committed, or real danger of public injury from individuals. . . ."[27]

In his research into the founding-era debates over the Constitution, Don Kates was surprised to find that states that recommended adding a guarantee of the right to have guns outnumbered those that recommended adding other rights thought to be central to American law. "Amending the constitution to assure the right to arms was endorsed by five state ratifying conventions. By comparison, only four states suggested that the rights to assemble, to due process, and against cruel and unusual punishment be guaranteed," he wrote in his landmark *Michigan Law Review* article, while "only three states suggested that freedom of speech be guaranteed."[28]

In response to the suggestions by so many states that various protections be added to the proposed Constitution, Madison drafted a Bill of Rights. He initially proposed twelve amendments. Some people assume that Madison put the freedom of speech in the first amendment because it was the most important. Yet that provision was really the third amendment Madison proposed. The first two, which related to compensation for elected officials and the apportionment of seats in Congress, did not receive sufficient support and were dropped. Just behind the new First Amendment was Madison's proposal to protect the right to keep and bear arms. The Second Amendment reassured wary Americans that Congress would not have the power to destroy state militias by disarming the people. "A well regulated Militia, being necessary to the security of a free State, the right of the people to keep and bear Arms, shall not be infringed."[29]

Although the wording of the Second Amendment confused generations of Americans, Kates sought to understand what those words meant to the founding fathers. Supporters of the militia theory saw the grant of the right to keep and bear arms to "the people" as indicating a collective right. That is, the people could assemble collectively and form a militia, and, as such a group, they had the right to bear arms. Kates's *Michigan Law Review* article offered a rebuttal. The Bill of Rights included many other examples of provisions where the framers took "the right of people" to mean individual rights. The First Amendment, for example, referred to "the right of the people . . . to petition the Government for a redress of grievances." The Fourth Amendment referred to the "right of the people to be secure in their persons, houses, papers, and effects, against unreasonable searches and seizures." The Tenth Amendment explicitly distinguished "the people" from "the States," providing that the "powers not delegated" to Congress "are reserved to the States respectively, or to the people." Any reading of the Second Amendment that didn't acknowledge an individual right had to assume the framers meant completely different things by the exact same phrase used just a few words apart.[30]

The Second Amendment's preamble—"A well regulated Militia, being necessary to the security of a free State"—was not in tension with the individual-rights reading. "The 'militia,'" Kates argued, "was the entire adult male citizenry, who were not simply *allowed* to keep their own arms, but affirmatively *required* to do so." The Virginian George Mason, who along with Madison is considered one of the "Fathers of the Bill of Rights," addressed the question: "Who are the militia? They consist now of the whole people." The Virginia Declaration of Rights of 1776, which, as written by Mason, stated that "a well regulated Militia, composed of the body of the People, trained to Arms, is the proper, natural, and safe Defense of a free State." The right was not limited to a select group of citizens but was enjoyed by all. To the framers, we the people were the militia.[31]

Supporters of the militia theory argued that the Second Amendment's reference to "keep and bear Arms" meant that the right was limited to military exercises or battle. The problem with this view, according to Kates, was that the founders used the term "keep arms" to mean private possession of weapons at home, even in contexts far removed from military service. Laws of the time provided, for instance, that "no slave . . . shall *keep* any such weapon." Other laws that exempted people from militia service—such as clergy, men over a certain age, and seamen—still required them to "keep" arms in their homes. If need be, these weapons would be available for war or for law enforcement. Not only did the founders lack a standing army; they also had no organized police departments. For decades after the Revolution, when crimes were committed, ordinary individuals were expected to respond to the "hue and cry," armed if necessary, and bring criminals to justice.[32]

The founders also used the words "bear arms" in nonmilitary contexts. In 1785, for instance, a "Bill for Preservation of Deer" was proposed in the Virginia legislature, which would have imposed a fine on anyone "for every deer by him unlawfully killed." For one year after such an offense, additional fines were to be imposed on the person if he "shall bear a gun out of his inclosed ground, unless whilst performing military duty." Every "such bearing of a gun shall be a breach," the bill provided. The author of the proposed law was also the author of the Second Amendment, James Madison.[33]

Kates didn't deny that the founding fathers were concerned primarily with the militia when they adopted the Second Amendment; that much was obvious. Yet this was not contrary to the idea that the provision protected the right of individuals to have guns. "Indeed, the evidence suggests it was precisely by protecting the individual that the Framers intended to protect the militia," he wrote. "[T]he one thing all the Framers agreed on was the desirability of allowing citizens to arm themselves." The modern-day debate over whether the Second Amendment was about militias or individual rights was, in Kates's view, a distraction. The provision was designed to keep the government from disarming the civilian population.[34]

Years later, Clark Neily, who came up with the original idea to bring the lawsuit to reinvigorate the Second Amendment, would call Kates's *Michigan Law Review* article the "seminal work" on the individual-rights theory. At first, however, Kates's argument was given short shrift by mainstream constitutional scholars. The Second Amendment was not taught in constitutional law classes, and none of the leading casebooks or treatises even mentioned it, except in passing. Kates himself didn't carry that much weight because he was a gun lawyer, not an academic affiliated with a university. Kates himself later recognized that "many early (pre-2000) scholarly publications" endorsing the individual-rights reading of the Second Amendment weren't taken seriously, since they "came from practicing lawyers, some of them gun lobby officers or employees." Scholars respect the work of other scholars, not of practicing lawyers whose fees are paid by clients with something at stake in the dispute.[35]

Then, in 1989, a law professor named Sanford Levinson published an article in the highly esteemed *Yale Law Journal* endorsing Kates's view of the Second Amendment. Levinson, one of the foremost liberal constitutional law professors in the country, titled his article "The Embarrassing Second Amendment." What was so embarrassing was that no mainstream law professors paid this longstanding provision any attention, not even those who considered themselves zealous champions of individual rights. Levinson maintained that the elite bar was so opposed to the idea of private gun ownership that it simply ignored the Second Amendment and Kates's powerful argument.[36]

Levinson certainly wasn't ignored. The nationally syndicated columnist George Will wrote about his article, as did the *Washington Post* and the *New Republic*. Leading law professors, including liberals, also took note. Laurence Tribe—frequently mentioned as a potential Supreme Court nominee and called by *USA Today* "probably the most influential living American constitutional scholar"—weighed in on the side of Kates and Levinson. "I've gotten an avalanche of angry mail from apparent liberals who said, 'How could you?'" Tribe noted. "But as someone who takes the Constitution seriously, I thought I had a responsibility to see what the Second Amendment says, and how it fits."[37]

Levinson's article drew attention not simply because he was a liberal, although that certainly enhanced the story. Between 1983, when Kates's article was published, and 1989, when Levinson's came out, the gun issue had exploded onto the national political scene. In the 1988 presidential election, the NRA actively campaigned against the gun control supporter Michael Dukakis, running ads in twenty states featuring Charlton Heston and distributing "Defeat Dukakis" bumper stickers. Despite an early two-digit lead in the polls, Dukakis lost the election to George H. W. Bush, and political analysts pointed to guns as one of the primary reasons. Dukakis's running mate, Senator Lloyd Bentsen of Texas, blamed the loss on "the incredible effect of gun control." In the West and South, Bentsen lamented, "we lost a lot of Democrats on peripheral issues like gun control and the pledge" of allegiance. As another commentator said, "the gun issue turned what might have been a very close election into an electoral landslide."[38]

Some historians, like Jack Rakove, winner of a Pulitzer Prize, continued to argue that the Second Amendment was only about protecting militias. Others, like Saul Cornell and David Konig, rejected the traditional militia theory and argued that, while the amendment did guarantee an individual right, it was only a right to serve in militias. These latter scholars likened the right to keep and bear arms to jury service: more a civic duty than a libertarian right rooted in personal self-defense. These accounts emphasized the paucity of explicit discussions in the founding era about the importance of guns for protection against ordinary criminals.[39]

Yet the vast majority of the Second Amendment scholarship published since Don Kates first wrote his groundbreaking article made it increasingly seem that there was a standard model for the Second

Amendment, as there was for human evolution. "The resurgence of academic interest in the Second Amendment," Clark Neily observed, "produced a body of scholarship that could neither be ignored nor dismissed by opponents of the individual-rights model—or, it turns out, by the federal courts."[40]

• • •

IN THE Revolutionary Era, gun laws were strict. Because there was no standing army, the national defense depended upon an armed citizenry capable of fighting off invading European powers or hostile Native tribes. With national defense becoming too important to leave to individual choice or the free market, the founders implemented laws that required all free men between the ages of eighteen and forty-five to outfit themselves with a musket, rifle, or other firearm suitable for military service. It didn't matter whether someone didn't like guns or already had a shotgun good for hunting birds. Every man of age was legally mandated to acquire a militarily useful gun. This mandate was enforced at "musters," public gatherings held several times a year where every person eligible for militia service was required to attend, military gun in hand. At the musters, government officials would inspect people's guns and account for the firearms on public rolls—an early version of gun registration.[41]

In some states, like New Hampshire and Rhode Island, government officials conducted door-to-door surveys of gun ownership in the community. In case of an attack, the government needed to know where the guns necessary to mount a defense were. If the government decided that a privately owned gun was needed, the founding fathers used a temporary form of gun confiscation known as "impressment" to seize the gun from its owner. Ten of the thirteen colonies impressed privately owned firearms for the war effort against England. Impressed guns would eventually be returned to their owners, but the seizure itself might leave the owner without a firearm to defend himself against an ordinary criminal attack. To the founding fathers, leaving an individual without a gun to defend himself was immaterial in light of the public need for that firearm. Guns were privately owned, but, in a sense, they were assets to be used if necessary for the public good.

The Revolutionary-era militia laws alone amount to a set of onerous gun laws that few modern-day gun rights advocates would ever accept. Imagine the outcry if Massachusetts announced that every gun owner of a certain age was required to appear with his or her guns at a public gathering where government officials would inspect the weapons and register them on state rolls.

The founders believed that ordinary people should have guns and that government shouldn't be allowed to completely disarm the citizenry. Yet their vision was certainly not that of today's gun rights hard-liners, who dismiss nearly any gun regulation as an infringement on individual liberty. Although the fact is rarely discussed in the individual-rights literature, the founding generation had many forms of gun control. They might not have termed it "gun control," but the founders understood that gun rights had to be balanced with public safety needs.

Government efforts to enhance public safety by regulating guns are as old as guns themselves. Credit—or blame—for inventing the first gun is often given to a Franciscan monk named Berthold Schwarz, who lived in Germany in the late 1200s and early 1300s. The exact dating of the invention is far from certain. Explosive powder goes back nearly a thousand years earlier. The Chinese reportedly had a handheld device made of bamboo that used gunpowder to shoot arrows in the 1100s. Guns, however, began to appear in Europe in the first decades of the 1300s, and laws restricting weapons quickly followed. In 1328, England enacted the Statute of Northampton, which provided that "no man great nor small, of what condition soever he be," shall "come before the King's justices, or other of the King's ministers doing their office, with force and arms" or "ride armed by night nor by day, in fairs, markets, nor in the presence of the justices or other ministers . . . upon pain to forfeit their armour to the King, and their bodies to prison at the King's pleasure." The law was intended mainly to limit traditional arms, like swords and knives, which were far more numerous at the time, but it applied equally to Berthold Schwarz's new invention.[42]

After gun control was abused by James II, the English Bill of Rights adopted in his wake didn't put an end to regulation of guns. Although that bill recognized the right to bear arms, the right was clearly limited. It applied only to Protestants, and even they were merely allowed guns "suitable to their conditions and as allowed by law." Soon after the English Bill of Rights was adopted, Parliament passed a law restricting the stockpiling of weapons by Catholics, whom the Protestant majority thought untrustworthy.[43]

Gun safety regulation was commonplace in the American colonies from their earliest days. The threat of hostile Native tribes led to government policies on gun ownership and use. In 1611, Governor Lord De La Warr of Virginia—after whom the state of Delaware is named—responded to a drawn-out battle with the Powhatan by ordering that all of the Jamestown settlers' muskets were officially part of the colony's public arsenal. By the end of that century, Massachusetts and Connecticut had both outlawed "matchlocks"—an early type of gun with a mechanism to ignite the firearm's gunpowder, freeing the shooter from having to lower the burning wick by hand—because they weren't effective enough in confrontations with the Natives. More dependable was the "wheel lock," an invention of Leonardo da Vinci that, like a modern-day lighter, used the rotation of a small wheel pressed against a flint to throw off sparks. In numerous colonies, governments used their regulatory authority to require men to carry guns to church and public meetings in order to, as a 1643 law in Connecticut explained, "prevent or withstand such sudden assaults as may be made" by Natives. Colonial laws frequently barred gun owners from selling firearms to the Natives. The right to bear arms in the colonial era was not a libertarian license to do whatever a person wanted with a gun. When public safety demanded that gun owners do something, the government was recognized to have the authority to make them do it.[44]

Selective disarmament was well within that authority, at least in the view of the founding fathers. They supported forcible disarmament of slaves, free blacks, and people of mixed race out of fear that these groups would use guns to revolt against slave masters. Even if free blacks and people of mixed race were completely law-abiding, they were prohibited from owning or carrying guns. Certain states were more liberal, like Virginia, where an 1806 law permitted "every negro or mulatto" who wasn't a slave to own a gun. Even here, however, they had to obtain permission from local officials, who had complete discretion over whether to grant the request.[45]

American colonists didn't bar only racial minorities from having guns. White people, too, were the target of gun control. Before the Revolution, at least one colony, Maryland, passed a law barring Catholics from possessing firearms. Other colonial governments prohibited any white person unwilling to affirm his allegiance to the British Crown from collecting firearms. Then, when the political winds shifted, people who didn't support the Revolution were ordered to turn over their guns. Only those prepared to swear their loyalty to the cause were entitled to keep and bear arms. The Loyalists disarmed by these rules, like those in Pennsylvania, weren't criminals or traitors who took up arms on behalf of the British. They were ordinary citizens exercising their fundamental right to freedom of conscience.[46]

The number of people eligible for disarmament by founding-era gun control was considerable. In some states, slaves and free blacks far outnumbered the white population. Some historians estimate that Loyalists opposed to the Revolution constituted up to 40 percent of the white population. Adding these groups together leaves only a small minority of people who fully enjoyed the right to keep and bear arms. The founders didn't think government should have the power to take away everyone's guns, but they were perfectly willing to confiscate weapons from anyone deemed untrustworthy—a category so broadly defined that it included a majority of the people.[47]

The burdensome militia laws and the disarmament of select groups were not the only forms of gun control in early America. The pressures to implement gun control in urban areas were intense even back then. Some cities and states adopted equivalents of today's "safe storage" laws. In several places, laws required that gunpowder be stored on the top floor of a building. The explosive power, which was being sold at the time by a start-up company named DuPont, was considered a safety hazard. In South Carolina before the Revolution, safe storage requirements were imposed on slave owners, who were required to keep their firearms locked up. Just as modern-day laws seek to prevent children from gaining access to guns, southern states sought to ensure that slaves couldn't get hold of a firearm.[48]

When public safety demanded it, the founding fathers were willing to go even further. In Boston, city leaders determined that the combustibility of gunpowder posed such a danger that all loaded firearms had to be kept out of buildings. A law from 1783 imposed a fine on "any person" who "shall take into any dwelling-house, stable, barn, out-house, ware-house, store, shop, or other building, within the town of Boston, any . . . fire-arm, loaded with, or having gunpowder." A second provision of the law effectively prohibited keeping a loaded firearm even in one's own home: "all . . . fire-arms . . . of any kind, that shall be found in any dwelling-house . . . or other building, charged with, or having in them any gun-powder, shall be liable to be seized" and forfeited. Given how time-consuming the loading of a gun was in those days, these two provisions imposed a significant burden on one's ability to have a functional firearm available for self-defense in the home. Yet there is no record of anyone's complaining that this law infringed the people's right to keep and bear arms. Even though the inspiration for this law was prevention of fires, not, say, protecting children from accidental shootings, the lesson remains the same: pressing safety concerns led Bostonians to effectively ban loaded weapons from any building in the city.[49]

The individual-rights literature that arose in the wake of Don Kates's article featured countless confident claims that gun control was a modern, twentieth-century invention. The facts suggest otherwise. The founding fathers had numerous gun control laws that responded to the public safety needs of their era. While our own public safety needs are different and require different responses, the basic idea that gun possession must be balanced with gun safety laws was one that the founders endorsed.

Don Kates, for one, recognized that many forms of gun control wouldn't conflict with the Second Amendment. His article was one of the few endorsing the individual-rights reading that would also discuss permissible forms of gun control. If liberals ignored the long tradition of gun rights because of their politics, conservatives ignored the long tradition of gun control because of theirs. Liberals didn't like the idea that "the people" had a right "to keep and bear arms," and conservatives didn't like the idea that gun owners could be "well regulated." Kates, however, thought mandatory gun registration, bans on rifles and machine guns, and restrictions on carrying firearms in public were all consistent with the Second Amendment. The true diehards in the gun rights movement didn't want to hear this part of Kates's argument. They instead wanted to talk about the founding fathers' guns, not their gun control. In *American Rifleman*, Steve Halbrook, the NRA lawyer who would later try to scuttle Alan Gura's lawsuit, dismissed Kates's endorsement of some forms of gun control as "Orwellian Newspeak."[50]

• • •

WHEN ALAN GURA was preparing for his appeal in the D.C. gun case, he relied heavily on Don Kates's Second Amendment scholarship. Gura planned to use the history Kates uncovered as proof that the founding generation intended the Second Amendment to protect the right of ordinary individuals to own guns.

Litigants in federal appeals court don't get to choose which judges will hear their cases. Each federal appellate "circuit"—a geographical region in which all appeals go to the same court—has half a dozen or more judges. Traditionally, three judges are chosen at random to hear an appeal. A court clerk picks them by lottery.

In the D.C. gun case, the selection process worked in Gura's favor. The three judges impaneled to hear his case were Karen Henderson, Thomas Griffith, and Laurence Silberman. Henderson was a Reagan appointee who, in one of her best-known cases, pleased conservatives by voting to strike down a landmark campaign finance law. Bob Levy, who financed the libertarians' lawsuit, said he "was convinced that Karen Henderson would be on our side." Griffith was also a reliable conservative. A Mormon, he was nominated to the bench by President George W. Bush. Prior to that, he served as counsel to the Senate during the impeachment trial of Bill Clinton. It was, however, the selection of Laurence Silberman that made it seem that Gura had indeed won the lottery.[51]

Appointed in 1985 as part of President Reagan and Ed Meese's effort to remake the federal bench, Silberman was known to be a die-hard conservative. He had defended Richard Nixon as acting attorney general during Watergate and later, as a federal judge, voted to void the convictions of Colonel Oliver North, the central figure in the notorious Iran-Contra arms-for-hostages controversy, a scandal that clouded the final years of the Reagan presidency. Accused by liberal groups of being "the most partisan and most political federal judge in the country," Silberman was feted by the right. The Federalist Society awarded him the group's "Distinguished Service" and "Lifetime Service" awards for his work to promote conservative legal ideas. To Gura, Silberman's conservatism was welcome, but equally important was Silberman's approach to interpreting the Constitution. When asked in an interview whether he was an originalist, Silberman replied, "Absolutely."[52]

In early December 2006, Gura appeared before the three judges to argue his case. Although Gura had never before made an argument in a federal court of appeals, it was Todd Kim, the lawyer for the District of Columbia, who appeared outmatched. A graduate of Harvard Law School and former editor of the prestigious *Harvard Law Review*, Kim was undoubtedly smart—an attribute he once used to win half a million dollars on the game show *Who Wants to Be a Super Millionaire*. Yet the gun case wasn't his case. Another lawyer in his office was slated to make the argument but came down with appendicitis three days before the scheduled hearing. Kim stepped in as a last-minute replacement, with little time to prepare.[53]

Kim started his presentation to the judges by insisting that none of the plaintiffs had really been hurt by the D.C. gun laws. (This was before the court ruled that all of Gura's plaintiffs except Dick Heller lacked standing to sue.) Each of them should have sought a license and then, if denied, should have attempted to get review of that decision through the D.C. government's administrative process. Having not done everything possible under D.C. law to obtain a license to own a gun, they didn't have any right to complain.[54]

Only moments into Kim's presentation, Judge Silberman interjected. "Suppose the District of Columbia passed a statute similar to this one but simply stating that no African American may get a license to have a handgun. Would there be standing to an African American who challenged a refusal to give him or her a license?"

The courtroom went silent. Kim, obviously surprised by Silberman's question, just stood there searching for an answer. Bob Levy, who was in the courtroom, estimated Kim took "maybe four minutes" to figure out an answer. Levy was admittedly exaggerating, but, he explained, when a lawyer is "silent at the podium for almost a minute, it seems like an hour and a half."[55]

Silberman was playing lawyer's chess with Kim. He wanted to push Kim into acknowledging that a black resident of D.C. would have the right to sue on the basis of the restriction in the law itself, without having to jump through procedural hoops. The person should be able to claim injury because the law, on its face, said he couldn't obtain a license. Once Kim admitted that, however, he would have a hard time arguing that some other person absolutely had to exhaust his administrative appeals before bringing a lawsuit.

Kim, unable to find a good response, eventually answered that D.C. would never enact such a statute. That wasn't good enough for Silberman, who then made it a bit more personal. What if, he asked the Korean American lawyer, D.C. barred Asians from having guns because the city government thought that too many Korean store owners were shooting blacks? Would an Asian person be able to bring suit? Yes, Kim responded, falling into Silberman's trap.

Silberman jumped at Kim's admission. From the perspective of the law, the reason for the statute's denial didn't matter, only the fact that the law said one couldn't obtain a license. If the Asian in Silberman's hypothetical was injured enough to bring suit, so was anyone who wanted to register a handgun under D.C.'s current law. The "injury is the denial of the license" by the statute, said Silberman.

Kim immediately realized his mistake and tried to backtrack, saying that he was wrong earlier, that the Asian store owner wouldn't be able to sue. By then, however, Kim had lost any credibility he had with Silberman, who peppered his remaining questions with sarcastic and dismissive remarks. Silberman almost wouldn't let Kim speak, interrupting him after almost every sentence. "No, no, no," the conservative judge insisted several times. Silberman even laughed out loud in response to what he saw as the logical implications of Kim's position. Judges argue and cajole, criticize and castigate, but rarely do they laugh at a lawyer's argument. Kim had begun the hearing with only a small hope of winning over Silberman. By the end, it was clear he had lost at least one of the three judges' votes.

Three months later, in February 2007, the D.C. Circuit handed down its decision in *Parker v. District of Columbia*—the case still bearing the name of the lead plaintiff, Shelly Parker. The decision was 2–1 against the District. The majority opinion, which strongly endorsed the individual-rights theory of the Second Amendment, was written by Silberman. The "Second Amendment protects an individual right to keep and bear arms," the opinion said. Silberman's contempt for Todd Kim's argument came through in the written opinion, which dismissed important points Kim made as "frivolous" and "strained." Karen Henderson, despite the libertarian lawyers' confidence that she'd vote with them, dissented. She thought the court was bound by the longstanding case law that interpreted the Second Amendment to be only about state militias.[56]

Silberman's opinion hewed closely to the arguments made twenty-five years earlier in Don Kates's *Michigan Law Review* article. The "right to keep and bear Arms" was not limited to military service; the "people" whose right is guaranteed were the same individuals who enjoyed First and Fourth Amendment rights; and the "Militia" meant all able-bodied citizens, who were expected to have their own guns when called to service. Silberman agreed with Kates that arming the

militia was the primary reason the founding fathers wrote the Second
Amendment, but it was not the only one. The right to bear arms the
founding fathers inherited from England also included the right to
defend one's home from violent attack. Because D.C.'s law completely
barred the use of a firearm for self-defense, it was unconstitutional.

For almost seventy years, the federal courts had consistently
turned away challenges to gun control on the basis of the militia
theory of the Second Amendment. Although one other recent decision had agreed that the Second Amendment protected an individual
right to have guns—the *Emerson* decision that originally inspired
Clark Neily to bring a Second Amendment case—even that court
had upheld the challenged law in the end. Neily, Levy, and Gura had
achieved something almost no one thought they could—persuade
a federal appeals court to strike down a gun control law on Second
Amendment grounds.

While the libertarian lawyers were ecstatic, the ruling only applied
in the District of Columbia. It didn't stand as binding precedent
anywhere else in the country. From the beginning, their goal was
to obtain a definitive ruling by the U.S. Supreme Court. There was,
nonetheless, a downside to their victory in the D.C. Circuit. Because
the losing party is the one with the legal right to file an appeal, it was
up to D.C.'s lawyers, not Alan Gura, to seek review by the Supreme
Court of the ruling on the constitutionality of D.C.'s law. Although
D.C. officials had vowed to fight until the end, rumors began to circulate that D.C. might not appeal after all. Gun control advocates
were urging the District to drop the case and avoid risking an adverse
decision by the Supreme Court, which could be devastating to gun
control nationwide. If the gun control advocates won out, Gura's case
would be over.

CHAPTER 5

CIVIL WAR

ALAN MORRISON NEVER FIT IN AT STANFORD UNIVERsity. The lush, oak-studded California campus was too serene for a New Yorker accustomed to a faster pace. One of the leading lawyers of his generation, Morrison had argued twenty cases before the Supreme Court, many of them landmark victories still studied in first-year law school courses. For years, he was the head of the litigation arm of Public Citizen, the public interest organization founded by Ralph Nader that was at the forefront of the consumer rights movement in the 1970s. Accompanied by his wife, Morrison had moved to Stanford to teach at the law school in 2001, but after five years of the relentless quietude and sunshine, the energetic Morrison was ready to return east.

In January 2007, he received a call from Linda Singer, the attorney general for the District of Columbia and Todd Kim's boss. Singer wanted Morrison's help with the D.C. gun case. "It was argued in the D.C. Circuit Court of Appeals a few weeks ago, and it looks very bad," she said.[1]

Morrison didn't know much about guns. A liberal urbanite, Morrison hadn't been around a gun since he was in the navy in the early 1960s. He still had a photograph of him posing with Charlton Heston, who visited Morrison's ship, the USS *Helena*. The photo shows Morrison, the young ensign, standing with the man who would become the face of the NRA. Towering behind them in the photo are three of the heavy cruiser's enormous guns.

Morrison's lack of gun knowledge was counterbalanced by his almost encyclopedic understanding of the Supreme Court. Not only had he argued many cases before the justices; he was a past president of the American Academy of Appellate Lawyers and the founder of an organization that helped inexperienced lawyers with cases at the high court. Morrison also counted several of the justices as friends, including Stephen Breyer, a jogging buddy, and David Souter, an old law school classmate. He had grown close, too, with Antonin Scalia when the two taught together years before at a summer law program in Rhodes, Greece. Their friendship, however, had soured. Morrison represented a group seeking to force the vice president at the time, Dick Cheney, to reveal who participated in secret meetings of an energy task force. When reports surfaced that Cheney had gone on a duck hunting trip with Scalia, Morrison filed a motion requesting Scalia to recuse himself from the case. Scalia refused and took offense at Morrison's implicit suggestion that Scalia couldn't be impartial. After that, Morrison said, Scalia "refused to say 'Hello' to me, shake my hand, anything like that."[2]

Linda Singer, whom Morrison knew from his Washington days, asked him to become her special deputy in the Office of the Attorney General for the District of Columbia. His role would be to advise Singer on legal strategy, especially in high-profile cases like the D.C. gun case. Morrison would also be the ideal person to argue the gun case in the Supreme Court, should the controversy go that far. It was far from clear, however, that the case would make it to the Court. Gun control groups were quietly seeking to persuade Singer to drop the case. The consequences of an adverse ruling by the Supreme Court were too great. If the Supreme Court issued a strong ruling endorsing the individual right to bear arms, "I think you can rest assured that virtually every gun law in the country would be at risk," predicted Kristen Rand, the legislative director of the Violence Policy Center. That was why the Brady Center to Prevent Gun Violence, the nation's leading gun control advocacy group, pushed the District behind closed doors not to appeal.[3]

Gun control groups had good reason to be worried. Over the preceding two years, the Court had taken a dramatic shift to the right. Bob Levy, who was financing the challenge to the D.C. gun laws, had predicted that by the time the case made it to the Supreme Court, President George W. Bush would have appointed several new conservative justices to the bench. After waiting in vain his entire first term for an opening on the Supreme Court, Bush had two vacancies arise over the span of six weeks in 2005. First Justice Sandra Day O'Connor, a moderate, retired so that she could take care of her ailing husband. Then the chief justice, William Rehnquist, died in office. President Bush's chance to alter the balance of the closely divided Court had finally arrived. He nominated Samuel Alito, whose views were so much like Justice Scalia's that critics derisively referred to him as "Scalito," and John Roberts, a federal judge known for his conservative rulings, to fill O'Connor's and Rehnquist's respective seats. Both of the new appointees were longtime members of the Federalist Society who had worked under Ed Meese in the Reagan administration.[4]

During his confirmation hearings before the Senate, Roberts stressed that he thought judges should respect precedent and not impose their own views on the nation. "Judges are like umpires," he told the senators. "Umpires don't make the rules; they apply them." Soon after joining the Court, however, Roberts and Alito voted to break with precedent in several high-profile cases—from abortion to affirmative action to workplace discrimination—each time moving the law in a direction favored by political conservatives. Referring to the impact of the new appointees, Justice Stephen Breyer lamented in one case, "It is not often in the law that so few have so quickly changed so much."[5]

Roberts and Alito formed a reliable bloc of conservative votes with

Antonin Scalia and Clarence Thomas. Justice Anthony Kennedy was the swing vote, and he often sided with the conservatives. Court watchers were predicting that if D.C. appealed the gun case, the justices would rule in favor of a broad reading of the Second Amendment. "Dominated as it is by Republican appointees, the court will adopt the individual-rights interpretation," warned Harvard law professor Cass Sunstein. Dennis Henigan, the legal director of the Brady Center, also thought that was the likely outcome. "There are obvious risks to taking this particular case before this particular court," he warned. Although the federal courts had read the 1939 *Miller* case as limiting the Second Amendment to militias, the Roberts Court, regardless of the chief justice's testimony in the Senate, had shown itself perfectly "comfortable disregarding very old precedents," Henigan observed.[6]

Among the lawyers for the District of Columbia, there was a spirited debate about whether to take the case to the Supreme Court. Perhaps chastened by his own experience defending the law before Judge Silberman, Todd Kim argued that D.C. should just take its losses. The District could revise its gun laws while keeping them very strict. For example, handguns could be allowed, but only under very restrictive licensing requirements. Or the District could keep its handgun ban and eliminate the trigger lock requirement for long guns. While this wouldn't stop Alan Gura from filing a new lawsuit challenging these revised restrictions, he would have to start over in the trial court and spend another three or four years litigating the case.[7]

Alan Morrison thought D.C. had to appeal. "To my way of thinking, we didn't have any choice." The lawyers had an obligation to their client, the District of Columbia and its residents. The handgun ban was one of the very first laws passed after the District was granted home rule. Because there were plausible arguments to defend the law, the lawyers should fight as hard as they could. Besides, it was up to the city council, not the lawyers, to decide what laws D.C. should have. The mayor, Adrian Fenty, who had the final say on whether to appeal, thought the people of the District supported *this* law. "The handgun ban has saved many lives and will continue to do so if it remains in effect," said the mayor. "Wherever I go, the response from the residents is, 'Mayor Fenty, you've got to fight this all the way to the Supreme Court.'" "So," explained Fenty and Singer in a *Washington Post* op-ed, "we will fight."[8]

On September 4, 2007, the District of Columbia filed its "petition for writ of certiorari"—legal terminology for a motion requesting the Supreme Court to review the case. It was Alan Morrison's first official day at work, although he had been advising Linda Singer informally for months.

Meanwhile, the infighting between the NRA and the libertarian lawyers broke out again. Despite the favorable ruling by the D.C. Circuit, the NRA still didn't want to risk an unfavorable one by the Supreme Court. If anything, Judge Silberman's opinion made it even more likely that the Supreme Court would decide to hear the D.C. gun case. The justices take very few appeals, but one of the best predictors of whether they will take one is if there is a "split" in the federal courts. If different federal courts around the country are issuing inconsistent rulings on the same legal question, the Supreme Court often steps in to resolve the conflict. *Emerson*, the judicial decision adopting the individual-rights view that motivated Clark Neily to consider a lawsuit against D.C., had created a split with the federal courts subscribing to the militia theory of the Second Amendment. Yet because the *Emerson* court didn't strike down any laws, the ruling didn't create a particularly meaningful split. Judge Silberman's decision, by contrast, struck down a gun control law and promised to open up many others to challenge. There was now a clear and consequential split among the federal courts.[9]

The NRA renewed its effort to have Congress pass the District of Columbia Personal Protection Act. If that federal law was passed, D.C.'s gun laws would be overturned and the very law Gura was challenging would be taken off the books.

When the libertarian lawyers heard that the NRA was once again pushing its Capitol Hill allies on the D.C. Personal Protection Act, they were outraged. They decided to do everything they could to persuade the NRA brass to let their case go to the Supreme Court. Bob

Levy, who had some friends high up in the NRA leadership, arranged for a meeting at the gun group's headquarters. In March 2007, Alan Gura, Clark Neily, and Bob Levy met with NRA leaders, including Wayne LaPierre, the executive vice president; Chris Cox, the director of the NRA's lobbying arm, the Institute for Legislative Action; Robert Dowlut, the general counsel; and others. The NRA tried to reassure the libertarian lawyers that it wasn't going to interfere with their lawsuit. LaPierre told them, "You can take it to the bank. The NRA will not do anything to prevent the Supreme Court from reviewing" the D.C. gun case. The proposal in Congress was just a show put on for members, a signal that the NRA still opposes D.C.'s draconian laws. "If it looks like it's going to pass, we'll pull the plug on it, don't worry," the NRA leaders insisted.[10]

The NRA's assurances were understandably hard to believe. Having tried to persuade the libertarian lawyers not to file suit and then mounting a hostile takeover attempt of the litigation, the NRA leaders had squandered their credibility to now say they wouldn't stand in the way. "I didn't believe it for a minute," recalled Clark Neily.[11]

Not more than a minute or two after the meeting ended, the libertarian lawyers were just outside of the NRA building when they received word that the D.C. Personal Protection Act was moving to the floor of the House of Representatives for a vote. The lawyers, Levy recalled, were "livid." Instead of the NRA pulling the plug, the bill was being fast-tracked. Just then, someone from the NRA came running out of the office and caught up to the libertarian lawyers. He "assured us that they were not responsible" for the decision to move forward with the law, remembered Levy.[12]

Gura, Levy, and Neily couldn't afford to take any chances. That same day, they went down to Capitol Hill to meet with congressional staffers and lobby against the NRA's bill. They met with people from the offices of several important senators in the Republican leadership, including Jim DeMint, Tom Coburn, James Inhofe, and Sam Brownback. Their pitch was simple: the NRA's bill looks good at first but would be a serious threat to the Second Amendment. The law was only a short-term fix. Once Democrats retook power in

Washington, they might overturn the law. A ruling by the Supreme Court was more durable—and could eventually extend to the whole country. The Supreme Court, they argued, was going to hear a Second Amendment case sooner or later, so better to hear the libertarian lawyers' case than one brought by a crack dealer or gangbanger.

Gura, Levy, and Neily spent the next few weeks working with lawmakers to stop the NRA's bill. While they had proven themselves effective lawyers, when it came to legislative politics, they would be no match for the NRA, one of the great powerhouses in Washington.

Three weeks after the meeting at the offices of the NRA, however, a mentally disturbed student named Seung-Hui Cho went on a rampage through the campus of Virginia Tech University in Blacksburg, Virginia, killing thirty-two innocent bystanders. Carrying a 9mm semiautomatic Glock 19, a .22-caliber Walther P22 handgun, and four hundred rounds of ammunition, Cho chained the main entrance doors to one of Virginia Tech's science buildings shut, went up to the second floor, and began to gun down professors and students. One professor, Liviu Librescu, a Holocaust survivor, barricaded the doorway to his classroom to allow students to escape out the window. While Librescu was holding the door closed, Cho fired multiple shots straight through the door, killing the heroic professor.

The Virginia Tech massacre was one of the deadliest peacetime shootings in American history. One casualty of the rampage was the D.C. Personal Protection Act. The extraordinary media attention devoted to the incident focused on how easily Cho was able to purchase guns despite his history of mental illness, dissipating the political will to pass a law liberalizing access to firearms.

•   •   •

THE NRA's reluctance to support Gura's lawsuit was due in part to uncertainty about how the justices of the Supreme Court would vote. The Court had become more conservative, but none of the justices had ever decided a Second Amendment case before. "Nobody had a track record on this," observed Alan Morrison.[13]

Of the nine justices, only Clarence Thomas had taken a firm stand
in favor of the individual-rights reading of the Second Amendment.
Thomas's view was expressed in a concurring opinion he wrote in
Printz v. United States—the case discussed in chapter 3 involving
a challenge to the 1993 law requiring background checks for certain gun purchases. In that case, the NRA's lawyer, Steve Halbrook,
didn't argue that the law was unconstitutional on Second Amendment grounds. He instead argued that the federal government had no
authority to require state and local police departments to spend their
own time and money conducting background checks. The Supreme
Court agreed, although the importance of the decision was mini-
mized by the switch the following year to instantaneous background
checks conducted with a computerized system run by the federal government. The change meant local officials wouldn't be required to do
anything.[14]

Justice Thomas, the most conservative justice to sit on the Court
since the 1930s, not only agreed with the outcome in the *Printz* case
but also filed a separate opinion, in which he wrote that the Court
should take a second look at the Second Amendment. "Marshaling
an impressive array of historical evidence, a growing body of scholarly commentary indicates that the 'right to keep and bear arms' is,
as the Amendment's text suggests, a personal right," Thomas wrote.
"This Court has not had recent occasion to consider the nature of
the substantive right safeguarded by the Second Amendment. If,
however, the Second Amendment is read to confer a personal right
to 'keep and bear arms,'" the federal background check law might
violate that provision. Making no effort to hide his view, Thomas
wrote, "Perhaps at some future date, this Court will have the opportunity to determine whether Justice Story," a well-respected judge
of the early 1800s, "was correct when he wrote that the right to bear
arms 'has justly been considered as the palladium of the liberties of
a republic.'"[15]

It was no small irony that the one justice most likely to vote to
overturn D.C.'s law was also the lone African American on the Court.
D.C. has one of the highest concentrations of blacks in America, and

gun violence nationwide disproportionately affects African Americans. Blacks make up only 13 percent of the American population, but over half of all gun-related homicide victims. In 2004, all but 2 of the 137 firearms homicide victims in D.C. were black. D.C.'s gun laws were designed by mostly black lawmakers to help out a predominantly black community. Thomas, however, knew that many of the most extreme gun control efforts in American history were intended to oppress blacks.[16]

●   ●   ●

THE GROUND shook as the hooves of fifty horses galloped through the pine thickets of York County, South Carolina. It was the dark of night in March 1871, and a local posse of Klansmen was on its way to the home of Jim Williams, a former slave. Led by Dr. J. Rufus Bratton, a prominent local physician, the night riders wore flowing gowns and cone-shaped hoods typical of the KKK. In the early years, Klansmen didn't all wear the distinctive plain white robes now so closely identified with this racist band. Instead, members wore a variety of different-colored regalia. Some wore red, brown, or yellow, while others preferred black so that they would be harder to spot in the dark. Hoods were often adorned with horns, beards, or long red cloth tongues to evoke a devilish visage.[17]

On the way to Williams's cabin, the posse stopped at the homes of other freedmen to terrorize them. Andy Tims, one of the victims, recalled, "They said: 'Here we come—we are the Ku Klux. Here we come, right from hell.' . . . Before I got the door they busted the latch off, and two came in, and one got me by the arm and says, 'We want your guns.'" Tims turned over his rifle. As the Klansmen departed, they said they were off to find Jim Williams. They wanted to get his guns too.

Worried that slaves and free blacks would rise up and start a race war, many white southerners were terrified at the prospect of black men with guns. Nat Turner's rebellion in 1831, which led to the deaths of fifty-five whites, is the most well-known uprising, but slave revolts

were common throughout the South in the early 1800s. The largest took place outside of New Orleans in 1811, the year before Louisiana became a state. Led by a mixed-race slave known as Charles
Deslondes, several hundred blacks formed military-style companies,
taking up guns and swords stored on plantations. Some on horseback, others on foot, the slaves headed toward the city, setting fire
to residences as they passed. To quell the uprising, the governor of
the territory, William Claiborne, called out the militia and distributed the cache of firearms stored in a local arsenal to whites. Within
forty-eight hours, the revolt was quashed and nearly one hundred
slaves were killed—far more than the two dozen or so killed in retribution for Turner's revolt. Deslondes, the leader, had his hands cut
off and, according to one witness, "before he had expired was put in
a bundle of straw and roasted." Others were decapitated, their heads
secured onto poles planted along the Mississippi River as a warning
to other slaves.[18]

These sorts of incidents convinced southern leaders that guns were
for whites only—an attitude reflected in the hardening of founding-
era laws restricting gun ownership for blacks. Slaves were already
barred from possessing firearms without their owner's permission, so
after the 1811 uprising New Orleans passed a law forbidding slaves
from carrying so much as a "cane or stick" in public. Elsewhere,
restrictions on free blacks were also tightened. Where they had once
been allowed to have guns if they obtained permission from local
officials, free blacks were increasingly prohibited from possessing any
type of firearm. As the North Carolina Supreme Court explained,
the "only object" of disarming the black population "is to preserve
the peace and safety of the community from being disturbed by an
indiscriminate use on ordinary occasions, by free men of color, of fire
arms and other arms of an offensive character." Whites believed they
were doing what was necessary to ensure public safety.[19]

The denial of blacks' right to keep and bear arms was enforced
by the other feature of the Second Amendment: states' well-regulated militias. In the decades after the Revolution, Americans came
to believe that militias composed of ordinary citizens were not suf-

ficiently reliable for national defense. Militias weren't adequately trained, and despite a federal law mandating they arm themselves— the founding fathers' version of an individual mandate—not enough people showed up for service with guns. The turning point was the War of 1812, when state militias were forced to fight the British for three years. The performance of the militias was so poor that Britain's army was able to burn Washington, D.C., to the ground despite its preoccupation with a far more important war in Europe against Napoleon. Opposed to the conflict, New England states refused to supply money or militias to support the war effort. Americans came to realize that militias could be helpful to respond to emergencies, but a long, drawn-out campaign required a more permanent and dependable army.[20]

In the South, militias were transformed into slave patrols. Posses of armed whites would hunt down escaped slaves and terrorize free blacks. Laws, like the one enacted in Florida in 1825, specifically authorized patrols to "enter into all negro houses" and to "lawfully seize and take away" any "arms, weapons, and ammunition."[21]

As blacks were being further disarmed, the constitutional right to have guns was, ironically, expanding in other ways. Between 1790 and 1860, twenty states joined the Union, and fourteen of them included in their state constitutions the right to bear arms. In this period, the traditional militia justification for the right to bear arms was increasingly replaced by the notion that the right was primarily about personal defense against criminal attack. This was reflected in the fact that many of these new state constitutional law provisions were phrased as protections for individuals to use guns to defend themselves. "Every citizen shall have the right to bear arms in defence of himself and the republic," declared Texas's constitution, adopted in 1845.[22]

Blacks, however, were not "citizens"—certainly not in the view of Roger Taney. In 1857, Taney, the chief justice of the United States, wrote the opinion for the Supreme Court in the infamous case of *Dred Scott v. Sandford*. Blacks, he said, were "unfit to associate with the white race" and "had no rights which the white man was bound to respect."

That this depraved view would come from Taney was surprising, considering his own past. As a young man, he had voluntarily freed eight of the ten slaves he inherited from his father; the two he kept on were elderly and, liberated from forced labor, were supported by Taney with monthly pensions for the rest of their lives. Slavery, he had said, was "a blot on our national character." Yet Taney was at his core a southerner. According to the renowned historian Don Fehrenbacher, "Taney's real commitment was not to slavery, for which he had no great affection, but to southern life and values, which seemed organically linked to the peculiar institution and unpreservable without it."[23]

Taney and many white southerners believed that blacks simply could not be citizens, because if they were, they would be entitled to all the rights and privileges guaranteed by the Constitution. As Taney wrote in *Dred Scott*, recognizing the citizenship of blacks would mean affording them "the full liberty of speech," the right "to hold meetings upon public affairs," and even the right "to keep and carry arms wherever they went." Taney knew that southerners would never stand for this. To protect the South and its way of life, he wrote an opinion that he hoped would put an end to the conflict over the future of slavery that was tearing the country apart in the 1850s.

Dred Scott didn't accomplish Taney's goal. It not only strengthened the North's resolve to impose its will on the South but also helped get a man who made his fame criticizing the ruling elected to the presidency in 1860. Even though Taney despised Abraham Lincoln, he did the honorable thing and agreed to administer the oath of office to the newly elected president. The South, meanwhile, reacted with far more hostility to the election results. Five weeks after Taney swore Lincoln in, South Carolina called out its constitutionally recognized militia and opened fire on Fort Sumter.[24]

•   •   •

BORN AND raised a slave, Jim Williams was freed by the Civil War—more by the chaos on the ground than by the formalities of Lincoln's Emancipation Proclamation. After the attack on Fort Sumter,

Williams escaped his plantation and joined the Union army, where he served in a black unit under the command of General William Tecumseh Sherman. Sherman, who coined the phrase "War is hell," led his troops in the late summer of 1864 into Atlanta, the heart of the Confederacy. His victorious march is often credited with saving the presidency of Lincoln and paving the way for the ultimate surrender of the South at Appomattox Courthouse the next spring.

Williams must have thought that Lincoln's promise of a "new birth of freedom" was about to be fulfilled. In the eyes of many northerners, blacks like him had earned the rights of citizenship by bearing arms in defense of the Union. When Williams returned home, he found that the whites of York County didn't agree.

Williams may not have had the respect of local whites, but he, like many blacks, now had guns. Some blacks fought for the Union army, which allowed soldiers to take home their rifled muskets for a reasonable price. Southern blacks intent on returning to their hometowns knew what was waiting for them and wanted the protection. As one activist in Louisiana advised, "I would say to every colored soldier, 'Bring your gun home.'" Even blacks who didn't serve were able to buy guns cheaply. Hundreds of thousands of firearms were produced for the war, and once the war ended the market was flooded with cheap guns. For the first time, southern blacks were armed.[25]

Almost immediately after the war ended, southern states adopted the "Black Codes"—laws designed to reestablish white supremacy by dictating what the freedmen could and couldn't do. If you were black in the South, the codes ordered you to get a job; anyone without one was deemed a vagrant and fined. You were required to sign an annual labor contract—by mid-January of a given year—that effectively made you a slave again. You had to work six days a week, from sunrise to sunset. If you tried to leave your job, you would be arrested and returned to your employer, who was legally allowed to whip you as punishment. You were not allowed to vote, sit on a jury, or own a gun.[26]

The old slave patrols reemerged to enforce these rules and terrorize the black community. Posses went by different names: the Men of

Justice and the Black Cavalry in Alabama, the Knights of the White
Camellia in Louisiana, the Knights of the Rising Sun in Texas. In
January 1866, *Harper's Weekly* reported that in Mississippi the whites
"have seized every gun found in the hands of the (so-called) freedmen of this section of the country."[27]

The most infamous of these disarmament posses was the Ku Klux
Klan. The KKK was formed in 1868 when six white men, all of whom
had fought for the Confederacy, gathered one night in the law office
of Judge Thomas M. Jones in Pulaski, Tennessee. The young men,
all well educated and from good families, were, as one of them later
described, "hungering and thirsting" for amusement. Civilian life
brought a boredom that paled in comparison with the danger and
excitement of war. The young men needed something to keep them
busy. Secret societies like the Freemasons were popular, and the men
decided to form one of their own. At first they were satisfied playing
practical jokes on blacks, like spooking them on back roads by dress-
ing up in white sheets and pretending to be ghosts of Confederate
soldiers. Making fun of blacks was already a well-established pastime
for the young white men of the South. In this case, however, violence
and terror soon followed.[28]

The six Pulaski men adopted the name Ku Klux Klan because they
liked its alliteration. Years later, people speculated that the name Ku
Klux was chosen to evoke the sound made by a rifle being loaded.
More likely, the Pulaski six just followed the common practice of
using Greek words to name fraternal organizations, like Phi Beta
Kappa. *Kuklos* is Greek for circle, band, or group of people. At the
time, the best-known collegiate fraternity in the South was Kuklos
Adelphon, founded in 1812 at the University of North Carolina and
known colloquially as Old Kappa Alpha. Ku Klux Klan was just a
variation on a theme.[29]

The name quickly caught on. Before long, there was a Ku Klux
little league baseball team in Nashville, Ku Klux Smoking Tobacco,
and a popular song called "Ku Klux's Midnight Roll Call." Medicines,
paints, theater shows, and circus acts all borrowed the label. Some
southerners loved the name and all that it came to stand for.[30]

Groups of former Confederate soldiers began calling themselves KKK with or without Pulaski's permission. In its early days, the Klan was so decentralized that it couldn't really be considered a single entity. The original founders had no control over the scores of local groups—or businesses, for that matter—that used the name. When white gangs calling themselves Klansmen became increasingly violent, some of the Pulaski six tried to disband the group altogether. By then, however, the name had become so popular that any band of whites striking fear into their black neighbors was called the Ku Klux Klan.[31]

Milus Smith Carroll was one of the Klansmen from York County who set out to raid Jim Williams's home. As he recalled, "The Klan was made up of ex-Confederate officers and we hoped to take the place of the patrol system used before the war to keep the slaves in order." Whether in South Carolina or Texas, the goal of the former rebel soldiers in flowing robes was to reestablish white supremacy in the South. However decentralized the Klan was, these bands shared the same strategy: strike terror into the hearts of the freedmen and take away their guns so they couldn't fight back.[32]

•   •   •

"DR. BRATTON and myself were the only ones who knew just where Jim Williams lived," Milus Carroll later told investigators. The fifty-odd Klansmen "followed a blind sort of road leading in back of where he lived. When we got in three or four hundred yards of his house, we halted and here we selected ten or twelve men to go to the house and left the rest of the men with the horses. We proceeded on foot to the house and knocked on the door. The door was opened by Rose, Jim's wife, and we went in. The only occupants of the house were Jim's wife and one Negro man. When asked where Jim was, his wife said she did not know. He had gone off somewhere, she said. We made a thorough search of the house but did not find him."

J. Rufus Bratton, the leader of the group, thought something wasn't right. Just the day before, Williams had told a gathering in York

County that he had a cache of guns and threatened to fight back if the KKK attacked him. That was one of the reasons the Klan decided to mount the raid—and why their group was over fifty strong.

Then Bratton was struck by a realization. Pull up some of the plank flooring, he told his men. "He might be under there." They started tearing up the floor of Williams's cabin. "And sure enough," remembered Milus Carroll, "there was Jim crouched down under the floor." Williams may have had a cache of arms, but no matter how many guns he owned, Williams would not be able to fight off a posse fifty strong. Williams decided that he and his wife were more likely to survive if he hid under the floorboards rather than take up arms and fight back.

Before the Civil War, abolitionists had extolled the virtues of gun ownership for blacks who wanted to defend themselves. In the 1840s and 1850s, antislavery advocates like Lysander Spooner and Joel Tiffany argued that blacks had a natural right to use guns to defend themselves from southern outrages. They also thought that slavery must end, even if it meant taking up arms to stop it. In 1856, the most famous preacher in America, Henry Ward Beecher—the brother of Harriet Beecher Stowe, author of *Uncle Tom's Cabin*—wrote in the *New York Tribune* of the need to supply antislavery men in Kansas with guns. A mini–civil war had broken out in that territory over whether to enter the Union slave or free. Despite being a man of the cloth, Beecher thought that only firearms, not the Good Book, would settle the question. "You might just as well read the Bible to Buffaloes," he said. Slavery people respected only "the logic that is embodied in Sharp's rifle." Beecher promoted efforts to send hundreds of rifles to Kansas in crates marked as containing bibles. Sharp's rifles became known as Beecher's Bibles.[33]

When Senator Andrew Pickens Butler of South Carolina, an ardent proponent of slavery, argued that the federal government should disarm the settlers in Kansas, Senator Charles Sumner of Massachusetts took to the floor of the Senate to denounce Butler's plan as a violation of the Second Amendment. The rifle, said Sumner, "has ever been the companion of the pioneer, and under God, his tutelary protector against the red man and the beast of the forest." Never "was this efficient weapon more needed in just self-defense, than now in Kansas, and at least one article in our National Constitution must be blotted out, before the complete right to it can in any way be impeached." Sumner went on to suggest that Butler himself was a disgrace. He had "chosen a mistress to whom he has made his vows and who, though ugly to others, is always lovely to him; though polluted in the sight of the world, is chaste in his sight. I mean the harlot, Slavery."[34]

Preston Brooks, a thirty-six-year-old congressman from South Carolina and Butler's cousin, took exception to Sumner's speech. Two days later Brooks went into the Senate chamber and viciously beat the Massachusetts senator with a gutta-percha cane. The incident itself is much better known than the reason the other senators didn't come to Sumner's aid. In fact, they tried. Brooks, however, was accompanied by Laurence Keitt, another representative from South Carolina, who drew a pistol and yelled, "Let them alone, God damn you!" Protected by Keitt's firearm, Brooks continued to bludgeon Sumner until his cane broke in half. With Sumner bloodied and limp on the Senate floor, Brooks and Keitt calmly walked out.

Even after losing the Civil War, southern whites were determined to make sure that blacks were disarmed and returned to their power-less state. That effort, like many overly aggressive efforts to take away people's guns, sparked a backlash. The North saw the right to bear arms as one of the freedmen's fundamental rights and sought to stop the southern aggression.

With much of the South under the occupation of the Union army, the North first attempted to protect the freedmen's right to have guns for self-defense with military orders. In South Carolina, where Jim Williams lived, General Daniel E. Sickles issued a command in January 1866 insisting "the constitutional rights of all loyal and well-disposed inhabitants to bear arms will not be infringed." Although his order recognized that gun safety laws were valid, they could not be applied solely to disarm the freedmen. The Union army's military occupation of the South, however, was so ineffective that South Carolinians just ignored Sickles's order.[35]

Radical Republicans in Congress then pushed for federal laws that

would guarantee the freedmen's fundamental rights. In the Freedmen's Bureau Act of July 1866, Congress declared that the freedmen
were entitled to the "full and equal benefit of all laws and proceedings
concerning personal liberty, security, and the acquisition, enjoyment,
and disposition of estate, real and personal, including the constitutional right to bear arms." The same year, Congress passed the
nation's first Civil Rights Act, which defined the freedmen as citizens
of the United States and made it a federal offense to deprive them of
their rights on the basis of race. Senator James Nye, a supporter of
both laws, told his colleagues, "As citizens of the United States," the
freedmen "have an equal right to protection, and to keep and bear
arms for self-defense."[36]

Andrew Johnson, who assumed the presidency after Lincoln's
assassination, did not support such efforts. Like the KKK, Johnson
was born in Tennessee and harbored sympathies for the South. He
vetoed both laws, but the support in Congress, in which the states that
seceded were no longer represented, was strong enough to override
Johnson. The president's opposition to Reconstruction eventually led
Congress to make Johnson the first president ever to be impeached.
He survived removal by a single vote.

One of the prosecutors in Johnson's impeachment trial was the
Ohio representative John Bingham. Ohio in the mid-nineteenth century was, like Massachusetts, a beacon of liberalism and abolition-
ist thought. The state was a major thoroughfare for the Underground
Railroad, which helped escaped slaves make their way to freedom
in Canada. Bingham, who was raised in the small frontier town of
Cadiz, became a lawyer known for his soaring oratory, which was
described by a contemporary as "a steady, strong, onsweeping wind,
roaring through and over a great old forest." Nothing meant more to
Bingham than his country and its Constitution. A frequent tagline in
his speeches was "One people, one Constitution, and one country!"
In 1865, Bingham's childhood friend from Cadiz, Edwin Stanton,
who was then secretary of war, appointed him to be one of the judges
in the military commission investigating the conspiracy to kill President Lincoln. That commission gave rise to eight convictions; one of

the defendants, Mary Surratt, became the first woman ever executed by the U.S. government. Throughout his life, Bingham hinted that there were details about the Lincoln conspiracy that, for the healing of the country, he could never reveal. On his deathbed, he told his doctor, "The truth must remain sealed."[37]

Bingham thought that the only way his beloved country would recover from the Civil War was to amend the Constitution. While he revered the founding fathers' handiwork, he recognized that because the Bill of Rights was not enforceable against the states, the South was exploiting it to deny the freedmen their rights, including the right to bear arms. Southern attempts to deny blacks equal rights, he said, were turning the Constitution—"a sublime and beautiful scripture— into a horrid charter of wrong." Bingham supported the Freedmen's Bureau and Civil Rights acts, but he held that it would take nothing less than a constitutional amendment to protect the former slaves. In December 1865, Bingham introduced a proposal to do just that.

In what would come to be recognized as the single most important provision in the Constitution, Bingham's proposal for the Fourteenth Amendment promised to overturn Roger Taney's decision in the *Dred Scott* case by declaring that blacks were citizens. "All persons born or naturalized in the United States . . . are citizens of the United States and of the State wherein they reside." The amendment also corrected what Bingham saw as the Constitution's greatest mistake. From now on, the states couldn't trespass on the fundamental rights of individuals listed in the Bill of Rights. "No state shall make or enforce any law which shall abridge the privileges or immunities of citizens of the United States; nor shall any state deprive any person of life, liberty, or property, without due process of law; nor deny to any person within its jurisdiction the equal protection of the laws."

The key phrase was "privileges or immunities." According to Bingham, "the privileges and immunities of citizens of the United States" were "chiefly defined in the first eight amendments to the Constitution." These fundamental rights "never were limitations upon the power of the States, until made so by the Fourteenth Amendment." In the Senate, Jacob Howard of Michigan was the chief sponsor of Bingham's amendment. He said the privileges and immunities included "the personal rights guaranteed and secured by the first eight amendments of the Constitution; such as the freedom of speech and of the press," "the right to be exempt from unreasonable searches and seizures," and "the right to keep and bear arms."[38]

The founding fathers may have thought the Second Amendment was first and foremost about protecting state militias, but the authors of the Fourteenth Amendment defined the right to keep and bear arms primarily in terms of individual self-defense. The freedmen had a right to defend themselves from the racist state militias and marauding Klansmen. Yale law professor Akhil Reed Amar has written, "In short, between 1775 and 1866 the poster boy of arms morphed from the Concord minuteman to the Carolina freedman."[39]

Because the southern states weren't likely to agree voluntarily to these provisions, Congress conditioned the termination of military occupation on the South's ratification of the Fourteenth Amendment. Congress, Senator James Rood Doolittle of Wisconsin explained, would "force them to adopt it, at the point of the bayonet."[40]

Congress may have had the authority to force its will on the South with its Klansmen in white robes, but it wasn't as easy to control the Supreme Court with its justices in black ones. Over the next few years, the high court would insert itself into the controversy over congressional attempts to help the freedmen just as it had inserted itself into the slavery question during Roger Taney's tenure. African Americans would find the post–Civil War Court almost as hostile to their constitutional rights.

• • •

ONCE J. RUFUS BRATTON, Milus Carroll, and their crew pulled Jim Williams up from beneath the floor, they demanded his weapons. He handed over two guns and said he had no more. The Klansmen weren't satisfied. "We hauled him out and placed a rope around his neck," Carroll recalled. "We had got back about half way to the horses when someone spied a large tree with a limb running out ten or twelve feet from the ground and suggested that that was the place to finish the job." The Klansmen told Williams to climb up the tree and fasten the rope around his neck to the tree limb. When they told him to jump from the tree, however, Williams refused. One of the Klansmen climbed up the tree and pushed Williams off. As he fell, Williams managed to grab hold of the branch. The Klansman who climbed the tree took out a knife and stabbed at Williams's fingers until the freedman couldn't hold on any longer.

In the thirty years after the Civil War broke out, white mobs lynched an estimated five thousand African Americans in the United States. The practice took its name from a Virginia Quaker named Charles Lynch, a justice of the peace in the Revolutionary era known for handing down summary, extralegal convictions of Loyalists to the Crown without proper trials. Before the Civil War, southern lynch mobs targeted whites primarily, murdering those who supported abolition. It was only after slaves won their freedom that lynch mobs turned to blacks. The Klan used mob violence to reassert white supremacy and dissuade blacks from exercising the constitutional freedoms, like the right to vote and the right to bear arms, that federal law insisted they enjoyed.[41]

In response to the growing white violence, blacks began to organize "Negro militias." The North and sympathetic Reconstruction governors in the South set about arming these militias to defend against white racist attacks. When the pro-Union governor of Florida purchased two thousand muskets and forty thousand rounds of ammunition to distribute to the black militias, Klansmen alerted by railroad employees seized the shipment en route. Similar seizures occurred elsewhere, such as in Arkansas after that state's governor bought the black militias four thousand guns from New York.[42]

Although black militias were occasionally able to repel the racists, they more often fared no better than Jim Williams, who was also the head of an informal black militia in York County.

Take, for example, the black militia of Grant Parish, Louisiana. The 1872 election in Grant Parish was marked by widespread fraud and intimidation of black voters. When whites claimed to have won in the majority black district, the black militiamen decided to stop them from seizing the county's seat of government, located in a courthouse in the parish town of Colfax. They occupied the courthouse and dug a large trench around the building. On Easter Sunday 1873 more than 300 whites armed with rifles arrived and ordered the blacks to turn over their guns and evacuate the courthouse. The blacks refused and a battle ensued. The black militia fought valiantly and was able to hold its position until the whites brought out a cannon. The militiamen inside the courthouse waved a white flag in surrender, but the whites set the building afire. Blacks able to escape the blaze were hunted down by the mob and executed. In all, 150 blacks and 3 whites were killed.[43]

One of the white men responsible for what became known as the Colfax Massacre was Bill Cruikshank, a local cotton planter. When Louisiana officials refused to press any charges, the federal government stepped in. Cruikshank and ninety-seven others were indicted for murder and conspiracy to violate the freedmen's civil rights, including their "right to keep and bear arms for a lawful purpose." A jury acquitted the defendants of most of the charges, but three of the men, including Cruikshank, were convicted of conspiracy. Cruikshank appealed to the Supreme Court, arguing that the federal government lacked the authority to prosecute them.

Roger Taney was no longer on the Supreme Court, having died the same day in 1864 that his home state of Maryland passed a law abolishing slavery. Yet the Court remained hostile to the program of Reconstruction. In *Ex parte Milligan*, decided in 1866, the Court held unconstitutional the North's policy of using military tribunals instead of civilian courts to try citizens charged with attempting to sabotage the war effort. In *Ex parte Garland*, decided the next year, the Court struck down a law barring former members of the Confederacy from serving in federal office. In Bill Cruikshank's case, the Court disregarded that what John Bingham said was the very purpose of the Fourteenth Amendment and held that it did not in fact make the Bill of Rights enforceable against the states. "The second amendment declares that it shall not be infringed; but this . . . means no more than it shall not be infringed *by Congress*," the Court explained. Congress hadn't infringed the rights of freedmen; Cruikshank had. Because the Second Amendment "has no other effect than to restrict the powers of the national government," the Court ordered Cruikshank set free.

The Court's decision in *United States v. Cruikshank*, along with others of the period, delayed the promise of Bingham's amendment for decades. As Pulitzer Prize–winning historian Leonard Levy remarked, "*Cruikshank* paralyzed the federal government's attempt to protect black citizens by punishing violators of their Civil Rights and, in effect, shaped the Constitution to the advantage of the Ku Klux Klan."[44]

Cruikshank was still a few years off when, after lynching Jim Williams, J. Rufus Bratton and Milus Carroll returned to where the other Klansmen were waiting with their horses. One man asked Bratton where Williams, the black militiaman, was. Bratton replied, "He is in hell, I expect." The posse then rode off to confiscate the guns of other blacks in the area. As the sun began to rise, the Klansmen stopped at the house of Bratton's brother John. There they drank whiskey, laughed about their night, and had a celebratory feast. Later that morning, Williams's body was found with a note pinned to his clothes. It read, "Jim Williams gone to his last muster."

●   ●   ●

ON NOVEMBER 20, 2007, the lawyers in the Office of the Attorney General for the District of Columbia received word that the Supreme Court had agreed to hear their appeal in the D.C. gun case. Alan Morrison, the experienced Supreme Court lawyer whom Attorney General Linda Singer had brought in, was writing D.C.'s brief and preparing for oral argument. He couldn't have known that the Office of the Attorney General was about to experience a civil war of its own.

Earlier that year, Adrian Fenty, D.C.'s mayor, had appointed his longtime family friend Peter Nickles to be his general counsel and special adviser. Nickles and Fenty had known each other since Fenty's childhood. Nickles, a marathon runner, used to frequent Fleet Feet, an athletic shoe store in the District owned by Fenty's father, Philip. The mayor had complete trust in Nickles, even though Nickles was abrasive and rubbed many others, including Linda Singer, the wrong way. "Nickles's view from the day he started was that *he* was the attorney general," recalled Alan Morrison. "He was issuing orders theoretically on behalf of the mayor to people in the office and to Linda."[45]

The bad blood between Singer and Nickles boiled over in early December. Singer was preparing a lawsuit against Bank of America to recover millions of dollars stolen from the District a few years earlier by a bank employee. Nickles sent Singer an email. "Stop work on this . . . we are not rushing into lawsuits," it said. When news leaked out, legal experts were shocked. D.C. wasn't rushing into the suit. In fact, the statute of limitations on some of the claims was set to expire, meaning that the District had to bring suit soon or potentially lose its ability to sue at all. Singer told Nickles, "We owe it to the Government and the taxpayers to pursue this," but Nickles shot her down. "The mayor has spoken, and I trust you will listen." Jim White, a nationally recognized expert on bank liability, said that dropping the bank lawsuit at this late date was "devastating." "I don't understand why the city would not proceed," he said. The *Washington Post* noted that Bank of America was one of the major clients of the law firm in which Nickles had been a partner for many years.[46]

Ten days after receiving Nickles's email about the Bank of America case, Linda Singer resigned. The *Washington Post* jumped on the story. The paper ran a piece saying that Nickles's meddling had forced Singer to step down. The story accused Nickles of being "so active that some in the city's legal community wondered whether he was overstepping" his authority. In two recent lawsuits over D.C. public school policies, for example, "Nickles appeared in court numerous times as if he were the attorney general." The *Post* noted that the federal judge presiding over one of the cases "asked Nickles in one status conference why he was doing all the talking when he wasn't recognized as a lawyer in the case."[47]

Mayor Fenty nevertheless named Nickles, his good friend and con-

U.S. Supreme Court, March 18, 2008: A sign is held up by a protester on the day the justices heard arguments in *District of Columbia v. Heller*, the landmark Second Amendment case. *(Bloomberg / Getty Images)*

Above: Dick Heller and the libertarian lawyers: Alan Gura (far left), Dick Heller (second from left), Clark Neily (far right), and Bob Levy (second from right) outside the Supreme Court after oral argument in the D.C. gun case. (*Bloomberg / Getty Images*)

Left: Walter Dellinger, the lawyer representing the District of Columbia in the D.C. gun case, travels to the Supreme Court on his bicycle. (*Photo: Jay Mallin*)

Non-Violence, a sculpture of a knotted revolver by Carl Fredrik Reuterswärd, is located at the United Nations in New York City. *(AP Photo / Harry Koundakjian)*

A sticker reflecting the Second Amendment Foundation's belief that America should have no gun control. *(Second Amendment Foundation)*

THE "MINUTE-MEN" OF THE REVOLUTION.

The minutemen of the Revolution.

Ku Klux Klan members on horseback seek to disarm black militiamen in this image from
The Birth of a Nation, directed by D. W. Griffith, 1915. *(Hulton Archive / Getty Images)*

Dodge City, Kansas, in 1879, with a street sign warning, "The Carrying of Firearms Strictly Prohibited." *(Kansas State Historical Society)*

NRA president Charlton Heston, who famously said that the government would have to pry his gun from his "cold, dead hands." *(AP Photo / Ric Feld, FILE)*

American outlaw Bonnie Parker playfully points a shotgun at her partner, Clyde Barrow, in 1932. *(Bettmann/Corbis)*

The Black Panthers at the California statehouse to protest a proposed gun control law in 1967. *(AP Photo)*

The justices of the U.S. Supreme Court in 2008. Seated, from left to right: Anthony Kennedy, John Paul Stevens, John Roberts, Antonin Scalia, David Souter. Standing, from left to right: Stephen Breyer, Clarence Thomas, Ruth Bader Ginsburg, Samuel Alito. *(Steve Petteway, Collection of the Supreme Court of the United States)*

fidant, to replace Singer as the attorney general. Many people in D.C. city government were so upset with Fenty's choice that a panel of the D.C. council initially rejected the nomination. One council member cited Nickles's "lack of independence, legal temperament, and questionable dedication to the rule of law." Fenty's support for Nickles, however, was strong enough eventually to push him through.[48]

The first thing Nickles did when chosen by Fenty was fire Singer's people, including her chief of staff and her press person. Morrison, having already spent months working on the D.C. gun case, thought his position was secure. Not only was he the chief strategist on the framing of the briefs the District was planning to file with the Supreme Court, but the hearing itself was only months away. More reassuring still was the fact that the mayor held a press conference and reaffirmed that Morrison would be the one to argue the case in the Supreme Court.

Then Nickles asked Morrison to meet with him. "Now I haven't decided who's going to argue this case," Nickles announced, to Morrison's surprise. "I want to talk to you about that. But I just want to tell you one thing in the beginning. If you are part of this cabal, then you're automatically disqualified." At first Morrison didn't know what "cabal" Nickles was talking about.[49]

"Do you want to know if I talked to the press about Linda's resignation?" Morrison asked. That *Washington Post* story had apparently bothered Nickles. "If that's your question, the answer is I absolutely, positively did not."

"If I find out that you did," Nickles replied, "you're gone."

A few days later, Morrison received an email from one of Nickles's people. "Peter has decided that your services are no longer needed." Nickles was moving into Singer's office in one week, and Morrison was to clear out by then. Morrison hadn't talked to the press, but he thought he knew why he was really fired. "I was seen as a Linda loyalist."[50]

Morrison's firing occurred just as he was preparing to file the District's brief with the Supreme Court. His last day in office, January 4, 2008, was the same day D.C.'s brief in the gun case was due to be filed. Nickles insisted Morrison's termination had nothing to do with Singer. "Alan is a very good lawyer, but I decided to move in a different direction," he explained. "It's not as if one person is indispensable." Others disagreed. "This is a case that requires an unusual amount of preparation," said David Vladeck, a law professor at Georgetown University. "In addition to needing a good lawyer and appellate advocate, you need someone who has immersed himself in very complex historical sources. Alan has been doing that for two or three months by now." The libertarian lawyers on the other side had been working on the case for five years. "Whoever takes over this case," Vladeck warned, "will start many, many, many laps behind where he ought to be."[51]

D.C. council member Phil Mendelson, who chaired the committee that oversaw the attorney general's office, was bewildered by Nickles's decision. "We are in the middle of preparing for a Supreme Court case," he said in exasperation. Firing Morrison now, he said, was "like committing hari-kari."[52]

Meanwhile, the pro-gun diehards weren't going to rely on the disarray in the District of Columbia's Office of the Attorney General to protect the Second Amendment. While the lawyers were preparing for oral argument, Montana lawmakers passed a resolution demanding the Court hold that the Second Amendment guaranteed an individual right to bear arms. The resolution said that when Montana agreed to join the Union in 1889, Montanans believed that the Constitution protected the right of individuals to possess guns, not some militia-based right. A Supreme Court ruling rejecting the individual-rights reading of the Second Amendment would, the resolution continued, "violate Montana's Compact with the United States," and Montana "reserves all usual rights and remedies under historic contract law if its Compact should be violated." In other words, Montana was threatening to secede from the Union. A victory by the D.C. lawyers in the Supreme Court, Montana lawmakers were suggesting, might justify nothing less than another Civil War.[53]

CHAPTER 6

THE WILD WEST

"OYEZ! OYEZ! OYEZ!" SHOUTED THE MARSHAL OF THE Supreme Court. The circus of reporters, lawyers, and spectators packed into the courtroom fell silent. The hearing in the D.C. gun case was called to order. Looking down on the proceedings from high up on the soaring forty-four-foot walls were the great lawgivers of history: Hammurabi, the Babylonian king whose code, which bound even him, is thought to be one of the first written constitutions; Solomon, king of Israel, the epitome of wisdom, who once coyly resolved a custody dispute by suggesting that the baby two women were fighting over be divided in half, frightening only the real mother; Draco, the Athenian whose punishments for even minor offenses were so severe that over two thousand years later unusually harsh penalties are still called draconian. "All persons having business before the Honorable, the Supreme Court of the United States, are admonished to draw near and give their attention, for the Court is now sitting," the marshal continued. "God save the United States and this Honorable Court!"[1]

The nine justices emerged from a partition in the red velvet curtains hanging behind the raised mahogany bench. Led by Chief Justice John Roberts, who looked a decade younger than his fifty-three years, the black-robed jurists filed in past the four imposing marble columns. The chief justice sat in the center, with the other members of the Court arranged around him in order of seniority. At each end sat the two most junior associate justices, the jocular Stephen Breyer on the left and the earnest Samuel Alito on the right—positions that happened to reflect the two men's politics. On the floor next to each justice's high-backed leather chair was a green ceramic spittoon, a holdover from an earlier era. The last justice to chew tobacco—Sherman Minton, once derisively referred to as the "spokesman against freedom"—retired in 1956. Over fifty years later, the spittoons are still there, only now used as wastebaskets.[2]

The spectators were packed in shoulder to shoulder on the long wooden benches that filled the courtroom. The three libertarian lawyers, Alan Gura, Bob Levy, and Clark Neily, brought with them five of the original plaintiffs, including Dick Heller, the security guard with strident antigovernment views. Todd Kim, the D.C. lawyer who had argued the case in the court of appeals, sat near Peter Nickles, his boss and triggerman for the abrupt firing of Alan Morrison, the lawyer originally hired to argue the case in the Supreme Court for the District. Wayne LaPierre of the NRA showed up, although he had done everything to keep such a hearing from occurring. Steve Halbrook, the lawyer hired by the NRA to mount a hostile takeover of the litigation, was there along with Nelson Lund, the law professor aligned with the NRA who tried to persuade the libertarians not to bring this case in the first place. The nation's foremost leading gun control advocates, like Dennis Henigan of the Brady Center, were on hand. David Kopel, a leading gun rights expert, sat with the libertarian lawyers. The only major player in the case who was absent was Morrison. It would have been too painful for him to be there as a spectator.

Now one of the most majestic halls in the country, the highest courtroom in the land was for most of its history anything but. Before the Supreme Court Building opened in 1935, the justices heard cases in a windowless room in the basement of the Capitol. In 1929, Chief Justice William Howard Taft persuaded Congress to give the Court a building of its own, befitting its status as a coequal branch of the federal government. As the only Supreme Court justice ever to have also served as president of the United States, Taft had unusual sway in political circles. He too, as onetime leader of the country, didn't enjoy working in a basement. A Supreme Court led by a man such as Taft deserved a dramatic marble temple equivalent in grandeur to the Capitol and the White House.[3] To accomplish this, Taft charged Cass Gilbert, the architect of the Woolworth Building—then the tallest in the world—to design "a building of dignity and importance suitable" for such an influential institution.

"We will hear argument today in Case 07-290, District of Columbia versus Heller," announced Chief Justice Roberts. "Mr. Dellinger." Walter Dellinger rose from his seat and stood at the lectern immediately in front of the justices. He was the man Peter Nickles chose to replace Alan Morrison as the District of Columbia's lawyer before the Supreme Court. Because D.C. had been the party that filed the appeal, its lawyer would speak first.

At sixty-six, Dellinger looked every bit the part of a distinguished lawyer. His full head of gray hair, round wire-rimmed glasses, and jowly cheeks perfectly complemented his dark suit, white shirt, and red tie. Dellinger's charm was such that he had once persuaded a famously demure Janet Reno, then the attorney general of the United States, to join him on the dance floor at a White House Christmas party. Just before the justices entered the courtroom in the gun case, Dellinger walked over to Alan Gura to shake his hand. This was Gura's first appearance in the highest court in the land, and Dellinger figured the rookie was anxious. Rather than feed the anxiety, the gracious Dellinger tried to relieve it. There was nothing to fear, Dellinger told him. His own first argument at the high court had been, he said, his best. "You'll do great."[4]

"Good morning, Mr. Chief Justice, and may it please the Court," Dellinger began in a southern drawl, strong enough to give away his

North Carolina upbringing. Neither Dellinger nor anyone else in the courtroom could have predicted the enormous role geography was going to play in the drama about to unfold in the courtroom.

"The Second Amendment," Dellinger told the justices, "was a direct response to concern over Article I, section 8 of the Constitution, which gave the new national Congress the surprising, perhaps even shocking, power to organize, arm, and presumably disarm the state militias." When the founding fathers were debating the Second Amendment, "every person who used the phrase 'bear arms' used it to refer to the use of arms in connection with militia service." Then, invoking the Second Amendment's opening phrase, "A well-regulated Militia, being necessary to the security of a free State," Dellinger added, "And even if the language of keeping and bearing arms were ambiguous, the amendment's first clause confirms that the right is militia-related."

In some ways, Dellinger was the antithesis of the man he replaced, Alan Morrison. Dellinger was a southern gentile, while Morrison was an intense Jewish New Yorker. Dellinger was charming, Morrison direct and outspoken. Dellinger was a highly paid partner at O'Melveny & Myers, one of the nation's preeminent white-shoe law firms; Morrison spent most of his career as a public interest lawyer earning a pittance. They were, however, both experienced Supreme Court advocates. Dellinger served as solicitor general, the federal government's top appellate lawyer, under President Clinton and once argued and won a case in the Supreme Court against Morrison. Since then, Dellinger had become one of the select few "go to" lawyers for the specialized role of arguing before the Supreme Court. He had argued twenty cases in the hallowed courtroom, with numerous victories to his name.[5]

Morrison was friends with Dellinger and didn't hold a grudge against him. Prior to his firing, Morrison had consulted with Dellinger on strategy in the gun case. After his firing, Morrison did everything he could to help Dellinger prepare for the Supreme Court argument, even holding a one-person moot court with Dellinger—a practice run-through of the hearing. Their meeting was kept a secret because Peter Nickles didn't want Morrison to have anything more to do with the case. "Alan is not only one of the best lawyers I have ever known; he is also a real class act," Dellinger said.[6]

There was some speculation that Dellinger wasn't the first person Peter Nickles considered as Morrison's replacement. Rumors in Washington circulated that Nickles intended to give the case to one of his former law firm partners, a man named Bob Long. Long had argued cases in the Supreme Court before, and the *Washington Post* was poised to write a harsh editorial suggesting that Nickles was sacrificing the case to help one of his cronies. Nickles may have realized that to avoid public embarrassment he needed to hire a top-shelf advocate, not a friend with no Supreme Court experience.

Considering the circumstances, Dellinger was a good choice for the case. The only drawback was his overly demanding schedule. He was already slated to argue two other major Supreme Court cases in the weeks just prior to the hearing in the gun case. One included representing Exxon in a challenge to a $2.5 billion punitive damages award arising out of the *Exxon Valdez* oil spill in Alaska's Prince William Sound. Dellinger hadn't been able to devote himself full-time to D.C.'s case—not when another client had $2.5 billion at stake. Dellinger recognized that he was stretched thin. To have three Supreme Court arguments—all of which were, he admitted, "really hard cases and really complicated"—in a span of less than thirty days was, he said, "very, very tough." He worked nonstop for several months. "It was the hardest thing I've done since I got out of law school in 1966."[7]

•   •   •

ON THE closely divided Supreme Court before which Walter Dellinger and Alan Gura were appearing, Anthony Kennedy was the swing vote. The tall, seventy-one-year-old justice was a westerner at heart, having grown up in Sacramento, California. The son of a prominent local attorney, he was born to be a lawyer and shared the lawyer's love of argument. As a college student, he studied abroad at the London School of Economics, where political debate was prized. "At the political union, you had to sit in the room according to your place on the ideological spectrum, and, to give you an idea of what it was like, the Communists—the Communists!—were in the middle," Kennedy recalled. "It was a different world, and I loved it."[8]

Like Dellinger, Kennedy wasn't supposed to be in the Supreme Court when the D.C. gun case was heard. In 1987, President Reagan first nominated Robert Bork to the Supreme Court seat now occupied by Kennedy. Bork, an outspoken conservative and vigorous critic of the liberal Warren Court, was strongly opposed by Senate Democrats. Less than an hour after he was nominated, Senator Ted Kennedy condemned the nomination. "Robert Bork's America is a land in which women would be forced into back-alley abortions, blacks would sit at segregated lunch counters, rogue police could break down citizens' doors in midnight raids," warned the Massachusetts senator. At Bork's confirmation hearings, led by Senator and later Vice President Joe Biden, Bork faulted Supreme Court decisions like *Roe v. Wade*, which legalized abortion, for relying on the right of privacy—a right nowhere clearly mentioned in the Constitution's text.[9]

After a bruising confirmation battle, Bork's nomination was voted down by the Senate. President Reagan then nominated Douglas Ginsburg, a judge and former law professor, to fill the vacant seat. That nomination also hit a snag. The news media reported that Ginsburg had smoked pot as a young professor at Harvard Law School. Although past drug use would soon become a nonissue in national politics after both the second President Bush and President Obama admitted to having been young and irresponsible with drugs, Ginsburg's marijuana use caused an uproar at the time. Ginsburg's wife, a doctor, had also done some things conservatives regarded as apostasy. When it came out that during her residency she had performed abortions, Ginsburg withdrew his name from consideration.[10]

Anthony Kennedy was the third person nominated to fill the seat. In his confirmation hearings, he avoided making the mistake that Bork made. He heartily endorsed the right of privacy, calling it a "zone of liberty, a zone of protection, a line that's drawn where the individual can tell the Government, 'Beyond this line you may not go.'" Although some liberal groups worried that Kennedy, a Roman

Catholic, was just telling the senators what they wanted to hear, he was confirmed by a 97–0 vote.[11]

On the Court, Kennedy's embrace of the right of privacy was proven to be sincere, earning him the ire of conservatives. For years, Republican presidents nominated justices with the goal of overturning the Court's most controversial privacy decision, *Roe v. Wade*. In 1992, after the first President Bush replaced two of the Court's most liberal members, William Brennan and civil rights icon Thurgood Marshall, with David Souter and Clarence Thomas, the administration asked the Court to overrule *Roe*. Following oral argument in that case, *Planned Parenthood v. Casey*, the justices met in their private conference and took an initial vote. Five justices, including Kennedy, voted to effectively overturn *Roe*. No Supreme Court case had energized the conservative legal movement more than *Roe*, and the Court, now controlled by a conservative majority, was going to reverse it at last.[12]

A few weeks later Kennedy was approached by Justices Souter and Sandra Day O'Connor, who proposed a compromise that would uphold *Roe* but give states more leeway to regulate abortion. The justices are allowed to change their votes at any time before the official publication of an opinion, and *Casey* was still being drafted. Kennedy sought out the advice of Justice Harry Blackmun, the author of the original *Roe* decision. The two men met alone in the justices' library at the Supreme Court. "Justice Kennedy seemed deeply concerned about being saddled with this issue for the rest of his career," recalled Blackmun. In the end, Kennedy changed his vote to affirm women's right to choose, igniting a firestorm of criticism by anti-abortion crusaders.[13]

Conservatives were also bitterly disappointed with Kennedy for his votes in gay rights cases. In 1996, Kennedy wrote an opinion for the Court striking down a provision of Colorado's constitution that prevented gays and lesbians who were the victims of discrimination from seeking legal redress. Seven years later, Kennedy wrote the Court's opinion in *Lawrence v. Texas*, which held that the right to privacy barred states from punishing consensual sex among gay adults. Many constitutional scholars believe that Kennedy's opinions in these cases will be the foundation for the Court to one day declare that same-sex couples have a constitutional right to marry.[14]

Because of what they saw as his betrayals, conservatives labeled Kennedy "America's worst justice." He was accused of "judicial lawlessness" and of being a prime illustration of the "Greenhouse effect"—the apparent pattern of justices moving to the left to appeal to the mainstream media, in particular to the longtime Supreme Court reporter for the *New York Times* Linda Greenhouse. James Dobson, the founder of Focus on the Family, an evangelical group influential in the conservative movement, went as far as to call Kennedy "the most dangerous man in America."[15]

To win the D.C. gun case, Walter Dellinger would need that dangerous man to veer to the left and disappoint conservatives once again. There were four reliable conservatives on the Court and four reliable liberals. Although Dellinger didn't know exactly how any of them would vote—with the exception of Clarence Thomas, who had expressed his views earlier—he thought he needed Kennedy. "Your best guess," Dellinger said, "is that Kennedy's vote is likely to be decisive."[16]

Alan Gura, meanwhile, felt confident that Kennedy would side with him. Gura, a libertarian who believed in small government and expansive individual rights, saw Kennedy as a fellow traveler. "The fact is that if you look at Justice Kennedy's voting pattern, the cases where he tends to disappoint the so-called conservative bloc—in almost all those cases, Justice Kennedy sides with a claim of an individual right being held by a person against the government," Gura observed. Indeed, data on the justices' voting behavior showed that Kennedy voted against the government in individual rights cases more often than any other justice.[17]

Gura and Dellinger weren't alone in believing that Kennedy's was likely to be the deciding vote in the D.C. gun case. The reporters who covered the Court were focused intently on the justice from Sacramento. They were prepared to measure his every word to gain some insight into whether he thought the Second Amendment protected an individual right to have guns for self-defense or just a right associated with service in state militias.

Only a few minutes in, Kennedy tipped his hand. Just as Dellinger began his argument that the "right of the people to keep and bear Arms" was limited to service in "a well regulated Militia," Kennedy interrupted him. The amendment, Kennedy announced, "says we reaffirm the right to have a militia, we've established it, but in addition, there is a right to bear arms." The two clauses of the Second Amendment were separate. "And in my view," he continued, the amendment's second clause meant "there's a general right to bear arms quite without reference to the militia either way." The swing vote had just swung decisively in Alan Gura's favor.

If Kennedy's expansive understanding of individual rights was not a shock, the reasons the justice articulated for why the Second Amendment should be read in this way were surprising. Kennedy suggested that the Second Amendment arose out of "the concern of the remote settler to defend himself and his family against hostile Indian tribes and outlaws, wolves and bears and grizzlies and things like that."

To Kennedy, born and raised in the West, the Second Amendment was about the frontier. It wasn't primarily for people living in the cities of the eastern seaboard at the time of the Revolution. It was for people on the edges of the western wilderness who needed firearms to battle gun-toting bandits, scalpel-wielding Natives, and teeth-baring animals. The Second Amendment wasn't designed for the minutemen of the colonies to fight off a tyrannical government; it was designed for the people of the frontier to fight off the tyranny of outlaws.

• • •

AMERICANS' VIEWS of the importance of guns to the lawmen of the western frontier were shaped by famous incidents like the one that occurred at about three o'clock in the afternoon of October 26, 1881, in Tombstone, Arizona. Tombstone was hailed as the "wickedest place in the West," and the events that transpired that day on Fremont Street would only enhance its reputation.

On one side of the street were five outlaws. Featuring the Clanton brothers, Ike and Billy, and the McLaurys, Tom and Frank, the gang was known as the Cowboys. Today, cowboys are often romanticized as chivalrous men of honor who protected the women and children of the frontier from hostile Natives. These Cowboys, however, were cattle rustlers and thieves. Three brothers, Wyatt, Virgil, and Morgan Earp, along with their good friend John Henry "Doc" Holliday, lined the other side of Fremont Street. Virgil Earp was the town's marshal, and in that capacity he had deputized his brothers and Holliday to help him enforce the law. Yet the only thing the marshal and his deputies seemed to be looking for at that moment was a fight.[18]

The bad blood between the Clanton/McLaury gang and the Earps began, as many things did in the Old West, with a horse. After a prized steed of Wyatt's disappeared, it was found in Billy Clanton's possession. Billy claimed he hadn't known the horse was stolen and returned it promptly. The Earps' suspicions about the Cowboys, however, were exacerbated when six mules stolen from an army post were discovered on Tom McLaury's ranch. Tom was forced to return the mules and pay a fine. Ike Clanton then infuriated the Earps by reneging on a deal Wyatt claimed they had made whereby Ike agreed to identify the men behind a recent stagecoach robbery in return for reward money. Wyatt, who was planning to run for county sheriff against the incumbent, Johnny Behan, thought catching the criminals would burnish his reputation with voters. After the deal fell through, Ike told locals that Wyatt tried to pay him to lie about who committed the crime.

The night before the two groups of men met on Fremont Street, Doc Holliday and Ike Clanton had an argument at the Occidental Saloon. Holliday eventually left, but Ike stayed through the night drinking and playing poker. In the morning, Ike, inebriated and angry, toured Tombstone's numerous saloons telling anyone who would listen that he was going to get Holliday and the Earps. Awoken by friends who reported the threats, Virgil and Morgan set out to find Ike, whom they soon spotted stumbling down the street with a rifle in one hand and a pistol in the other. The two Earp brothers sneaked up behind him, grabbed his guns, and pistol-whipped him in the head. Then they arrested him. In the small town that Tombstone was, Ike's court date was that same afternoon. While Virgil was out rounding up the local judge, Ike made the mistake of repeating his threat to exact revenge on the Earps, this time directly to Morgan and Wyatt.

The judge fined Ike twenty-five dollars and set him free. Just outside of the courthouse, an angry Wyatt ran into Tom McLaury and the two men argued. Wyatt smacked Tom in the head with a pistol and left him on the ground bleeding. A few hours later, Ike and Billy Clanton, Tom McLaury, Tom's brother Frank, and another member of their gang, Billy Claiborne, were spotted in a gun shop. The Earps took this as a sign that the Cowboys were gearing up to make good on Ike's threats. A little while later, the Cowboys were approached by Behan, the county sheriff, who had heard about the pistol-whippings and the threats. Predicting trouble, Behan asked the men to turn over their guns. Ike and Tom replied that they were unarmed. Frank McLaury admitted he was carrying firearms but refused to turn them over unless the Earps were also disarmed. Behan, who didn't much like the Earps, let the Cowboys be.

Moments later, the two sets of men confronted each other on Fremont Street. With guns drawn, Virgil and his brothers commanded the Clanton gang to put their hands up. Instead, the outlaws reached for their guns. No one knows for sure who fired the first shot, but most witnesses gave the dubious honor to Doc Holliday. When the shooting stopped, Frank McLaury, Tom McLaury, and Billy Clanton were dead. Virgil Earp, Morgan Earp, Doc Holliday, and Billy Claiborne were wounded, but not fatally. Only Wyatt and Ike, two of the main protagonists, emerged unscathed from the Shootout at the O.K. Corral.

Over time, this battle became the most famous gunfight of the Wild West. Perhaps no other event in American history has been featured in as many movies, television shows, and books. Many of Hollywood's leading men have starred as one of the protagonists: Randolph Scott in *Frontier Marshal* (1939), Henry Fonda in *My Darling Clementine* (1946), Burt Lancaster in 1957's *Gunfight at the O.K.*

Corral (1957), Kurt Russell in *Tombstone* (1993), and Kevin Costner in *Wyatt Earp* (1994). Even James T. Kirk and Captain Spock re-created the gunfight in one of the original *Star Trek* episodes. Every day in Tombstone, tourists are treated to a reenactment of the battle. As one writer has noted, the gunfight "is so much a part of America folklore that scarcely a public confrontation of any kind can occur without someone evoking it." The Shootout at the O.K. Corral, as one of the central myths of the western frontier and of America's gun culture, has helped shape how Americans understand themselves and their shared history. It has taught us that once there was a time when people settled their differences with guns, not lawsuits; when men were willing to risk their lives to defend their honor; when everyone was armed and gun violence was an accepted fact of life. Like many myths, however, the lessons often taken from the Shootout at the O.K. Corral are profoundly misleading.[19]

•   •   •

THE WILD WEST was filled with guns. Throughout the 1800s, settlers headed west by the thousands in search of a new life or the economic prosperity that eluded them back home. The Civil War, surprisingly, gave new impetus for migration to the frontier. Veterans whose war-time experiences left them too scarred to return to the humdrum life of their hometowns moved west in large numbers. Increasingly, they came armed with handguns. Although long guns were always com-monplace in America, the small, repeating handgun became popular in the mid-1800s, largely because of the efforts of a marketing genius named Samuel Colt. Colt took advantage of the remarkable techno-logical innovation in firearms during the early nineteenth century that produced new, lighter, and more powerful guns almost every year. He helped to develop and perfect a pistol with a rotating barrel that could hold multiple rounds of ammunition. His "revolver," as he called it, was not the only six-shooter available to people heading into the frontier, but he sold his at a discounted price and drummed up sales with direct advertising and an unyielding thirst for publicity.

Often heard on the frontier was one of Colt's promotional tag lines: "God created men. Colonel Colt made them equal."[20]

At the world's fair of 1893, held in Chicago, the frontier remained very much on people's minds, even as the automobiles, urbanization, and flying machines of the twentieth century were quickly approaching. Called the World's Columbian Exposition, the fair was dedicated to the 400th anniversary of Christopher Columbus's "discovery" of the Americas—the moment that gave life to the idea that liberty could be found in the untamed lands of a new world. Twenty-four million people attended the fair, more people than had ever come to a single event in all of human history. One of those people was a thirty-two-year-old historian from Portage, Wisconsin, who was little known even in academic circles. His name was Frederick Jackson Turner, and he was there to speak to a gathering of scholars about how the frontier shaped the American identity. Although he had never been to the West himself, Turner told his audience that the frontier was "the meeting point between savagery and civilization," where the "forces dominating American character" could be found. The American, Turner argued, began as a European, civilized and respectful of authority, but the frontier "strips off the garments of civilization and arrays him in the hunting shirt and the moccasin." The frontier breeds a "tendency" to be "anti-social. It produces antipathy to control." It was the vast physical and cognitive space, Turner insisted, that gave Americans their rugged individualism, independence, and democratic ethos. The frontier, in short, was the birthplace of America.[21]

The paper Turner delivered at the Chicago world's fair, entitled "The Significance of the Frontier in American History," was not itself thought to be all that significant at the time. Yet Turner's timing was ideal. The U.S. census of 1890 concluded that the American frontier had now been officially closed, that the country had expanded all the way to the Pacific Ocean, and that there was nowhere left to go. The closing of the frontier was, for some, a distressing fact. If Turner was right that America's strength of character and democratic ideals were a function of the frontier, Americans needed to find new lands to conquer. One amateur historian in particular, Theodore Roosevelt, thought that the closing of the frontier meant that America's leaders had to push for territorial expansion abroad. Less than a decade after Turner's speech in Chicago, Roosevelt would be president, and colonial imperialism—the search for new frontiers—would become a national obsession.[22]

Ever since the frontier was closed, cultural observers have argued that the frontier was not only the root of the American character but also the origin of America's propensity for violence. In the 1920s, the Pulitzer Prize–winning social historian James Truslow Adams—the man who coined the term "the American dream"—wrote in the *Atlantic Monthly* that "lawlessness" was "one of the most distinctive American traits." Life on the frontier carried much of the blame. "Until thirty years ago, America has always had a frontier, and that fact has been of prime importance in many respects for the national outlook," Adams explained. "For our purpose we may merely note that in the rough life of the border there is scant recognition for law as law. Frequently remote from the courts and authority of the established communities left behind, the frontiersman not only has to enforce his own law, but he elects what laws he shall enforce and what he shall cease to observe." On the border of civilization where people were constantly threatened—as Justice Kennedy would recall in the oral argument over the D.C. gun laws—by outlaws, Indians, bears, and wolves, the only law that mattered was, a later historian would write, "the law a man carried on his hip."[23]

The late historian W. Eugene Hollon wrote that "generations of Americans have grown up accepting the idea that the frontier during the closing decades of the nineteenth century represented this country at its most adventurous as well as its most violent." In frontier towns, the story goes, "mobs of mounted cowboys 'took over' by day, their six-shooters roaring while respectable citizens cowered behind locked doors," as the historian Ray Allen Billington put it. In this image of the frontier, disputes were settled by duels at high noon, and just about any poker game could ignite a deadly barroom brawl. Crime ran rampant, and the only reliable form of protection was the gun that every man wore.[24]

The truth, however, is that the famous gun havens of the Wild West were not nearly as violent as usually imagined. Moreoever, frontier towns like Tombstone had some of the most restrictive gun control laws in America.

• • •

ROBERT DYKSTRA'S shock of white hair, rugged face, and neatly trimmed white beard gave him the appearance of a nineteenth-century Tombstone native. In fact, he spent most of his life in upstate New York as a professor of history at the University of Albany, where he conducted groundbreaking research into life on the frontier. Dykstra set out to re-create what frontier towns were really like in the late 1800s, the heyday of the Wild West. What he found completely contradicts the narrative that generations of Americans have been told.

Dykstra's study focused on cattle towns on the frontier in Kansas. Examining local newspapers and other documentary records, Dykstra compiled statistics on all the homicides in notorious Dodge City between 1877 and 1886—its height as a cattle town. Astonishingly, he found that homicides were few and far between. In those ten years, only fifteen murders—a rate of 1.5 per year—were reported in Dodge. Its most violent year, 1878, saw a grand total of five killings. In most years, however, there were no homicides or only one. It turns out there really wasn't much need to get out of Dodge.[25]

Other scholars have made similar findings about the frontier in the late 1800s. Richard Shenkman found that during Tombstone's most violent year only five people were killed. That year happened to be 1881, and three of those people were Frank McLaury, Tom McLaury, and Billy Clanton. In Deadwood, South Dakota, four people were killed in its most violent year. These towns had small populations, and thus their murder rates, if calculated, might not be much lower than those of the big cities the East. Still, the paucity of homicides is hardly what one would expect in places thought to be taken over every day by gun-slinging cowboys.[26]

Virginia City, Nevada, was another frontier town known for

its violence. It was said that in Virginia City someone was gunned down every day before breakfast. Contemporary accounts of people who visited the town in the late 1800s, however, reported otherwise. With some disappointment, visitors recounted nothing but "the most perfect order and decorum." By 1900, most cowboys admitted that they had never even seen a killing, much less killed a man themselves. According to Shenkman, "many more people have died in Hollywood westerns than ever died on the real frontier."[27]

Crime generally was rare in frontier towns. Although stagecoaches out in the vast, unpoliced open spaces of the wilderness were frequent targets—so much so that drivers took to hiring an armed guard to sit next to them in the front of the carriage, "riding shotgun"— armed robbery, petty theft, rape, and assault within city limits were extremely rare. The very crimes that Americans today consider a legacy of the Wild West were almost unheard of in frontier towns. People didn't even lock their doors; one historian who studied the frontier town of Colorado City, Texas, found that, other than the bank's, none of the doors in town had locks to bolt.[28]

In the great American tradition, the popular mythology of gun-toting cowboys having a shootout over a poker game gone awry was more a product of marketing than anything else. According to Dykstra, the notoriety of frontier towns for gun violence was "born . . . of vigorous sensationalism." No small part of the blame belongs to one of America's greatest entertainers, William Frederick Cody, more commonly known as Buffalo Bill. When Chicago held its world's fair, Cody set up camp next door for performances of his show, "Buffalo Bill's Wild West and Congress of Rough Riders of the World." The extravaganza, which starred the famous crack shot Annie Oakley, featured mock shootouts, Indian attacks, and stagecoach robberies. Cowboys were always the good guys, and guns were always the key to their success. The show was so famous that more than a century later not only do schoolchildren still learn about Buffalo Bill but the show's distorted image of frontier violence, helped along by a century of films like *High Noon* and television shows like *Gunsmoke*, continues to define the Wild West. For entertainers, emphasizing violence on the frontier was a surefire way to sell tickets. Even today, blockbuster films and pop-ular videogames sensationalize a western frontier that, according to W. Eugene Hollon, was in truth "a far more civilized, more peaceful, and safer place than American society is today."[29]

To gun rights hard-liners, the paucity of gun deaths in the Wild West must have been a product of easy access to guns. In their image of the West, where guns dangled from the hips of sheriffs, cowboys, and outlaws, few people were crazy enough to commit a crime when they knew they would be instantly met by the barrel end of a Colt .45. An armed society is a polite society, the saying goes. Like almost everything about the history of guns in America, however, the reality was far more complicated.[30]

Dykstra discovered something in the Wild West that, given our popular mythology, shouldn't have been there. He found gun control, and lots of it. Guns were widespread on the frontier, but so was gun regulation. Almost everyone carried firearms in the untamed wilder-ness, which was full of dangerous Natives, outlaws, and bears. In the frontier towns, however, where people lived and businesses operated, the law often forbade people from toting their guns around. Frontier towns, Dykstra reported, adopted "blanket ordinances against the carrying of arms by anyone." The "carrying of dangerous weapons of any type, concealed or otherwise, by persons other than law enforce-ment officers," he found, was nearly always proscribed.[31]

Frontier towns handled guns the way a Boston restaurant today handles overcoats in winter. New arrivals were required to turn in their guns to authorities in exchange for something like a metal token. Certain places required people to check their guns at one of the major entry points to town or leave their weapons with their horses at the livery stables. A visitor arriving in Wichita, Kansas, in 1873 would have seen signs declaring, "LEAVE YOUR REVOLVERS AT POLICE HEADQUARTERS, AND GET A CHECK." A grainy, black-and-white photograph of Dodge City taken around 1879 shows a huge wooden billboard posted in the middle of the main road through town that says, "THE CARRYING OF FIREARMS STRICTLY PROHIBITED." Visitors were welcome, but their guns were not.[32]

In frontier towns, cowboys couldn't walk around like John Wayne in *The Man Who Shot Liberty Valance*, two six-shooters holstered on his belt and a rifle in his hand. In many places on the frontier, if a cowboy wanted to have his guns on him, he'd have to be out in the wilderness, away from town folk. If he wanted to drink some whiskey and play some poker at the saloon, he had to leave his guns behind. On Main Street at high noon, holsters carried no guns.

•   •   •

WHEN DODGE CITY residents originally organized a government in 1873, the very first thing they did was adopt a resolution supporting gun control. They resolved that "any person or persons found carrying concealed weapons in the city of Dodge or violating the laws of the State shall be dealt with according to law."[33]

No gun control law was more common in the late 1800s—on the frontier and elsewhere—than bans on concealed firearms. According to the gun rights historian Clayton Cramer, concealed carry laws were among the earliest types of gun control laws adopted in the years after the American Revolution. The first bans on possession of concealed weapons in public were adopted in Kentucky and Louisiana in 1813. Indiana banned concealed carry in 1820, Tennessee and Virginia in 1838, Alabama in 1839, and Ohio in 1859. "Most people are surprised when I tell them that the South led the nation in the development of gun control laws," remarked Cramer. "Especially to the cultural elite of American society, the South is stereotyped as a place of rednecks, huntin' dogs, and gun racks in pickup trucks. But when you examine the history of laws regulating firearms and other deadly weapons, the South was decades ahead of the rest of the United States."[34]

The southern roots of concealed carry laws might suggest that these laws, like the Klan raids after the Civil War, were designed to oppress African Americans. Cramer, however, concluded that this was not the case—even though he had plenty of motivation to find that racism was to blame. Cramer was a strong supporter of gun rights, and if he could show that concealed carry laws were tainted by racism that would provide even more reason to reject that type of law today.

The facts, however, led Cramer to a different conclusion. The first clue was that the statutes involved were phrased in racially neutral language. By their terms, the laws applied equally to everyone, regardless of color. At that time in the South, lawmakers who wanted to discriminate on the basis of race could easily do so by writing the discrimination into the statute. If they wanted to ban blacks from carrying concealed weapons, they could have just written the laws to apply to blacks. They didn't need to hide it in racially neutral language. These were, after all, slave states. Ever since the Revolution, many states had banned slaves and free blacks from possessing firearms in laws that were racially discriminatory.

After Cramer examined the legislative history behind the rash of concealed carry laws adopted in the first half of the 1800s, he came to a startling conclusion. These laws were designed to diminish exactly what the Wild West would later become famous for: dueling, gunfights, violence. The southern culture of the time, Cramer found, dictated that when "someone insulted you publicly, or cast doubts about your honor, you challenged them to a duel." Or even worse, you pulled out a hidden gun and shot them immediately, before the insulter could fight back. At the slightest offense, a man was expected to protect his honor. "In response, Southern governments passed increasingly stringent laws regulating the concealed carrying of deadly weapons, as well as measures to ban the sale of such weapons." The intent of these laws was the same as that of many forms of gun control today. As Governor James Stephen Hogg of Texas said at the time, the "mission of the concealed deadly weapon is murder. To check it is the duty of every self-respecting, law abiding man."[35]

Reducing public violence has led to restrictions on carrying weapons in public places for ages. Six hundred years before the birth of Christ, the Greek lawmaker Solon, who made it his mission to stop the moral and political decline of Athens, criminalized the indiscriminate wearing of arms in the city. Easy access to weapons, Solon believed, led to murder, thievery, and unnecessary dueling. In the years before the American Revolution, the Crown barred the rebellious Highlanders of Scotland from bearing arms in public. William Blackstone, the leading eighteenth-century expert on English law, noted that throughout England "riding or going armed, with dangerous or unusual weapons, is a crime against the public peace" whenever such acts would be "terrifying the good people of the land."[36]

Bans on the carrying of firearms, especially hidden ones, gave rise to the very first court cases dealing with the constitutionality of gun control. Today, people often bemoan that our society has become so litigious that every political disagreement ends up in court. Yet the phenomenon is anything but new. When southern states adopted laws barring concealed carry of firearms in the early 1800s, gun owners brought legal challenges to the bans, asserting they infringed the right to bear arms guaranteed by state constitutions. Most courts ruled that even total bans on concealed carry were constitutionally permissible. As an Alabama court explained, the right guaranteed by the state's constitution "is not to bear arms upon all occasions and in all places," and the legislature was within its power to try to "suppress the evil practice of carrying weapons secretly." Concealed weapons, according to a Louisiana court, improperly created a "tendency to secret advantages and unmanly assassinations." In Kentucky, when a state court ruled the other way and struck down the state's ban on concealed carry, the state constitution was quickly amended to provide explicitly that the individual right to bear arms was "subject to the power of the general assembly to enact laws to prevent persons from carrying concealed weapons."[37]

These early state cases introduced two important concepts to the emerging jurisprudence of the right to bear arms, each of which remains strong to this day. The first is that the right was about personal self-defense against criminal attack. Whereas the founding fathers emphasized a broader conception of self-defense against the machinations of a tyrant or invading force, personal protection became a more prominent justification for gun rights in the early 1800s. These cases also differentiated between "regulation" of the right to bear arms, which was permissible, and complete "destruction" of the right, which was not. A ban on carrying hidden weapons didn't undermine the underlying right, because, some courts said, people could still carry firearms openly, which was viewed at the time as a less pernicious and, equally important, more manly practice. Still, by the end of the 1800s, several states with constitutional protections for gun rights, including Texas, Florida, and Oklahoma, restricted or banned open carry, too.[38]

Bans on concealed carry spread to the frontier. In 1887, Montana banned the concealed carry of any "deadly weapon" within city limits, including pistols, daggers, slingshots, and brass knuckles. Violators received six months in jail or a hefty fine. In 1890, Oklahoma passed an even broader law that applied throughout the territory, not just in cities and towns. It made it unlawful, with exceptions for law enforcement, "for any person in the territory of Oklahoma to carry concealed on or about his person, saddle, or saddle bags, any pistol, revolver, bowie knife, dirk, dagger, slung-shot, sword cane, spear, metal knuckles, or any other kind of knife or instrument manufactured or sold for the purpose of defense." This type of gun control was sufficiently widespread that the Washington State Supreme Court could write in 1907, "Nearly all the states have enacted laws prohibiting the carrying of concealed weapons." Although the pro-gun literature often insists that gun control was first enacted in the twentieth century, in reality this kind of law was well established in the nineteenth century.[39]

One of the more popular concealed guns of the time was the palm-sized "Philadelphia Deringer," which was designed by gunsmith Henry Deringer and manufactured between 1852 and 1868. The tiny pistol with a short barrel fit easily into a man's pocket or secured underneath his pant leg without any noticeable bump. The gun became so popular that, over time, "Derringer"—misspelled with an extra *r*—became the generic name for any small pocket handgun. Though sales were good, the gun gained a dubious reputation as the weapon of choice for assassins, cheats, and criminals. Only a dishonorable man would hide his gun from view and surprise his victim with it at the last minute. The Derringer's reputation was sealed when, on Good Friday in 1865, a disaffected Confederate sympathizer named John Wilkes Booth sneaked up behind Abraham Lincoln one night in Ford's Theatre and shot the president in the head with one.[40]

Restrictions on the concealed carry of firearms inspire more controversy at the turn of the twenty-first century than they did a century earlier. Over the past two decades, concealed carry laws have once again swept through the states. This time, however, it's been a wave of liberalization. No fewer than thirty-six states have adopted "shall-issue" permitting laws that enable almost anyone with a clean record to get a permit to carry a hidden gun in public. Supporters of these laws reason that criminals avoid potential victims who might secretly be armed. Critics insist that allowing more people to have guns on the streets will lead inevitably to huge spikes in violence, with minor incidents having the potential to escalate into fatal gun battles.

The claims of proponents and opponents of shall-issue concealed carry laws can be tested with the rigorous methods of social scientific research. In 1997, John Lott and David Mustard published a study that found that liberal carry laws reduced violent crime. (Lott, you will recall, was dicussed earlier, in chapter 3.) In states that followed Florida's lead, the authors found, homicide dropped 8.5 percent, rape dropped 5 percent, and aggravated assault dropped 7 percent. Lott and Mustard estimated that if every state had allowed liberal concealed carry during the period of their study, there would have been 1,500 fewer murders, 4,200 fewer rapes, and 60,000 fewer aggravated assaults. Legislator after legislator cited these findings in debates over allowing more liberal concealed carry of firearms.[41]

Lott and Mustard's study has been the subject of considerable study itself, and some scholars believe it to be inaccurate. Two Yale professors, Ian Ayres and John Donahue, ran their own tests and concluded that shall-issue concealed carry laws had no statistically significant effects on crime, and "if anything, there is stronger evidence for the conclusion that these laws increase crime than there is for the conclusion that they decrease it." Another study concluded that

carry laws lead to a decrease in homicides committed with guns, but
to an increase in homicides committed by other means. Some have
suggested that Lott and Mustard's results were radically skewed by
data from a single state, Florida. A few years after Florida adopted
shall-issue permitting for concealed carry, it also adopted a number
of other gun control laws, like background checks and waiting periods, that might also have contributed to that state's drastic drop in
violent crime. Take Florida out of the Lott and Mustard study, Ayres
and Donahue argue, and the evidence that concealed carry reduces
crime disappears.[42]

Ayres and Donahue's study has also been challenged. Yet, for all the
controversy over concealed carry laws, the only clear outcome from
the dueling statistics is that the most extreme claims of both supporters and critics of shall-issue permitting are exaggerated. The laws lead
to neither stark increases nor decreases in violent crime. Ayres and
Donahue admit "these laws have not led to the massive bloodbath of
death and injury that some of their opponents feared." The rise they
detected was slight. Even under Lott and Mustard's analysis, liberal
concealed carry laws aren't exactly a boon to law enforcement. Their
study found significant increases in a host of crimes other than homicide, rape, and aggravated assault. If all states had adopted shall-issue
permitting, they estimated there would have been almost 250,000
additional property crimes.[43]

It is hard to assess the effectiveness of gun laws because there are
already so many guns in circulation that no law can be properly
enforced. The same was true in the Wild West. The whole point of hiding a gun is to make it hard for anyone, including the local marshals,
to know that you are carrying one. Robert Dykstra found nonetheless
that the second most common cause of arrest in frontier towns was,
after drunk and disorderly conduct, the illegal carrying of concealed
weapons. Wild West lawmen took gun control seriously and frequently
arrested people who violated their town's gun control laws.[44]

Frontier communities liked gun control because small towns on
the border of civilization wanted to become bigger towns filled with
civilized people. The growth and economic development they wanted

required attracting investors, who were going to come only if the towns were stable and crime was low. If a businessman on his way to deposit the week's earnings in the bank was liable to be shot down by a drunken cowboy, he was going to find somewhere else to open his business. A newspaper editor in the cattle town of Caldwell, Kansas, put it simply: "People who have money to invest go where they are protected by law, and where good society and order reign."[45]

Frederick Jackson Turner, the historian who spoke about the frontier at the Chicago world's fair, said that the Wild West was quintessential America. Yet as Calvin Coolidge once memorably remarked, "the chief business of the American people is business." It was this desire for economic development that led to both gun control laws in frontier towns and town boosters who, in the decades after the West had been tamed, made up outrageous tales of a violent past. Exaggerating the gunfights of the old days was a way to draw tourists and immigrants seeking a piece of Americana, along with the businesses to serve them. That same spirit can be seen today in Tombstone, Arizona, in the daily reenactments of the Shootout at the O.K. Corral.

Americans have long celebrated that shootout as a defining incident in our cultural heritage of guns. Less often recognized, however, is the central role gun control played in that day's events. Two years before the gunfight, the Tombstone city council adopted a law known as Ordinance No. 9. The title of the ordinance was "To Provide against the Carrying of Deadly Weapons."[46]

It was the failure of the Clantons and McLaurys to abide by the requirements of Ordinance No. 9 that provoked the shootout. Recall that Ike Clanton was arrested and fined twenty-five dollars, not a trivial amount in 1881. The fine was the penalty imposed on Ike for walking around the town armed, in violation of Ordinance No. 9. When Wyatt Earp beat Tom McLaury on the street, it wasn't just out of anger. Wyatt demanded that Tom turn over the concealed firearm that Earp believed Tom was carrying, again in violation of the ordinance. Instead of depositing their guns upon their arrival in Tombstone, the Clanton/McLaury gang was still armed when spotted at the gun shop loading up on ammunition just a few minutes before the shootout. At the later inquest into the shooting, Virgil Earp testified that when the gunfight erupted, he was just innocently trying to enforce the ban on possession of guns on the public streets. "Throw up your hands," he claimed he told the Cowboys. "I have come to disarm you." While few people believed Virgil's self-serving testimony, no one doubts that the Cowboys had broken the law—a gun control law.

Few stories of the Wild West have played a more formative role in shaping the mythology of America's gun culture than the Shootout at the O.K. Corral. On the frontier, people did need guns, as Justice Anthony Kennedy suggested to Walter Dellinger, to fight outlaws, Natives, wolves, and grizzly bears. Yet frontier communities also needed gun control laws to limit violence and encourage economic development. The Shootout at the O.K. Corral, then, is not only a story about America's gun culture. It is also a tale about America's gun *control* culture.

●   ●   ●

HAVING APPEARED before the justices before, Walter Dellinger, D.C.'s lawyer, knew that oral argument at the Supreme Court was the lawyer's version of a Wild West shootout—only a very lopsided one. The lawyer stands alone at the lectern facing off against the nine justices, who look down from an elevated bench. From their perch the justices ambush the lawyer with questions, often interrupting him with another question before he finishes answering the previous one. The successful advocate is quick on his feet, able to shift focus in an instant and provide short, clear answers to the justices' inquisitions. No matter how hostile the justices become, decorum requires the lawyer to be courteous and deferential. To be successful, one needs a steely carapace.

Perhaps the lawyer's only advantage is first draw. The lawyer is allowed to make an opening statement of prepared remarks. Within moments, however, the justices start firing off probing questions in an effort to expose the weaknesses of the lawyer's argument. Dellinger was given less than a minute and a half to tell the justices why the Second Amendment should be read to protect state militias before he was interrupted.

"If you're right, Mr. Dellinger, it's certainly an odd way in the Second Amendment to phrase the operative provision," Chief Justice John Roberts interjected. Roberts, who was appointed by President George W. Bush, was known to lean to the right ideologically. "If it is limited to State militias, why would they say 'the right of the people'? In other words, why wouldn't they say 'State militias have the right to keep arms'?"

"Mr. Chief Justice, I believe that the phrase 'the people' and the phrase 'the militia' were really in sync with each other," Dellinger answered. Referring to "Federal Farmer," the pseudonym of a Revolutionary-era author whose identity is still contested to this day, Dellinger said, "'Farmer' uses the phrase 'the people are the militia, the militia are the people.'"

"But if that's right," asked the chief justice, "doesn't that cut against you? If the militia included all the people, doesn't the preamble that you rely on not really restrict the right much at all? It includes all the people."

Justice Antonin Scalia, the darling of conservatives who was so instrumental in the formation of the Federalist Society, voiced his skepticism too. "I don't see how there's any, any, any contradiction between reading the second clause as a personal guarantee and reading the first one as assuring the existence of a militia," the self-assured and outspoken justice said emphatically. The framers "knew that the way militias were destroyed by tyrants in the past was not by passing a law against militias, but by taking away the people's weapons. . . . The two clauses go together beautifully: Since we need a militia, the right of the people to keep and bear arms shall not be infringed." Scalia wasn't asking Dellinger a question. As Scalia often does, he just wanted to tell the lawyer he was wrong.

Dellinger's response was quickly cut short by a different question from Justice Kennedy. Before Dellinger could give his answer to that question, Scalia shot another one at him. From the right side of the bench, Justice Samuel Alito asked about something else. Then Justice Ruth Bader Ginsburg piped up. Dellinger was cut off in midsentence more than thirty times: "No, I think . . . Now, the . . . I think the better . . . Yes, but if, well. . . ." It is said that a successful lawyer doesn't win oral argument at the Supreme Court. He survives it.

The only justice who didn't speak was Clarence Thomas, who was notorious for his consistent refusal to ask questions from the bench. From 2006 to 2010, Thomas didn't ask a single question or make a single statement during oral argument. "You don't have to ask all those questions to judge properly," he told an audience in 2007. "We are there to decide cases, not to engage in seminar discussions." He joked, "My colleagues should shut up!" Yet, because Justice Thomas had already made it clear that he thought the Second Amendment guaranteed an individual right to own guns, Dellinger took no solace in his silence.[47]

Indeed, there was not much solace to take in anything Dellinger was hearing from the bench. Chief Justice Roberts, Justice Scalia, and Justice Alito had indicated their support of the individual-rights reading of the Second Amendment by their unfriendly questions and statements. Add Justice Thomas and Justice Kennedy, who said the Second Amendment was intended to protect settlers on the frontier who needed guns to fight off outlaws, Natives, bears, and wolves, and there were five votes against the militia theory.

Dellinger decided to change tack. Instead of continuing to defend the militia theory, he decided to focus on a fallback argument that might be more appealing to Justice Kennedy. Dellinger said that D.C.'s law could still be upheld as a "sensible regulation of dangerous weapons" even if the Second Amendment protected an individual right to own guns. The right to bear arms was not an absolute right to have any guns a person wants, anytime a person wants them. In the over forty states that protect the right to bear arms in their state constitutions, courts usually upheld any reasonable regulation short of a complete prohibition of firearms ownership by civilians.[48]

"What is reasonable about a total ban on possession?" asked the chief justice.

"What is reasonable about a total ban on possession is that it's a ban only on the possession of one kind of weapon, of handguns, that's been considered especially dangerous," replied Dellinger.

"So if you have a law that prohibits the possession of books, it's all right if you allow the possession of newspapers?" Roberts shot back. Clearly, Dellinger's fallback argument was also going to be an uphill battle.

The D.C. laws that Dellinger was defending really appeared like a total prohibition on the use of guns for self-defense. All handguns were banned, and long guns—shotguns and rifles—had to be kept disassembled or secured with a trigger lock. By the terms of the law, a homeowner could assemble or unlock his long guns only for "lawful recreational purposes," like target shooting or hunting. Within the D.C. city limits, however, there were no hunting grounds or publicly accessible rifle ranges. More importantly, the law made no exception for self-defense. If you woke up one night to find a potentially violent intruder breaking into your home, you were not allowed to use your shotgun to defend yourself or your family, because that wasn't a "recreational" use of the gun.

In an attempt to salvage the D.C. gun laws, Dellinger told the justices that the D.C. government respected the right of residents to use long guns in self-defense. For centuries, the law has allowed a person to defend himself with deadly force if he is threatened in his own home, and D.C. hadn't intended to limit that right, according to Dellinger. "It is a universal or near universal rule of criminal law that there is a self-defense exception," he said. The D.C. laws weren't a total ban on the use of guns for self-defense, because the D.C. government would never prosecute someone for unlocking his shotgun and using it to shoot an intruder. "We have no argument whatsoever with the notion that you may load and have a weapon ready when you need to use it for self-defense."

The problem, Justice Alito pointed out, was that the law didn't explicitly provide such an exception. The text of the statute clearly stated that a resident could unlock or assemble a long gun only for "lawful recreational purposes." Not only was the language of the statute straightforward, but when the gun case was in the trial court D.C.'s lawyers had agreed that the proper interpretation of the law was to prohibit non-recreational uses of long guns. It is a common principle of the law that once a party stipulates to a set of facts, that party can't dispute those facts later on. Dellinger was now in the uncomfortable position of trying to distance himself from the stipulation made by D.C.'s other lawyers years earlier. The Court, he argued, should interpret the statute to have a self-defense exception.

Adrian Fenty, D.C.'s mayor, could have kept Dellinger out of this situation had he been willing to revise the city's gun laws. Fenty could have pushed the D.C. council members to rewrite the statute to permit unambiguously the use of long guns for self-defense in the home and rectify its other problematic provisions. Alan Gura and the libertarian lawyers would likely have to go back and file a new lawsuit against the revised law. Fenty, however, was a politician—a position that didn't necessarily encourage this sort of compromise. Perhaps it was better to be seen as a fighter.

As a result, Dellinger was stuck defending a law that the more you looked at it, the broader it seemed. He could tell that the justices were sympathetic to the notion that the Second Amendment guaranteed the right to have a gun for personal self-defense. His best hope was to persuade the justices that D.C.'s law permitted some use of firearms for self-defense, even if the text of the statute didn't provide much support for that view. In practice, Dellinger argued, the law was not nearly the burden it appeared to be. The trigger lock requirement for long guns, for example, was nothing more than a minor inconvenience, he said. If an intruder was breaking in late one night, a homeowner could easily and quickly remove the lock. In his characteristic, country-lawyer way, Dellinger said he had tried it himself. "The version I have—you can buy them at 17th Street Hardware—has a code, like a three-digit code. You turn the code and you pull it apart. That's all it takes," he told the justices. "It took me three seconds."

Chief Justice Roberts wasn't swayed by Dellinger's personal experience. Conjuring up the image of a D.C. resident awakened in the middle of the night by the sound of an intruder, Roberts responded, drawing out each syllable slowly: "So then you turn on the lamp, you pick up your reading glasses. . . ." The staid courtroom audience burst out in laughter.

Seated at a table facing the justices, Alan Gura stayed emotionless. He didn't laugh, he didn't smile, he didn't cheer. He didn't react in any noticeable way, even though the hearing was going his way. For Gura, the turning point was when Justice Kennedy, the Court's swing vote, made his statement about frontier settlers needing to fight off outlaws and bears. When asked later about what he was thinking at that moment, Gura lifted both arms straight up in the air with fists clenched. For one moment, in the highest court in the land, the young, inexperienced lawyer was Rocky Balboa, standing triumphant at the top of the steps. Like that iconic underdog, Gura sensed that he was on the verge of overcoming all the odds, of doing something no one believed he could do.[49]

Although few people remember it, Rocky Balboa actually lost his boxing match in the Academy Award–winning film. Rocky was way out of his league, and his sole goal was to stand toe-to-toe with the heavyweight champion of the world for the full fifteen rounds. Victory, to him, was to go the distance, to avoid being knocked out, no more. Gura's makeup was different. He was going to be satisfied with nothing short of winning this case. He didn't come all this way to stand toe-to-toe with the great Walter Dellinger; he came here to trounce him. In Gura's mind, a 9–0 unanimous decision in his favor was just good enough.

The hearing was going well, but Gura hadn't won anything yet. After Dellinger finished, the justices would hear from Paul Clement, the solicitor general of the United States, the federal government's designated advocate before the Supreme Court. In cases where the federal government's interest is significant, the justices permit the solicitor general to participate in oral argument, even though the United States isn't technically a party to the dispute. Because this case involved important questions that could impact a range of federal gun control laws, Clement was given fifteen minutes to address the Court.

When Alan Gura first heard that the solicitor general planned to share the administration's views with the justices, he had every reason to be thankful. George W. Bush was the most pro-gun president in decades. Bush had run for office as a strong defender of gun rights, and it was his former attorney general, John Ashcroft, who had announced that the administration officially subscribed to the individual-rights view of the Second Amendment. That's why Gura was shocked to read Paul Clement's brief, which advised the justices to partially reverse Gura's victory in the lower court. While Clement's brief endorsed the individual-rights reading, it also argued that D.C.'s law might be a reasonable regulation consistent with the demands of the Second Amendment. When it came down to the ultimate question posed by the case—were the D.C. gun laws unconstitutional?—Gura and many others in the gun rights community thought the Bush administration was siding with Walter Dellinger and the District of Columbia. And now the administration's lawyer, who was known for his persuasive prowess, was stepping up to the lectern.

CHAPTER 7

GANGSTERS, GUNS, AND G-MEN

THE SOLICITOR GENERAL OF THE UNITED STATES IS ONE of the many positions in the federal government whose influence is belied by the anonymity of the office. Few outside of Washington, D.C., know who the solicitor general, or SG, is. As the national government's top appellate lawyer, however, the solicitor general not only coordinates all appeals throughout the country involving the U.S. Department of Justice but also appears before the justices whenever significant federal interests are involved in a case. As a result, the solicitor general argues more cases at the high court each year than anyone else. Although a political appointee of the president, the SG has long had a special relationship and credibility with the justices— factors reflected in the fact that his is the only executive branch office in the Supreme Court Building itself. In court, the SG's role as spokesperson for the executive, a coequal branch of the federal government, entitles him to a degree of deference.

Studies consistently show that the justices are much

more likely to hear a case the SG recommends, and far more likely
to decide a case in favor of a party supported by the SG—even if the
outcome deviates from the prior policy positions of the justices. "It
just is impossible to overstate the influence of the Solicitor General's
office and their advocates and how much the justices look to them for
guidance," says Tom Goldstein, a Supreme Court specialist. Indeed,
among constitutional lawyers, the SG is often called the "tenth justice" because of his sway on the Court. Alan Gura knew about those
studies, and as Paul Clement, the current holder of the post, walked
up to the lectern to address the justices, Gura couldn't help wonder-
ing about what they meant for his own case.[1]

At forty-one, Clement was young to have such a critical position.
When appointed four years earlier, he was the youngest person named
to that office in half a century. Clement looked even younger than his
years, with wispy light brown hair and an angular face untouched
by wrinkles. Standing before the justices in his small wire-rimmed
glasses and the black, long-tailed morning coat traditionally worn by
the SG, he looked like a youthful groom waiting at the altar.[2]

Clement was being groomed—to be a justice on the Supreme
Court. He was a rising star in conservative legal circles, where he
was viewed as an eventual nominee to the nation's highest court.
A longtime member of the Federalist Society, Clement was called
a "true believer" and a "movement conservative across the board."
He had what one writer termed "a perfectly appointed conservative resume": graduate of Georgetown University, editor of the *Harvard Law Review*, and law clerk to the noted conservatives Laurence
Silberman—the federal judge who wrote the lower court opinion in
the D.C. gun case—and Supreme Court Justice Antonin Scalia. The
only setback in Clement's meteoric rise happened when, in a terrorism case a few years earlier, Clement assured the justices that the U.S.
government did not engage in torture. That same evening, CBS News
aired the first photographs of U.S. soldiers abusing prisoners at the
Abu Ghraib prison in Iraq.[3]

Clement did not have to pay for his gaffe, in part perhaps because
the justices may have thought that he had not been told what was

really happening. They may also have given him a pass because he was such an outstanding lawyer. Renowned for his clarity and persuasiveness, Clement argued even the most complicated cases without any notes. Viet Dinh, a former head of the Office of Legal Counsel who worked with Clement, called him "the perfect solicitor general." Former Attorney General John Ashcroft described him as "one of the brightest legal minds in the country." Even liberals, like Justice John Paul Stevens, praised him. Walter Dellinger, D.C.'s lawyer in the gun case, said Clement was "one of the best" he had ever seen.[4]

Gura was unhappy with Clement because of the "friend of the court" brief Clement's office filed in the case. "Friend of the court," or "amicus," briefs are documents filed with the Court from people other than the two parties to the dispute. They offer the Court perspectives on a legal issue that aren't offered by the named parties. In a small case, there might be one or two such briefs. In the high-profile gun case, there were seventy. Briefs were filed by historians, social scientists, gun rights groups, gun control groups, public health officials, prosecutors, police associations, state legislators, the NRA—everyone with a lawyer seemed to think his or her opinion might sway the justices. (Even I wrote one.)[5]

While most amicus briefs are notable mainly for their lack of influence on the outcome of the dispute (like my own in the gun case), in unusual instances they've had a profound effect. In 2003, the Court's landmark decision upholding affirmative action in graduate school admissions relied on an amicus brief filed on behalf of retired military officers, who insisted that racial diversity was essential for the smooth functioning of the armed services. Such influential amicus briefs are, however, the exception. Another exception is when the solicitor general files an amicus brief.[6]

Clement's brief, filed two months before the hearing in the Supreme Court, said that the proper construction of the Second Amendment was as guarantee of an individual's right to have a gun even outside of service in a state militia. The catch was that Clement thought that the D.C. law did not necessarily run afoul of that right. In language he could have borrowed straight from D.C.'s own briefs, Clement wrote that the right to keep and bear arms was "subject to reasonable restrictions" and that D.C.'s gun laws might indeed be reasonable. The lower-court opinion had misapplied the Second Amendment and interpreted the right to be far stronger than it should have. The opinion of Laurence Silberman, the judge Clement had clerked for, was wrong and should be overturned. In Clement's view, the Supreme Court should return the case to Silberman's court with instructions to reconsider the law and be more deferential to the D.C. city council.[7]

When Gura read Clement's brief, he was dumbfounded. The president was considered a strong supporter of gun rights, yet the solicitor general's brief, in Gura's view, "advocated for a meaningless individual right." The administration recognized a right to bear arms, but it was one that was to be governed by a standard "so lenient that even this law, which is the worst in the country by far" might survive. If a complete ban on handguns and effective prohibition on the use of all other firearms for self-defense by civilians were permitted, then no gun control would run afoul of the Second Amendment. Clement, Gura said, was "basically siding with the District of Columbia."[8]

Others in the gun rights community were equally indignant. "Behold a traitor to the Constitution," exclaimed the *Liberty Zone*, a conservative blog, over a picture of Clement. Gun rights advocates denounced Clement's brief as "outrageous" and "a betrayal." The *Wall Street Journal* editorial page called it "nothing short of astonishing." The gun lovers who had voted for Bush saw Clement's brief as "an abandonment" of their cause. David Hardy, a leading gun rights advocate, said the whole episode illustrated the all-too-common beltway phenomenon of "screw your friends and appease your enemies."[9]

The conservative columnist Robert Novak wrote a piece soon after the SG's brief was filed, claiming that even President Bush and his senior staff "were stunned to learn, on the day it was issued," of Clement's position. That brief, however, was not really *Clement's* brief. It was the *administration's* brief. It reflected the legal position of the executive branch, not Clement's personal views. Whoever was feeding Novak his information was just doing damage control. While the

SG could influence the legal position of the executive branch, it was the president, the White House counsel, and the attorney general who determined how to handle a high-profile case like this—especially when it dealt with one of the most salient issues in the president's political platform. The SG may have an office in the Supreme Court Building, but he meets almost daily with the attorney general, who meets almost daily with the White House counsel, who meets almost daily with the president. "In a case of this magnitude," observed one former government lawyer, "it is difficult to imagine that the White House Counsel was not brought into the loop much sooner—or that the White House Counsel did not give the President and 'senior staff' notice" of what Clement intended to say in his brief.[10]

What the White House was really stunned to learn was that its position would cause such an uproar. Years earlier, the Bush administration had taken basically the same public position on the Second Amendment and was celebrated by gun rights supporters. Back in 2001, gun people were ecstatic about Attorney General John Ashcroft's letter to the NRA and the subsequent memorandum to Justice Department prosecutors announcing the administration's support of the individual-rights view of the Second Amendment. Perhaps they hadn't read Ashcroft's words closely. Ashcroft had explicitly noted that "the existence of this individual right does not mean that reasonable restrictions cannot be imposed." In fact, he continued, the administration "will continue to defend vigorously the constitutionality, under the Second Amendment, of all existing federal firearms laws." The Bush administration might support a new reading of the Second Amendment, but it was a reading that didn't create many new barriers to gun control. President Bush and his senior staff should not have been surprised by Clement's brief, since it was in line with what the administration had been saying for years.[11]

Although written years earlier, the Ashcroft memorandum contained an additional clue that top officials in the administration were well aware of what Clement was doing. Ashcroft specifically directed federal lawyers to "promptly advise" higher-ups in the Department of Justice "of all cases in which Second Amendment issues are raised, and coordinate all briefing in those cases." To claim that this instruction was not followed in the biggest Second Amendment case to reach the Supreme Court in seventy years strains credibility.

Even if the White House was more involved with Clement's filing than officials wanted to admit, there were clearly dissenters within the top ranks of the administration. In an unprecedented move, Vice President Dick Cheney responded to Clement's brief by signing onto a friend of the court brief that directly challenged the solicitor general's position. The brief, which was written by Steve Halbrook—the gun lawyer who first worked with the libertarian lawyers and then tried to take over their case on behalf of the NRA—and signed on to by 55 U.S. senators and 250 representatives, said the Supreme Court should affirm the lower-court ruling that D.C.'s law was unconstitutional. In contrast to Clement's, Cheney's brief argued that "no purpose would be served by remanding this case for further fact finding or other proceedings." Cheney joined the brief in his capacity as president of the Senate, but never before had the vice president of the United States filed a brief disagreeing with the official position of his own administration in the Supreme Court.[12]

In light of the political fallout from the SG's brief, some Washington insiders predicted that Paul Clement would change his position at oral argument in the Supreme Court. "Don't count on it," advised a former Justice Department lawyer. The "institutional cost to the office of such a reversal" would be great. According to the former solicitor general (and later Clinton Whitewater prosecutor) Ken Starr, Clement was a man with a "very strong sense of institutional arrangements and institutional integrity." Besides, Clement had already survived one major gaffe, and he wasn't likely to risk his reputation before the justices again. Still, he did take his orders from the White House.[13]

There was another reason for Paul Clement to stay the course—the same reason the administration had always said that gun control was consistent with the Second Amendment. The primary responsibility of the executive branch is to enforce the law. A broad Second Amendment ruling could undermine the vast array of federal gun control laws that prosecutors were using routinely to put criminals in jail. In his brief, Clement argued that the reasoning used by Judge Silberman in the lower court "could cast doubt on the constitutionality of existing federal legislation prohibiting the possession of certain firearms, including machineguns." Anyone serving a criminal sentence for violating a federal gun law might suddenly be able to challenge his conviction. The executive branch was all for recognizing an individual right to bear arms in the Second Amendment, just so long as it didn't interfere with law and order.

As oral argument in the D.C. gun case approached, Court watchers wondered what Clement would do. The administration had badly miscalculated the political consequences of its position in the gun case. Maybe the pressure from the gun rights community—and from Dick Cheney himself—would be enough to force the administration's, and Clement's, hand. Now that Clement stood at the lectern in front of the nine justices, the spectators in the courtroom were eagerly anticipating what he would say.

●   ●   ●

THE FEDERAL gun control laws that Paul Clement and the Bush administration were worried about had their roots in the 1930s. That's when the federal government first involved itself seriously in the business of regulating guns. During the Revolutionary era, it was primarily state and local governments that mandated musters, banned disloyal people from possessing guns, and required safe storage of gunpowder. It was they that banned concealed carry of firearms in the mid-1800s. It was they that banned possession of guns on the public streets of frontier towns in the Wild West. The federal government had required people to outfit themselves with military-style firearms in the Militia Acts of the late 1700s, but otherwise it mostly stayed out of the business of regulating guns or gun owners.[14]

Gun control became a federal issue in the 1930s because President Franklin Delano Roosevelt, who was elected in 1932, had a crime problem. Criminal law was an area of law traditionally left to states and cities. As the historian Mary Stolberg has noted, "For most of U.S. history, politicians believed that crime was a local matter." From time to time, federal officials proposed to increase the involvement of the federal government in crime control, but states' rights proponents consistently and successfully objected. When FDR's fifth cousin Teddy was president, Attorney General Charles Joseph Bonaparte—himself the great nephew of Emperor Napoleon Bonaparte—lobbied to create a federal police agency in 1907, but members of Congress weren't interested. The dominant view held that crime wasn't a federal problem. It was a state and local problem, with little room for federal interference. This antiquated understanding of criminal law came under enormous pressure in the years just before FDR was elected.[15]

The trouble began with the U.S. Constitution itself. On January 16, 1919, Americans ratified the Eighteenth Amendment, which prohibited "the manufacture, sale, or transportation of intoxicating liquors." Inspired by the moralistic reformers of the temperance movement, the amendment was intended to reduce the social costs of alcohol, from the abuse of women and children to workplace absenteeism, barroom brawling, and crime. While the Eighteenth Amendment did not ban the consumption of alcohol directly, it was designed to make alcohol hard to come by. Or so those who drafted the amendment hoped.[16]

Moralistic reform usually founders on the shoals of dissent. Those who don't share the moral outrage—or, worse, find great enjoyment in the activities targeted for reform—won't give in simply because a law is passed, even if that law is a constitutional amendment. Anti-gun reformers in Washington, D.C., found this out when they tried to get rid of all the guns in the nation's capital. Proponents of Prohibition, the "Noble Experiment," as it was called, discovered the same thing. Banning the production, sale, and transportation of alcohol didn't stop people from producing, selling, and transporting alcohol. It just drove opponents of Prohibition to do those things underground, where men like Al Capone thrived.

Alphonse Gabriel Capone was born in 1899 in Brooklyn, New York. He left public school at the age of fourteen to attend Harvard—that is to say, the Harvard Inn, a Coney Island nightclub and brothel run by the mob. A large, round, strong man, Capone worked as a bouncer. One night he insulted a woman at the club, whose brother turned out to be a well-connected mobster named Frank Gallucio. Capone was made to pay for his gaffe. Gallucio took a bottle opener and cut several deep gashes in Capone's left cheek. The resulting marks never went away. From then on, and much to his embarrassment, the vain Capone was known as Scarface.[17]

Coincidentally, Capone celebrated his twenty-first birthday in 1920, the day after the Eighteenth Amendment went into effect. The decade that followed would be his own personal Roaring Twenties. He moved to Chicago, where he came under the tutelage of "Papa Johnny" Torrio, the head of a gambling and prostitution ring called the Chicago Outfit. Torrio was one of the first gangsters to realize the incredible profit potential of Prohibition. The moment the Eighteenth Amendment went into effect, he added bootlegging to his résumé. Soon, he began to teach Capone everything about his business, which flourished thanks to the public's unquenchable thirst for liquor. Capone was being groomed—to be capo of the biggest crime syndicate in the Midwest.

The Chicago Outfit controlled the downtown area (the "Loop") and the South Side. Its main competitor was the North Side Gang, a mostly Irish mob run by Dion O'Banion. The Irish looked down on the Italians for trafficking in prostitution, which they thought was beneath them. They preferred to spend their money bribing politicians and buying police protection. In the Prohibition era, more money was to be made making whores out of cops and public officials. Chicago police officers were known to escort members of the North Side Gang into local distilleries so that the gangsters could steal illegal whiskey in peace.[18]

Chicago's Irish mob controlled the part of town in which nearly all the old distilleries and breweries in Chicago were located. At first, Torrio and Capone tried to form an alliance with O'Banion and the North Side Gang. O'Banion, however, had nothing but disdain for the Italians. He took pleasure in slurring Torrio and Capone to their faces. After a negotiation over the sale of a brewery turned sour, the Chicago Outfit had had enough. In November 1924, three of Torrio's men marched into a flower shop owned by O'Banion and shot him. A few months later, the North Side Gang struck back. Torrio and Capone were ambushed on separate occasions, though both survived the attacks. The brush with death led Torrio to retire. He returned to Italy and crowned Capone, then twenty-six, capo.

Over the next five years, the Chicago Outfit and the North Side Gang would wage the worst gang war in American history, one that would have a profound effect on gun control legislation and the Second Amendment—and help bring the NRA into the political fight over gun legislation. The NRA, surprisingly, would be on the side of gun control.

The gangsters' weapon of choice was the "Tommy Gun"—a compact, easy-to-carry submachine gun named after its designer, John T. Thompson. Thompson was the chief engineer of the Remington Arms Company when World War I broke out. He devoted himself to developing a gun that would help the Allies defeat the Germans in the horrendous trench warfare that came to characterize the war in Europe. Thompson wanted a small, automatic gun with which one could clear out a ditch quickly. His "trench broom," as he called it, would enable a single soldier to fire scores of rounds with a single pull of the trigger.[19]

Machine guns were not new, but existing designs were bulky and hard to use. The Gatling gun, designed by Richard Gatling for use in the Civil War, was the first functioning and effective firearm capable of firing continuously. Like a mega-sized six-shooter, its multiple barrels had to be spun around by a hand crank, and its enormous size and weight required a two-wheeled cart to move it around. In 1884, an American-born inventor named Hiram Maxim devised the first real automatic machine gun. After a friend in Vienna advised him, "If you want to make a pile of money, invent something that will enable these Europeans to cut each others' throats with greater facility," Maxim set out to build a better mousetrap, literally. Not only did he figure out a way to use the power generated from the recoil of a fired round to load and fire another one—making Maxim's the first gun capable of shooting multiple rounds with nothing more than a single pull of the trigger—Maxim also invented the modern, spring-loaded mousetrap still widely used today.[20]

Maxim's gun, however, was so large that, like Gatling's, it had to be mounted on a cart or placed on the ground to be fired effectively. Thompson wanted a continuous-fire gun that a single soldier could easily carry by himself. The gun he designed looked a bit like a rifle, with a short, thick buttstock. It had two pistol grips, one behind the trigger and another midway down the barrel, and could be equipped with a round drum magazine to hold loads of ammunition. It weighed only eight and a half pounds and could fire at a rate of nearly a thousand rounds per minute. Unfortunately for the Allied forces, Thompson's gun, dubbed a "sub" machine gun because of its small size and use of pistol ammunition, was not ready for manufacture until 1920, just after the Great War ended.

Gangsters readily took advantage of the weapon that Allied soldiers never had the chance to use. The Tommy Gun, or, as some mobsters called it, the "Chicago piano"—because it fired like a finger running quickly up the keys—or the "chopper"—because it cut people in half—was the perfect firearm. Available for purchase by anyone through mail order or at a sporting goods store, the gun retailed for $175 (or $2,000 in current dollars), which was expensive but affordable to a thriving criminal syndicate. It was well worth the money. The Tommy Gun could be carried around easily, hidden under a coat or in the trunk of a car. It fired .45-caliber ammunition so quickly that the Tommy Gun not only did the job fast but also gave the shooter time to flee the scene. Thompson's invention was said to be "the gun that made the Twenties roar."[21]

On Valentine's Day in 1929, the volatile mixture of the Tommy Gun, bootlegging, and an all-out gang war exploded into what has been called "the most famous machine-gun incident of all time." A mobster gang allied with Capone lured seven members of the North Side Gang to the S.M.C. Cartage Company warehouse in the Lincoln Park neighborhood of Chicago with the promise of a cheap shipment of hijacked Canadian whiskey. Unknown to the North Side Gang, no liquor was heading to the warehouse. Several out-of-town hitmen hired by Capone were.[22]

Capone wanted the hit to look like a police raid, so his hired guns dressed the part. Two of the gunmen wore police uniforms, and the other two dressed up in trench coats to look like detectives. They arrived at the warehouse in a stolen police car, with siren blaring. Once inside, Capone's men ordered the members of the North Side Gang to raise their arms up high and line up against the back wall. The seven members of the North Side Gang did as they were told. They had nothing to fear from a police raid. Given all the public officials that were in their pockets, an arrest was just a minor inconvenience. The gangsters didn't dare fight back, since killing a police officer could bring real heat down on them. Instead, they lined up against the wall, smug in the knowledge that they would be out of jail before nightfall.

Capone's men ruthlessly unleashed the firepower of two Tommy Guns, one shotgun, and a pistol. They sprayed bullets across the North Side Gang men's heads and chests until the victims tumbled to the floor. In ten seconds, Capone's men fired over seventy rounds and two shotgun blasts. To make it look good for any people who might have heard the disturbance, two of the men disguised as police officers escorted the two other killers out of the building at gunpoint. Neighbors testified that they saw police arrest two men and drive off in a police car.

When the real police arrived at the scene of the St. Valentine's Day Massacre, what they found was horrific. The victims were sprawled out on the floor in pools of blood. The back wall of the warehouse was riddled with bullet holes. Scores of spent shells littered the floor. One victim, Frank Gusenberg, was still alive, despite having been hit twenty-two times. A detective asked who shot him, but Gusenberg, ever the mobster, replied, "No one—nobody shot me," just before taking his last breath. In part because Gusenberg hadn't talked, no one was ever prosecuted for the crime.

Tony Berardi, a photographer for the *Chicago Evening American*, arrived at the warehouse minutes after the police, possibly tipped off by Capone himself. His gruesome photos of the dead men were syndicated in newspapers across the country.

Violent confrontations between gangsters and with the police were becoming so common that a new sense of urgency about crime was starting to emerge. The era saw what one historian described as an "explosion of information technologies, particularly newsreels, radio, and syndicated news services," and they were all filled with crime stories. Never before, however, had the nation seen an execution of seven men all at once, sprayed with machine-gun fire. That the killers committed their horrible crime disguised as police officers was all the more unsettling.[23]

Armed with Tommy Guns, the gangsters of the Prohibition era were radically more violent than the criminals of yore, like the Clantons and the McLaurys. Newspapers and radio only heightened the public's distress. Local law enforcement, meanwhile, was increasingly shown to be ineffective in combating the modern-day outlaw. Many local police forces were corrupted by the easy money doled out by bootleggers. Those that weren't bought off were simply outmatched. In 1929, the Chicago Police Department owned only five submachine guns. Although Chicago was one of the largest cities in the country, its police didn't have the firepower to keep up with the Capones.[24]

•   •   •

Prohibition-era criminals made a mockery of state and local police departments by relying on two of the early twentieth century's most important developments: the national highway system and the automobile. The Federal Aid Road Act of 1916 provided a massive infusion of federal money to the states to pave the nation's mostly dirt roads and to build highways connecting cities. Soon, there were 300,000 miles of blacktop from coast to coast. In 1924, Rand McNally published the first national road atlas to help drivers navigate this newly paved terrain. There were plenty of takers. Thanks largely to Henry Ford's "progressive assembly" line, automobiles were being made cheaply, and ownership spread widely into the middle class. By the early 1920s, Americans owned over ten million automobiles. These cars were the seeds of highway robbery—a crime problem only the federal government could solve. Part of that solution would be newly designed laws to take the most dangerous weapons out of the hands of the desperados who traversed state lines in search of banks, gas stations, and grocery stores to rob.[25]

The most infamous desperados of the day were so well known that people referred to them by their first names, Bonnie and Clyde. Bonnie Parker and Clyde Barrow weren't Mafiosi, although they did occasionally rely on organized crime for shelter, supplies, and medical attention. Bonnie and Clyde were white Protestant bandits who grew up in the slums of West Dallas, Texas. They weren't bootleggers, like Capone and the urban mobsters. They were thieves whose heists were aided by the unending highways of the American West.[26]

Between 1932 and 1934, Bonnie and Clyde went on a crime spree, each heist garnering more publicity than the last. They weren't the only "rob 'em and run" outlaws of the day. The original "Public Enemy No. 1," John Dillinger, robbed at least ten banks in 1933 alone, often using a spray of machine-gun fire to provide cover for his car as he sped away. Others included George "Machine Gun" Kelly, George "Baby Face" Nelson, Charles "Pretty Boy" Floyd, and Kate "Ma" Barker. A crime writer in 1924 estimated that a car was used in three of every four crimes. The car and the highway system offered bandits on the run an easy route to freedom. Because state and local police had no jurisdiction to arrest someone across state lines, officers would stop at the border even as the bandits drove on. Today, police can just radio ahead to police in the neighboring state. In the 1920s and 1930s, however, there were no radios in police cars. With an easy way to avoid getting caught, criminals were more willing than ever to use their new high-powered firearms like the Tommy Gun.[27]

Bonnie and Clyde stood out from the criminal crowd for two reasons. The first was Bonnie herself—or, rather, Bonnie's sex. Crime was thought to be a man's game. Nevertheless, Bonnie was a notoriously willing and eager participant in the robberies and shootouts.

That a woman was a cold-blooded killer scandalized the country. Many Americans expected women to be barefoot and pregnant, not locked and loaded.

The second reason was Clyde's penchant for shooting people. *Time* magazine reported in 1934 that Clyde seemed "to find sport in shooting down, without provocation, people who got in his way—filling station men, constables, plain citizens." If Clyde was approached by a policeman, he didn't try to talk his way out of the jam. He shot his way out. In their two-year run, Bonnie and Clyde were "credited" with twelve murders, earning the pair the dubious title of "the worst killers of the Southwest."[28]

Guns, of course, were key to Bonnie and Clyde's success. In Oklahoma, Clyde broke into a National Guard armory and came out with an arsenal of firearms. One of his gang later told police, "Clyde brought back so many guns it looked like a gun factory." The take, he said, included "some 46 government automatics, .45 [caliber] pistols, several rifles and two or three cases of ammunition." When police discovered one of Bonnie and Clyde's hideouts, they found numerous photographs of the pair and their gang posing with Tommy Guns, pistols, and shotguns. The police released some of the photos to the press, which circulated them across the country. One photo showed Bonnie playfully "sticking up" Clyde with a shotgun. Another had her posing with a stolen car, a pistol in her hand, and a cigar in her mouth. It's not clear whether the public was more taken aback by a woman holding a gun or by a woman smoking a cigar.[29]

Bonnie and Clyde's armed withdrawals came to an inglorious end on May 23, 1934, on a dirt road outside of Arcadia, Louisiana. Police had been lying in wait for the pair, who eventually drove right into a hailstorm of bullets. In one minute, 167 rounds were fired, at least 50 of which hit the two outlaws. When police stopped shooting long enough to approach the vehicle, they found Bonnie with a submachine gun in her lap and Clyde holding a sawed-off shotgun. Inside the car were two more machine guns, another sawed-off shotgun, seven handguns, and a half-eaten sandwich.

It was a reflection of their notoriety that nearly thirty thousand spectators attended their funerals. People were eager to have a piece of them. Right after they were gunned down, bystanders ran up to the scene and, seeking a souvenir, dipped clothing in Bonnie and Clyde's spilled blood. One person ripped out strands of Bonnie's hair, while another tried to cut off one of Clyde's ears.[30]

Despite the success of the Louisiana police in ending Bonnie and Clyde's murderous spree, the pair's criminal adventures helped to solidify the belief that the time had come to enlist the help of the federal government in fighting desperados and their guns. While the pleas of Charles Bonaparte, Teddy Roosevelt's attorney general, had gone unheeded, people were now willing to listen when Homer Cummings, FDR's attorney general, insisted that Bonnie and Clyde "illustrate the manifest need of federal assistance in a cooperative effort to suppress this kind of crime." Modern criminals thrived in the jurisdictional cracks between the states, what Cummings called "the twilight zone, a sort of neutral corridor, unpoliced and unprotected."[31]

Local police, the traditional locus of crime control, were no more capable of bringing desperados to justice than of containing the Al Capones of the underworld. The gangsters and the desperados didn't confine themselves to one locale. They and their high-powered guns moved around the country from state to state, their crimes stretching across state lines. These types of criminals were a national problem, and it was going to require the national government to combat them.

•   •   •

THE ASSERTION of federal power over guns and crime fit perfectly with Franklin D. Roosevelt's philosophy of using the government to protect ordinary Americans from the hazards of modern society. In 1929, the year of the St. Valentine's Day Massacre, the Great Depression began. In October, the stock market crashed and in one week erased $30 billion in assets—ten times more than the annual budget of the federal government. Unemployment soared from 4 percent in 1929 to 25 percent in 1933. When Roosevelt accepted the Democratic Party's nomination for president in 1932, he famously announced, "I pledge myself to a new deal for the American people." From then on, FDR's plan to extend the hand of big government to secure a more prosperous, less risky future for all Americans was known as the New Deal.[32]

The New Deal was nothing short of a radical restructuring of American government. Traditionally, the states had been in charge of virtually all aspects of government affairs other than diplomacy and war. FDR sought to have the federal government take on unprecedented authority over the economy, agriculture, and industrial production. In his first few years in office, he pushed through Congress an incredible array of landmark legislation—each law expanding federal power at the expense of the states: the Emergency Banking Act and the Glass-Steagall Act to reform financial services; the Agricultural Adjustment Act to control the price and supply of commodities like corn, rice, and wheat; the National Industrial Recovery Act to manage the economy, stabilize prices, and control wages; the National Labor Relations Act to protect unions; the Securities Act and the Securities Exchange Act to regulate the stock markets; and, most important of all, the Social Security Act to provide universal retirement pensions, unemployment insurance, and welfare for the poor. Programs like the Tennessee Valley Authority were set up to deliver electricity and economic development to impoverished rural communities. The Public Works Administration financed infrastructure development and quasi-public employment policies on a scale never before seen.[33]

Roosevelt portrayed gun control and crime fighting as simply one more element of the New Deal—indeed, of the new America. "During the past two years," he said in a speech in late 1934, "there have been uppermost in our minds the problems of feeding and clothing the destitute, making secure the foundations of our agricultural, industrial, and financial structures, and realizing and directing the vital forces that make for a healthy national life. As a component part of that larger objective we include our constant struggle to safeguard ourselves against the attacks of the lawless and criminal elements of our own populations." Because crime drained the economy, federal crime control, he argued, was essential for national recovery.[34]

Roosevelt understood that, like many of his other New Deal reforms, a federal push in the field of guns and crime would face opposition from traditionalists committed to states' rights. At that juncture in history, however, what he called "the essentially nation-wide character of the crime problem" left the country no choice. "The consequences of lax law enforcement and crime-breeding conditions in one part of the country may be felt in cities and villages and farms all across the continent."[35]

The situation required a "New Deal for Crime." Just as Roosevelt sought to expand the power and reach of the federal government over the economy, he determined to expand its power and reach over criminals and their weapons. The man Roosevelt tapped to lead the push was his attorney general, Homer Cummings. A bald man with a round face and piercing blue eyes, Cummings was a close confidant of the president. He wasn't the first person you'd expect to lead a rev-olution. One of Roosevelt's speechwriters called Cummings "the least dramatic man in the whole world." As a three-time former mayor and former chair of the Democratic National Committee, however, Cum-mings was well versed in politics, and Roosevelt knew he wouldn't back down in the face of public or political opposition.[36]

Cummings first gained national attention in 1924 when he was a prosecutor in Fairfield, Connecticut. He refused to press charges against a man accused of murdering a priest, despite a public clam-oring for vengeance. The accused was in the vicinity of the crime when it was committed, was identified by witnesses as the killer, was caught with the gun used in the crime, and confessed to police. Yet Cummings's own investigation convinced him that he didn't have the right man and that the police had coerced the confession. He explained that "it is just as important for a state's attorney to use the great powers of his office to protect the innocent as it is to convict the guilty." Cummings also might have been more dramatic than Roosevelt's speechwriter thought. Once, when he was a young lawyer in Connecticut, he made a closing argument so eloquent that people in the courtroom were reported to have spontaneously burst out in applause.[37]

The first task for Attorney General Cummings was repeal of Prohibition. Teetotalers had tried to reinforce the ban on liquor in the
same way that later generations would try to reinforce bans on illegal
drugs, through harsher penalties for users. The strategy was equally
unsuccessful then. Even more troubling, thought Cummings, was
that "the illegal traffic in liquor" had created "new forms of crime."
"We are engaged in a war," he said. "A war with the organized forces
of crime." Victory wasn't going to come from stiffer penalties for
drinkers; it required making liquor lawful again and eliminating the
illegal profiteering that was enriching the mob.[38]

By 1933, with crime ascendant and illegal liquor easily available,
Cummings didn't face nearly the opposition one would expect when
seeking to overturn an amendment to the Constitution. Civic leaders, both wet and dry, recognized that Prohibition was a failure. The
famous industrialist and Prohibition advocate John D. Rockefeller
wrote in 1932, "When Prohibition was introduced, I hoped that it
would be widely supported by public opinion and the day would
soon come when the evil effects of alcohol would be recognized. I
have slowly and reluctantly come to believe that this has not been
the result. Instead, drinking has generally increased; the speakeasy
has replaced the saloon; a vast army of lawbreakers has appeared;
many of our best citizens have openly ignored Prohibition; respect
for the law has been greatly lessened; and crime has increased to
a level never seen before." In congressional hearings, respected
journalist Walter Liggett testified that Prohibition brought about
"wholesale crime, more drunkenness, more debauchery, disorder of
every sort."[39]

In March 1933, one of the first bills signed into law by Roosevelt
was the Cullen-Harrison Act, which redefined what counted as
"intoxicating liquor" for purposes of the Eighteenth Amendment.
The law made it lawful to manufacture and sell low-alcohol beer (3.2
percent alcohol by weight, or what was known as "three point two
brew") and certain wines. As he affixed his signature to the bill, Roosevelt announced cheerily, "I think this would be a good time for a
beer." Public support for Roosevelt's measure was strong enough to

propel ratification of the Twenty-first Amendment, repealing the Eighteenth, by the end of that year. The Noble Experiment was over, but the war on crime and heavily armed gangsters was still in its infancy.[40]

Cummings realized that he needed troops to wage war—in this case, a truly effective federal police force. The Justice Department already had what passed for law enforcement agents in the Bureau of Prohibition and the Bureau of Investigation. Yet the former was being disbanded in the wake of the legalization of liquor, and the latter was an underfunded agency devoted mainly to information gathering. The agencies were also hamstrung by the states' rights tradition. Because policing was a state function, federal agents didn't have the power to arrest people and weren't allowed to carry guns. Soldiers in the war on crime couldn't be effective armed only with notepads.[41]

As part of the New Deal for Crime, Cummings lobbied for a significant reorganization of the Bureau of Investigation. The number of field offices was more than doubled, as was the agency's budget. Two hundred new agents were added, and they were permitted to carry weapons, including submachine guns. Their charge was to fight interstate criminals like Bonnie and Clyde and mobsters like Al Capone and John Dillinger. When gun-toting federal agents arrested Machine Gun Kelly at a Memphis hotel after a manhunt in September 1933, the outlaw allegedly raised his hands in surrender and shouted, "Don't shoot, G-men!" The name, short for "government men," stuck.[42]

Two years later, Cummings had the agency itself renamed the Federal Bureau of Investigation to emphasize the new role of the federal government in fighting crime. Under its gifted but aggressive founding director, J. Edgar Hoover, the FBI would become the leading crime-fighting force in the country. At least for a time, one historian has observed, his agents became "symbols of national generation and a powerful state that was well organized, honest, and resolved to serve the people." Hoover thought that his professional lawmen should be trained in new scientific methods and equipped with the latest technology—an image of the G-men immortalized in popular culture by the comic hero *Dick Tracy* and his two-way radio wristwatch. Strong laws restricting the most dangerous weapons were also necessary. "What excuse can there possibly be for permitting the sale of machine guns?" Hoover asked. A master of public relations, at least in his early years, Hoover prepared the nation for federal gun control through the stories he wrote for the *American Magazine*. They emphasized the exploits of his agents and the pathologies of the modern criminal, under appropriate titles such as "Gun Crazy."[43]

Gun control required legislation, not just good public relations. Prior to being elected president, FDR had served on the executive committee of the National Crime Commission, a citizens' group formed in 1925 to investigate the roots of the Prohibition-era crime wave. The commission was an early advocate for the creation of a federal police force and the passage of federal gun control laws. Roosevelt's passion for gun control was enhanced in February 1933 when an anarchist named Giuseppe Zangara used a .32-caliber revolver to fire five shots at the president from less than fifteen yards away. Zangara was a poor shot and Roosevelt wasn't hurt, but five others were hit, including the mayor of Chicago, who was killed.[44]

Other than the Militia Acts of the founding era, there was little precedent for federal gun legislation. Congress had imposed a 10 percent excise tax on gun makers in the War Revenues Act of 1919, the primary purpose of which was to raise money to fight World War I, not to reduce the availability of guns. In 1927, Congress did have public safety in mind when it banned shipment of handguns through the U.S. mail. Like many of the gun controls that would follow in the twentieth century, however, this law was rendered ineffective by a gaping loophole. Only the U.S. mail was covered, which meant that people could still lawfully send handguns through private carriers, like the United Parcel Service.[45]

As Homer Cummings knew too well, there was ample precedent for the Supreme Court to strike down federal regulation. For the preceding forty years, the Court had repeatedly invalidated federal laws on the ground that Congress had exceeded its limited authority under the Constitution. The text of Article I, section 8, offered a list of areas in which Congress had power to act: "raise and support armies," "coin money," "fix the standard of weights and measures," "establish post offices," "punish piracies and felonies committed on the high seas," and "declare war." There was no provision authorizing the federal government to restrict guns or enhance public safety. One potentially broad enumerated power—"to regulate commerce . . . among the several states"—was narrowly construed by the Court to mean that Congress could not do much more than regulate the shipment of goods across state lines. Just because a good was manufactured in one state and shipped to another, however, did not empower Congress to regulate the production or use of the good.[46]

This jurisprudence of the early twentieth century, known to constitutional scholars as the "*Lochner* era," after a 1905 decision striking down a maximum-hours law for bakers, was the main impediment to many of Roosevelt's New Deal reforms. During the first three years of Cummings's tenure as attorney general, the Supreme Court struck down numerous landmark bills enacted to speed economic recovery. It was this dilemma that led Roosevelt in 1937 to propose his infamous Court-packing plan. The idea, which turned into a major embarrassment, was originally suggested by Homer Cummings.[47]

The Court-packing plan was still several years off when, in 1934, Cummings first sought to get the federal government involved in gun control. Needing to find a way to restrict criminals' access to guns without being overturned by the Supreme Court, Cummings ingeniously proposed raising taxes on firearms. One of Congress's clearly enumerated powers was "to lay and collect taxes." Even during the *Lochner* era, the Supreme Court held that the federal power to tax was very broad. So while Congress didn't have the power to ban guns directly, Cummings knew that, as the great Chief Justice John Marshall himself had noted over a century earlier, "the power to tax involves the power to destroy."[48]

By the spring of 1934, nearly everyone, even traditional states' rights advocates, was willing to destroy the guns favored by criminals. During deliberations over Cummings's anticrime bills, including a federal gun control law, the newspapers were headlined by stories of John Dillinger's yearlong crime spree. The need for federal intervention was acutely felt. State and local authorities had proven their ineffectiveness; Chicago police were rumored to be on the take, and Dillinger had easily escaped a highly touted "escape proof" county jail in Indiana by brandishing a piece of wood carved to look like a pistol. Texas congressman Hatton Sumners, a states' rights man through and through, announced that it was time for the federal government to "smash the criminal gangs and make another Dillinger impossible."[49]

The gun control law adopted by Congress was entitled the National Firearms Act of 1934. The law imposed an onerous tax on machine guns and on short-barreled (or "sawed-off") shotguns and rifles. Every time one of these guns were manufactured, sold, or transferred, the federal government imposed a tax of $200 on the transaction (more than $2,000 in 2010 dollars). Few law-abiding people had much interest in machine guns or short-barreled shotguns, especially when the tax more than doubled the price. Legitimate sales of these guns dried up almost immediately.[50]

The National Firearms Act didn't rely on a tax alone. It also required that owners of machine guns and short-barreled long guns register with federal authorities and submit to fingerprinting within sixty days. Cummings defended registration and fingerprinting as necessary to help enforce the tax. Mobsters and desperados might be able to afford the tax, but they wouldn't want to register and get fingerprinted. While no one expected them to comply with those requirements, their predictable failure to do so meant that anytime one of them was caught with a Tommy Gun or a sawed-off shotgun, he could be put in jail for up to five years simply for noncompliance. The government wouldn't have to prove that the person had killed anyone, only that he hadn't paid his taxes or properly registered his weapon.[51]

A similar strategy had already proven effective against Al Capone, who in 1932 was tried, convicted, and sentenced to eleven years in prison for tax evasion. Federal agents weren't able to gather up enough evidence to arrest him for killing the seven members of North Side

Gang on Valentine's Day or for illegally distributing alcohol through-out the Midwest, but they could charge him for failing to pay income taxes on the money he had in his accounts—money made from boot-legging and gambling. Capone was one of the first prisoners sent to Alcatraz, the forbidding maximum-security prison in the middle of San Francisco Bay that would become infamous for its harsh con-ditions and rigid enforcement of discipline. Turning Alcatraz into a federal prison was another piece of the Cummings and Roosevelt New Deal for Crime.[52]

When FDR signed the National Firearms Act into law he expressed his concern that law enforcement officers "are constantly facing machine-gun fire in the pursuit of gangsters." Yet within a few years, civilian ownership of machine guns and short-barreled shotguns and rifles became rare, and those who did own them weren't criminals. Criminals still had guns, but it had become much harder to obtain and riskier to keep some of the more dangerous weapons around. The first major federal gun control law was deemed so successful that four years later Congress once again asserted its authority over guns by passing the Federal Firearms Act of 1938. This law was essentially a licensing and record-keeping law for gun dealers, but it also barred felons from receiving firearms.[53]

Just after Congress passed the New Deal for Crime legislation in 1934, John Dillinger was finally stopped. Acting on Homer Cum-mings's order "Shoot to kill—then count ten," fifteen federal agents gunned down Public Enemy No. 1 outside of the Biograph Theatre in Chicago. The proud attorney general posed for photographs with the gangster's hat and gun. There were even rumors that he took a photo posing with one of Dillinger's severed ears.[54]

*   *   *

IN THE early twentieth century, state and local governments also turned their attention to gun control. While the federal government focused on the unusually dangerous weapons of gangsters and des-perados, state and local governments directed their efforts to handguns—what one New York judge called "the greatest nuisance in modern life." New York was at the forefront of the regulation, adopting in 1911 one of the strictest gun laws in the nation, the Sullivan Dangerous Weapons Act. The law took the name of its sponsor, "Big Tim" Sullivan, a Tammany Hall leader who represented the slums of lower Manhattan in the state senate. Sullivan was familiar with violence, having been born in 1863, a week after the Draft Riots, the worst civil unrest in New York history. Beaten often by his father, he was raised in the infamous Five Points district, below Fourteenth Street, reputed to be one of the poorest and most violent neighborhoods in the country. At the age of twenty-three, Sullivan won his first election to the state assembly buoyed by a reputation earned one day when, after seeing a noted prizefighter beating up a woman on the street, he stepped in and gave the boxer a thrashing of his own.[55]

Sullivan spent the rest of his life in electoral politics, becoming "the political ruler of down-town." Like many machine politicians of his day, he dipped his fingers into such profitable vices as gambling, prostitution, and indecent playhouses. Nevertheless, Sullivan often took things a step further than his counterparts. His interest in popular entertainment led him to form a chain of vaudeville theaters in which performers like Charlie Chaplin and Will Rogers got their start. He eventually sold the chain to an entrepreneur named Marcus Loew, who used them to create the first nationwide chain of movie houses, still in existence today, as Loews Theatres.[56]

The most innovative provision in Sullivan's gun control law was a requirement that anyone who wanted to possess a handgun, even at home, had first to obtain a permit. Dealers were prohibited from selling any concealable firearm to a person without a permit and were required to keep records of all gun sales. The law also made it illegal to give or sell a gun to someone under the age of sixteen. Gun control, Sullivan promised, "will do more to carry out the commandment thou shalt not kill and save more souls than all the talk of all the ministers and priests in the state for the next ten years."[57]

The Sullivan Act is often characterized in gun literature as an attempt to disarm immigrants. Racism and nativism were certainly part of the story behind the law. New York's gun problem was often blamed on immigrants who brought with them to America a fondness for pocket pistols and habit of using them at the slightest provocation. One provision of the Sullivan law barred aliens from carrying guns in public, though unlike aliens in numerous other states, those in New York were allowed to keep handguns at home. Other provisions were framed neutrally but applied by police chiefs discriminatorily against immigrants—in that era, a phenomenon hardly unique to gun control.[58]

The motivations behind the Sullivan law were, however, far more tangled than simple racism. Everything about Big Tim's political career suggests that he wanted to help, not hurt, immigrants—if for no other reason than his own continued political success. He was an immigrant himself, from one of the many Irish families that joined the dense concentration of German, Jewish, Irish, Italian, Chinese, and Greek newcomers who filled lower Manhattan. Sullivan's political influence over the years was due largely to his appeal to immigrant communities. He was famous for serving free Christmas dinners to the poor and dispossessed of the Bowery; thousands came every year, and Sullivan never turned anyone away. Each summer he organized popular community festivals in his district, where downtrodden constituents would feast on chowder, chicken, and beer while enjoying music, parades, and pie-eating contests. Big Tim thought gun control was necessary not to disarm immigrants, but to make those in his district safer from what he called "the tough men, the men who tote guns and use them far too frequently."

Moreover, the main provisions of the Sullivan law applied to all civilians regardless of where they hailed from. New York's gun problem was not limited to immigrants. Guns, especially handguns, were involved in an alarming number of incidents. In 1901, William McKinley became the third U.S. president to be assassinated when, during a visit to Buffalo, he was shot by a pistol-bearing anarchist— that era's brand of terrorist. In 1910, a disgruntled city employee used a pistol to shoot the popular mayor of New York City, William Jay Gaynor, at point-blank range. Although Gaynor survived, the incident was captured in a photograph that was especially disheartening to Americans. It showed the wounded mayor stumbling, blood all over his face and coat as he was being helped by another man. That other man was Robert Todd Lincoln, the only living son of the first U.S. president to be assassinated.[59]

Although political assassinations made the most headlines, gun violence was being felt by ordinary citizens too. In 1911, the New York City chief medical examiner reported that gun-related murders had jumped 50 percent the preceding year. "This city is like a wild Western town. The gun men rule," he wrote. Although this statement, as we've seen, exaggerated gun violence in frontier towns, the coroner's recommendation of "severe measures for the regulation of the indiscriminate sale and carrying of firearms" was influential. Across the country, reformers, including John Wanamaker, the nation's leading merchant, and John D. Rockefeller, began pushing for gun control legislation. A 1925 article in the *American Bar Association Journal*, entitled "Legislatures and the Pistol Problem," reported that a "current of public opinion is setting against the right of individuals to possess and carry freely revolvers capable of being concealed, and there is strong police sanction of this opinion." Enhancing public safety by regulating guns was of a piece with the progressive ferment that pushed for minimum-wage laws, child labor laws, and food quality legislation.[60]

The U.S. Revolver Association, a pro-gun organization formed, like the NRA, to promote marksmanship and competitive shooting, proposed in 1923 a Revolver Act for states to adopt. Under this proposal, civilians would have to obtain a permit to carry a concealed weapon. Anyone who committed a crime while in possession of a handgun would receive an extra five years in prison, and noncitizens would be prohibited from possessing handguns entirely. Gun dealers would have to deliver to police detailed records of all handgun sales. The proposal also included a one-day waiting period that meant dealers could not deliver a handgun to the purchaser until the day after the sale. While these last two types of gun control—turning over records of sales to the police and waiting periods—are vigorously opposed by gun rights advocates today, the Revolver Act was quickly enacted by numerous states, among them West Virginia, New Jersey, Michigan, Indiana, Oregon, California, New Hampshire, North Dakota, and Connecticut.[61]

The Revolver Act was the first important "model" gun control law. Around the turn of the century, lawyers and public officials increasingly saw the problems inherent in the patchwork of disparate laws in the then forty-odd states. Each state had its own set of laws and regulations. The wide variation among states bred inconsistency and confusion, especially for interstate businesses and an ever more mobile population. A movement began to promote consistency in the law among the states. In 1889, the American Bar Association resolved to work for "uniformity of the laws." Three years later, the first meeting of the National Conference of Commissioners on Uniform State Laws was held in Saratoga Springs, New York. By 1912, every state in the Union appointed commissioners to the national conference.[62]

In the 1920s, the National Conference of Commissioners turned its attention to gun control. Charles Imlay, one of the commissioners, wrote in 1926, "That there is need of more careful regulation of the use of firearms and in particular small firearms . . . is evidenced from the daily newspaper records of crimes of violence committed with the revolver." Imlay believed that the "same exigencies which demand the regulation of the sale and use of firearms require that the laws upon the subject be uniform." Because guns are easily transported across state lines, it was vital to enact consistent regulation so that the laws of one state were not undermined by the laxer laws of its neighbors.[63]

The model legislation endorsed by the National Conference of Commissioners was called the Uniform Firearms Act, and it borrowed liberally from the earlier Revolver Act. The Uniform Firearms Act's primary purpose was to "make it difficult for any person not a law-abiding citizen to obtain a pistol or revolver." The commissioners recommended that states require a license to have a concealed weapon in public and that a license be issued only to a "suitable person" with a "proper reason for carrying" a firearm. Dealers were to maintain records of sales and automatically forward them to law enforcement officials. The Uniform Firearms Act also included a one-day waiting period for handgun sales, later extended to two days in a revised version of the act. Anyone who sold a handgun was to be licensed by the state and was prohibited from selling such a weapon to those convicted of crimes of violence, drug addicts, drunkards, and minors. Aliens weren't singled out and, assuming they met the ordinary standards, could possess a concealed weapon just like citizens.[64]

The commissioners did not seek to get rid of all the guns. Most of the provisions of the Uniform Firearms Act applied only to handguns, which were thought to be especially prevalent in ordinary street crime. Ownership of shotguns and rifles, useful for hunting or protecting one's home from criminals, remained untouched. The commissioners were mindful of people's need to have firearms available for self-defense. The statement of principles that accompanied the act said the commissioners did not want to hamper "the facility of a law-abiding citizen to secure arms for the protection of his home."

The Uniform Firearms Act was eagerly adopted by numerous states, North and South. Alabama, Arkansas, Maryland, Montana, Pennsylvania, South Dakota, Virginia, Washington, and Wisconsin joined the states that had previously enacted the similar Revolver Act. By 1932, an article reviewing the spread of gun control legislation concluded that laws requiring a license to carry a concealed weapon "are in effect in practically every jurisdiction." Not all states adopted the Uniform Firearms Act in its totality. Some legislatures thought the model legislation went too far and supported only individual provisions. Legislatures in other states thought the act didn't go far enough. In Hawaii, Massachusetts, Michigan, West Virginia, and New Jersey, laws were passed requiring all purchasers of handguns, not just those who wanted to carry them concealed in public, to obtain a license first.[65]

New York was among the few states that didn't adopt one of the model gun control laws. Although a bill incorporating the Uniform Firearms Act passed both houses of the state legislature in 1932, the governor vetoed it. He thought that the Sullivan law was more restrictive and that the new law would have made it easier for people to carry guns. The governor at the time was a presidential candidate named Franklin D. Roosevelt.[66]

●   ●   ●

REMARKABLY, THE NRA, which today fights against nearly any gun control law, supported the restrictive gun laws of the early twentieth century. The NRA's president in the 1930s was Karl T. Frederick, a New York lawyer and graduate of Princeton University and Harvard Law School. Frederick was called "the best shot in America"—a title earned when, in the 1920 summer Olympic Games in Antwerp, Belgium, he won three gold medals in pistol-shooting events. Like many shooters of his generation, Frederick was an avid conservationist. Preserving the wilderness was necessary to ensure there would still be wild animals to hunt. He was vice president of the National Wildlife Federation and president of the Campfire Club, an early environmental group made up of East Coast bluebloods who, among other things, sought protection for baby seals. To this day, a wildlife management area in North Dakota is named after Frederick.[67]

Frederick was also a proponent of gun control. Indeed, as vice president of the U.S. Revolver Association, he helped draft the Revolver Act. Later, Charles Imlay of the National Conference of Commissioners brought Frederick on board as a special consultant to help draft the Uniform Firearms Act. The NRA, under Frederick's leadership, promoted this model legislation nationwide. Frederick himself said the NRA "sponsored" the Uniform Firearms Act. In other words, the NRA was behind a nationwide push for more restrictive gun control.[68]

When Frederick testified in congressional hearings over Homer Cummings's proposed National Firearms Act, he commended the states for the recent wave of gun laws restricting the carrying of guns. "I have never believed in the general practice of carrying weapons," he said. Although in special situations one might need a firearm for self-defense, "I do not believe in the general promiscuous toting of guns. I think it should be sharply restricted and only under licenses." His view was shared by other leaders of the NRA. The executive vice president at the time, Milton A. Reckord, told a congressional committee that the association he represented was "absolutely favorable to reasonable gun control." Years later, *American Rifleman*, the NRA's leading publication, touted the organization's efforts to ensure passage of both the National Firearms Act of 1934 and the Federal Firearms Act of 1938, laws that curtailed rather than expanded gun rights.[69]

Frederick and the NRA did not blindly support any and all gun control. They supported what he called "reasonable, sensible, and fair legislation," not "drastic proposals." The NRA opposed the Sullivan law because it went too far, restricting the ability of a law-abiding citizen to defend himself in his own home. While intended to take guns out of criminals' hands, the New York law was said—in words that continue to echo loudly in today's gun debate—to "have the effect of arming the bad man and disarming the good one to the injury of the community." For years, Frederick lobbied for repeal of New York's law. It wasn't because he was opposed to New York's controlling guns. He simply thought New York should adopt the Uniform Firearms Act he helped write instead.[70]

The organization also successfully fought to have the most "drastic" provisions of Cummings's original proposals stripped from the National Firearms Act of 1934. Roosevelt's attorney general initially sought to impose prohibitive taxes and registration requirements not just on machine guns and sawed-off shotguns but on handguns too. It was, after all, a handgun that had been used in the attempt to assassinate the president. Cummings wanted to tax handguns out of existence, along with the Tommy Guns favored by the Al Capones and Bonnie and Clydes. In his congressional testimony, Frederick and other leaders of the NRA said the handgun provisions would interfere with the ability of ordinary citizens to defend themselves and their homes from criminals, especially in rural communities with little police protection. The NRA organized a massive letter-writing campaign urging Congress to drop the handgun provisions. Members of Congress were inundated by letters from hunters, gun collectors, target shooters, and people concerned about their personal safety. Cummings backed down, and the final version of the law applied only to gangster guns. In the House report on the bill, Congress expressed its agreement with Karl Frederick that "there is justification for permitting the citizen to keep a pistol or revolver for his own protection."[71]

Conspicuous in its absence from the NRA's advocacy during this period was the Second Amendment. In an article on handgun regulation at the state level published in 1933, Karl Frederick posed the question of whether laws like the Uniform Firearms Act infringed the Constitution. He noted that the Second Amendment "is believed by many laymen to afford general protection" against laws that "abolish or restrict the possession and use of pistols." Yet that amendment, wrote Frederick, "applies only to the Federal Government. It has nothing to do with laws which may be passed by the respective States for the regulation or abolition of pistols." Frederick didn't even believe that the Second Amendment posed a significant hurdle to federal gun control. When asked during his testimony on the National Firearms Act whether the proposed law violated any constitutional provision, he responded, "I have not given it any study from that point of view." The president of the NRA hadn't even considered whether the most far-reaching federal gun control law to date was affected by the Second Amendment.[72]

To Frederick, preserving people's access to guns for self-defense was not a matter of the Second Amendment. It was a policy matter, to be debated on the merits. Protection for guns "lies in an enlightened public sentiment and in intelligent legislative action," he argued. "It is not to be found in the Constitution."

•   •   •

EVEN IF the president of the NRA didn't spend much time thinking about the impact of the Second Amendment on gun control, Homer Cummings did. The fact that the Supreme Court had never decided a Second Amendment case before didn't mean the proposed federal gun laws were on sure legal footing. The justices were hardly shy about striking down federal laws they didn't like. Indeed, Cummings knew that most of Roosevelt's first term was wasted fighting for landmark New Deal legislation that the Court held unconstitutional.

One reason the Supreme Court hadn't ever decided any Second Amendment cases was that it didn't have to. Prior to the twentieth century, gun control laws were typically adopted by state and local governments, not Congress. As Karl Frederick suggested, the amendment did not apply to state and local governments—a result of the Court's Reconstruction-era decisions, like *United States v. Cruikshank*, discussed earlier. There was no case law on how the new federal gun control might be impacted by the Second Amendment.

To protect the National Firearms Act from being overturned, Cummings had designed the law as a tax bill. He knew, however, that this strategy wouldn't protect the law from being overturned on Second Amendment grounds. Even if tax laws were within Congress's power generally, everything the federal government did was still limited by the Bill of Rights. Congress, for example, couldn't tax newspapers at exorbitant rates without running afoul of the First Amendment freedom of speech. If the Supreme Court thought that the Second Amendment protected an individual's right to have machine guns or sawed-off shotguns, then the tax imposed by the National Firearms Act would likely be invalidated.

Cummings needed a test case. Like Alan Gura and the libertarian lawyers decades later, he understood that judges can be swayed by the facts or circumstances of a lawsuit. It wouldn't be a good idea to prosecute some rural farm owner who used a sawed-off shotgun to kill an armed burglar trying to invade his home. Just as the libertarian lawyers wanted sympathetic plaintiffs to make their case as strong as possible, Cummings needed an unseemly character, someone who would give the justices pause before declaring that he had a right to especially dangerous weapons. Cummings found his ideal defendant in Jack Miller.

In the early 1930s, Miller had been part of a crew of bank robbers called the O'Malley Gang. Like so many desperados of the day, members of the gang used machine guns to get their money and cars to make their escapes. When the group was finally caught, Miller agreed to testify against his brothers in arms in return for his own freedom. Yet Miller didn't stay out of trouble long. In April 1938, he and his friend Frank Layton were pulled over outside of Siloam Springs, Arkansas. Inside their car, police found an unregistered sawed-off shotgun. The two men were arrested and charged by federal prosecutors with violating the National Firearms Act.[73]

Cummings's test case failed its first test. The trial judge, Hiram Heartsill Ragon, held that the National Firearms Act violated the Second Amendment. Despite being an ardent New Dealer and advocate for gun control before he joined the bench, Judge Ragon ruled that individuals have a right to possess guns and that the federal government can't require those guns to be registered. The judge ordered Miller and Layton to be released immediately—a move some say was designed to ensure an appeal to the Supreme Court.

As expected, Cummings's Department of Justice appealed the decision, and the Supreme Court agreed to hear the case. Unfortunately, the moment Judge Ragon had set Miller and Layton free, the two men disappeared. Their lawyer, who was appointed by the judge to represent the men free of charge, had no interest in devoting any more uncompensated time to their cause. He sent the clerk of the Supreme Court a telegram: "Unable to obtain any money from clients to be present and argue case." The justices, he suggested, should decide the case based solely on the government's brief.

Roosevelt's solicitor general at the time was Robert H. Jackson, who later gained prominence as a Supreme Court justice and, after World War II, as the chief prosecutor in the Nuremberg war crimes trials. He did everything exceptionally well. The progressive reformer and Supreme Court justice Louis Brandeis once said that Jackson was so good as the nation's leading advocate, he should be appointed "Solicitor General for life." One thing that helped make Jackson such a fine lawyer was his pragmatism; he wasn't given to grand theories but sought out practical solutions to his client's problems instead. In the *Miller* case, Jackson's brief to the Court offered a workable way

around Judge Ragon's constitutional objection to the National Firearms Act.

Jackson emphasized the first clause of the Second Amendment.
The right to bear arms "had its origin in the attachment of the people to the utilization as a protective force of a well-regulated militia
as contrasted with a standing army which might possibly be used
to oppress them." That right is "restricted to the keeping and bearing of arms by the people collectively for their common defense and
security. . . . Indeed, the very declaration in the Second Amendment that 'a well-regulated Militia, being necessary to the security
of a free State,' indicates that the right . . . is not one which may
be utilized for private purposes but only one which exists where
the arms are borne in the militia or some other military organization provided for by law and intended for the protection of the
state." The brief concluded by referencing the type of gun owners
targeted by the challenged federal law: "The firearms referred to in
the National Firearms Act, i.e., sawed-off shotguns, sawed-off rifles,
and machine guns, clearly have no legitimate use in the hands of
private individuals but, on the contrary, frequently constitute the
arsenal of the gangster and the desperado."[74]

In May 1939, two months after Homer Cummings stepped down
from his post as attorney general, the Supreme Court upheld his
landmark gun control law. The decision in *United States v. Miller*
was unanimous: the National Firearms Act did not violate the Second Amendment. The Court's opinion was written by Justice James
McReynolds, a Kentucky native and one of the most despicable men
ever to sit on the bench. Chief Justice William Howard Taft called him
"fuller of prejudice than any man I have ever seen." After Brandeis
became the first Jew on the Supreme Court in 1916, McReynolds
refused to talk to him for three years. Whenever Brandeis would
speak in the justices' conferences, McReynolds reportedly stood up
and left the room.[75]

McReynolds's opinion in the *Miller* case was hardly the epitome
of clarity, but some of his language suggested that the Court had
accepted the solicitor general's view that the Second Amendment was

designed only for state militias. "With obvious purpose to assure the continuation and render possible the effectiveness of such forces the declaration and guarantee of the Second Amendment were made. It must be interpreted and applied with that end in view." Because the sawed-off shotgun Jack Miller and Frank Layton had been caught with did not have any "reasonable relationship to the preservation or efficiency of a well regulated militia," the Second Amendment was inapplicable.

A few months later, Miller and Layton resurfaced. Miller was found in Oklahoma, his body, riddled with bullet holes, decaying on the bank of a stream. Layton had a better fortune. Still alive, he was charged again with violating the National Firearms Act. He pled guilty, but Judge Ragon, perhaps still waging his own personal war against the federal law, gave him probation.[76]

The Court's opinion in *United States v. Miller* didn't explicitly state that there was no individual right to have guns or that the right guaranteed by the Second Amendment applied only in the context of state militias. The opinion focused on the fact that a sawed-off shotgun wasn't a typical weapon used by a militia and thus wasn't protected by the Second Amendment. The reasoning seemed to suggest that weapons typically used by militias might be protected. Yet after *Miller* was handed down, the federal courts consistently read the Supreme Court's opinion to mean that the Second Amendment gave individuals no protection from ordinary gun control. As one federal appeals court put it in 1996, in *Miller* "the Court found that the right to keep and bear arms is meant solely to protect the right of the states to keep and maintain armed militia. . . . Following *Miller*, it is clear that the Second Amendment guarantees a collective rather than an individual right."[77]

That's how it stood for seventy years. Robert Jackson's militia-based view of the Second Amendment was the law of the land. The Supreme Court had any number of opportunities to clarify the meaning of the Second Amendment—there was no shortage of prosecutions for gun crimes, many of which were appealed to the Court—but the justices always chose to remain on the sidelines. Now, however, with

Alan Gura and the libertarian lawyers' challenge to D.C.'s gun laws, the Court was once again set to rule on the meaning of the Second Amendment.

·   ·   ·

Paul Clement began his presentation to the justices by distancing himself from the views of his predecessor, Robert Jackson. "The Second Amendment to the Constitution, as its text indicates, guarantees an individual right that does not depend on eligibility for, or service in, the militia." The Second Amendment right to keep and bear arms also encompassed the right of individuals to have guns for their own personal self-defense.[78]

No one in the courtroom was surprised by Clement's endorsement of the individual-rights reading of the Second Amendment. The Bush administration had clearly and often expressed its support for that view. Still, the spectators remained curious about what Clement would say regarding the government's ability to restrict that right in the name of public safety. They wondered whether he would stick to the argument made in his brief—that legislators should have broad leeway to regulate guns—or reverse course and advocate for strict limits on gun control. That latter position was what the betrayed gun enthusiasts, including Vice President Cheney, demanded. Almost certainly, career prosecutors at the Department of Justice were pushing Clement the other way.

Before Clement could address the issue that intrigued the Court watchers, the liberal justices took issue with Clement's claim that the Second Amendment protected an individual right. Justice John Paul Stevens, at eighty-eight the oldest member of the Court and the leader of its liberal wing, asked Clement how his individual-rights reading of the Second Amendment fit with state constitutional provisions on the right to bear arms in the founding era. Wasn't James Madison, the author of the Second Amendment, "guided at all by contemporaneous provisions in State constitutions?" Stevens asked.

"I'm sure he was influenced by that," Clement answered.

"And how many of them protected an individual right? Just two, right?" asked Stevens. There were thirteen original states.

"I think Pennsylvania and Vermont are the ones that most obviously protected" the right of individuals, agreed the solicitor general.

"They are only two," said Stevens. "And the others quite clearly went in the other direction, did they not?" The "other direction" meant limiting the right, if any, to service in the militia. If the majority of states didn't guarantee a personal right unrelated to the militia, that might suggest James Madison wasn't intending to protect such a right either.

"Well, I don't know about 'quite clearly,'" replied Clement. "The textual indication in state amendments that probably most obviously goes in the other direction is the phrase 'keep and bear arms for the common defense.'" In early America, several state constitutions that guaranteed the right to bear arms used that language. These state provisions, Clement suggested, were not the models for the Second Amendment. He pointed out that "there was a proposal during the debate over the Second Amendment to add exactly those words to the Second Amendment, and the proposal was defeated," never making it into the Constitution. The founding fathers had considered restricting the right to the militia, in other words, but decided against it.

Justice Ruth Bader Ginsburg asked Clement whether he thought the Second Amendment protected a right to have any type of gun a person wanted, or only particular firearms. The *Miller* decision had suggested that if any guns were covered by the amendment, they were only those with a reasonable tie to militia service. That might mean that firearms predominantly used for personal self-defense, like the handguns banned by the District of Columbia, weren't protected. Did Clement believe that the Second Amendment permitted the government to prohibit individuals from possessing some types of guns?

"Absolutely, Justice Ginsburg," he answered. The administration "would take the position that the kind of plastic gun or guns that are specifically designed to evade metal detectors that are prohibited by Federal law are not 'arms' within the meaning of the Second Amendment and are not protected at all." Here Clement was revealing his concern with preserving existing federal gun laws. Exempting from the Second Amendment weapons with no obvious military purpose, like plastic pistols, was one way to do that. Yet it wasn't enough, in Clement's view. Other federal gun control laws did target weapons with a military purpose like the machine guns regulated by the National Firearms Act.

"I think to make the same argument about machine guns would be a much more difficult argument, to say the least," Clement insisted, "given that they are the standard-issue weapon for today's armed forces and the State-organized militia." Because machine guns were commonly used by the military, such guns did have a reasonable relationship to militia service. If the Second Amendment guaranteed individuals access to some firearms, as Clement thought, the line *Miller* could be read to draw—militia guns were protected but personal self-defense weapons were not—was untenable. It would have the perverse result of permitting citizens to own the most dangerous firearms in existence, but not ordinary handguns.

The Court didn't necessarily have to identify which firearms were protected by the Second Amendment. Instead, it could assume that all "arms" are covered and apply what lawyers call a "standard of review," which is essentially a test to determine whether a given law is constitutional. A lenient standard of review would allow lawmakers considerable leeway on what guns to restrict. Walter Dellinger, D.C.'s lawyer, had argued for this as part of his fall-back position. The Court, he said, could apply a relatively deferential test that would require only that a challenged gun control law be "reasonable." Alan Gura, by contrast, had argued for a test that would be harder for lawmakers to meet—a standard known as "strict scrutiny." Under his test, a gun control law could survive only if it was absolutely necessary for public safety. Reasonableness wasn't enough; the law would have to be supported by compelling justifications. It was certainly possible that some gun control laws would be upheld even if the courts applied the strict scrutiny standard, but most laws subjected to such a test in other areas of constitutional law are invalidated. Legal scholars often say that strict scrutiny is "strict in theory and fatal in fact." Strict scrutiny was the standard applied in Judge Silberman's opinion for the federal court of appeals.[79]

Before Paul Clement was able to address which standard of review he thought most appropriate for the Second Amendment, a white light on the lectern went on, indicating his allotted time was about to end. Oral argument in the Supreme Court is run on a tight schedule. Chief Justice Roberts's predecessor, William Rehnquist, was famous for cutting off lawyers in midsentence when their time was up.[80]

The time clock was not always so severe. Early in the Court's history, oral argument was leisurely—and apparently far more entertaining. In 1819, for example, the Court heard arguments in the case of *Dartmouth College v. Woodward* over the course of three days. That case involved a legal challenge by Dartmouth to an effort by the state of New Hampshire to take over the private school and effectively turn it into a public college. Dartmouth was represented by Daniel Webster, considered the greatest advocate the Supreme Court has ever known. No one before or since has argued as many cases in the nation's highest court. Webster's gifts of oratory were legendary. Contemporaries joked that when he went fishing, the trout would leap from the water right into his pocket because they knew there was no fighting him. One speech he gave on the floor of the Senate was called "the most eloquent speech ever delivered in Congress." Webster's gifts were on full display in the three days the Court afforded to oral argument in the *Dartmouth College* case.[81]

Webster began his presentation by recognizing the power and authority of the justices. "You may destroy this institution, it is weak, it is in your hands." Then he won their sympathy by reminding them that Dartmouth was only "a small college and yet there are those who love it." As he finished his argument, Webster likened the plight of the school to Shakespeare's Julius Caesar—a victim at the hands of those who were trusted for protection. His emotions welled up. Spectators said his lips quivered, his voice cracked, and he trembled with emotion. His presentation was so moving it brought Chief Justice John Marshall to tears. After Webster spoke, Justice Joseph Story recalled that it was several minutes before the silence in the courtroom was broken: "The whole seemed but an agonizing dream, from which the audience was slowly and almost unconsciously awakening." The Court ruled unanimously in Webster's favor.[82]

Paul Clement might not have moved anyone to tears, but he also didn't have the luxury of three days to make his case. Because the United States wasn't formally a party to the dispute, the solicitor general was given just fifteen minutes. When the white light on the lectern clicked on, it signaled to Clement that he had only one minute left to wrap up. Fortunately for Clement, Chief Justice Roberts was more lenient than Chief Justice Rehnquist and permitted him and each of the two other lawyers in the gun case to go a few minutes over. The issues on the table were sufficiently important to warrant a bit more time.

"I would like to talk about the standard and my light is indeed on, so let me do that," said Clement. The spectators shifted and sat up in curiosity, waiting to hear whether Clement would stick with the position he took in his brief—in favor of a deferential test—or endorse the strict scrutiny test the gun rights people wanted. "I think there are several reasons why a standard as we suggest in our brief rather than strict scrutiny is an appropriate standard to be applied in evaluating these laws." Clement called his proposed standard "intermediate scrutiny," although it looked a lot like the reasonableness test Dellinger was advocating.

The right to keep and bear arms, Clement argued, "always coexisted with reasonable regulations of firearms." Even back in England before the American Revolution, where the right to bear arms was guaranteed by the English Bill of Rights, "the right was conditioned" on "what class you were, and also subject expressly to . . . the laws of Parliament." The right was not absolute. Just as Parliament could adopt laws regulating guns, so could the District of Columbia's lawmakers—and, more important in Clement's view, so could Congress.

Before Supreme Court justices make a rule or adopt a standard of review, they want to understand the implications, how today's decision will impact tomorrow's controversies. Justice Ginsburg noted that "there is a whole panoply of federal laws restricting gun possession." She asked Clement, "Would any of them be jeopardized under your standard?"

"In our view, it makes a world of difference" what standard applies under the Second Amendment, Clement replied. "[W]e certainly take the position, as we have since—consistently since—2001 that the federal firearm statutes can be defended as constitutional," Clement explained. "If you apply strict scrutiny, I think that the result would be quite different unfortunately." Clement was reaffirming the position of the Bush administration dating back to the memorandum by Attorney General Ashcroft. Yes, there is an individual right to bear arms for purposes of self-defense, but none of the existing federal gun laws are unconstitutional. The Supreme Court, he argued, should adopt a standard for judging gun control laws that would not undermine the panoply of federal gun control laws Ginsburg asked about.

Clement's argument put the conservative justices most open to the individual-rights view in a difficult position. As a general matter, they were also all proponents of the tough "law and order" stance popular in Republican circles ever since Richard Nixon railed against the coddling of criminals by the liberal Warren Court. Justices like Antonin Scalia and John Roberts didn't want to issue a ruling that would significantly undermine the gun laws used to keep criminals off the streets. If the nation's gun control laws were ruled unconstitutional, every criminal ever convicted of violating those laws could have his or her convictions overturned. Clement's approach provided a way out—but one that led many people to say, as Alan Gura did, that Clement's right to bear arms was a "meaningless" one.

Justice Samuel Alito thought perhaps the Court could avoid the whole question. Even under Clement's standard, Alito suggested the D.C. law should be struck down. "If the amendment is intended, at least in part, to protect the right to self-defense in the home, how could the District code provision survive under any standard of review where they totally ban the possession of the type of weapon that's most commonly used for self-defense," the handgun? Alito also noted that shotguns and rifles, while permitted in D.C., "have to be unloaded and disassembled or locked at all times, even presumably if someone is breaking into the home." It's one thing to permit reasonable regulation of guns, quite another to completely prohibit their use for self-defense. D.C.'s law was not a regulation of the right, Alito argued. It was a total denial of it.

Chief Justice Roberts said that it wasn't necessary to adopt any standard at all. "I wonder why in this case we have to articulate an all-encompassing standard. Isn't it enough to determine the scope of the existing right that the amendment refers to, look at the various regulations that were available at the time" of the founding and compare "how this restriction and the scope of this right looks in relation to those?" He went on, "I mean, these standards that apply in the First Amendment just kind of developed over the years. . . . But I don't know why when we are starting afresh, we would try to articulate a whole standard that would apply in every case?"

"I don't know what you're worried about," Scalia said to Clement. "Machine guns, what else?"

"I think it is more than a little difficult to say that the one arm that's not protected by the Second Amendment is that which is the standard issue armament for the National Guard, and that's what the machine gun is," Clement answered.

"But this law didn't involve a restriction on machine guns," Chief Justice Roberts shot back. "Why would you think that the opinion striking down an absolute ban" on the use of weapons for self-defense "would also apply to a . . . narrower one directed solely to machine guns?"

"I think, Mr. Chief Justice, why one might worry about that is" that the lower court opinion "said: Once it is an arm, then it is not open to the District to ban it." A machine gun was clearly an arm, and, ever since a law passed by Congress in 1986, the federal government had prohibited the sale of new machine guns to civilians.

"But that passage doesn't mean once it's an arm in the dictionary definition of 'arms,'" Justice Scalia insisted. For Second Amendment purposes, the term "arm" is used in a "specialized sense": a weapon "that was used in militias and . . . nowadays commonly held." Handguns are commonly owned by civilians; machine guns are not. Scalia was saying that only guns in common use by ordinary citizens were protected. There were the types of guns the founding fathers expected people to bring with them when called to serve in the militia. "If you read it that way, I don't see why you have a problem."

What Scalia omitted was the reason why machine guns were not in common use. In the New Deal for Crime, Homer Cummings and Franklin Roosevelt had pushed through Congress onerous restrictions on machine guns, with the stated goal of taking them off the streets. Machine guns weren't in common use at least in part because of decades of federal gun control. Paul Clement wanted the Court to recognize the right of individuals to own guns, but only so long as the ruling didn't call into question the federal gun control laws that made machine guns rare and other such laws that the Department of Justice used every day to prosecute criminals.

Clement's time, however, was up. "Thank you, General," said the Chief Justice. As Clement returned to his seat, Roberts looked over at the Supreme Court rookie challenging the D.C. law and nodded, "Mr. Gura."

CHAPTER 8

BY ANY MEANS NECESSARY

THE SEATING IN THE SUPREME COURT IS NOT DESIGNED well for spectators. The floor has no pitch, so when the courtroom is crowded you can see only the justices up on their raised bench and the back of everyone else's head. When Alan Gura rose from his seat and walked toward the podium, people in the rear of the room sat up tall and craned their necks to get a better view. Most people there didn't know what he looked like. The slender thirty-seven-year-old with the tousled black hair wasn't a prominent member of the local bar, and, in contrast to Paul Clement and Walter Dellinger—who combined had argued scores of cases in the Supreme Court—Gura was making his first appearance at the high court's lectern. In fact, he hadn't argued many appeals in any court, anywhere.

"No, not too much," Gura said when asked whether he had previous experience in the appellate courts. "Two, maybe three" prior cases, he estimated. In fact, his argument before Judge Silberman and the other judges in the D.C. Circuit was his first argument in a federal court of

appeals. When he was a government lawyer in California just out
of law school, he had "been to court plenty of times. Of course the
task of arguing to a judge is very different from arguing to a jury," he
admitted. He just hadn't had the chance to make many arguments in
front of a panel of judges before. "Most things settle," he said.[1]

In the months leading up to the oral argument, people in the gun
rights community were pressuring Bob Levy, who was financing the
case, to replace Gura with a more experienced Supreme Court advocate. They wanted him to hire a heavyweight like Ted Olson, who
won the *Bush v. Gore* case, or Ken Starr, the former solicitor general
and Whitewater prosecutor. Levy refused. Early on, when Gura was
willing to work on the case for almost no money, Levy had promised
Gura he could see this case through to the end. Such a deal was easy
to make back then, when most lawyers would have thought the lawsuit would never make it to the Supreme Court. Levy, however, not
only was a man of his word but thought Gura knew this case "better
than anybody in the world." Yet, it was still a big risk. If Gura fum-
bled, Levy, who had defied the NRA from the very beginning of the
lawsuit, would be heavily criticized by his friends in the gun rights
community for years to come.[2]

For Gura, the stakes were even higher. A misfire in such a high-profile case would probably make this his last Supreme Court appearance.
To make matters worse, Gura was up against two legal titans in Dellinger and Clement. Clement was widely recognized as one of the top
appellate advocates in the country, and Dellinger was a seasoned veteran who, as the *Washington Post* put it, "was winning arguments in
the Supreme Court when Gura was still studying for the bar exam."[3]

The self-assured Gura claimed to be nothing but confident. "I won
the case in the circuit court. I've written the pleadings. I've made
the arguments before. I've devised the strategy," he said. Some high-
profile Supreme Court veterans could have been brought in, but this
wasn't "their case." He insisted he "was not nervous."[4]

"Thank you, Mr. Chief Justice, and may it please the Court,"
Gura began—words required by Supreme Court etiquette. Gura
then launched into his argument, speaking so rapidly that the words

melted together. "All fifty states allow law-abiding citizens to defend
themselves and their families in their homes with ordinary functional firearms including handguns." Then, barely a sentence in, he
suddenly veered from his prepared remarks. "Now, I'd like to respond
to one point that was raised lately by the General. . . ." To the spectators in the courtroom, Gura seemed nervous after all.[5]

Justice Antonin Scalia stopped the overheated young lawyer. "Talk
a little slower, I'm not following you." For a moment, the courtroom
was completely silent. Gura took a deep breath and nodded, "Certainly, Justice Scalia."

He started over, this time articulating every word carefully and
slowly. "I'd like to respond to the point about the District of Columbia's position over the years with respect to the functional firearms
ban." The District, he said, had conceded in the trial court that gun
owners were banned from using "lawfully owned firearms for self-
defense within the home, even in instances when self-defense would
be lawful by other means." The District's lawyers had always insisted
that using guns in self-defense was not permitted. They shouldn't be
allowed to change their story this late in the game.

In every Supreme Court hearing, there are dozens of arguments
the lawyers can make. The briefs they file with the Court address all
the important ones. When it comes to oral argument before the justices, a skilled lawyer has to be able to figure out what he needs to
focus on in his limited time. Only half an hour is allotted for each
side, and much of that time is spent answering questions. The successful advocate has to be adept at responding to the justices' questions, while also steering the justices to the most persuasive points in
his favor.

Alan Gura didn't need to spend his time focusing on the history
behind the Second Amendment. It already seemed clear to everyone
in the courtroom that there were at least five justices willing to say
the Second Amendment guaranteed the right of individuals to own
guns for personal self-defense. That, the biggest question in the case,
was settled by Justice Anthony Kennedy's early remarks. Gura had
to emphasize two other points instead. The first was that the justices

shouldn't accept Walter Dellinger's reading of D.C. law to allow self-defensive uses of long guns. This was key. The heart of Gura's argument was that D.C.'s law was unconstitutional because it didn't allow for self-defense. If the justices read the D.C. gun law to allow rifles and shotguns to be used in this manner, he might well lose.

Gura's second objective was to allay the fear raised by Clement about the continuing validity of federal gun control. The Second Amendment might have guaranteed a right to keep and bear arms, but Gura needed to assure the justices that an individual right to bear arms didn't mean anyone could have any type of weapon he wanted. The Second Amendment did not present a permanent barrier to any and all gun control. Gura knew that some of the justices would share Clement's concern about the implications of a decision striking down D.C.'s law. To win those justices over, he had to persuade them that they could rule in his favor without spelling the end of gun control in America.

Government "can ban arms that are not appropriate for civilian use," Gura told the justices. "There is no question of that."

"For example?" asked Justice Ruth Bader Ginsburg.

"For example, I think machine guns," Gura answered. Machine guns are "arms" but the Second Amendment should not be read to guarantee civilians access to them.

"But why wouldn't a machine gun qualify?" Ginsburg responded. "General Clement told us that that's standard issue in the military."

"But it's not an arm of the type that people might be expected to possess commonly in ordinary use," explained Gura. The *Miller* case "spoke very strongly about the fact that people were expected to bring arms supplied by themselves of the kind in common use at the time. So if in this time people do not have, or are not recognized by any court to have, a common application for, say, a machine gun or a rocket launcher," then those weapons would not be protected by the Second Amendment.

In fact, Gura argued, a whole host of gun control laws would be consistent with the Second Amendment. D.C. could "require safe storage" of guns, "for example, in a safe." D.C. could require a license to possess a firearm and condition that license on what he called "demonstrated competency" with the weapon. It could also require "background checks" or prohibit minors from possessing guns. Indeed, Gura counseled, D.C. should have "a great deal of leeway in regulating firearms."

These concessions led to an avalanche of criticism of Gura by the gun rights extremists after the oral argument. Vin Suprynowicz, an opinion writer for the *Las Vegas Review Journal* who calls himself "America's Champion of Liberty," accused Gura of being a stooge for the gun controllers. "Why go to the trouble of getting the Supreme Court to rule on whether the Second Amendment says what it says, and then offer to help the gun-grabbers pleasure themselves in court, selling out our God-given, constitutionally protected right to keep and bear machine guns?" Suprynowicz asked. "Was it a failure of nerve under pressure, or did somebody get to this guy?" A man in Michigan dashed off a letter to Gura comparing the lawyer to Osama bin Laden and Benedict Arnold. History, the letter warned, would condemn Gura for his compromises. The man, it turned out, was currently serving time for illegal possession of a machine gun.[6]

As Gura recalled, "I received a very negative reaction from the real far-out anti-gun control crazies, who were very angry with me." They accused him, he said, of "high treason and conspiring with the city to destroy the Second Amendment." In particular, they were upset "because I told the Court that machine guns were not protected by at least our conception of the Second Amendment, and that was very, very infuriating to a lot of people. I received some just vicious, nasty responses."[7]

Larry Pratt, the head of Gun Owners of America, one of the more extreme gun rights groups, worried that the Court was set to protect only a "watered-down individual right to keep and bear arms." With Gura clearly in mind, Pratt lashed out at those "who seem to be on our side" but "then turn around and concede government's author-ity" to enact restrictions on guns. People like that are "slowly suck-ing the life out of our constitutional rights." The NRA also voiced its opposition to the idea that machine guns could be banned. Rachel Parsons, a spokesperson for the NRA, came out and announced that because machine guns are not usually involved in crime, anyone without a criminal record should be able to own one. "The NRA stands firmly by the notion that law-abiding citizens are not the problem," she said.[8]

Gun rights hard-liners firmly oppose many of the types of restrictions that Gura conceded were permissible. According to Richard Poe, a former journalist who writes on guns, the "real purpose" of licensing is to collect data to enable government to confiscate all the guns. "Those who advocate licensing are implicitly acknowledging that Americans have no right to keep and bear arms. Rather they regard gun possession as a special favor or privilege that can be granted or revoked for almost any reason." The pro-gun zealot, former rock star, and NRA board member Ted Nugent insisted that all safe storage requirements were unconstitutional. A right to "bear" arms means, "I've got it right here, on me, either in my grasp or damn near. This does not mean locked away in some safe," he wrote.[9]

"These people are crazy," said Gura. "I could have, if I wanted to, stood up before the Court and said, 'Yes, *shall not be infringed* means you may never have any gun laws, and of course we need to all have machine guns in case we want to overthrow the government, and while we're at it we should have rocket launchers and stinger missiles. And that would have probably made me very popular in some cabin somewhere out there in the woods." He added, "Of course, I would have lost 9–0." Gura said that you "win constitutional litigation by framing issues in as narrow a manner as possible. I could not tell the justices honestly that I hadn't thought about machine guns." Strategically, Gura had no choice but to concede that some gun restrictions were consistent with the Second Amendment. He wasn't out to appease the radicals in the modern gun rights movement. He was trying to win his case—by any means necessary.[10]

●   ●   ●

THE HARD-LINERS in the modern gun rights movement who were so upset with Alan Gura's concessions in the Supreme Court can trace their roots to, of all people, the Black Panthers. If it hadn't been for the Black Panthers, a militant group of Marxist black nationalists committed to "Black Power," there might never have been a modern gun rights movement. The Black Panthers and other extremists of the 1960s inspired some of the strictest gun control laws in American history. These laws, aimed largely at disarming urban black leftist radicals, led to a backlash by rural white conservatives.

The Black Panther Party for Self-Defense, as it was officially called, was formed in October 1966 by two African Americans in their twenties, Huey Newton and Bobby Seale. The two had met a few years earlier as students at Merritt College, a community college in the hills of Oakland, California. They were part of a group of politically active students who pushed the school's administration to add its first course on black studies. Newton and Seale had similar backgrounds. Both were born in the South and brought to Oakland in the 1940s by their parents, who were seeking to escape discrimination and find work in the burgeoning wartime industries of California. What their parents found instead was that racism, poverty, and unemployment followed them west.[11]

By 1966, many in the black community had grown frustrated with the failed promise of the civil rights movement. The Supreme Court had decided *Brown v. Board of Education* more than a decade earlier, but most schools were still racially segregated. Dr. Martin Luther King Jr. was a certified American hero, but his strategy of nonviolent resistance had yet to deliver equal opportunity. The Civil Rights Act of 1964 and the Voting Rights Act of 1965 were landmarks, but for unemployed blacks living in the ghetto they hadn't yet made much of a difference.

Among the few tangible things the civil rights movement had delivered to blacks were beatings, arrests, and death. In 1961, the "freedom riders" took seats on the buses and trains the Supreme Court said were constitutionally theirs to ride, only to be imprisoned in Mississippi and firebombed in Alabama. In 1963, the KKK bombed the Sixteenth Street Baptist Church in Birmingham, killing four young girls attending Sunday school. That same year, Medgar Evers, an NAACP field secretary, was shot in the back by an Enfield M1917 rifle fired by a white supremacist. Thousands of civil rights workers descended upon Mississippi to register black voters in the "freedom summer" of 1964; four were killed, three of them when local police arrested them and then turned them over to the Klan.[12]

Peaceful protests and Supreme Court victories had done little to improve the economic conditions of blacks, who had an unemployment rate twice that of whites. Those who were employed made about half as much as their white counterparts. Blacks felt unfairly burdened by conscription into military service in Vietnam; those still at home felt unfairly burdened by the police, who seemed more determined to harass and beat blacks than protect and serve them. These ingredients combusted in August 1965 when a six-day riot broke out in Watts, a minority neighborhood in Los Angeles. The spark was a police confrontation with an allegedly intoxicated black driver. When the officers refused to allow the driver's sober brother to take the car home—impounding it instead—an angry mob began to hurl rocks and insults. Before long, thirty-four people were killed, over a thousand injured, and hundreds of buildings damaged or destroyed.[13]

Police abuses were often entwined with Klan violence. In 1961, Birmingham Police Commissioner T. Eugene "Bull" Connor promised the local Klan fifteen minutes to beat freedom riders with iron pipes before police would step in. Two years later, Connor unleashed police dogs and high-pressure fire hoses on civil rights marchers—events that, when televised, shocked the nation. Throughout much of the South, police departments were heavily populated by Klansmen. In some counties, Klan dues were even paid and collected right at the local police station.[14]

In Oakland, Huey Newton and Bobby Seale committed themselves to fighting back against the police. The almost exclusively white Oakland police force had recently increased its presence in minority neighborhoods to combat juvenile delinquency, angering residents. As one Panther said, "the primary job" of the police "was to keep black folks down and corralled" in the poor part of town. Only months before the Black Panther Party was started, Bay Area police killed three black men engaged in petty crimes; one was shot seven times in the back by Oakland police officers for trespassing. The courts didn't provide much justice for victims of police abuse. Grand juries usually ruled that police shootings were "justifiable homicides," even when the victims, like the three in the Bay Area in 1966, were unarmed when they were shot. Self-help seemed the only available option. As one Panther said, it didn't make any sense "to report the police to the police."[15]

Inspired by the teachings of Malcolm X, "Huey was on a level where he was ready to organize the black brothers for a righteous revolutionary struggle with guns and force," recalled Seale. Before he was assassinated in 1965, Malcolm X preached that the nonviolent resistance of Martin Luther King was a failure. Because the government was "either unable or unwilling to protect the lives and property" of blacks, they had to defend themselves "by whatever means necessary." The phrase was borrowed from the French existential philosopher Jean-Paul Sartre, who used it in his 1948 play *Les Mains Sales* ("Dirty Hands"), about the assassination of a political leader. To Malcolm X, the phrase meant that blacks were justified in doing whatever they had to in order to bring about racial justice. He illustrated the idea for *Ebony* magazine by posing for photographs in suit and tie, peering out a window with a rifle—an M1 Carbine semiautomatic—in his hand.[16]

"Malcolm's spirit is in us," explained Newton. It was impossible, he said, to overstate "the effect that Malcolm has had on the Black Panther Party." The group was "a living testament to his life work." When asked why they didn't first try King's nonviolence, Seale responded, "Nonviolence on the part of whom? On the part of the racists who've infested the police department? Who continue to brutalize and murder black people in the streets? No, we must defend ourselves, like Malcolm said, by any means necessary." And, like their hero, they characterized their right to use guns in self-defense in constitutional terms. "Article number two of the constitutional amendments," Malcolm X had argued, "provides you and me the right to own a rifle or a shotgun."[17]

Just as Malcolm X had borrowed "by any means necessary" from Sartre, Newton and Seale borrowed the name Black Panthers from the Lowndes County Freedom Organization. The LCFO was an Alabama group started by Stokely Carmichael—who coined the phrase "Black Power"—as a political alternative to the all-white Democratic Party in the state. Its symbol was a pouncing black jungle cat, with sharp teeth and outstretched claws. Newton thought the LCFO's panther was an ideal symbol for black people determined to fight, rather than wait, for racial equality. "The panther is a fierce animal but he will not attack until he is backed into a corner," Newton explained. "Then he will strike out."[18]

Guns were central to Newton and Seale's philosophy and to the public image of the Panthers. They taught their early recruits that the gun "is the only thing the pigs will understand. The gun is the only thing that will free us—gain us our liberation." According to Newton, "Black People can develop Self-Defense Power by arming themselves from house to house, block to block, community to community throughout the nation." They bought some of their first guns with proceeds earned from selling copies of Mao Zedong's Little Red Book to left-wing students at the University of California at Berkeley. The Panthers liked the Chinese manifesto in part because of Mao's famous statement, "Political power grows out of the barrel of a gun." In time, the Panthers' arsenal included machine guns, rifles, handguns, explosives, grenade launchers, and "boxes and boxes of ammunition," recalled Elaine Brown, one of the first female members of the party, in her memoir. Some of the guns and ammo came from the federal government. The Panthers had connections with people at Camp Pendleton, a military base in Southern California, who would sell them anything for the right price. One Panther said that they could have bought an M-48 tank and driven it right up the freeway.[19]

Every member of the Black Panthers was expected to know how to use a firearm. Along with political education classes on black nationalism and socialist theory, Newton made sure recruits were taught how to clean, handle, and shoot guns. Their instructors were sympathetic black veterans who had recently returned home from Vietnam. For their "righteous revolutionary struggle," the Panthers were armed and trained, however indirectly, by the U.S. government.

Guns became part of the official uniform of the Black Panthers: black beret, black leather jacket, powder blue shirt, black pants, and a firearm. The black leather jackets were chosen because "it seemed like everybody had one anyway," said an early member, Elbert "Big Man" Howard. Once Newton and Seale began recruiting "brothers off the block"—pimps, drug dealers, numbers runners—the new recruits brought their own guns too. They "had been shooting their pistols Friday and Saturday night anyway," said one Panther. "So we'd get them and politicize them."[20]

Civil rights activists had long appreciated the value of guns for self-protection. In 1956, after his house was bombed but before he fully adopted Gandhian nonviolence, Martin Luther King Jr. applied for a permit to carry a concealed firearm in Montgomery, Alabama. Because the local police chief had discretion over who could receive a permit—decades earlier, the state had adopted the NRA-endorsed Uniform Firearms Act—King's application was denied. Yet, from then on, armed supporters took turns guarding King's home. King truly believed that love was the best answer to violence. Nevertheless, he endorsed the right to defend one's home and family when attacked. Glenn Smiley, an adviser to King, described the civil rights leader's home as "an arsenal." Once, when he was visiting King's parsonage, William Worthy, a black reporter who covered the Southern Christian Leadership Conference, went to sit down on an armchair in the living room and almost sat on a loaded gun.[21]

While they weren't the first civil rights activists to have guns, the Panthers took it to the extreme. They carried their guns in public, openly displaying them for everyone—especially the police—to see. Newton, who had attended classes at San Francisco Law School, discovered that California law allowed people to have guns in public so long as they were visible. You needed a license only to carry a concealed firearm. Anyone was allowed to carry a handgun holstered on the outside of his clothing or walk around with a rifle or shotgun in hand, so long as it wasn't carried in a threatening manner—that is, pointed at anyone. No one ever toted guns around this way in the cities of California, but it was perfectly legal to do so.

One day in February 1967, an Oakland police officer saw Newton, Seale, and some other Panthers loading into a car with an assortment of guns. The officer wasn't used to seeing civilians openly carrying firearms, much less black residents. He suspected that the Panthers had some criminal intent. He called for backup and cautiously approached the car. Newton was in the driver's seat with an M1 rifle—the same gun Malcolm X had posed with in the famous photographs. Seale had a 9-millimeter handgun on the seat beside him. The policeman asked Newton to hand over his driver's license. Newton complied. When additional officers arrived a few moments later, one looked into the Panthers' car and asked to inspect one of the guns. This time, Newton refused.

"I don't have to give you anything but my identification, name, and address," Newton insisted. This, too, he had learned at law school.

"Who in the hell do you think you are?" the officer responded.

"Who in the hell do *you* think *you* are?" said Newton indignantly. He told the officer that they had a legal right to have these guns.

The officers asked Newton to get out of the car. Newton did, but while getting up he simultaneously loaded a round of ammunition into his M1. Newton was careful to keep the gun pointed upward and not aimed at any of the officers.

"What are you going to do with that gun?" asked one of the stunned policemen.

"What are *you* going to do with *your* gun?" Newton replied.

By this time, the scene had drawn a crowd of onlookers. The police told the people to move on, but Newton shouted to them to stay. California law, he informed them, gave civilians a right to observe police officers making arrests so long as they didn't interfere—another thing he had learned in law school. Newton played it up for the crowd. In a loud voice, he told the police officers, "If you try to shoot at me or if you try to take this gun, I'm going to shoot back at you, swine."

The officers must have been confused by Newton's audacity. Yet they also knew the law—and that Newton was right about everything

he said. Although a black man with Newton's attitude would usually find himself handcuffed in the back of a police car in seconds,
the officers were not about to do anything foolish. The people on the
street were watching them, and Newton appeared to be serious about
that M1 in his hands. The officers decided to let Newton and the others go on their way.

The people who witnessed the scene were amazed. Not even Bobby
Seale could believe it. Right then, he knew that Newton was the "bad-
dest motherfucker in the world." Everyone there that day understood
what Seale said was Newton's message: "the gun is where it's at and
about and in." After the February incident, the Black Panthers began
a practice of policing the police. Thanks to an army of new recruits
inspired to join when they heard about Newton standing up to the
cops, groups of armed Panthers would drive around following police
cars. When the police stopped a black person, the Panthers would
stand off to the side and shout out legal advice. You have the right
to remain silent and to have a lawyer appointed for you, they would
yell. If the police turned their attention to the Panthers, the party
members would recite verbatim the provisions of the California penal
code that authorized them to carry guns openly and observe arrests.
Such encounters served two purposes. They informed the persons
being harassed by the police of their rights and, because the confrontations inevitably attracted the attention of curious bystanders, they
also advertised the Black Panthers to potential new members.

The organization was less than a year old, but Newton sensed that
his Panthers and their guns were changing the relationship between
blacks and the Oakland police. With "weapons in our hands, we were
no longer their subjects but their equals."[22]

•   •   •

IT WAS a sunny day in Sacramento, the lily-white hub of California
politics, when, on May 2, 1967, a group of twenty-four men and six
women, all black and between the ages of sixteen and thirty-one,
parked in front of the Capitol Building. As they got out of their cars,

they loaded their guns, which included .357 Magnums, 12-gauge shotguns, and .45-caliber pistols. During the eighty-mile drive from Oakland, the guns had remained unloaded because California law prohibited possession of a loaded firearm in a vehicle. What California law didn't prohibit, however, was carrying a loaded, visible firearm in any public place. So the Panthers holstered their loaded pistols, grabbed their loaded shotguns, and looked up at the majestic statehouse. Bobby Seale motioned to the others, "All right, brothers, let's roll."[23]

It was three months after the February incident with police, and the Black Panthers were now out to change the relationship between blacks and California legislators. Huey Newton decided that the Panthers should take their guns to the state Capitol and declare that blacks were no longer just subjects. They had a say in politics too. One of their first demands was that lawmakers respect their right to keep and bear arms.

California's statehouse, a neoclassical building constructed between 1860 and 1874, looks much like the building it was modeled after, the Capitol Building in Washington, D.C. A wide rectangular base sports granite archways and fluted Corinthian columns, topped in the center by a towering dome that rises 220 feet in the air. This being California, the mostly white granite building is surrounded by tall palm trees and thick evergreen pines. Both houses of the California legislature—the assembly and the senate—are located in the building, as is the governor's office.[24]

In front of the Capitol is the West Lawn, a large, flat expanse of grass used for special events. This is where a group of mostly white eighth-graders were gathering for a fried chicken lunch with the governor, the former actor and future icon of the conservative movement, Ronald Reagan. The students stopped and stared in amazement as the Black Panthers marched right by. News crews there to cover the governor's event saw the better story developing and rushed to follow the heavily armed Panthers.

The idea of visiting the statehouse had come to Newton a few weeks earlier. In April, the Panthers had organized a series of rallies in

North Richmond, California, to protest the killing of Denzil Dowell, a young black resident who was shot by sheriff's deputies one night while allegedly trying to flee arrest. Predictably, Dowell's killing was ruled a "justifiable homicide." At the request of the Dowell family, Newton, Seale, and a few other Panthers went to see the local sheriff to demand an investigation. The sheriff wasn't particularly interested and told the men that if they didn't like the way the law worked, they should take their complaints to the state assembly.[25]

In May, Newton saw the perfect opportunity to do just that. Don Mulford, a conservative Republican state assemblyman from Alameda County, which includes Oakland, had introduced legislation inspired by the Panthers to outlaw the open carrying of loaded firearms within city limits. Mulford had a history of fighting radicals; when the Berkeley campus was in the throes of the student "free-speech movement," Mulford backed a new law that allowed state universities to remove from campus anyone who wasn't a student. Although the campuses were traditionally open to the public, Mulford's law permitted security to forcibly remove people who came onto school grounds only to protest.[26]

Mulford had special contempt for the Panthers, who he thought were undermining law and order in his district. After the Dowell rallies, Newton was invited to appear on a local radio talk show. Mulford called in, irate. He promised that he would "get" the Panthers and put an end to their armed police patrols. Not long thereafter, the state assembly scheduled debate on Mulford's gun control proposal.[27]

When Newton found out about this, he told Seale, "You know what we're going to do? We're going to the Capitol." Seale was incredulous, "The *Capitol?*" Newton explained, "Mulford's there, and they're trying to pass a law against our guns, and we're going to the Capitol steps." Newton's plan was to take a select group of Panthers "loaded down to the gills," he said, to send a message to California lawmakers about the group's opposition to the proposed law. Newton, a showman by nature, realized that the public show of force, like the armed police patrols, would generate attention for the group.[28]

The Panthers loved the plan, but decided it was too dangerous for

Newton to go. He was their leader—their "Minister of Defense," they called him—and if anything bad happened, they wanted him to be safe. Instead, Bobby Seale led the group to Sacramento. Even though Newton wasn't with them, his teachings about California's guns laws were. The Panthers held their guns in a nonthreatening manner, pointed straight down to the ground or straight up in the air. To white people in Sacramento, however, a group of young blacks carrying guns was threatening no matter where the guns were pointed. The 1965 race riots in Watts were still fresh in people's memories. Seale recalled the business people and tourists around the statehouse gawking at the Panthers. "A lot of white people were shocked, just looking at us. I know what they were saying: 'Who in the hell are those niggers with these guns?'"

When Seale and the others reached the top of the Capitol steps, the Panthers stopped and Seale read some prepared remarks to the gathering crowd of journalists and curious onlookers. The Black Panther Party for Self-Defense "calls on the American people in general and the black people in particular to take careful note of the racist California legislature . . . aimed at keeping the black people disarmed and powerless at the very same time that racist police agencies throughout the country are intensifying the terror and repression of black people," Seale announced. "Black people have begged, prayed, petitioned, demonstrated and everything else to get the racist power structure of America to right the wrongs which have historically been perpetuated against black people. All of these efforts have been answered by more repression, deceit, and hypocrisy." He said the "time has come for black people to arm themselves against this terror before it is too late. The pending Mulford Act brings the hour of doom one step nearer."

Then Seale turned to the other Panthers. "All right, brothers, come on," he said loud enough to be heard over the commotion. "We're going inside." He opened the door, and the Panthers walked into the most important building in the state, guns in hand. No security officers stopped them, and there were no metal detectors to pass through.

Once inside, they headed for the assembly chamber. The only hitch was that they had no idea where it was. They began to wander the hallways of the Capitol with a growing throng of cameramen and journalists swarming around them. Employees and other visitors stood to the side, mouths agape at the spectacle. Jerry Rankin, a reporter for the *Los Angeles Times*, wrote, "It was one of the most amazing incidents in legislative history—a tumultuous, traveling group of grim-faced, silent young men with guns roaming the Capitol surrounded by reporters, television cameramen, stunned state police and watched by incredulous groups of visiting school children."[29]

Reporters, many of whom had probably never heard of the Black Panthers before, were eager to find out more. They shouted questions at Seale and the others, but the Panthers kept walking on without saying a word. Suddenly, Seale stopped and broke the silence. "Anybody here know where you go in and observe the Assembly making these laws?" Someone shouted back to go upstairs, so the Panthers made their way to the staircase.

Gaining the attention of the press was all part of Huey Newton's plan. Bobby Seale recalled "how smart Brother Huey was when he planned Sacramento." Newton figured that when the press called the armed Panthers "thugs and hoodlums," it would only heighten the group's appeal to "the brothers on the block, who the man has been calling thugs and hoodlums for 100 years." Blacks would see the Panthers and say, "'Them's some out of sight thugs and hoodlums up there. Who is these thugs and hoodlums?'" The media frenzy the Panthers were causing would be a recruiting boon to the new party, and put them on America's cognitive map.

The guns were mainly for show, although not entirely. Newton instructed Seale and the others to be prepared to return fire if anyone shot at them. The Panthers were not violating any law, and they had the right to defend themselves if attacked. Even so, the guns were primarily to garner the group media attention. The Panthers didn't plan to take hostages or to start a shootout. This was a political protest. If Capitol police tried to arrest the Panthers, as Newton and Seale imagined they would, the Panthers were to refrain from using their guns and allow themselves to be taken into custody peacefully.

Initially, the guards didn't give the Panthers much trouble. Several members of the Capitol police came to see what all the commotion was about, but the crowd was large enough, and the situation so unexpected, that the officers didn't know what to do. Amazingly, no one tried to stop a large group of self-proclaimed revolutionaries from parading around the hallways of the statehouse with loaded guns and looking for the state's legislators.

Eventually, Seale found the way to the official viewing area for people to watch the legislative proceedings. Six of the Panthers went inside and stood in the back quietly. Inside the assembly chamber, the Panthers were quiet and respectful, saying nothing and standing still. The crowd of reporters who followed them in with cameras and bright lights, however, were noisy and noticeable, drawing the attention of lawmakers. Carlos Bee, the speaker pro tem, saw the lights and shouted for security to remove the camera crews immediately. He didn't even notice the Panthers standing there with loaded rifles. Nonetheless, the security officers close to the viewing area forced the Panthers to leave.

Officers escorted the Panthers downstairs to the first-floor office of the Capitol police. There the officers checked the guns and were surprised to discover they were loaded. However, because it was legal to have a loaded gun in the Capitol, it didn't seem that the Panthers had done anything unlawful. They hadn't threatened anyone and hadn't gone anywhere they weren't allowed to go. The only trouble came when the Panthers thought the Capitol police weren't going to give them back their guns. Then the Panthers became angry, calling the officers "racist dogs" and assertively insisting on their lawful authority to be there armed. The officers unloaded the guns, returned them to the Panthers, and told the protesters to leave.

When Seale first read his prepared statement prior to entering the statehouse, the reporters were just beginning to notice the entourage. Now, half an hour later, the newsmen realized that this was a headline-grabbing story, so they asked Seale to read his prepared remarks again. He did, this time captured on film that would be shown on television news programs nationwide. After he finished, the Panthers left the building, descended the stairs, piled into their cars, and left. No shots were fired, no arrests were made, no one was harmed—there was only a huge spectacle captured by camera crews.

On their way out of town, the Panthers were forced to stop at a gas station when one of their cars began to overheat. The police had followed them. When Seale got out of his car, he saw an officer walking straight toward him gun drawn. "Now wait a minute," Seale said. "Now first thing you have to do is you have to put that gun away. Put it back in the holster. If you want to make an arrest you can make an arrest, but you better put that gun away." Seale stared down the officer with his best don't-mess-with-an-angry-black-man look. Then the officer heard a familiar sound coming from the other cars. Chick-chuck. Chick-chuck. It was the sound of rounds being jacked into the chambers of shotguns. The officer looked around and quickly realized he was outnumbered and outgunned. He nervously slid his handgun back into his holster.

"What are you, a gun club?" the officer asked Seale. "No, we're the Black Panther Party. We're black people with guns. What about it?" Seale replied with bravado. Within moments, a slew of additional police officers arrived and arrested twenty-five of the Panthers. They were charged with disturbing the peace, among other misdemeanors, and eventually six of the Panthers, including Seale, pled guilty and served short prison sentences.

The Sacramento "Invasion," as the papers called it, was a huge success for the Panthers—and a historic event that came to define the bold, assertive protest mentality of late 1960s radicals. Their visit to the Capitol made headlines across the country and television news broadcast film of the event over and over. The incident and the resulting media coverage "catapulted the party into the living rooms of millions of Americans," according to one expert. "It's All Legal," observed one newspaper headline, in referring to the Panthers' public display of firearms. The reaction of Americans depended largely on their race. Whites were horrified and began to call for the government to take more aggressive action to stop the Panthers. Blacks, emboldened, inundated the Black Panther office in Oakland with calls seeking information on how they could form chapters in their own neighborhoods. Newton said they "could hardly keep track of the requests. In a matter of months, we went from a small Bay Area group to a national organization."[30]

• • •

THE EXTREME methods of the Black Panthers were guaranteed to cause a backlash by those fearful of what seemed to be an impending revolution. The day the Panthers staged their protest in the California Assembly, Speaker Pro Tem Carlos Bee said their actions would speed enactment of Don Mulford's proposed bill. Mulford himself announced that he would now seek to make the law even tougher. He added a provision to the bill prohibiting anyone but police from bringing a loaded firearm into the state Capitol.

The Mulford law would give California an unusually strict set of gun control laws. It was already illegal to have a loaded rifle or shotgun in a motor vehicle and to fire a gun within 150 yards of an occupied building without the building owner's consent. It was already illegal to carry a concealed firearm without a license and for ex-felons, noncitizens, and drug addicts to have a handgun. And it was already illegal for gun dealers to deliver a gun to someone without first waiting five days, during which time authorities conducted a background check on the purchaser.[31]

In most states, however, a person could carry a firearm so long as it was done openly. Most states restricted concealed guns, but it was generally lawful to have a gun that was visible. Earlier laws, like those in western frontier towns barring possession of all guns in public, had lapsed or still applied only in specific cities. Yet even though it was usually lawful to have a visible gun in public, few people walked around town with a loaded gun in their hands. This was a matter more of decorum than of law. In most places, toting around a loaded shotgun on Main Street was a sure way to provoke the enmity of neighbors.

Mulford later denied that his gun control law was aimed at the

Black Panthers. The law, he said, applied to everyone regardless of skin color. San Francisco Democrat Willie Brown scoffed at Mulford's denial. The text of the legislation all but pointed a finger at the Panthers when it said, "The State of California has witnessed, in recent years, the increasing incidence of organized groups and individuals publicly arming themselves for purposes inimical to the peace and safety of the people of California." Brown noted that Mulford had previously opposed similar gun control proposals and came around only when "Negroes showed up in Oakland—his district— with arms."[32]

Mulford was not the only Republican to support the ban on public possession of loaded guns. Another was California's conservative governor, Ronald Reagan, who strongly supported the gun control law. On the day the Panthers visited Sacramento, Reagan emerged from his office in the Capitol Building after the Panthers left and spoke briefly to reporters. "There's no reason why on the street today a citizen should be carrying loaded weapons." Guns, he said, were a "ridiculous way to solve problems that have to be solved among people of good will." In a later press conference, Reagan said that he didn't "know of any sportsman who leaves his home with a gun to go out into the field to hunt or for target shooting who carries that gun loaded." The Mulford Act, he said, "would work no hardship on the honest citizen."[32]

On July 28, 1967, less than three months after the Panthers' visit to Sacramento, Governor Reagan signed the Mulford Act into law. Most laws don't go into effect for months, but Don Mulford saw to it that his bill had an emergency provision that made the law effective the moment Reagan affixed his signature. The Panthers had to be disarmed immediately. At the signing ceremony, the governor joked to reporters, "Everybody get ready to unload their guns!" From that moment on, anyone caught carrying a loaded gun on a public street in California would face five years in prison.[34]

The Mulford Act succeeded in ending the Black Panthers' armed police patrols, but some members continued to carry firearms illegally, leading to arrests and confrontations with police. In October

1967, Huey Newton was taken into custody after a gun battle that led to one police officer's death, the serious wounding of another, and four bullets in Newton's abdomen. Over the next few years, the shootouts between Panthers and police would become commonplace, cementing the image of the Panthers as the latest incarnation of the Depression-era gangsters and desperados who were misusing firearms to undermine order and stability in society.[35]

In late 1967, with Newton in jail and Seale also incarcerated on an unrelated charge, leadership of the Panthers fell to Eldridge Cleaver. Cleaver, who was more radical than Newton and Seale, was the author of *Soul on Ice*, a collection of essays he wrote in prison that detailed his criminal past—including his serial rapes of women, which he justified as "insurrectionary." With increasingly militant rhetoric, Cleaver built up the party, going on a national speaking tour in 1968 that spurred the creation of dozens of additional chapters across the country. Instead of urging self-defense against racist cops, he suggested that blacks go out and hunt down police officers during their coffee breaks. The Panthers' guns should be used on offense—a shift reflected in the party's dropping "for Self-Defense" from its name. Newton later said Cleaver's "forceful personality would be the rock on which the movement foundered."[36]

As the Black Panthers went national, the federal law enforcement agency created in the 1930s to fight interstate crime sought to disarm them. The FBI, still under the leadership of its founding director, J. Edgar Hoover, began what the *New York Times* called a campaign of "domestic spying, psychological warfare, and dirty tricks." Hoover, reflecting the views of many Americans, insisted that "the Black Panther Party, without question, represents the greatest threat to the internal security of the country." A counterintelligence program run by the FBI, known by its acronym COINTELPRO, infiltrated the Panthers, promoted dissention among the members, conducted warrantless searches, and planted false information about them and other groups to create destructive rivalries. The FBI was even tied to the murder of a high-ranking Panther in the Chicago chapter. A U.S. Senate committee report found that "the FBI's tactics were clearly intended to foster violence." Though "charged by law with investigating crimes and preventing criminal conduct," the FBI "itself engaged in lawless tactics." Hoover also subscribed to Malcolm X's motto: by any means necessary.[37]

•   •   •

THE MULFORD ACT signed into law by Governor Reagan was among the strictest gun controls of the late 1960s, but equally important to the rise of the modern gun rights movement was the federal Gun Control Act of 1968 and its companion bill, the Omnibus Crime Control and Safe Streets Act. These gun laws marked Congress's first attempts at serious gun regulation since the 1930s, and, like California's law, they also represented a backlash against armed blacks who were seen to be undermining social order.

Since the late 1950s, gun control advocates had been trying unsuccessfully to push new restrictions on firearms through Congress. Guns were more widespread than ever, driven largely by the interest in firearms among soldiers who returned home from World War II. Many brought home European guns, began collections, or took to hunting, which witnessed a postwar boom. Guns were also cheap, the market saturated by firearms manufactured for wars around the world and imported into the United States. It was, one gun owner recalled, "the golden age of choice in arms" when people enjoyed "a freedom of essentially unrestricted purchase." We've already seen why that statement is hyperbole—the federal and state laws discussed in chapter 7 limited purchases in a number of ways. Still, it accurately reflects the relative ease by which a law-abiding adult willing to jump over small hurdles could buy guns. The serious problem posed by the easy availability of inexpensive firearms was that those who didn't intend to obey the law could also obtain them, helping to fuel a surge in crime.[38]

In 1958, Senator John F. Kennedy of Massachusetts introduced a bill to restrict the importation of surplus military firearms—guns from foreign countries that were increasingly ending up in Americans' hands. The bill, however, was seen more as a protectionist measure to benefit northeastern gun manufacturers, and it failed to obtain the broad, national support necessary in Congress. Five years later, a man going by the name of "A. Hidell" ordered a $19.95 Mannlicher-Carcano bolt-action rifle from an ad he saw in the NRA's *American Rifleman*. Hidell used the Italian military surplus firearm to shoot Kennedy from a window of the Texas Book Depository in Dallas, making his real name, Lee Harvey Oswald, infamous.[39]

Kennedy's assassination led Senator Thomas Dodd of Connecticut, a Democrat who had been studying gun violence for several years, to commit himself to enacting stricter gun control. Five days after Kennedy's death, Dodd proposed legislation to restrict mail-order sales of shotguns and rifles like the one Oswald bought through *American Rifleman*. The federal government needed to step in and stop people from using fake names and skirting state gun laws by purchasing through the mail.[40]

Dodd had what was described as a "chiseled countenance and silver mane" that "lent him the air of a person Hollywood might cast for the role of a Senator." If, however, one were to typecast a senator for Connecticut, one wouldn't make him an advocate of gun control. Connecticut is a small state where gun manufacturers play a large role. Historically, Connecticut was the heart of the American gun industry. Colt made its famous six-shooters in Hartford. New Haven was home to the Winchester Repeating Arms Company, the maker of a line of rifles so popular that they were nicknamed the "Guns That Won the West." O. F. Mossberg & Sons, the world's largest manufacturer of pump-action shotguns was also located in Connecticut. Senators don't usually go against the major industries in their state and live to see reelection.[41]

A fierce anti-Communist, fervent supporter of the Vietnam War, and good friend to J. Edgar Hoover, Dodd was a law-and-order man who thought crime was out of control. Early in his career, he learned the value of gun control. When he was a special agent for the FBI in the 1930s, he worked with the unit charged with bringing John Dillinger to justice. In that role, he saw the damage done by guns in the hands of the wrong people. On a frigid April night in 1934, Dodd and fourteen other agents raided the Little Bohemia Lodge in northern Wisconsin, where Dillinger was hiding out. The ensuing machine-gun shootout left two men dead. Dodd went on to serve as an assistant to Attorney General Homer Cummings, the father of the first modern federal gun laws, and helped prosecute war crimes in Nuremberg under Robert Jackson, who successfully persuaded the Supreme Court to uphold the National Firearms Act in *United States v. Miller*.[42]

Even after the Kennedy assassination, Dodd found that many members of Congress weren't interested in new legislation to keep guns out of the hands of crazed killers like Lee Harvey Oswald. Beginning in 1965, Dodd's close ally, President Lyndon Johnson, annually proposed sweeping gun measures, including mandatory federal registration of all firearms and federal licensing for those who wished to carry guns on the street. Although Johnson enjoyed remarkable success at pushing through legislation—he had more major laws passed and a higher percentage of his proposals enacted than any other president in history—his gun control reforms languished in committee.[43]

In 1967, the momentum for gun control began to shift thanks to the Black Panthers and the wave of race riots that engulfed the nation—what the historian Harvard Sitkoff called the "most intense and destructive wave of racial violence the nation had ever witnessed." Starting in July, there were eight major riots and thirty-three other serious incidents of civil unrest. "North and South, from coast to coast," Sitkoff wrote, "authorities reported unprecedented numbers of blacks throwing Molotov cocktails, looting and burning stores, and firing upon police." Images of Detroit's riot, the worst civil disorder of the twentieth century, were featured on the nightly news and stoked Americans' fears. Forty-one people were killed and two hundred square blocks of the city were destroyed; it took nearly a week for police to restore order. One witness reported that "everywhere you turned and looked, you could see nothing but flames." In one incident, a man threw a Molotov cocktail into a business establishment, and the hot summer winds quickly spread the flames to neighboring buildings. Within an hour, the entire block was on fire, including the home of the man who threw the Molotov cocktail. Ironically, this was the summer hippies in San Francisco would remember as the "summer of love."[44]

Police and National Guardsmen were hindered in their attempts to quell the riots by a steady stream of hostile gunfire. Firefighters who came to douse the flames instead found themselves in a blaze of sniper fire. Rioters with guns controlled the Kercheval area of Detroit for three days. Many of the rioters took their cue from black radicals like H. Rap Brown, who told a rally in Cambridge, Massachusetts, "You'd better get you some guns. The man's moving to kill you. The only thing the honky respects is force. . . . [D]on't be trying to love that honky to death. Shoot him to death." To whites, it seemed that the guerrilla warfare of the Vietcong had found its way onto the streets of America.[45]

A federal report on the riots put at least part of the blame on the easy availability of guns. In the years just before 1967, the number of handguns registered in Michigan had increased 128 percent. Newark had seen a 300 percent increase in permit applications in the preceding two years alone. Because potential rioters could use guns to protect themselves while committing unlawful acts, the recent spike in firearms sales and permit applications was, the report concluded, "directly related to the actuality and prospect of civil disorders." The report came to "the firm conclusion that effective firearms controls are an essential contribution to domestic peace and tranquility."[46]

In Senate hearings, Thomas Dodd emphasized the dramatic increase in the number of guns in America. Between 1958 and 1968, over 30 million firearms were added to the civilian stockpile of weapons. Even though handguns only constituted about 30 percent of the guns in civilian hands, they were linked to 75 percent of the gun-related homicides. Dodd cited FBI statistics that showed a 51 percent increase in the number of murders committed with guns, an 84 percent increase in aggravated assaults with guns, and a 57 percent increase in armed robbery—all within the preceding three years. Imports of handguns had grown from a trickle of 67,000 guns in 1955 to a torrent of over 1 million in 1968.[47]

Dodd was gaining votes, but still fell short. Though he was dedi-

cated to the cause, gun control advocates weren't especially well
served by having Dodd lead their charge. In 1967, Dodd became hob-
bled politically by an ethics scandal involving the improper use of
campaign funds, charges so serious that his became the very first ethics case ever investigated by the Senate Ethics Committee. The committee recommended that Dodd be censured for "conduct which is
contrary to accepted morals, derogates from the public trust expected
of a Senator and tends to bring the Senate into dishonor and disre-
pute." In June 1967, the Senate censured Dodd by a vote of 92–5.[48]

The gun control effort was reinvigorated by events of the next
spring. In April 1968, as Congress was pondering the causes of the
1967 riots, another wave of urban violence broke out after James
Earl Ray, a white racist, used a Remington Gamemaster deer rifle to
shoot and kill Martin Luther King in Memphis, Tennessee. King's
assassination—and the sniper fire once again faced by police trying
to quell the resulting riots—gave gun control advocates an especially salient example of the need for new restrictions on firearms.
Two months and one day after King's killing, another was provided
by the fatal shooting of Robert Kennedy in Los Angeles by a man
wielding a .22-caliber Iver-Johnson Cadet revolver. The political
will to enact gun control shifted literally overnight. The very next
day, Congress passed the Omnibus Crime Control and Safe Street
Act of 1968, the first federal gun control law in thirty years.[49]

The new law was amended and added to a few months later by
the Gun Control Act of 1968. Together, these gun laws had several
components. The first was a ban on gun shipments across state lines
to anyone other than federally licensed dealers and collectors. The
second was a ban on all gun sales to "prohibited persons," which
included felons, the mentally ill, substance abusers, and minors. A
third was the expansion of the federal licensing system first established in the Federal Firearms Act of 1938.

Gun dealers bore the brunt of the new controls. Now anyone
"engaged in the business" of selling guns had to have a federal license.
This language was designed to exclude the person who sold a rifle left
to him in his father's will. Anyone who made a business of selling

guns, however, had to be licensed and had to maintain records of all gun sales, including the name and address of the purchaser and the type of firearm sold. With some exceptions, dealers were restricted to selling guns to in-state residents and required to verify the buyer's residency. None of these burdens on dealers seriously limited gun sales. Rather, they gave law enforcement new tools to oversee gun transactions. If a gun was used in a crime, these new provisions gave the government hope of tracing the firearm to a particular buyer.

The one type of gun that Congress was eager to reduce access to was the so-called Saturday night special. This was the blanket name first given by Detroit police to small, cheap, poor-quality handguns often associated with youth crime, which spiked on the weekends. Because these inexpensive pistols were popular in poor—read, minority— communities, one critic said the new federal gun control, which banned their importation, "was passed not to control guns but to control blacks." Even so, the law wasn't well thought out. Domestic production of cheap handguns wasn't impacted, and imports of easily reassembled handgun parts continued. Like assault weapons twenty-five years later, the type of weapon was so ambiguously defined that only symbol-ism was served. That ambiguity was highlighted when agency officials declared that among the guns subject to the Saturday night special rules was the Walther PPK—a relatively high-quality pistol famous as the firearm of choice of Ian Fleming's fictional spy James Bond.[50]

The gun laws fell far short of the ambitious federal registration and licensing proposals endorsed by President Johnson. Gun rights advocates managed to defeat registration and licensing by arguing that such measures would lead eventually to confiscation of all civil-ian guns. In the House of Representatives, the Michigan Democrat and NRA board member John Dingell warned his congressional col-leagues that the Nazis adopted mandatory registration and used the records to disarm the Jews and political dissidents. This law, too, could be the first step toward a holocaust. While others dismissed the analogy to the Nazis, it didn't help that Thomas Dodd had in fact asked the Library of Congress to provide him with a translation of the German gun laws of the 1930s when he was drafting his bills.

Dodd probably first learned of the Nazi laws when he served under Robert Jackson as a prosecutor in the Nuremberg war trials.[51]

In an era that would become known for the aggressive, bold federal legislation enacted to combat a variety of social ills—from the Civil Rights Act to Medicare—the gun control laws of 1968 were notable for their timidity. According to the political scientist Robert Spitzer, "the Gun Control Act was the most sweeping federal gun regulation enacted up to that time. Yet its scope was modest and, as a consequence, its impact was minimal." President Johnson recognized the reform's limited potential when he signed the act into law. "Today, we begin to disarm the criminal and the careless and the insane," he said. Still, the new law "falls short because we just could not get the Congress" to enact "national registration of all guns and the licensing of those who carry those guns."[52]

●   ●   ●

THE NEW federal gun laws and their state law counterparts like the Mulford Act came just as the modern gun rights movement was beginning to form. These laws gave the movement the catalyst it needed to crystallize, paving the way for the NRA to become the political powerhouse it is today.

The NRA was an early supporter of Senator Dodd's push for new federal gun laws. After the assassination of President Kennedy, Franklin Orth, the executive vice president of the NRA, testified before Congress in favor of banning mail-order sales of rifles. "We do not think that any sane American, who calls himself an American, can object to placing into this bill the instrument which killed the president of the United States." Orth and the NRA weren't in favor of stricter proposals, like the national registration that President Johnson favored, but when the final version of the Gun Control Act was finally adopted in 1968, Orth stood behind the legislation. While certain features of the law "appear unduly restrictive and unjustified in their application to law-abiding citizens, the measure as a whole appears to be one that the sportsmen of America can live with," he

said. An article in *American Rifleman* noted with approval that the
act included numerous provisions supported by the organization.[53]

Some rank-and-file members, however, were vigorously opposed
to the new law and were furious with Orth. This emerging group of
internal critics was motivated less by opposition to the particulars of
the new laws than by opposition to the very idea of gun control. Their
attitude was reflected in the editorial pages of the specialized gun
magazines of the day—*Guns and Ammo, Gun Week, Guns*—where
anti-gun control screeds were fast becoming the norm. In the view of
these nascent gun hard-liners, Orth and the current NRA leadership
were focused too much on the sporting uses of guns and not enough
on personal self-defense and the Second Amendment. In a time of
rising crime rates, easy access to drugs, and the breakdown of the
inner city, the NRA should be fighting to secure Americans the ability to defend themselves against criminals. The NRA, they thought,
"needed to spend less time and energy on paper targets and ducks
and more time blasting away at gun control legislation." The faction
even tried to have Orth fired. They failed, but the controversy over
the gun control laws of the 1960s was, as one writer noted, "just the
opening volley in what was to become an all-out war, one that would
split the gun group wide open over the next decade."[54]

The avid gun enthusiasts merely grew more enraged as the laws
went into effect. The laws were riddled with loopholes. There was the
provision that banned imports of Saturday night specials but allowed
domestic manufacture of these guns and the importation of foreign
parts, which were easily reassembled here. As a result, the law did
little to restrict access to cheap handguns. The Saturday night crook
could just buy an American-made gun. The only people affected by
the law were collectors who favored imported guns. Other critics
wondered why the federal regulations defined a Saturday night special in part by its price. A short-barreled pistol that sold for over fifty
dollars was legal, but one that sold for forty-nine was not. Line drawing is an inevitable part of lawmaking, but the price of a firearm says
nothing about how dangerous or lethal it is. Gun lovers—especially
those in rural areas, where the urban crime problem wasn't felt—

increasingly saw gun control laws as little more than a way to make
life difficult for them without significantly enhancing public safety.[55]

It was a sentiment that was only compounded by the federal agency
charged by the Gun Control Act with enforcing the new laws, the
Alcohol and Tobacco Division of the Treasury Department—soon to
be renamed the Bureau of Alcohol, Tobacco, and Firearms. Like the
Second Amendment, ATF traced its roots back to the American Revolution. Alexander Hamilton first proposed taxing imports of liquor
to pay off the new country's war debts, and Congress vested authority to collect the tax in the Treasury Department. In the 1930s, the
department's jurisdiction extended to firearms as a result of the tax
collection provisions of Homer Cummings's National Firearms Act.
The federal gun laws of 1968 put ATF in charge of overseeing the federal firearms-licensing process covering gun dealers. It was a mission
ATF was not well equipped to handle.[56]

Gun owners accused ATF of emphasizing "technical violations"
among otherwise law-abiding gun lovers instead of cracking down
on real criminals. The new laws were ambiguous about exactly who
was required to have a license. The laws referred to people who were
"engaged in the business" of dealing firearms, but didn't provide any
details about how to define those terms. Was it fifty sales a year? Ten?
Five? At the same time, the laws set the price of the license at ten dollars, so low that many people applied for one, figuring they could sell
or buy guns across state lines when they wanted to. Stories circulated
of ATF agents rescinding a license because the licensee had sold just
three guns recently and thus wasn't really "engaged in the business"
of dealing firearms. Then ATF agents would charge someone else
with unlawfully selling firearms without a license after they discovered he had recently sold three guns.[57]

In contrast to the 1960s, when government was seen as the solution
to America's social ills, the 1970s began a period of increasing hostility to government regulation. When Ronald Reagan famously said that
"government is not the solution to our problem; government is the
problem," he was giving voice to a sentiment that was already strong
in the gun rights community. ATF came to embody for gun owners

the idea that government was divorced from the concerns of the average person and too eager to impose its will upon the individual. In an incident highly publicized in gun circles, ATF agents in 1971 raided the home of the longtime NRA member Kenyon Ballew and shot him. ATF suspected he was making illegal hand grenades and sent agents to his apartment to search for the explosives. According to articles in *American Rifleman*, the agents broke down the door without warning, shot Ballew for no reason, and found nothing in the apartment to warrant their suspicion. Ballew, the articles claimed, was merely taking a bath with his wife when agents barged in. Years later, a federal court determined that this version of the facts was wrong in almost every respect—the agents did knock and announce their presence; Ballew's door had been heavily barricaded; when officers entered the apartment, Ballew pointed a gun at them; the woman was not his wife; and he did have illegal, unregistered grenades in the apartment. Given the circumstances, the court ruled that the officers' actions were reasonable. The damage to ATF's reputation, however, had already been done. After the Ballew incident, the NRA board member and newspaper writer William Loeb took to calling ATF the "Treasury Gestapo" in his articles.[58]

By the mid-1970s, NRA leaders were openly calling for the repeal of the Gun Control Act. In a far cry from Franklin Orth's statement that the act was "one that the sportsmen of America can live with," Woodson D. Scott, the new president, issued a statement to members in *American Rifleman* calling for complete repeal. The law, he said, was "a legislative monstrosity saddled upon the people in a period of emotionalism." Congressman John Dingell fatefully advised the NRA to set up a full-time professional lobbying arm to fight off regulation and roll back the laws of the 1960s. That advice would shape gun politics for decades to come.[59]

The new NRA-led gun rights movement was not only fueled by the laws passed to disarm the Black Panthers and other black radicals; it also echoed many of the principles espoused by the Panthers. Like the Panthers, modern gun enthusiasts didn't view guns as valuable for sporting purposes; guns were about personal self-defense. Though justified as a way to fight crime, gun control laws were, in reality, just another way for elites to harass and oppress. Guns were not only for protecting your home; people should be allowed to carry them on the street for protection. Law enforcement was demonized as the enemy, prone to abusive behavior and disregard for the rights of the people. The Panthers went to Sacramento to make their voices heard; the NRA's lobbyists went to Washington.

In conservative circles, the 1970s and 1980s were a time to roll back the excesses of the 1960s. While other conservatives were trying to reverse environmental laws and consumer protection laws, the NRA was focused on the recent wave of gun control legislation, which was another example of big government gone awry. The gun laws that were a response to the extremists of the day—from the Black Panthers to the urban race rioters in Detroit, from Lee Harvey Oswald to James Earl Ray—were themselves perceived among the leaders of the gun rights movement as extreme and sparked a backlash of their own.

One element of that backlash was constitutional reform in rural states. There, where urban crime was not a pressing problem, gun ownership was widespread—as was a growing hostility to the federal government. Prompted by the NRA, numerous states that lacked explicit guarantees for the right to bear arms in their own constitutions began to add them: Nevada and New Hampshire in 1982, North Dakota and Utah in 1984, West Virginia in 1986, Nebraska in 1988, Alaska in 1994, Delaware in 1997, and Wisconsin in 1998. These enactments illustrated the growing split between urban and rural on guns. Although none of these states had unusually restrictive gun laws in the years before the amendments, the constitutional reforms made a symbolic statement about the strong pro-gun, pro–states' rights sentiments of rural America. To many in these communities, federal gun laws represented a distant national government that seemed concerned only with the pathologies of big cities.

The gun rights movement that arose in the wake of the 1960s gun control would see to it that the Gun Control Act was the last national gun law for years. The next significant gun bill passed by Congress was the Firearms Owners Protection Act in 1986. That law, as its name suggests, largely expanded the rights of gun owners and watered down the provisions of the Gun Control Act.

•   •   •

SEVERAL OF the justices who looked down upon Alan Gura from the raised bench had been appointed by Republican presidents elected on a platform of cutting back on the excesses of the 1960s. Few had endorsed that conservative backlash more heartily than Justice Antonin Scalia. Gura's case had special interest to him. He agreed that the Second Amendment protected the right of individuals to own guns, and he was willing to do whatever necessary to ensure that his view won out in the D.C. gun case.

Some justices like oral argument because it affords them the opportunity to ask the lawyers hard questions that aren't answered in the briefs. It is their chance to fill in the gaps in their own knowledge so that they can make the right decision. Scalia, however, often used oral argument not to elicit information from the lawyers but to express his own views and try to persuade the other justices. He didn't ask questions out of curiosity so much as make statements reflecting his certainty. Indeed, this is exactly what he did in the D.C. gun case. He might not be able to rely on Gura, a Supreme Court neophyte. If Scalia had to tell Gura what to say or answer the questions other justices asked of the libertarian lawyer, that's what he would do. So when he stopped Gura barely a minute into Gura's presentation to tell him to slow down, he wasn't trying to embarrass the young lawyer. Scalia was genuinely trying to help him. A nervous advocate rushing through his remarks was not going to convince the other justices.[60]

Oral argument in the Supreme Court can provide a window into the personalities of the justices. Scalia, for example, is humorous on the bench, cracking jokes and making wry observations. A study of transcripts of oral argument in the Supreme Court found that he was the justice who made spectators laugh out loud the most.[61]

Justice Stephen Breyer was a professor at Harvard Law School before

he joined the bench, and he remains ever the academic, given to posing
long, detailed questions typical of a first-year law school class. He likes
to use complicated hypothetical situations to tease out the implications
of an argument and test the advocate's reasoning. If x happens, then
what? What if y occurs? Or z? What should the rule be if x, y, and z
are present? What about x and z, but not y? Studies showed that Breyer
didn't ask as many questions as some of his colleagues, yet his questions took up the most time to ask. A Breyer question can stretch on for
more than a minute before coming to the question mark.[62]

Breyer put one of his legendary law professor questions to Alan
Gura. Breyer wanted to know why D.C.'s ban on handguns wasn't a
reasonable restriction under the Second Amendment, even assuming
an individual right to bear arms. He asked Gura,

> Assume two things with me, which you probably don't agree with,
> and I may not agree with them either. But I just want you to assume
> them for the purpose of the question. All right. Assume that there
> is an individual right, but the purpose of that right is to maintain a
> citizen army; call it a militia; that's the basic purpose. So it informs
> what's reasonable and what isn't reasonable. . . . As I read these 80
> briefs—and they were very good, I mean really good and infor-
> mative on both sides—and I'm trying to boil down the statistics
> where there is disagreement, and roughly what I get—and don't
> quarrel with this too much, it's very rough—that 80,000 to 100,000
> people every year in the United States are either killed or wounded
> in gun-related homicides or crimes or accidents or suicides, but
> suicide is more questionable. That's why I say 80,000 to 100,000. In
> the District, I guess the number is somewhere around 200 to 300
> dead; and maybe, if it's similar, 1,500 to 2,000 people wounded.
> All right. Now in light of that, why isn't a ban on handguns, while
> allowing the use of rifles and muskets, a reasonable or a propor-
> tionate response on behalf of the District of Columbia?

Gura was prepared for this sort of question from Breyer. He
answered simply. A handgun ban hurt military preparedness, he said,

citing some briefs filed by military officers. It's good for people to know how to fire a gun. Perhaps, Breyer responded, but to maintain military preparedness, people need "to understand weapons, to know how to use them, to practice with them. And they can do that, you see, with their rifles. They can go to gun ranges, I guess, in neighboring states. But does that make it unreasonable for a city with a very high crime rate, assuming that the objective is what the military people say, to keep us ready for the draft if necessary, is it unreasonable for a city with that high crime rate to say 'No handguns here'?" Before Gura could answer, however, Justice Scalia interjected, "You want to say, 'Yes.' That's your answer."

Justice John Paul Stevens asked Gura whether, in light of his concessions about machine guns and safe-storage laws, "we can simply read" the Second Amendment to say "'shall not be *unreasonably* infringed'"? When Gura began to say yes, Scalia once again stepped in. "You wouldn't put it that way. You would just say it is not being infringed" when certain kinds of limitations—perhaps machine gun bans—are enacted. Gura took the hint: "That's another way to look at it, Your Honor. Certainly."

At another point in the argument, Gura and Justice Ruth Bader Ginsburg were discussing how the first clause of the Second Amendment—referring to the "well regulated Militia"—informed the second clause—referring to "the right of the people to keep and bear Arms." Gura agreed with Ginsburg that the first clause was, in his words, "a limitation" on the second clause; only weapons useful for the militia were protected. Scalia corrected him. "The principal purpose here is the militia, but the second clause goes beyond the militia and says the right of the people to keep and bear arms," he insisted. "So why not acknowledge that" the right "is broader than the first clause?" Gura backtracked and signaled his agreement with Scalia.

Even without Scalia's help, Gura was holding his own. Justice David Souter, a liberal who had been appointed to the Court by President Bush because he was thought to be more conservative than the other person in the final running for the job, the eventual Whitewater prosecutor Ken Starr, asked Gura whether legislatures should be able to look at modern-day statistics, such as crime and murder rates, in devising gun safety laws. Gura replied that "the object of the Bill of Rights is to remove certain judgment from the legislature." Lawmakers can't just "say, 'Well, we've decided as a matter of policy that the right to keep and bear arms is no longer a good idea and, therefore, we are going to have restrictions that violate that stricture in the Bill of Rights.'" No statistics can support infringing the rights guaranteed by the Second Amendment. The Constitution has a procedure for changing it: Article V of the text, which requires an amendment passed by the states or a constitutional convention. "At some point," Gura continued, "you have to go to Article V if you think that the Constitution is impractical."

None of the justices seemed particularly interested in the only potentially controlling precedent involved in the case, *United States v. Miller.* Although that case had long been read to endorse the militia theory of the Second Amendment, most of the justices seemed to agree with Justice Kennedy, who called the decision "deficient." At least no one seemed to think it dictated a result in Gura's case.

When Chief Justice John Roberts announced that Gura's time was up, the libertarian lawyer returned to his seat knowing that he had won on the big question of whether or not the Second Amendment guaranteed an individual right to have guns for personal self-defense. He had also done all that he could to allay the justices' fears about the future of gun control.

Walter Dellinger, counsel for the District of Columbia, had come to the same realization. As is standard for appellate courts, Dellinger was allowed a few minutes for "rebuttal." This was his chance to respond to Gura's arguments and address any open issues. Dellinger skipped right over the individual rights/militia debate and went straight to discussing the extent of the government's power to enact gun control assuming an individual right to bear arms. Once again, he emphasized that reasonable regulations of guns should be permit-

ted. D.C.'s law, he argued, was reasonable in light of the city's murder rate. Maybe he could sway Justice Kennedy's vote on this issue
and still pull out a victory for the District—and secure defeat for the
modern gun rights movement that, in so many ways, was influenced
by the Black Panthers. The chief justice soon cut him off. "Thank
you, Mr. Dellinger. The case is submitted."

PART III

CHAPTER 9

DECISION

CASES IN THE SUPREME COURT ARE ARGUED IN PUBLIC
but decided in private, in an oak-paneled room on the
other side of the red velvet curtains. Once a week, the justices gather there, surrounded by hundreds of books filled
with judicial decisions and watched over by the legendary
Chief Justice John Marshall, an 1830 portrait of whom
hangs above the fireplace. Here, in what they call the conference, the justices discuss their views of the case and cast
tentative votes in total seclusion. No one else is allowed in
the room, not even the justices' law clerks, secretaries, or
stenographers. Servants used to be permitted inside, but
that ended in 1910, when two waiters were accused of leak-
ing the outcome of a business case and the news triggered
a panic on Wall Street. Today, a security officer is stationed
in the hallway outside the door, where pages wait to receive
requests from the justices for a case file, a legal treatise, or
a sandwich.[1]

With no one else allowed inside, the job of delivering
the justices' requests to the pages or answering the door if

the security officer knocks falls to the justice with the least seniority—
in the D.C. gun case, Samuel Alito. Tom Clark, who was the junior
justice for several years in the 1950s, jokingly called himself "the
highest paid doorkeeper in the world." Clark was only half right.
The junior justice is also the highest-paid scorekeeper in the world,
because he is responsible for keeping count of the justices' votes as
well. In 1981, when Sandra Day O'Connor was appointed the first
female justice, the other members of the Court considered exempting
her from these responsibilities out of fear that forcing a woman to do
such menial tasks would appear sexist. In the Supreme Court, however, traditions endure, and O'Connor was required to carry out the
duties of the junior justice like the men who had come before her.[2]

At the conference to discuss the D.C. gun case, the justices began
with ritualistic handshakes, each justice greeting all the others—
a practice dating back to the late 1800s, when Chief Justice Melville
Fuller instituted it to emphasize camaraderie in the potentially contentious decision-making process. After shaking hands, the justices,
wearing business attire but no robes, took their places around a long
mahogany table, their seats determined by seniority. At the head of
the table sat Chief Justice John Roberts. Justice John Paul Stevens, the
most senior associate justice, faced him from the other end of the table.
Roberts spoke first, summarizing the issues of the case and indicating
how he was likely to vote. Once Roberts finished, the justices shared
their views of the case, in descending order of seniority. The justices
don't interrupt one another, and there is usually little give-and-take,
just a seriatim presentation of perspectives, at least until everyone
has had the opportunity to speak. In most cases, the senior justices
do most of the talking; by the time the junior justices are allowed to
address the matter, the important points have all been made.[3]

In the early days of the Court, the justices' deliberations were far
less sober, in all senses of the word. The justices, who lived in Washington only part-time, roomed together in a common boardinghouse
when the Court was in session and used to debate the cases over dinner and Madeira. Justice Joseph Story—a colleague of John Marshall's who once called the Second Amendment "the palladium of the

liberties of the republic"—recounted how the justices would "deny [them]selves wine except in wet weather." Occasionally Marshall would ask Story to go to the window to see whether rain was coming. "And if I tell him that the sun is shining brightly, Judge Marshall will sometimes reply, 'Our jurisdiction extends over so large a territory that the doctrine of chances makes it certain that it must be raining somewhere,'" and the Portuguese wine would be poured.[4]

Although the justices do not disclose how they voted in the conference, the journalists who covered the Court were certain that a majority was going to rule in Alan Gura's favor. All five of the conservative justices, including Anthony Kennedy, the swing vote, had voiced strong support for the individual-rights view, save for the silent-as-always Clarence Thomas. In their stories, the reporters speculated that Gura's strategy of conceding the legitimacy of some forms of gun control, like licensing and bans on machine guns, was wise and greatly increased his chances of winning. In light of these reports, the libertarian lawyers were ecstatic. Walter Dellinger and the lawyers for the District of Columbia, by contrast, were gloomy and pessimistic. "I didn't see a fifth vote to uphold the law," recalled Dellinger.[5]

Experienced Supreme Court advocates like Dellinger also know, however, that oral argument in the Supreme Court can be misleading. The justice who seems most skeptical of a lawyer's argument can end up writing a strong opinion in that lawyer's favor. Or a justice who treats the lawyer's argument gingerly could have already made up his mind to rule against him. In one of the landmark school desegregation cases, for instance, several justices aggressively challenged the lawyers for the NAACP while the argument of John W. Davis, representing a school board, was interrupted only twice, both times by relatively friendly questions. The Court eventually ruled 9–0 in favor of the NAACP.

Decisions of the Court are not announced until several months after the justices' conference. During that time, the justices write up drafts of their opinions and circulate them to the others. The votes tallied at the conference are not final, and, on occasion, justices change their votes—as Anthony Kennedy did in *Planned Par-*

enthood v. Casey, the abortion case discussed earlier in which the Court backed away from overturning *Roe v. Wade* at the last minute. More commonly, however, a justice in the majority will suggest small changes in the language or tone of a draft opinion. If the matter is serious enough, the justice may threaten to withhold his vote unless the opinion is revised.

All that happens in private, however, and until the final opinion is released, the public receives no information about how the justices voted on the case. Court watchers eager to learn the outcome rely on any clues they can find, no matter how indirect or ambiguous. In the D.C. gun case, some legal bloggers thought they spotted one such clue when the Court released a set of opinions in early June 2008—a hint that related to who was writing the majority's opinion. As much as possible, the workload of the Court is divided evenly. Usually, no justice will receive additional writing assignments until every other justice has been assigned one for a given "sitting" (a group of cases heard around the same time). Alan Gura's case was heard during the Court's March sitting. When the Court issued that set of opinions in early June, bloggers realized that all of the decisions from that sitting had been released except the gun case. Moreover, every justice had written an opinion from the March sitting except one—and that was exactly the justice Alan Gura had hoped would author the decision in his case: Antonin Scalia.[6]

•   •   •

IN NOVEMBER 1997, a large crowd dressed in black tie gathered inside a ballroom at the grand Waldorf-Astoria Hotel on Park Avenue in New York City. Built by the Astor family, the luxurious hotel was once a progressive force in New York; it was one of the first upscale hotels to allow women to stay the night unescorted by a man. On this evening, however, conservatives filled the ballroom, guests of the Manhattan Institute, a right-leaning public policy think tank. Much of the chatter among the guests focused on the featured speaker. Although most Supreme Court justices are dull speakers who diligently avoid saying anything newsworthy, such a description could never be applied to Antonin Scalia. He was known for his biting, sarcastic sense of humor, which he frequently employed to deride those who disagreed with his often controversial views.[7]

A speech by Scalia is like "a rock concert," wrote Margaret Talbot in a *New Yorker* profile. People line up to hear what he will say and, even more, how he will say it. With his blunt and colorful language, Talbot noted, "Scalia is most likely to offer the jurisprudential equivalent of smashing a guitar on stage." He is a natural entertainer, whether guest-starring with the Washington National Opera or singing Christmas songs for hours with carolers who happen upon his home. On a camping trip once, Scalia put on a wig and a dress and sneaked up on the other campers pretending to be "the wild woman of the marsh." His playfulness extends even to the otherwise serious world of the law, as evidenced by his frequent laughter-inducing comments during Supreme Court arguments. "Life is dull enough," Scalia once said. "There's no reason why legal argument cannot be civilized with a little bit of wit and humor now and then."[8]

Scalia mixes his humor with what has been called a "street-fighter personality." An only child of Italian immigrants, "Nino," as he is known to his friends, grew up in a working-class neighborhood in Queens, New York. Ever since he was appointed to the Supreme Court in 1986 by President Reagan, he has been a hero to political conservatives. Railing against judicial activism, Scalia angrily denounced many of the landmark constitutional law decisions of the past half century, from *Roe v. Wade* to *New York Times v. Sullivan*, the Warren Court decision that gave journalists wide leeway to write about public figures without fear of libel suits. Every Republican presidential nominee since has invoked Scalia as the type of justice he would appoint to the Supreme Court.[9]

Introducing Scalia to the crowd at the Waldorf-Astoria, Peter Huber, a senior fellow at the Manhattan Institute, described him as "seductive, fierce, funny, charming, always brilliant." "Justice Scalia writes many dissents, sometimes acerbic ones. And when he does, he writes with the strength and passion of the great dissenters of the Court's history in the noble tradition of John Marshall Harlan and Oliver Wendell Holmes." Scalia's "intellect and convictions are as large, robust, resolute, rich, challenging, and generous as the city that raised him."[10]

Justice Scalia rose and took the podium to vigorous applause. "What I want to talk to you tonight about is what I will bend anybody's ear about," Scalia announced. "And that is what in the world we think we're doing when we interpret the Constitution of the United States. It's amazing that that should be a question after we've been doing this for over two hundred years. But it *is* a question, not only among the justices of the Supreme Court. Not only among lawyers. But also among the American people."

Filled with vague generalities like "due process" and "equal protection," the Constitution leaves to the Supreme Court the task of discerning what such phrases mean and how they apply in concrete cases. In the 1950s and 1960s, the Supreme Court read the ambiguities of the Constitution to end racial segregation, expand the right of privacy, and create new protections for criminal defendants. Although many of the new legal rules were not clearly provided for in the text of the Constitution, the Warren Court justices read the text expansively so that it reflected the values of an evolving society. Justice William Brennan, who died in 1997, was the strongest proponent of the Court's approach, known as the "living Constitution." "The genius of the Constitution rests not in any static meaning it might have had in a world that is dead and gone," Brennan said, "but in the adaptability of its great principles to cope with current problems and current needs."[11]

"The argument is something like this," Scalia told the Manhattan Institute crowd. "The Constitution, after all, is two hundred years old. *That's very old*," he said, stretching out the words in ridicule. "It is an organic document. It needs room to grow and develop with the society that it governs. And if it could not grow and develop it would become brittle and snap," he mocked. The Constitution is not really at risk of dying because of old age, Scalia insisted. It is at risk of dying because living constitutionalists treat it like "an empty bottle which we feel free to fill up with whatever liquid" today's society desires.

Justice Scalia, of course, championed a very different approach to constitutional interpretation, originalism. "What was that language understood to mean when it was adopted?" Scalia said courts should ask. The Constitution does not evolve. It bears a static meaning that doesn't change. To Scalia, originalism was the only legitimate way to interpret the Constitution. "You either take the original meaning as it was understood then or there is no criterion by which the judge may judge. Except his own prejudices."

Under originalism, decisions like *Roe v. Wade* would have to be overturned. The founders didn't aim to protect abortion rights. In fact, for much of American history, abortion was outlawed or restricted in many ways. Scalia liked to say that for over a hundred years, few people ever thought that the Constitution outlawed abortion. Abortion gained protection because in the 1970s the justices of the Supreme Court thought the freedom to choose whether to have children was a right that women ought to have. An honest originalist, however, will reach results contrary to his political preferences, according to Scalia. As an example, he cited his own vote to protect burning of the American flag as a form of constitutionally protected speech. "I don't like scruffy, bearded, sandal-wearing people who go around burning the United States flag," he admitted. Because Scalia believed that the founding fathers intended the freedom of speech to cover political protests, however, he had to cast his vote with the scruffy, bearded, sandal-wearing flag burners.[12]

Scalia joked that his approach to constitutional interpretation was out of step with mainstream legal thinkers. "I am now something of a dodo bird among jurists and legal scholars," he told the black-tie audience at the Waldorf. "You can fire a cannon in the faculty lounge of any major law school in the country and not strike an originalist." In other speeches, he said that people often asked him, "'Justice Scalia, when did you first become an originalist?' as though it's some weird affliction. You know, 'When did you start eating human flesh?'"[13]

It was true that for many years legal scholars rejected originalism. They believed it too difficult to determine what the founding fathers thought about many provisions of the Constitution and how those

provisions ought to answer today's controversies. Others argued
that originalism was defective because it couldn't explain the most
important Supreme Court decisions in American history, like *Brown
v. Board of Education*. The decision requiring desegregation of public schools was based on the Fourteenth Amendment's "equal protection" clause, but when that clause was added to the Constitution
in 1868 segregated public schools were commonplace. For almost a
hundred years, few people thought the Constitution outlawed racially
segregated schools. Still others rejected what they saw as the ideological motivations behind originalism's rise in tandem with the conservative movement of the 1970s and 1980s. Originalism, they suspected,
was promoted not because it was a better way to interpret the Constitution but because it could lead to a rollback of many of the decisions
of the modern-day Supreme Court, like *Roe*.

Originalism today is not as far outside the mainstream as Justice
Scalia likes to say. In part because of his influence, originalism has
become a more widely accepted method of constitutional interpretation, and even liberal scholars often invoke the original meaning of
the Constitution to explain the text's ambiguous terms. Polls show
that a solid majority of Americans believe that courts should follow
the original intention of the framers, regardless of the consequences.[14]

Scalia's influence, however, has been greater outside the Court
than within. When he was appointed to the Court, many conservatives expected that because of his forceful personality and intel-
ligence he would exert a strong pull on the other justices. He was
just the right person to lead a counterrevolution against the liberal
Warren Court. Yet, as the legal analyst Jeffrey Toobin argues, Scalia's
legacy on legal doctrine so far has been "modest." "In two decades
on a generally conservative Court, his number of important majority opinions was almost shockingly small," Toobin observes. The
outspokenness that makes him entertaining at the Waldorf-Astoria
isolates him in the Supreme Court. He laces his opinions with caus-
tic and disrespectful references to the arguments of the other justices: "beyond the absurd" or "sheer applesauce," he'll write in one
case; "cannot be taken seriously" or "nothing short of preposterous,"

in another. According to his biographer Joan Biskupic, "Scalia was notorious for pushing away other justices at critical points in the decision-making process. In a close case, when he was barely holding on to a majority, he could not resist brash comments that might alienate a key vote." For years, Chief Justice William Rehnquist assigned contentious cases to other justices so that Scalia didn't torpedo the majority.[15]

To the astonishment of some people outside of the Court, one of Scalia's closest friends is Ruth Bader Ginsburg, arguably the Court's most liberal member. The two travel together and join with their respective spouses each year to celebrate New Year's Eve. "I love him," she once said. "But sometimes I'd like to strangle him." She recognized, "It would be better if he dropped things like: 'This opinion is not to be taken seriously.' He might have been more influential around here if he did that."[16]

Scalia's sway was also undermined by his unwillingness to compromise. William Brennan, the liberal proponent of the living Constitution philosophy, used to ask his newly hired law clerks what the most important rule of constitutional law was. They would scratch their heads and fumble for answers—freedom of speech? equal protection of the laws? due process?—until Brennan would hold up one hand with his fingers outstretched. "Five," he would say; you need five votes to make a majority on the nine-member Court. With five votes, a justice could do anything. To get those votes, Brennan was willing to bargain, haggle, or deal. "Brennan would famously settle for half a loaf rather than get none," writes Biskupic. "Scalia had no interest in such compromises to reach the five needed for the majority. He believed it wrong, maybe even beneath him, to yield on the things that mattered—and most everything mattered."[17]

"The wins," Scalia once bemoaned. "Damn few."

Although well aware of Scalia's personality and history, Alan Gura was heartened by the prospect of Scalia's writing the opinion in the D.C. gun case. For Scalia to be assigned the opinion, he had to be in the majority. Gura had little doubt how Scalia was going to vote in this case. Not only had Scalia voiced his unambiguous support for the individual-rights reading of the Second Amendment during oral argument; he had also shepherded Gura through the hearing. If Chief Justice Roberts assigned the opinion to the sharp-tongued Scalia, it must also mean that Roberts thought the votes in Gura's favor were firm. Like Rehnquist, he wouldn't risk losing his majority in such a significant case.

Scalia, who was an avid hunter, was also known to be fond of guns. As a teenager growing up in New York, he was on the shooting team at Xavier High School, a Jesuit military academy in Manhattan, and he used to ride the subway to school from his home in Queens with a .22 carbine in hand. His Supreme Court chambers had so many stuffed animals shot by the justice, including the gigantic head of an elk with a six-by-six rack, that the office was described as a "veritable museum of taxidermy." In a speech to the National Wild Turkey Association, Scalia extolled the virtues of guns and hunting. "The hunting culture, of course, begins with a culture that does not have a hostile attitude toward firearms." Hunters, he said, need to work to change popular misunderstandings of guns. "The attitude of people associating guns with nothing but crime, that is what has to be changed," he said. "I grew up at a time when people were not afraid of people with firearms . . . I used to travel the subway from Queens to Manhattan with a rifle. Could you imagine doing that today in New York City?"[18]

Equally important was Scalia's jurisprudential philosophy. Gura had made a strongly originalist argument in the D.C. gun case. He said the Court should look to what the founding fathers thought was meant by the Second Amendment. Because they thought the amendment prevented the government from disarming the members of the state militias—that is, ordinary civilians with their own weapons—D.C.'s effective ban on all firearms had to be unconstitutional. Gura hadn't argued that the justices should consider how the Second Amendment had evolved like some living organism.

Scalia ended his speech at the Waldorf-Astoria with an invitation. "Come along with me and admire the *Dead* Constitution." The audience laughed. "It does not do all those wonderful things that maybe you think a Constitution should do. But it happens to be the way that a democracy ought to govern itself."

•   •   •

THE SUPREME COURT's term lasts from the first Monday in October to the last week of June the following year. The final days of June usually see a flurry of noteworthy decisions. For Court watchers, this adds a certain climactic drama to the term.

In June 2008, the Supreme Court wasn't foremost on people's minds, especially in Washington, D.C. Barack Obama was on the verge of a historic White House run after winning the Montana Democratic primary and forcing his main rival, Hillary Clinton, out of the presidential race. Then the gravity of the deepening economic downturn became increasingly evident when Wachovia, the nation's fourth-largest bank, fired its chief executive after massive write-downs tied to subprime home loans—joining the ranks of Citigroup, Merrill Lynch, and other financial powerhouses in crisis. General Motors announced four major plant closings, triggering fears of growing unemployment. In Afghanistan, the Taliban stepped up attacks against American troops, and a suicide bomber affiliated with al-Qaeda struck at the Danish embassy across the border in Pakistan. Anyone focused on the judiciary was looking west, where the California Supreme Court had just weeks before declared that same-sex marriage was a right guaranteed under the state constitution.

Alan Gura, Clark Neily, and Bob Levy, the three libertarian lawyers behind the challenge to D.C.'s gun laws, knew, however, that the U.S. Supreme Court's decision in their case could be announced any day. Having overcome so many obstacles over five years of litigation, especially those that gun rights proponents placed in their way, the three men wanted to be in the courtroom when the decision was handed down. Unfortunately, they didn't know when that would be. The Court never discloses when a decision will be released. When an opinion is ready to be issued, the justices come into the courtroom and, without much warning, announce their ruling.

The Court does reveal in advance the specific dates set aside for the issuance of opinions generally. The lawyers don't know which cases will be decided on a given day set aside for opinions, but they are told that some opinions will be released. When they were down to the last three opinion days of the term, Gura and the others decided to go the Supreme Court every morning until their decision, *District of Columbia v. Heller,* was announced. "You don't really know what day it's going to be on," said Gura. "All you can do is show up to court and hope."[19]

On the morning of June 23, after an unusual summer storm pelted the Washington area with hailstones and drenching rain, the libertarian lawyers arrived at the Supreme Court Building to wait. Once inside, they ran into William Suter, the official clerk of the Court. Not to be confused with the justices' law clerks, who research and draft opinions, the clerk of the Supreme Court is an employee responsible for maintaining the Court's docket and records. Certainly no one would ever have mistaken Suter for one of the justices' clerks. A tall, distinguished looking man in his seventies, Suter had the demeanor one might expect from a retired major general of the army, which he was. When Gura, Neily, and Levy saw him, Suter was wearing the clerk's traditional, long-tailed morning coat, similar to the one the solicitor general wears. Under his arm, he had a stack of papers that constituted the opinions that were going to be released that morning.[20]

Suter recognized the three right away. "You're the *Heller* lawyers," he acknowledged. Gura, Levy, and Neily engaged in small talk with Suter but couldn't keep their eyes off what was beneath his arm. They knew exactly what those papers were, yet it would have been a breach of etiquette for them to ask whether their opinion was among them. "Well, good luck," Suter wished them as he turned to walk away. "I hope your decision comes down today." Suter, of course, knew whether their case was going to be announced that day—or, more to the point, he knew it wasn't going to be announced that day.

The next morning, Gura, Neily, and Levy went back to the Supreme Court. Again, they ran into William Suter with that day's opinions under his arm. "Good luck. I hope your case comes down today," he said again. And once again, it did not.

The Court was not in session the next day, but the day after that, June 26, the libertarian lawyers were back in the courtroom. It was the very last day of the term. Although the justices could push off the decision until October, when the next term began, that would be unusual. Gura, Neily, and Levy took their seats on the benches in the courtroom, crossed their fingers, and waited. They were joined by Dick Heller, the security guard who was now their only remaining plaintiff.

The justices filed in and took their own seats. The first decision announced was a campaign finance case. Although the Supreme Court was traditionally somewhat deferential to legislators' efforts to cabin the role of money in politics, the more conservative Roberts Court was not. The campaign finance law, the Court declared, violated the First Amendment. Alan Gura recalled the scene: "Then Justice Scalia had an opinion in some extraordinarily boring case. I'm sorry. I am sure it was exciting to the people who were involved in it, but most people weren't really interested in it. And Scalia starts reading this really convoluted fact pattern that had something to do with some sort of energy regulation and then he looked up and looks down the middle of the courtroom and says, 'Are you still with me?'" The case was not boring to Walter Dellinger, D.C.'s lawyer; it was a major energy regulation case he had argued in the February sitting, just weeks before arguing the gun case, and the justices ruled in Dellinger's favor.[21]

Once Scalia was finished reading his opinion, Chief Justice John Roberts announced, "Justice Scalia will have our decision in 07-290." That was the docket number of the D.C. gun case. When Roberts said that Scalia was the author of the opinion, "that was when we knew," said Gura. What happened next was "just sort of a blur," Clark Neily recalled. "I don't remember anything about it." All he missed was the Supreme Court declaring for the first time in American history that a gun control law violated the Second Amendment to the Constitution.[22]

Like so many decisions of the ideologically divided Court, the

D.C. gun case was 5–4. The five justices in the majority were Antonin Scalia, John Roberts, Clarence Thomas, Sam Alito, and Anthony Kennedy. The Second Amendment, they held, protected the right of individuals to own guns for self-defense. Although one of the goals of the founding fathers was to secure state militias, the right to keep and bear arms was not limited to militia service. We the People were the militia, and so We the People had a right to keep our own guns and use them if necessary to protect ourselves from criminals. The four most liberal members of the Court—John Paul Stevens, Stephen Breyer, David Souter, and Ruth Bader Ginsburg—dissented.[23]

In his dissenting opinion, Breyer argued that even if the Second Amendment did guarantee an individual right to bear arms, the Court should uphold D.C.'s law. In considering the constitutionality of a gun control law, he wrote, courts should balance the individual's right against the government's interest in public safety. Scalia scoffed at Breyer's proposed balancing. "The very enumeration of the right takes out of the hands of government—even the Third Branch of Government—the power to decide on a case-by-case basis whether the right is *really worth* insisting upon," the majority opinion replied. "Constitutional rights are enshrined with the scope they were understood to have when the people adopted them whether or not future legislatures or (yes) even future judges think that scope too broad." In other words, public safety or any other governmental objective can't justify limits on a constitutionally guaranteed right. The very purpose of guaranteeing something in the Constitution, Scalia suggested, was to ensure that it would not be balanced against the contingencies of the moment.

With this, Scalia brushed aside all of the arguments offered by Alan Gura, Walter Dellinger, and Paul Clement about the standard of review that should be applied to judge the constitutionality of gun laws. The Court didn't embrace the hard-to-satisfy strict-scrutiny standard Gura proposed. Nor did the Court embrace the more lenient tests Dellinger and Clement endorsed. Scalia's opinion for the majority declined to commit to any set, determinate standard for courts to apply to future cases challenging gun control.

Scalia's opinion did, however, indicate that the justices deemed many forms of gun control to be constitutional. "Like most rights, the right secured by the Second Amendment is not unlimited," Scalia wrote. The opinion even offered a laundry list of Second Amendment exceptions. Nothing in the opinion should "be taken to cast doubt on longstanding prohibitions on the possession of firearms by felons and the mentally ill, or laws forbidding the carrying of firearms in sensitive places such as schools and government buildings, or laws imposing conditions and qualifications on the commercial sale of arms." Scalia also suggested that bans on "dangerous and unusual weapons," such as machine guns, were constitutionally permissible. While there was a right to bear arms for individual self-defense, the right was not "a right to keep and carry any weapon whatsoever in any way whatsoever and for whatever purpose." Indeed, in another important limitation, Scalia implied that the right recognized by the Court might be restricted to the home. Individuals did not necessarily have the right to possess a weapon in public.

Self-confident to the end, Alan Gura was not surprised at all that he had won the case that no one, not even the NRA, had thought he could win. He found it remarkable instead that he persuaded only five of the nine justices to side with him. "My biggest surprise was that it was 5–4," he recalled. "I thought the case was much stronger than 5–4."[24]

Once the justices finished reading their opinions and disappeared behind the red velvet curtains, the libertarian lawyers left the courtroom. As they were walking out, Gura spotted Steve Halbrook in the hallway. Halbrook was the lawyer first hired by Bob Levy to look into the feasibility of challenging D.C.'s gun laws. He had demanded too much money to continue on and then represented the NRA in its effort to sidetrack the litigation. Halbrook must have had conflicted emotions. He had spent much of his career advocating for the individual-rights view of the Second Amendment, and that view was just declared the law of the land. Yet he, not Alan Gura, was the leading gun lawyer in the country, and this should have been his case. He should have been the one standing at the lectern answering the justices' questions, and he should have been the lawyer who won new life for the Second Amendment. "I remember we just looked at each other and smiled," recalled Gura. They didn't speak, and Halbrook didn't offer any congratulations. Gura kept walking, out the huge bronze doors, past the towering marble columns, down the long flight of steps in front of the Supreme Court Building, and into the throngs of reporters and cameramen waiting outside for an interview.[25]

•   •   •

JUSTICE SCALIA'S opinion in *District of Columbia v. Heller* was immediately declared "a triumph of originalism." His opinion relied heavily on historical sources to determine that the Second Amendment was understood by the framers to protect a right to bear arms for private purposes. The lengthy opinion included roughly forty-five pages of discussion of the original meaning to resolve a host of issues: whether the amendment's reference to "the right of the people" meant an individual right or a state right; whether "keep and bear Arms" had a purely military connotation; how to construe the phrases "well regulated Militia" and "necessary to the security of a free State."[26]

Heller was said to be a triumph of originalism because even the dissenters adopted that methodology. Like Scalia's majority opinion, Justice Stevens's dissent argued at length about how the amendment was originally understood. The majority and the dissenters "came to opposite conclusions but proceeded on the premise that original understanding of the amendment's framers was the proper basis for the decision," wrote Linda Greenhouse, the Supreme Court reporter for the *New York Times*. Northwestern University law professor John McGinnis agreed. "All justices adopted an originalist approach, suggesting that originalism commands consensus support" on the Court.[27]

In a speech at Harvard Law School later that year, Justice Scalia credited the lawyers and the scores of amicus briefs for providing the Court with the historical data necessary for an originalist decision. "The court had before it all the materials needed to determine the meaning of the Second Amendment at the time it was written. With these in hand, what method would be easier or more reliable than the originalist approach taken by the Court?" he asked rhetorically. He must have forgotten for a moment that this easy and reliable method led the majority and the dissenters to diametrically opposed conclusions.[28]

Heller was even hailed as the crowning achievement in Justice Scalia's long battle for originalism. "This case really is his legacy," noted Supreme Court expert Tom Goldstein. "Not only is the issue fantastically important, but the way the case was decided—on the basis of history and the original understanding—is his great contribution to the law." Others called Scalia's opinion the "most important in his 22 years on the court," "easily the most significant opinion Scalia has written," and "a symbol of [his] influence."[29]

At Harvard, Justice Scalia himself recognized how much more often the justices and litigants rely on originalism today than when he first joined the Court. Recalling a case from 1987 in which his clerks were alone in seeking out historical materials to illuminate the original meaning of the Eighth Amendment's prohibition on "cruel and unusual punishment," Scalia said that the extensive reliance on history was "unthinkable" back then. Now, with *Heller*, Scalia's originalism reigned supreme.

Not surprisingly, liberals criticized Scalia's opinion, objecting to both the outcome and the originalism used to achieve it. They didn't favor gun rights generally and believed Scalia's methodology to be an unsound basis for interpreting rights that were designed to solve problems of a far different time. More unexpectedly, several noted conservatives and proponents of originalism also condemned the opinion.

In November 2008, the conservative law professor Nelson Lund—one of the people who tried to persuade the libertarian lawyers to drop the lawsuit—gave a speech on the *Heller* decision at the annual convention of the Federalist Society. Several hundred people were packed tight in two conjoined banquet rooms at the Mayflower Hotel in Washington, D.C. It was a Democrat, Harry Truman, who called the Mayflower the "Second Best Address" in Washington, behind the

White House, but it was conservatives who found the most to like about the historic hotel. Not only did the Federalist Society meet there every year, but the hotel was also once the home of Monica Lewinsky—the ingénue whose liaison with Bill Clinton almost brought down his presidency—and the site of a presidential inauguration gala every four years that usually feted the latest Republican victory. Yet even though the hotel's party planners were preparing for a party to celebrate the inauguration of Barack Obama, a Democrat elected along with strong majorities in both the House and the Senate, the mood at the Federalist Society convention was still gay. Libertarians in the Federalist Society were happy to be rid of George W. Bush, whom they considered a turncoat for overseeing a huge expansion of the federal government and treading on individual liberties in the War on Terror. The worries of other conservatives about the Democratic ascendancy were mollified, in a way, by the *Heller* case. That decision showed that the Supreme Court was still in conservative hands and could be counted on to police the excesses of Obama and the liberals in Congress.[30]

Lund had been asked to speak about the D.C. gun case because he was one of the nation's experts on the history and meaning of the Second Amendment. A devout originalist, Lund had written numerous articles arguing that the founding fathers intended the Second Amendment to protect an individual right to bear arms. Although he had advised the libertarian lawyers not to bring their lawsuit—for fear of seeing the argument he had spent years making lose in the Supreme Court—his expertise on the Second Amendment and commitment to originalism made him a worthy speaker to celebrate this major victory for gun rights. He would also be the perfect person to counter the criticism leveled at the Supreme Court by Richard Posner and J. Harvie Wilkinson III, two of the leading conservative legal thinkers in America.[31]

Both Wilkinson and Posner were federal appeals court judges who spoke out frequently about political and legal issues. Appointed to the federal bench by President Reagan, Wilkinson was known for his strong conservative views and was on the shortlist of potential

nominees President Bush considered to replace Chief Justice William
Rehnquist in 2004. Richard Posner was also appointed to the bench
by President Reagan but was even more influential among conservatives than Wilkinson. Lawyers often referred to Posner as the greatest
legal mind never to sit on the Supreme Court. As a professor at the
University of Chicago Law School in the 1970s, where Antonin Scalia
was one of his colleagues, Posner was a founder of what is known
as "law and economics." Analyzing legal rules through the lens of
economic theory—with tools like cost-benefit analysis and goals like
wealth maximization and market efficiency—the field of law and
economics was not only popular among conservative fans of the free
market but also grew into one of the most important forms of contemporary legal scholarship across ideological lines. Posner himself
used economic analysis to study any number of law topics, from the
obvious (contract law and regulation of business) to the unexpected
(family law and sexuality). Even after he became a judge in 1981,
Posner continued to write nearly a book a year on everything from
legal philosophy and national security to public intellectuals and the
impeachment of Bill Clinton. In fact, Posner was never appointed to
the Supreme Court largely because he was so prolific and opinion-
ated at a time when an increasingly politicized confirmation process
was becoming more favorable to candidates with little or no paper
trail.[32]

Few people were surprised that the indefatigable Posner turned
his attention to the Second Amendment after the Supreme Court
issued its ruling in *Heller*. His unyielding, harsh criticism of the
decision, however, stunned conservatives. Posner wrote that Scalia's opinion employed "faux originalism" and that, when it came to
the original meaning of the Second Amendment, Justice Stevens's
dissent had the better argument. The "motivation for the Second
Amendment" was only to protect state militias from being disarmed by the federal government, according to Posner. "The text
of the amendment, whether viewed alone or in light of the concerns that actuated its adoption, creates no right to the private
possession of guns for hunting or other sport, or for the defense

of person or property." Not only did the majority err in its historical inquiry, Posner said, but originalism itself was contrary to the
original intent of the framers, who favored instead what he called
"loose construction" of legal texts that sought to uphold the "spirit"
of the law in changing circumstances rather than calcify the text's
meaning to a given era. Originalism was just an ideological gloss to
a politically motivated decision. *Heller* is "not evidence of disinter-
ested historical inquiry," wrote Posner. "It is evidence of the ability
of well-staffed courts to produce snow jobs."[33]

Posner and Wilkinson both condemned *Heller* as a right-wing version of *Roe v. Wade*, the bête noire of conservatives for over thirty
years. Wilkinson wrote an article that spread quickly through conservative legal circles while still in draft form. In the piece, he accused
the Court of undermining states' rights and legislating from the
bench. "*Heller* represents a triumph for conservative lawyers. But it
also represents a failure—the Court's failure to adhere to a conservative judicial methodology in reaching its decisions." Wilkinson con-
tended that the historical evidence on both sides was equally strong
and that the Court's majority simply imposed its own values on the
text. "*Heller* encourages Americans to do what conservative jurists
warned for years they should not do: bypass the ballot and seek to
press their political agenda in the courts," he charged. *Roe* and *Heller*
"are guilty of the same sins."[34]

Standing before the Federalist Society crowd at the Mayflower
Hotel, Lund was not likely to agree with these critiques. He had
long endorsed the idea of using originalism to interpret the Second
Amendment to guarantee the right of individuals to own guns for
self-defense. Lund began his speech with assurances that, as a proponent of originalism, he agreed with both the majority's methodology and its basic interpretation of the text as protecting an individual
right. Lund then astonished the audience by launching into a lengthy
and harsh condemnation of Scalia's opinion. "Unfortunately, the
Court's performance is so transparently defective that it's quite possible that this decision will become Exhibit A when people seek to
discredit originalism as an interpretive method."[35]

To Lund, Scalia's opinion for the Court veered away from originalism in several important ways. Although the Court was right to see an individual right in the Second Amendment, the ultimate legal question in the case was whether D.C.'s law violated that right. It's one thing to identify a right in the Constitution, but the courts also have to determine what laws are prohibited by that right. Anyone can say that the First Amendment protects the freedom of speech. What lawmakers need to know is whether a ban on flag burning or on child pornography violates that right. What types of regulations are allowed? Which laws does the right invalidate? What are the exact limits on government imposed by the right? This is what really matters in constitutional analysis. If the Second Amendment is to be a meaningful constraint on government, then it must do more than simply identify a fundamental individual right in abstract terms. It must also separate what the government can do from what the government cannot. It was here that Lund accused Scalia's opinion of ignoring original meaning. An originalist, Lund said, would "have to ask, 'What does history tell us about *handgun bans*?' Oddly, Scalia has nothing to say about that at all."[36]

The reason D.C. couldn't ban handguns, Scalia's opinion said, was that this type of weapon was "in common use." Many Americans prefer handguns to shotguns or rifles because handguns are lightweight and easy to use. "Whatever the reason," Scalia explained, "handguns are the most popular weapon chosen by Americans for self-defense in the home and a complete prohibition of their use is invalid." Yet Lund responded that this argument "doesn't have much basis in the history of the eighteenth century," when the Second Amendment was adopted. A true originalist wouldn't care why people *today* like handguns, he would ask whether Americans in the late 1700s thought that the Second Amendment prohibited a ban on handguns. Lund didn't know the answer to that question—but neither did the Supreme Court. Scalia's argument "is not an originalist or historical argument. If it's any kind of argument at all, it's probably a disguised and incomplete form of the Breyer interest-balancing approach that Scalia disdainfully dismissed."

In fact, the founding fathers didn't always believe that the guns commonly owned by civilians were good enough. Many of the guns ordinary people owned were useful to shoot birds and other small animals for food or sport, but militias required military weapons. As a result, when Congress passed the Uniform Militia Act of 1792, it required militia members to outfit themselves with the specific firearms that weren't necessarily already in the closet: "every citizen, so enrolled and notified, shall, within six months thereafter, provide himself with a good musket or firelock, a sufficient bayonet . . . or with a good rifle . . . and that from and after five years from the passing of this Act, all muskets from arming the militia as is herein required, shall be of bores sufficient for balls of the eighteenth part of a pound." Such specificity was required because the guns commonly owned by civilians were often the wrong kind.[37]

"But things get worse," Lund complained, pointing to the list of Second Amendment exceptions recognized in Scalia's opinion. "Little analysis of any kind is provided . . . [so] with regard to these exceptions to the right to arms, we seem to have a case of verdict first and trial later, if at all." Scalia didn't cite a single historical source to support the listed exceptions, and if "Scalia couldn't provide an historical justification for striking down the D.C. handgun ban at issue in this case," Lund suggested, "it's not very likely that he really has historical justifications to back up" the listed exceptions.

Lund was right that there wasn't much evidence that the founding fathers understood the types of laws identified by Justice Scalia to be permissible restraints on the Second Amendment. The founders did have gun control, so there are historical precedents one can look to in determining what types of gun control laws the founding generation thought to be consistent with the right to bear arms. At the time of the founding, laws required the armed citizenry to report with their guns to militia musters, where weapons would be inspected and the citizens trained. Authorities often required that militia guns be registered. There were laws requiring gunpowder to be stored safely, even though the rules made it more difficult for people to load their guns quickly to defend themselves against attack. The founders also imposed more severe limitations, including complete bans on gun ownership by free blacks, slaves, and political dissenters.

What the founding fathers did not have much of was the type of gun control identified as Second Amendment exceptions by Justice Scalia. They had no restrictions on the commercial sales of firearms like the licensing of gun dealers, mandatory background checks, or waiting periods. The founders didn't have any laws banning guns in schools, government buildings, or any other sort of "sensitive place." Indeed, in some colonies, people were *required* to bring their guns to church—what many people today might consider to be precisely the type of sensitive place where guns ought to be excluded. The founding generation had no notion whatsoever of "mental illness" as a legal category, much less laws that barred the mentally ill from possession of firearms. Laws prohibiting ex-felons from buying firearms were longstanding, but they originated in the 1920s and 1930s, more than a century after the founding.

The irony of Scalia's opinion was that the heralded "triumph of originalism" in fact reflected a thoroughly modern understanding of gun rights. The primary justification for the right of individuals to bear arms, in Scalia's view, is self-defense in the home. At the time of the founding, however, the primary justifications for it were to preserve the right of the people to throw off a tyrannical government, to serve in a militia for national defense, or to go out into the wilderness and hunt. Few, if any, arguments for the right rested on the ability to defend your home against a criminal attack. The right envisioned by the founders was anything but homebound.[38]

The living constitutionalism underlying the decision was further illustrated in the explanation offered by the Court for why the government could ban machine guns but not handguns. In contrast to handguns, Scalia wrote, machine guns can be restricted because they are "dangerous and unusual weapons" not "in common use." As we saw in chapter 7, however, civilian ownership of machine guns has been heavily restricted by federal law since the 1930s. Federal gun control of the twentieth century has made machine guns unusual and uncommon, while the absence of serious restrictions on the availability of handguns has given people the opportunity to choose them for self-defense. The scope of the Second Amendment's protections was not, in other words, defined by the original meaning of the Constitution. The protections were shaped instead by the marketplace choices of twentieth-century consumers, made within the confines of contemporary government regulation.

Scalia's opinion makes "originalism look as lawless and result-oriented as the living constitutionalism that Scalia and many of us in the Federalist Society have been denouncing for years," said Lund, finishing his speech. "What a pity."

●   ●   ●

JOSEPH HELLER's satirical novel *Catch-22* is a classic of American literature. The novel, which follows the travails of a group of military airmen in World War II, offers an insightful and humorous account of the quagmires and incongruities of contemporary bureaucratic life. In the novel, a "Catch-22" is a nonexistent military rule that, by its self-contradictory logic, all service personnel must obey. The notion of a Catch-22 has since become famous as an idiom representing a no-win situation built on illogic and circular reasoning.

The Supreme Court's decision in the D.C. gun case bore the surname of *Catch-22*'s author and also some of the same ironic contradictions explored in the novel. One we've already seen: for a decision steeped in originalism, it relied largely on a modern conception of gun rights to determine what gun control laws are legitimate. Justice Scalia, who believes the courts must use originalism because that is the only way the judiciary can maintain its legitimacy, veered away from originalism in *Heller* because, most likely, a ruling that did not permit modern forms of gun control laws would not have been seen as legitimate. Originalism is required for public legitimacy, except when it isn't.[39]

There were other unexpected twists as well. For a decision celebrated by the gun rights community, its immediate effect on gun control was far less than what the gun rights hard-liners might have hoped for. *Heller* did spark a wave of lawsuits challenging every conceivable type of gun control; within two years, there were over 150 federal court rulings on the constitutionality of gun laws under the Second Amendment. Few laws, however, were invalidated. Despite some sky-is-falling rhetoric of gun control advocates after the case was decided, the Supreme Court did not undermine very many gun laws, at least in the short term. Instead, lower-court judges in Second Amendment cases consistently pointed to Scalia's list of exceptions and said that whatever law they were ruling on was sufficiently similar—and similarly constitutional. Employing this type of analysis, courts upheld everything from concealed carry permit requirements to bans on firearms possession by fathers who failed to pay child support.[40]

One of the few laws invalidated was Chicago's ban on handguns. Besides Washington, D.C., Chicago was the only major city in the nation to prohibit ordinary civilians from owning handguns. The day the *Heller* decision was announced, Alan Gura filed a lawsuit challenging Chicago's ban. In 2010, the Supreme Court in a case entitled *McDonald v. City of Chicago* held that the Second Amendment, like nearly all of the provisions in the Bill of Rights, applied with equal force to federal, state, and local laws. The amendment, in the terminology of constitutional doctrine, was "incorporated" through the Fourteenth Amendment to apply to the lower levels of government. Central to the Court's decision, in which the justices again split 5–4, was the history recounted in chapter 5: after the Civil War, the drafters of the Fourteenth Amendment intended to guarantee freedmen the right to keep and bear arms, among other fundamental rights, from state infringement. The *McDonald* decision repeated the list of exceptions earlier recognized by Scalia's opinion in *Heller*. "We made it clear in *Heller* that our holding did not cast doubt" on many forms of gun control, the majority wrote. "We repeat those assurances here."[41]

About Scalia's list of exceptions, Bob Levy said, "I would have preferred that that not have been there." Because of that paragraph, Scalia's opinion, in Levy's view, "created more confusion than light."

The problem, in fact, was the opposite. Scalia's opinion revealed that the Supreme Court thought most gun control laws currently on the books were constitutional regardless of the Second Amendment.[42]

Scalia's opinion also posed other hurdles for gun rights. To many in the gun rights community, the most important battlefield in the wake of *Heller* and *McDonald* was concealed carry restrictions. Although nearly every state allows people to carry concealed firearms if they have a permit, the requirements for obtaining such a permit vary. In some states, it is as easy as filling out a form; in others, the local chief of police or the sheriff has discretion to determine whether an applicant has sufficient need to carry a concealed gun. Back in the early twentieth century, the NRA promoted the idea that concealed carry permits should be limited; the Uniform Firearms Act drafted with the help of the NRA president Karl Frederick restricted licenses to "suitable" people with "proper reason for carrying." In the modern-day gun movement, however, such restrictions are viewed as profound infringements on one's right to have a firearm for self-protection at all times.

If the ability to carry a concealed firearm in public is one of the rights protected by the Second Amendment, then a law giving a government official unfettered discretion to withhold permits does raise troublesome questions. Over the course of American history, such discretion was often used against racial minorities and other disfavored groups—as, you may recall, Martin Luther King Jr. discovered when he applied to the Montgomery police chief for a concealed carry permit in his early days in the civil rights movement. *Heller*, however, makes challenges to concealed carry restrictions difficult. As Scalia's opinion recognized, the "majority of the 19th-century courts to consider the question held that prohibitions on carrying concealed weapons were lawful under the Second Amendment or state analogues." The laws he was referring to were complete bans on concealed carry—a greater burden than today's laws, which generally allow for carrying hidden firearms so long as one first obtains a permit.

It was for these reasons that some gun control advocates, like Dennis Henigan of the Brady Center to Prevent Gun Violence, called Scalia's opinion "a pleasant surprise." To be sure, Henigan disagreed with the Court's reading of the Second Amendment to guarantee an individual right to bear arms. Like any advocate, he also had incentive to minimize his side's loss in the Supreme Court. Yet Henigan insisted that *Heller*'s list of exceptions "encompassed our entire agenda." "It basically made it very easy for lower courts without a whole lot of difficulty to find that whatever gun law is at issue in the particular case in front of them . . . had been blessed" by the Court. "I'm sure it's been enormously frustrating to the gun rights community to see the lower courts upholding laws of a wide variety by simply citing" *Heller*'s list of exceptions.[43]

Ironically, gun rights advocates may be helped most by *Heller* outside of the courts. The threat of a lawsuit alone will force many lawmakers to reconsider ineffective or overly burdensome gun control laws currently on the books. They used to be confident that nearly any gun law would survive a Second Amendment challenge in the courts, but now they must be a bit more careful. In the wake of the Supreme Court's decisions, New York City, for example, revised its permitting laws to make it somewhat easier and quicker for applicants to gain approval. Although the mayor, Michael Bloomberg, is one of the nation's leading gun control advocates, his administration didn't want to make the same mistake as D.C. Mayor Adrian Fenty and cling to a law likely to be overturned—and risk creating new precedents that further undermine gun control.

Previously, gun control advocates were occasionally able to sway elected officials to vote for gun restrictions by arguing that the NRA and other gun rights proponents were misreading the Second Amendment. After *Heller*, that argument won't work. Undecided lawmakers may be more likely now to side with gun rights advocates. This would be an obvious blow to gun control groups, who are so often on the losing end of legislative battles anyway.

● ● ●

ONE OF the most famous photographs in American history was taken on September 4, 1957. That was the day the Little Rock Nine—

a group of African American teenagers—arrived at Central High School in Arkansas to integrate the all-white school. Three years earlier, the Supreme Court had decided *Brown v. Board of Education*, and the Little Rock school district, which represented one of the more progressive cities in the South, chose a handful of gifted black students to become the first to integrate a major southern high school. The photograph, taken on the street outside of the school, shows Elizabeth Eckford, a fifteen-year-old black girl in a pleated white skirt and dark sunglasses clutching a notebook tightly to her chest. She is being followed by a mob of angry white students, one of whom, Hazel Bryan, is seen following Eckford and yelling epithets. The hate-filled rage on Bryan's contorted face is palpable.[44]

Eckford is the only African American in the picture. She was alone because she was the first of the nine to arrive at Central High that morning. Daisy Bates, a local NAACP official, had wanted all of the students to meet first at Bates's house, from where they could all go to school together, accompanied by ministers and other civil rights workers. However, Bates was unable to get in touch with her because Eckford's parents didn't have a phone. Eckford arrived at the school alone, only to find the street in front of Central High filled with white racists. "Lynch her!" they shouted. "No nigger bitch is going to get in our school!" "Send that nigger back to the jungle!" The National Guard was there, but wouldn't let Eckford into the school. The guard had been called out by the governor, Orval Faubus, to keep the blacks out. Eckford saw an old woman with a welcoming face and turned to her for help. Instead, the older woman spat on her.[45]

For weeks thereafter, Daisy Bates wouldn't leave her home without a gun. The black students, meanwhile, eventually made it into the school, escorted by federal troops sent in by President Dwight Eisenhower. No strong supporter of integration, Eisenhower nevertheless believed in the rule of law. The Supreme Court had ruled that the Constitution required integration, and Eisenhower, as president, was obliged to follow the Court's decision. Elected officials in the South, however, didn't respect the Court in the same way. In 1958, rather than continue the preceding year's experiment in racial integration, Arkansas lawmakers simply closed down Central High altogether.

The battle over the integration in Little Rock reflected America's profound polarization over race in the 1950s. Each side, motivated by the sense that the other was threatening everything it held dear, was driven to the extremes. An observer could be forgiven for believing at the time that Americans would never bridge the racial divide. Yet, in 1999, Elizabeth Eckford and Hazel Bryan came together again, this time on a daytime television talk show, where the extremism that characterized their first encounter was much subsided. One measure of how far America had come was the television program itself; the highest-rated talk show in the country, watched by blacks and whites alike, was hosted by Oprah Winfrey.

Little Rock was put into motion by the Supreme Court's decision in *Brown*, and blame is often placed on the Court for polarizing Americans on issues ranging from abortion to religion to gay rights. J. Harvie Wilkinson, the conservative judge who criticized the Court's decision in the gun case, likened *Heller* to *Roe v. Wade*. Just as the justices should never have imposed their view of abortion rights on America, they should have left gun control to the political process. The Court's mistake in *Roe* was to attempt to "put to rest an extremely controversial issue of social policy." Instead, the Court only exacerbated the divide in America over abortion rights, preventing Americans from coming to a moderate consensus on the issue. If only the Court had stayed out of this controversy, the argument goes, Americans would have solved the abortion question through the normal process of political give-and-take. To Wilkinson, the Supreme Court in the gun case once again inhibited Americans' ability to find a satisfying middle ground.[46]

Wilkinson's view of politics, like that of many of *Roe*'s critics, is overly sanguine. For seventy years, the Supreme Court remained on the sidelines of the gun debate, and the result was anything but a gradual move toward consensus. Instead, the Court's absence allowed the forces of unreason to command the field. Without any Supreme Court decisions firmly protecting the right to bear arms and articulating the scope and limits of that right, extremists were free to cast the Second Amendment in their own preferred terms. Gun rights advocates, fearful that the right to bear arms could be legislated away completely, insisted that almost no forms of gun control were legitimate. Gun control hard-liners, eager to reduce gun violence, could say that "the right of the people to keep and bear Arms" meant no such thing. Debates over gun control proposals didn't focus on their merits as a matter of policy but instead became ensnared in arguments about the history and meaning of the Second Amendment. Neither side felt the need to compromise because total victory was still possible: one day the high court might make their extremist view the law of the land.

Rather than give either side in the gun debate a total victory, the Supreme Court's decision in *Heller* validated a compromise position on guns. Individuals have a right to possess a gun for self-defense, but that right can and should be subject to some regulation in the interest of public safety. Private ownership of guns cannot be completely banned, and the civilian disarmament long desired by anti-gun people is now constitutionally impossible. No one can come and take away all the guns, even if many other forms of gun control remain permissible. Unlike the radical right to keep and bear arms envisioned by gun rights and gun control groups—in which the right to own guns cannot coexist with gun safety regulation—*Heller* stands as a symbol of a truly reasonable right to bear arms in which we can have both.

By making civilian disarmament impermissible, the Court's decision has the potential to restore some measure of reason to the gun debate. Extremists on both sides have obsessed over disarmament for too long. In truth, disarmament has never been a realistic option. There is no political will for it; even if there were, there are just too many guns in America and too many gun owners who would never comply with a law requiring them to turn in their guns. Guns are permanent in America, and *Heller* will help all Americans, whether gun rights supporters or proponents of gun control, realize it.

Disarmament has distracted attention away from the significant public policy questions Americans need to ask. Instead of questioning whether we should have guns or not, we should accept the permanence of guns and focus instead on what types of policies can effectively and efficiently reduce gun violence. If we can move beyond the shouting match over whether guns are evil and lawless—as gun control hard-liners insist—or are the embodiment of liberty—as gun rights abso-lutists claim—perhaps we can begin careful discussions of the serious empirical work on gun crime that criminologists are doing. The solu-tions to America's gun violence are not going to be found by simplistic sloganeering about whether we should have more guns or fewer guns. What we need are better policies that, for example, do more to keep guns out of the hands of the gang members and recidivist offenders responsible for the bulk of gun crime.[47]

Paradoxically, by establishing a firmer foundation for gun rights, the Supreme Court could make it easier for Americans to identify and enact effective gun control laws. "By erecting a constitutional barrier to a broad gun ban, the *Heller* ruling may have flattened the gun lobby's 'slippery slope,' making it harder for the NRA to use fear tactics to motivate gun owners to give their time, money and votes in opposing sensible gun laws and the candidates who support those laws," wrote the Brady Center's Dennis Henigan. This view is not held only by hopeful gun control advocates. The pro-gun libertar-ian Jacob Sullum has written that, by eliminating the possibility of disarmament, *Heller* "could help calm the often vociferous conflict over gun policy." Prior to *Heller*, Glenn Harlan Reynolds, the conser-vative law professor who coined the standard-model terminology for the individual-rights view of the Second Amendment, predicted that a favorable individual-rights ruling by the Supreme Court would give gun owners "less reason to fear creeping confiscation, and sensible gun control laws—those aimed at disarming criminals, not ordinary citizens—would pass much more easily."[48]

Although lost in the overheated public debate that has bedeviled American political discourse on the Second Amendment since the 1960s, compromise on guns has a place. As the history of the right to bear arms and gun control shows, there is a middle ground in which gun rights and laws providing for public safety from gun violence can coexist. Ever since the founding of America, the right to own a firearm has lived side by side with gun control. Americans don't need to choose between two absolutes—between unfettered gun rights on the one hand and unfettered gun control on the other. As we've seen, Americans have always had both gun rights and gun control.

This is exactly what most Americans today want. Polls consistently show that three of every four Americans believe that the Constitution guarantees an individual right. Only 17 percent support the collective or states' rights view. According to a study by the National Opinion Research Center, just 11 percent of Americans support the kind of draconian ban on handguns struck down by the Supreme Court in the Washington and Chicago cases. *Heller*'s laundry list of Second Amendment exceptions raised the ire of some in the gun community, but those exceptions are also well aligned with popular sentiment, even among most gun owners. Surveying polling data, the study concluded that "[l]arge majorities back most general measures for controlling guns, policies to increase gun safety, laws to restrict criminals from acquiring firearms, and measures to enforce gun laws and punish offenders."[49]

One of the reasons Elizabeth Eckford and the other members of the Little Rock Nine needed federal troops to escort them was that the Supreme Court decision striking down segregation in schools ran counter to the deeply held beliefs of a wide swath of the country. Not only did the revolutionary opinion in *Brown v. Board of Education* reverse years of case law affirming the constitutionality of "separate but equal"; it upended the worldview of millions of people. Yet because of *Brown*'s ultimate success in ending formal legal discrimination, tearing down barriers that had divided the nation along racial lines for centuries, the decision is taken to epitomize the role and function of the Supreme Court. The Court in this view is at the vanguard of social reform, fighting to protect the downtrodden and powerless, securing the rights of minorities against the tyranny of the majority. *Heller*, by contrast, didn't protect helpless minorities so much as confirm a majority view of the Second Amendment that had already become entrenched in the public mind.

Constitutional scholars today argue that cases like *Heller* are far more typical than cases like *Brown*. Historically the Supreme Court lags behind social movements rather than leads them. From birth control to women's equality to gay rights, the Court tends to invalidate laws that are exceptional, outliers defying a broader national consensus. When the Court gets out in front of national commitments, as it did in *Roe v. Wade*, the justices invite uncomfortable charges of judicial activism and often provoke a backlash.[50]

It's hardly surprising that the Court is usually a laggard rather than a pioneer. While no justice thinks it appropriate to follow the election returns or slavishly manipulate constitutional law to match up with public opinion polls, certain institutional dynamics keep the Court's rulings within a broad mainstream of American political thought. The appointment process enables elected presidents and senators to nominate and confirm justices who reflect prevailing understandings about the law. A nominee with esoteric or publicly unappealing views—like a Robert Bork, who rejected the idea that any right of privacy was embedded in the Constitution—will not be easily confirmed. Justices are also influenced by the same cultural, social, and economic conditions that shape the views of all Americans. Whatever leads the vast majority of the populace to believe that the proper reading of the Second Amendment is to protect an individual right to possess a firearm also penetrates the Supreme Court's marble walls. Justices also prefer to stamp out outliers rather than carve new paths in order to protect the legitimacy of the Court. Without the power of the purse or the power of the sword, the Court relies on public respect to maintain its authority. That respect has been challenged at times— think *Bush v. Gore*—but one can understand why the justices usually stay away from the cutting edge.

The District of Columbia's law was a quintessential outlier. Other than Chicago, D.C. was the only major city in the country to outlaw the possession of handguns by ordinary civilians. Adopted in an effort to start a nationwide trend toward disarmament, the laws failed spectacularly; no national consensus against handgun ownership ever developed, and even within the few places where the laws were adopted, they were viewed as ineffective and symbolic measures. Washington's laws, which also banned the use of shotguns and rifles for self-defense in the home, were simply the most extreme set of gun laws in the nation—a fact that was not lost on the justices: "Few laws in the history of our Nation," Scalia wrote, "have come close to the severe restriction of the District's handgun ban."

In contrast to *Brown*, the immediate public response to *Heller* was predictably muted. Handed down in the heat of a presidential campaign, the Court's decision was endorsed by both of the major party nominees. Unlike *Roe*, *Heller* is not likely to create a backlash against the Court because the decision reflected a national consensus about the Second Amendment, though one easily hidden by the extremism of the gun debate. Another important reason why the decision is unlikely to incite a backlash is its affirmation of reasonable gun control laws. The need for laws to keep guns out of the hands of dangerous people and to reduce gun violence is also part of the national consensus about guns.

Heller was hailed as a major victory for the gun rights extremists. Like so much else about guns in America, however, this latest chapter in our nation's remarkable story of firearms is more nuanced. The wider public, which can now escape the pro-gun/anti-gun rut that trapped gun policy, was the real winner. *Heller* was the Supreme Court decision that the gun rights movement long hoped for. Yet other than the occasional outlier, most gun control laws are not likely to run afoul of the right recognized by the Court. Gun rights won, but so did gun control. *Catch-22*'s Joseph Heller would have been proud.

EPILOGUE

WHEN ALAN GURA FINISHED WITH THE REPORTERS OUTSIDE THE
Supreme Court Building the day *Heller* was decided, he turned on his
iPhone to find, by his own estimation, about "five thousand text mes-
sages and emails." It seemed everyone he knew, and a lot of people he
didn't, sent their congratulations.[1]

That night, Gura and his wife, Amy, took their young son out for a
celebratory dinner at one of their favorite neighborhood restaurants, a
Nuevo Latino fusion place called Café Salsa, in Alexandria, Virginia.
After a few mojitos, Gura suggested they head home. Amy, however,
insisted on walking across the street to stop by his office. "I didn't
want to go to the office, I had nothing to do there, and, c'mon, I'd
had a long day," Gura recalled. Amy wouldn't take no for an answer.
When Gura entered his office and turned on the lights, he saw why
she was so insistent. The walls were covered with scores of colorful
plastic squirt guns, all taped up alongside funny signs. Gura laughed,
"My office was basically converted into an armory of water pistols."

Bob Levy, who financed the case, went back to where he was staying
in town and did what he does best. He began to write up his thoughts
about the case and his experience. By the end of the year, he would be
named chairman of the Cato Institute, the libertarian think tank.[2]

Clark Neily, who along with his colleague Steve Simpson had originally come up with the idea of bringing a Second Amendment lawsuit during a happy hour, celebrated by having another one. Together
with friends from the Institute for Justice, Neily toasted the victory
at the Tortoise & Hare Bar and Grill, not far from his office. "We had
shots and, you know, it was just sort of one of those things where
you go celebrate. It was like winning the Super Bowl or something
like that. It was a culmination of a five and half year effort." The
bartender at the Tortoise & Hare created a special drink in Neily's
honor. It included rum, which had been the most common liquor in
the American colonies; Coke, the quintessential American beverage;
and Jack Daniels, "on the premise that that was the drink of choice
of gun-toting rednecks everywhere," Neily explained. The bartender
gave the concoction an evocative name: "The Shot Heard 'round the
World."[3]

ACKNOWLEDGMENTS

THE PEOPLE INVOLVED IN THE *DISTRICT OF COLUMBIA V. HELLER* lawsuit generously shared their insights and experiences with me. I owe them all my gratitude: Alan Gura, Clark Neily, Robert Levy, Walter Dellinger, Alan Morrison, Joseph Blocher, Matt Shors, Jon Lowy, Dennis Henigan, and Saul Cornell, in addition to a number of others who wish to remain anonymous. Any author who writes about a historical event is indebted to those who've written on it before; I was fortunate to supplement my own research with that of Brian Doherty, whose *Gun Control on Trial: Inside the Supreme Court Battle over the Second Amendment* is an excellent insider account of the *Heller* litigation. Our books are very different, although they both begin in the same place, with the scene outside the Supreme Court on the day of oral argument.

My research was also helped tremendously by the UCLA reference librarians, including Amy Atchison, Tammy Pettinato, Stephanie Plotin, June Kim, and John Wilson, and by a cadre of hardworking research assistants, including Tina Mehr, Gina Giacopuzzi, Sarah Levesque, Wesley Gorman, Rhianna Bauer, Beverly Bradshaw, and Jessica Moore, under the supervision of Linda O'Connor. Vicki Steiner was invaluable in finding the photographs used in the book.

Robin Lee, Rusty Klibaner, and Samantha Luu provided help in so many ways throughout the writing of this book, assisted by Kristin Kim, Timothy Lee, Mark Kim, and Julie Dinh. UCLA School of Law provided funds to support my research.

Indeed, many people provided guidance and suggestions along the way: Kent Greenfield, Frank Partnoy, Wah Chen, Kal Raustiala, Don Kates, Mitchell Duneier, Bradley Lewis, Eugene Volokh, Nick Pileggi, Jason Epstein, Andrea Stanford, Ed Renwick, Steve Wasserman, Jeff Lipsky, Ben Schwarz, William Clark, Sir Harry Evans, Elizabeth Knoll, Judge James Zagel, Peggy Zagel, Mort Zuckerman, Bob Bomes, Lucas Wittmann, Matt Feigin, Larry Paul, Renee Schwartz, Len Decof, Jack Chin, Rachel Salzman, Peter Jacobs, Dan Markel, Susan Kuo, Christopher Lund, Andrew Hessick, Carissa Hessick, Asli Bali, David Fagundes, Sonja West, Miriam Baer, Bill McGowan, Caleb Mason, Anne Kimball, Marli Garcia, Nicole Mutchnik, Mort Zuckerman, Marco DiMaccio, David Ginsburg, Chris Hirt, and David Messinger. Dave Kopel generously read the manuscript twice to hunt for mistakes and misinterpretations.

My agent, Lynn Nesbit, helped get this project off the ground and spent time with this first-time author that might have been better spent with one of her more profitable clients. At W. W. Norton, Philip Marino did an excellent job with line edits and handholding. Jessica Purcell and Angela Hayes worked diligently to publicize the book. Robert Weil, my editor, gave me spectacular advice and improved the manuscript enormously.

My parents, Irwin and Margo Winkler, devoured every word of every draft as only parents can; their love and support has made possible not just this book but nearly everything else I've ever accomplished.

Two people, however, deserve special mention: Melissa Bomes, who is both the love of my life and my Obi-Wan Kenobi for all things personal and professional, and Danny Winkler, my beloved daughter who made me want to make the world a better place in whatever small way I could. They embody the reason a law-abiding person might want to own a gun. There is nothing more precious to me than them.

NOTES

Chapter 1: BIG GUNS AND LITTLE GUNS
AT THE SUPREME COURT

1. I attended the oral argument and saw firsthand some of the signs and events recounted here. Information can also be found at Jan Crawford Greenburg, "Lining Up for Guns," *Legalities* (blog), ABC News, March 16, 2008, available at http://blogs.abcnews.com/legalities/2008/03/lining-up-for-g.html; Mary Beth Sheridan, "Braving Cold, Chants, Students Flock to Hear Gun Case," *Washington Post*, March 19, 2008, p. A8; interview with Jason McCrory, Oct. 19, 2010; Jason McCrory blog post available at http://www.ar15.com/forums/topic.html?b=1&f=5&t=688643. The scene is also described in Brian Doherty, *Gun Control on Trial: Inside the Supreme Court Battle over the Second Amendment* (2008), which inspired me to see the street scene as a microcosm of the gun debate in America.

2. On Dellinger's bike habit, see David L'Heureux, "People Who Ride: Walter Dellinger," *Bicycling*, available at http://tourdefrancefacts.com/article/0,661 0,s1-3-583-17104-1,00.html; interview with Walter Dellinger, Sept. 24, 2009.

3. Interview with Alan Gura, Jan. 24, 2009.

4. The 250–280 million estimate is derived from coupling the U.S. Department of Justice's estimate of 223 million firearms in 1995 with the estimated number of new firearms sold in America since then. See U.S. Dept. of Justice, Bureau of Justice Statistics, *Guns Used in Crime*, July 1995, available at http://www.ojp.usdoj.gov/bjs/pub/pdf/guic.pdf.

5. On polarization, see Alan I. Abramowitz and Kyle L. Saunders, "Is Polarization a Myth?," *Journal of Politics* 70 (2008): 542; Delia Baldassarri and Andrew Gelman, "Partisans without Constraint: Political Polarization and Trends in American Public Opinion," *American Journal of Sociology* 114 (2008): 408;

Peitro S. Nivola and David W. Brady, eds., *Red and Blue Nation?: Characteristics and Causes of America's Polarized Politics* (2006).

Chapter 2: "Gun Grabbers"

1. On the Hechinger Hardware robbery, see the testimony of John Hechinger at hearings before the Council of the District of Columbia, Committee on Judiciary and Criminal Law, June 6, 1975, pp. 32-33; William Raspberry, "What About the Old Law?," *Washington Post*, June 16, 1975, p. A23.
2. Hechinger urged the city council to adopt a gun control law. See Arnold L. Thibou, "Panel Opens Hearing on Gun Control Bills," *Washington Post*, June 7, 1975, p. B2.
3. See Juan Cameron, "The Washington Tourists Don't Visit," *Fortune*, March 1975, p. 142.
4. See Steven Brill, *Firearm Abuse: A Research and Policy Report* (1977), 12.
5. On Moore's opposition, see Paul W. Valentine, "Council Backs Gun Control," *Washington Post*, May 4, 1976, p. A1. On the NRA mailing, see Paul W. Valentine, "NRA Starts Drive to Defeat Proposed D.C. Gun Law," *Washington Post*, May 14, 1976, p. C1.
6. On the NRA boycott, see Paul W. Valentine, "Mayor Signs Stringent Gun Control Measure," *Washington Post*, July 24, 1976, pp. E1, E3. The D.C. law allowed existing owners of handguns to retain their firearms.
7. On Ron Paul, see Christopher Caldwell, "The Antiwar, Anti-Abortion, Anti-Drug-Enforcement-Administration, Anti-Medicare Candidacy of Dr. Ron Paul," *New York Times Magazine*, July 22, 2007.
8. On Ron Paul's effort to overturn the D.C. gun ban, see "D.C. Firearms Act Challenged," *Washington Post*, July 31, 1976, p. E3; La Barbara Bowman and Paul W. Valentine, "Gun Bill Votes Tied to NRA," *Washington Post*, Aug. 26, 1976, pp. C1, C10; Karlyn Barker and Paul W. Valentine, "Effort to Kill D.C. Gun Law Hits Snag," *Washington Post*, Sept. 18, 1976, pp. D1, D4.
9. On the recognized ineffectiveness of the D.C. law, see Joe Ritchie, "Gun Control Approved by Council Unit," *Washington Post*, April 16, 1976, p. C5; Eugene L. Meyer and Paul W. Valentine, "U.S. Study Casts Doubt on City's New Gun Law," *Washington Post*, Aug. 14, 1976, at B1; Paul Duggan, "Crime Data Underscore Limits of D.C. Gun Ban's Effectiveness," *Washington Post*, Nov. 13, 2007.
10. On the hope that D.C.'s ban would spark a nationwide trend, see Raspberry, "What About the Old Law?," A23; "Handguns and the City," *Washington Post*, Aug. 20, 1976, p. A26; Valentine, "Mayor Signs Stringent Gun Control Measure," E1, E3; Duggan, "Crime Data Underscore Limits." Hechinger's statement is quoted in Jan E. Dizard et al., "Living with Guns—Seeking Middle Ground in the Battlefield," in *Guns in America: A Reader* (1999), 447, 448.
11. On gun prohibitionists, see Gary Kleck, "Absolutist Politics in a Moderate Package: Prohibitionist Intentions of the Gun Control Movement," *Journal of Firearms and Public Policy* 13 (2001): 1.
12. For the annual number of guns manufactured in the United States (and not

exported), see Bureau of Alcohol, Tobacco, Firearms, and Explosives, *Annual Firearms Manufacturing and Export Report* (2007), available at http://www .atf.gov/firearms/stats/afmer/afmer2007.pdf. On the percentage of homes with guns, see *2001 National Gun Policy Survey of the National Opinion Research Center: Research Findings* (Dec. 2001), available at http://www .mindchanging.com/politics/guncontrolsurvey.pdf. On the U.K., see Alexander DeConde, *Gun Violence in America: The Struggle for Control* (2001), 119.

13. On noncompliance in California and Illinois, see Kleck, "Absolutist Politics in a Moderate Package," 14–15.

14. On drug use, see Office of National Drug Control Policy, *Drug Data Summary* (March 2003), available at http://www.whitehousedrugpolicy.gov/pdf/ drug_datasum.pdf.

15. On Tom Palmer's frightening encounter with gay bashers, see his interview in "Does Gun Control Reduce Crime?," ABC News, May 4, 2007. See also the account in Elissa Silverman and Allison Klein, "Plaintiffs Reflect on Gun Ruling," *Washington Post*, March 11, 2001, p. C1; Brian Doherty, *Gun Control on Trial: Inside the Supreme Court Battle over the Second Amendment* (2008), 30–32; Christian Davenport, "Plaintiff in Handgun Case Is Suing D.C. for Right to Carry Firearms in Public," *Washington Post*, Feb. 21, 2010.

16. For contrasting views of the frequency of self-defensive uses of firearms, compare Gary Kleck and Marc Gertz, "Armed Resistance to Crime: The Prevalence and Nature of Self-Defense with a Gun," *Journal of Criminal Law and Criminology* 86 (1995): 1 (estimating 2.5 million uses), and Philip J. Cook and Jens Ludwig, *Gun Violence: The Real Costs* (2000) (estimating 100,000 uses).

17. On the evolution of the Democratic Party platform's position on guns, see Robert J. Spitzer, "Gun Control: Constitutional Mandate or Myth?," in *Moral Controversies in American Politics*, ed. Byron W. Daynes, 3d ed. (2005), 179–80.

18. Kohn's statement comes from Abigail A. Kohn, "Beyond Fear and Loathing," *Reason*, May 2005, available at http://www.reason.com/news/show/32181 .html.

19. The account of Bellesiles's talk at Irvine comes from Jon Wiener, "Fire at Will," *Nation*, Nov. 4, 2002.

20. Michael A. Bellesiles, *Arming America: The Origins of a National Gun Culture* (2000), 445.

21. On polling data about the Second Amendment, see Joan Biskupic, "Do You Have a Legal Right to Own a Gun?," *USA Today*, Feb. 27, 2008, available at http://www.usatoday.com/news/washington/2008-02-26-guns-cover_N.htm.

22. On the militia theory of the Second Amendment, see Keith A. Ehrman and Dennis A. Henigan, "The Second Amendment in the Twentieth Century: Have You Seen Your Militia Lately?," *University of Dayton Law Review* 15 (1989): 5; Jack N. Rakove, "The Second Amendment: The Highest State of Originalism," *Chicago-Kent Law Review* 76 (2000): 103; David Yassky, "The Second Amendment: Structure, History and Constitutional Change," *Michigan Law Review* 99 (2000): 588.

23. *United States v. Miller*, 307 U.S. 174 (1939).

24. Chief Justice Burger's charge of fraud was recounted in *Silveira v. Lockyer*, 312 F.3d 1052, 1063 (9th Cir. 2002).

25. Edmund S. Morgan, "In Love with Guns," *New York Review of Books*, Oct. 19, 2000, pp. 30–32; Roger Lane, review of Bellesiles, *Arming America*, in *Journal of American History* 88 (2001): 614.

26. Brady Center to Prevent Gun Violence, "HCI/CPHV Congratulate Michael Bellesiles for Receiving the Bancroft Prize," April 18, 2001, available at http://www.bradycampaign.org/media/release.php?release=283.

27. On Bellesiles's talk at Irvine, see Wiener, "Fire at Will."

28. For Lindgren's account of his examination of Bellesiles's research, see James Lindgren, "Fall from Grace: Arming America and the Bellesiles Scandal," *Yale Law Journal* 111 (2002): 2195.

29. Linda Singer's view was quoted in Silverman and Klein, "Plaintiffs Reflect on Gun Ruling," C1. On Switzerland's guns, see David B. Kopel and Stephen D'Andrilli, "The Swiss and Their Guns," *American Rifleman*, Feb. 1990; David B. Kopel, *The Samurai, the Mountie, and the Cowboy: Should America Adopt the Gun Controls of Other Democracies?* (1992), 278–302; Don B. Kates, "Gun Laws around the World: Do They Work?," NRA-ILA, June 11, 2001, available at http://www.nraila.org/Issues/Articles/Read.aspx?ID=72.

30. On suicide with guns, see Andrew J. McClurg, "The Public Health Case for the Safe Storage of Firearms: Adolescent Suicides Add One More 'Smoking Gun,'" *Hastings Law Journal* 51 (2000): 953; Mark Duggan, "Guns and Suicide," in *Evaluating Gun Policy: Effects on Crime and Violence*, ed. Jens Ludwig and Philip J. Cook (2003), 41.

31. On criminals victimizing other criminals, see Philip J. Cook and Jens Ludwig, *Gun Violence: The Real Costs* (2000), chap. 2. The statistics about gang-related homicide in Los Angeles County come from the Los Angeles Almanac, "Gang-Related Crime in Los Angeles County," available at http://www.laalmanac.com/crime/cr03x.htm. See also Mark Greenberg and Harry Litman, "Rethinking Gun Violence," working paper available at http://papers.ssrn.com/sol3/papers.cfm?abstract_id=1531371.

32. On accidental shootings involving children, see Gary Kleck, *Targeting Guns: Firearms and Their Control* (1997), 293–322.

33. On the flood's alleged destruction of Bellesiles's yellow pads, see Jerome Sternstein, "'Pulped' Fiction: Michael Bellesiles and His Yellow Note Pads," History News Network, May 20, 2002, available at http://hnn.us/articles/742.html.

34. On Emory's review, see HNN Staff, "Summary of the Emory Report on Michael Bellesiles," Oct. 25, 2002, available at http://hnn.us/articles/1069.html. On Columbia's rescinding the Bancroft Prize, see Robert F. Worth, "Prize Is Taken Back from Historian," *New York Times*, Dec. 14, 2002.

35. On Burress's touchdown catch, see Tom Canavan, "Late TD Pass to Plaxico Burress the Difference," *USA Today*, Feb. 4, 2008, available at http://www.usatoday.com/sports/football/2008-02-04-1933864190_x.htm. The touchdown can be viewed at http://www.youtube.com/watch?v=uhW1DgHLqAQ.

36. On Burress's bad night at the club, see Mark Maske, "Burress Accidentally Shoots Himself in the Leg," *Washington Post*, Nov. 30, 2008, p. D7; Juliet Macur, "Burress Will Surrender to Authorities on Monday," *New York Times*,

Nov. 30, 2008, p. D1; David B. Kopel, "Free Plaxico Burress," *Wall Street Journal*, Dec. 4, 2008, p. A17. Burress also described the incident to ESPN's Jeremey Schapp in an interview available at http://www.youtube.com/watch?v=bKQzz7vmeYs.

37. See John Feinstein, "Time for Leagues to Do Something about Players with Guns," *Washington Post*, Dec. 1, 2008.

38. On the right to bear arms in state constitutions, see Adam Winkler, "Scrutinizing the Second Amendment," *Michigan Law Review* 105 (2007): 683.

39. On the Second Amendment and the living Constitution, see Eugene Volokh, "The Second Amendment and the Living Constitution," *Huffington Post*, Nov. 20, 2007, available at http://www.huffingtonpost.com/eugene-volokh/the-sec ond-amendment-and-_b_73606.html; David B. Kopel, "The Right to Arms in the Living Constitution," *2010 Cardozo Law Review De Novo* 99. Volokh cites forty-four states with right-to-bear-arms provisions, but one (Massachusetts) interprets its provisions to refer to a militia right, not an individual right.

40. "Repeal the Second Amendment," *Chicago Tribune*, June 26, 2008; Walter Shapiro, "Repeal the Second Amendment," *Salon*, April 18, 2007, available at http://www.salon.com/news/opinion/feature/2007/04/18/second_amend ment/.

41. On Shields, see Richard Harris, "Handguns," *The New Yorker*, July 26, 1976, p. 53. On Brady, see Erik Eckhom, "A Little Gun Control, a Lot of Guns," *New York Times*, August 15, 1993, p. B1.

42. On knives, see U.S. Department of Justice, "Crime in the United States 2008," Expanded Homicide Data Table 11, available at http://www.fbi.gov/ucr/cius2008/offenses/expanded_information/data/shrtable_11.html. On the lawsuits against gun manufacturers, see Timothy D. Lytton, ed., *Suing the Gun Industry: A Battle at the Crossroads of Gun Control and Mass Torts* (2005).

43. On gun control adopted in times of crisis, see Robert J. Spitzer, *The Politics of Gun Control*, 4th ed. (2008); Allen Rostron, "Incrementalism, Rationality, and the Future of Gun Control," *Maryland Law Review* 67 (2008): 513.

44. See Josh Sugarmann, *Assault Weapons and Accessories in America* (1988), 26–27.

45. The Handgun Control, Inc. advertisement ran in the *Washington Post* on July 27, 1990. On the National Matches at Camp Perry, see the competition's website, available at http://www.nrahq.org/compete/nm_campperry.asp.

46. For a critical analysis of the federal ban, see David B. Kopel, "Clueless: The Misuse of BATF Firearms Tracing Data," *Law Review of Michigan State University–Detroit College of Law* (1999): 180; Bruce H. Kobayashi and Joseph E. Olson, "In Re 101 California Street: A Legal and Economic Analysis of Strict Liability for the Manufacture and Sale of 'Assault Weapons,'" *Stanford Law and Policy Review* 8 (1997): 43.

47. On the history of the federal ban on assault weapons, see Spitzer, *Politics of Gun Control*, 130–33; Kopel, "Clueless," 180.

48. On Clinton's crediting the NRA with swinging the 1994 election, see "Clinton Detects Similarities between 2010, 1994, But Says Democrats Can Still Win," FoxNews.com, Feb. 22, 2010, available at http://www.foxnews.com/poli tics/2010/02/22/clinton-detects-similarities-says-democrats-win/.

49. James O'Toole, "Gun Control Efforts Going Nowhere," *Pittsburgh Post-Gazette*, April 19, 2009, p. A5.

50. For Tom Diaz's intemperate remarks, see Tom Diaz, "Invasion of the Chevron Mind-Snatchers," *Fairly Civil* (blog), Nov. 19, 2008, available at http://replay.waybackmachine.org/20090212062611/http://tomdiaz.wordpress.com/2008/11/. On New York's toy gun law, see DeConde, *Gun Violence in America*, 167. On Mayor Nickels of Seattle, see Second Amendment Foundation press release, "Mayor Nickles Admitted He Lacks Ban Authority in 2006 Letter," *PR Newswire*, Dec. 15, 2008. On the kindergartners suspended for finger guns, see "Pupils Suspended over Cops Game," BBC News, April 6, 2000, available at http://news.bbc.co.uk/2/hi/uk_news/education/703759.stm. On the community college in Texas, see Angela K. Brown, "Student Says College Violated Rights by Banning Protest," *Dallas Morning News*, May 23, 2008. On New Orleans gun confiscation, see Rostron, "Incrementalism," 523f.

51. See Sewell Chan, "Annie Hall, Get Your Gun," *City Room* (blog), *New York Times*, Dec. 2, 2008, available at http://cityroom.blogs.nytimes.com/2008/12/02/a-guide-to-city-gun-licenses/.

52. On New York's rules, see *Rules of the City of New York*, title 38, chap. 5, sec. 5-03 (2009); *New York Penal Law*, sec. 265.2 (2005); ibid., sec. 400 (2005); http://www.nyc.gov/html/nypd/html/permits/handgun_licensing_information.shtml.

53. On the Kentucky Courts, see Jim Myers, "Requiem for Kentucky Courts," *Washington Post Magazine*, July 1, 2001, p. 8.

54. On Dick Heller, see "Right to Bear Arms?," NBC News, March 18, 2008, available at http://www.youtube.com/watch?v=ATLvZfYrM10. On Kentucky Courts, see Jim Myers, *Washington Post Magazine*, July 1, 2001, p. 8. On Washington, D.C., in the mid-1970s, see Juan Cameron, "The Washington Tourists Don't Visit," *Fortune*, March 1975, p. 142.

55. On D.C.'s homicide rates, see Duggan, "Crime Data Underscore Limits."

56. On Parker's story, see Elissa Silverman, "Fight against Ban Grew Out of Fear, Frustration," *Washington Post*, April 8, 2007, p. C6; Brian Doherty, "How the Second Amendment Was Restored," *Reason*, Dec. 2008.

Chapter 3: "GUN NUTS"

1. On the happy hour conversation between Neily and Simpson, see Brian Doherty, *Gun Control on Trial: Inside the Supreme Court Battle over the Second Amendment* (2008), 24.

2. On the role of the NRA in the 2000 election, see Allan J. Cigler, "Interest Groups and Financing in the 2000 Election," in *Financing the 2000 Election*, ed. David B. Magleby (2002), 179; Anthony Corrado, "Financing the 2000 Presidential General Election," ibid., 96.

3. Ashcroft's letter to the NRA can be found at http://www.nraila.org/images/Ashcroft.pdf. The memorandum to federal prosecutors can be found at John Ashcroft, "Memorandum to All United States' Attorneys re: United States v.

Emerson, November 9, 2001," available at http://www.ccrkba.org/pub/rkba/Legal/AshcroftMemo.pdf.

4. On James Baker and the Ashcroft letter to the NRA, see Peter H. Brown and Daniel G. Abel, *Outgunned: Up Against the NRA* (2003), 296; speech by James Jay Baker to the 2001 NRA Annual Meeting, May 19, 2001, available at http://www.nraila.org/News/Read/Speeches.aspx?ID=21.

5. The decision in *United States v. Emerson* can be found at 270 F.3d 203 (5th Cir. 2001).

6. On Neily's hard-charging ways, see "Center's General Counsel Discusses Florida's School Voucher Program with Institute for Justice Attorney," Sept. 9, 2004, available at http://www.cfif.org/htdocs/freedomline/current/in_our_opinion/florida_school_voucher.htm.

7. On the Institute for Justice, see its website, www.ij.org.

8. On the libertarians, see David Boaz, *Libertarianism: A Primer* (1997); Stephen A. Newman, *Liberalism at Wits' End: The Libertarian Revolt against the Modern State* (1984); Brian Doherty, *Radicals for Capitalism: A Freewheeling History of the Modern Libertarian Movement* (2007). On the alliance of libertarians and social conservatives in the Republican Party, see Ryan Sager, *The Elephant in the Room: Evangelicals, Libertarians, and the Battle to Control the Republican Party* (2006). On the disappointment of libertarians with the presidency of George W. Bush, see Bruce Bartlett, *Imposter: How George W. Bush Bankrupted America and Betrayed the Reagan Legacy* (2006); Michael Tanner, *Leviathan on the Right: How Big-Government Conservativism Brought Down the Republican Revolution* (2007).

9. On the need for a Supreme Court ruling, see Robert A. Levy, "Anatomy of a Lawsuit: District of Columbia v. Heller," *Engage*, Oct. 2008, p. 27.

10. On the Supreme Court's shrinking docket, see David M. O'Brien, "The Rehnquist Court's Shrinking Plenary Docket," in *Judicial Politics: Readings from Judicature*, ed. Elliot E. Slotnick, 2d ed. (1999), 332; Robert Barnes, "Justices Continue Trend of Hearing Fewer Cases," *Washington Post*, Jan. 7, 2007, p. A4.

11. On Neily's interior designer case, see *Roberts v. Farrell*, 630 F. Supp. 2d 246 (D. Conn. 2009); Lynn Doan, "An Unfair Burden? Interior Decorators Challenge State Law That Limits Use of 'Designer' in Job Description," *Hartford Courant*, Sept. 10, 2008, p. A1. On the equine dentist case, see *Mitz v. Texas State Board of Veterinary Medical Experts*, 278 S.W.3d 17 (Tex. 2008); Clark Neily, "A Certain Lack of Horse Sense Here," *Fort Worth Star-Telegram*, April 23, 2008, p. B13. On the florist case, see *Meadows v. Odom*, 198 Fed. Appx. 348 (La. 2006); Joe Gyan Jr., "Would-be Florists Ask Court to Uproot Exam," *Advocate* (Louisiana), July 7, 2005, p. A7.

12. On the need for a harsh gun law to challenge, see Levy, "Anatomy of a Lawsuit," 27, 29–30.

13. To experience the institute's humor, see its website, www.ij.org.

14. On the Second Amendment being outside of the institute's scope, see Doherty, *Gun Control on Trial*, 24.

15. Mellor's discussions with Simpson and Neily were reported to me in an interview with Clark Neily, Sept. 25, 2009.

16. On Levy's background, see "Cato Institute Names Robert Levy as Chairman, Praises Chairman Emeritus William Niskanen," *PR Newswire*, Sept. 25, 2008. On the friendship between Neily and Levy, and Neily's decision to approach Levy to gain financing for the case, see Clark Neily, "*District of Columbia v. Heller*: The Second Amendment Is Back, Baby," p. 135, available at http://www.cato.org/pubs/scr/2008/Heller_Neily.pdf; interview with Clark Neily, Sept. 25, 2009.

17. See "Cato Institute Names Robert Levy as Chairman."

18. On George Mason's libertarian leanings, see John J. Miller, "A Law School with a Twist," *National Review*, March 13, 2006.

19. On Neily and Levy's shared philosophy, see Levy, "Anatomy of a Lawsuit," 27. Levy's analysis of gun control can be found in Robert A. Levy, "Pistol Whipped: Baseless Lawsuits, Foolish Laws," Cato Institute Policy Analysis Working Paper no. 400, available at http://ssrn.com/abstract=316459. Neily's characterization comes from Neily, "*District of Columbia v. Heller*," 135.

20. On Halbrook, see his website, http://www.stephenhalbrook.com; Robert Ver-Bruggen, "Self-Defense vs. Municipal Gun Bans," *Reason*, June 2005.

21. On Levy and Neily's relationship with Halbrook, see "Memorandum of Points and Authorities in Reply to Opposition to Motion for Recusal of Counsel," *Parker v. District of Columbia*, May 1, 2003, available at http://www.gurapossessky.com/news/parker/documents/Brief_Opposing_Consolidation.pdf. The exact amount Holbrook would have charged Bob Levy to represent the plaintiffs in the *Heller* case remains confidential.

22. Details about Gura's background were reported to me by Gura himself in interview with Alan Gura, Nov. 21, 2008; interview with Alan Gura, Jan. 24, 2009. See also James Taranto, "Alan Gura: How a Young Lawyer Saved the Second Amendment," *Wall St. Journal*, July 19, 2008, p. A7. Both Neily and Levy shared with me how they knew Alan Gura from libertarian circles. See interview with Clark Neily, Sept. 25, 2009; interview with Bob Levy, Sept. 22, 2009.

23. Gura recounted his early career to me in interview with Alan Gura, Jan. 24, 2009.

24. Levy's assessment of Gura's fee and the deal he made with Gura were recounted in Taranto, "Alan Gura," A7. Gura's comment about being the low bidder was told to me in interview with Alan Gura, March 17, 2009.

25. The August meeting with Lund and Cooper was recounted to me in interview with Bob Levy, Sept. 22, 2009. See also "Memorandum of Points and Authorities in Reply to Opposition to Motion for Recusal of Counsel."

26. For Levy's account of the NRA's concerns, see Levy, "Anatomy of a Lawsuit," 27, 30. On the NRA lobbyist's view of the perpetual, crisis-based fund-raising of the NRA, see Richard Feldman, "The NRA Has Lost Sight of Its Mission," *Dallas Morning News*, Jan. 6, 2008; Richard Feldman, *Ricochet: Confessions of a Gun Lobbyist* (2008), 2, 202. A complementary view was offered by the Supreme Court reporter Tony Mauro, who said that a successful Supreme Court case could deprive the NRA of its "loudest fund-raising drum." See Tony Mauro, "Both Sides Fear Firing Blanks If D.C. Gun Case Reaches High Court," Law.com, July 30, 2007, available at http://www.law.com/jsp/article.jsp?id=1185527215310.

27. On Levy's belief that the composition of the Court would likely change in the libertarians' favor, see Levy, "Anatomy of a Lawsuit," 27, 30; Robert A. Levy and Gene Healy, "Battle of the Ban," Cato.org, July 21, 2003, available at http://www.cato.org/pub_display.php?pub_id=3175. On Sandra Day O'Connor's disappointment with the news that Al Gore had been elected president, see Evan Thomas and Michael Isikoff, "The Truth behind the Pillars," *Newsweek*, Dec. 25, 2000, p. 46.

28. On Levy's rebuttal of the NRA's argument, see VerBruggen, "Self-Defense vs. Municipal Gun Bans"; Robert A. Levy and Gene Healy, "Battle of the Ban," July 21, 2003, available at http://www.cato.org/pub_display.php?pub_id=3175.

29. On Lund and Cooper's advice to include a trap door in the lawsuit, see "Memorandum of Points and Authorities in Reply to Opposition to Motion for Recusal of Counsel."

30. Gura's complaint in *Parker v. District of Columbia* can be found at http://www.gurapossessky.com/news/parker/documents/complaint.pdf.

31. On the *Seegars* case, see "Memorandum of Points and Authorities in Reply to Opposition to Motion for Recusal of Counsel"; Levy, "Anatomy of a Lawsuit," 27, 30–31; VerBruggen, "Self-Defense vs. Municipal Gun Bans."

32. For Halbrook's motion to consolidate the cases, see http://www.gurapossessky.com/news/parker/documents/NRAConsolidationMotion.pdf. Gura's view of the NRA's frustration was recounted in "Memorandum of Points and Authorities in Reply to Opposition to Motion for Recusal of Counsel." Levy's view was reported in Levy, "Anatomy of a Lawsuit," 27, 30.

33. On the meeting between Halbrook, Gura, Levy, and Neily, see "Memorandum of Points and Authorities in Reply to Opposition to Motion for Recusal of Counsel." Gura recounted the story of the meeting to me in a conversation on March 17, 2009, as did Levy in a conversation on Sept. 22, 2009.

34. Gura's motion can be found at "Memorandum of Points and Authorities in Reply to Opposition to Motion for Recusal of Counsel."

35. Judge Sullivan's decision not to consolidate the two cases can be found at http://www.gurapossessky.com/news/parker/documents/Second_Denial_of_Consolidation.pdf. On the District of Columbia Personal Protection Act, see Levy and Healy, "Battle of the Ban."

36. Levy's view of the D.C. Personal Protection Act was reported in "Cato Experts: NRA, Sen. Hatch Try to Prevent Supreme Court from Hearing 2nd Amendment Case," July 17, 2003, available at http://www.cato.org/new/07-03/07-17-03r.html. See also Levy, "Anatomy of a Lawsuit," 27, 31.

37. See the U.S. District Court for the District of Columbia, "Memorandum Opinion and Order Granting Defendants' Motion to Dismiss in *Parker v. District of Columbia*," March 31, 2004, available at http://www.gurapossessky.com/news/parker/documents/PARKER_DCT_OPINION.pdf and http://www.gurapossessky.com/news/parker/documents/PARKER_DCT_ORDER.pdf.

38. On the founding of the NRA, see the NRA's website at www.nra.org/aboutus.aspx; Jeffrey L. Rodengen, *NRA: An American Legend*, ed. Melody Maysonet (2002); Osha Gray Davidson, *Under Fire: The NRA and the Battle for Gun Control* (1998), 20–28; Josh Sugarmann, *National Rifle Association: Money, Firepower and Fear* (1992).

39. The quotation about the NRA's antigovernment rhetoric and details about the government subsidies come from Robert J. Spitzer, *The Politics of Gun Control*, 4th ed. (2008), 82–83. More on the government subsidies can be found in Davidson, *Under Fire*, 22–28.

40. The NRA's support of gun control in the early twentieth century is detailed further in chapter 7.

41. On the Second Amendment in *American Rifleman*, see Joan Burbick, *Gun Show Nation* (2006), 73. Burbick's findings were confirmed by reviewing copies of *American Rifleman* from the 1930s through the 1950s. On the NRA Fact Book, see Sugarmann, *National Rifle Association*, 48. On the formation of the Legislation Division, see James B. Trefethen, *Americans and Their Guns: The National Rifle Association Story through Nearly a Century of Service to the Nation* (1967), 292. On the motto on the 1957 NRA headquarters, see Davidson, *Under Fire*, 20.

42. On the NRA's shift from target competition to hunting, see Davidson, *Under Fire*, 28. On the nature of the membership before the 1970s, see Feldman, *Ricochet*, 4. On the decline of hunting, see Burbick, *Gun Show Nation*, 68. On the NRA plan to move west, see Davidson, *Under Fire*, 35.

43. On Harlon Carter's colorful background, see Davidson, *Under Fire*, 31–39; David B. Kopel, "Misfiring on Harlon Carter," *National Review Online*, Aug. 14, 2000, available at http://www.davekopel.com/NRO/2000/Misfiring-at-Harlon-Carter.htm.

44. On the opposition among hard-liners to the NRA plan to move west, see Davidson, *Under Fire*, 31–39.

45. On the ILA, see Feldman, *Ricochet*, 42–44; Davidson, *Under Fire*, 34. On Carter's "Potato Chip" theory of gun control, see ibid., 45.

46. On the ILA "Weekend Massacre," see Davidson, *Under Fire*, 35; Feldman, *Ricochet*, 44.

47. On the Federation of the NRA, see Sugarmann, *National Rifle Association*, 50–51.

48. On Carter and Knox's hostile takeover of the NRA, see Davidson, *Under Fire*, 37–39; Feldman, *Ricochet*, 45–47. On Knox's views about machine-gun laws, see ibid., 46, 75. On Knox's views of the King and Kennedy assassinations, along with his statement about the NRA leader as Monty Hall, see Davidson, *Under Fire*, 238, 300. For Knox's views in his own words, see Neal Knox, *The Gun Rights War: Dispatches from the Front Lines, 1966–2000* (2009).

49. On the growth of the NRA under Harlon Carter, the post-Cincinnati attitude of NRA leaders, and the new motto on the building, see Davidson, *Under Fire*, 134, 194. For more on the new hard-line approach of the NRA, see Spitzer, *Politics of Gun Control*, 86, 98–99; Robert Dreyfuss, "Political Snipers: How the NRA Exploited Loopholes and Waged a Stealth Campaign against the Democrats," in *Guns in America*, ed. Jan Dizard et al. (1999), 234.

50. On compromise as heresy to the new NRA, see Feldman, *Ricochet*, 2; Spitzer, *Politics of Gun Control*, 97.

51. On LaPierre's corporate executive appearance and his comment about being a hard-liner, see Davidson, *Under Fire*, 240–41.

52. LaPierre's statement, from a fund-raising letter, was reported in Morris Dees, *Gathering Storm: America's Militia Threat* (1997), 77.

53. Gingrich's statement was reported in Dreyfuss, "Political Snipers," 233. McCain's statement from the campaign trail was reported in Calvin Woodward, "McCain Says He Backs No Gun Control," Fox News, April 19, 2007, available at http://www.foxnews.com/printer_friendly_wires/2007Apr19/0,46 75,VirginiaTechGunControl2008,00.html.

54. On John Hinckley, see Debra A. Pinals, *Stalking: Psychiatric Perspectives and Practical Approaches* (2007), 239–40; Carol Oyster and David Kopel, "Hinckley, John Warnock, Jr.," in *Guns in American Society*, ed. Gregg Lee Carter, 2 vols. (2002), 1:294–95.

55. On Sarah Brady's gun control activism and involvement with the Brady bill, see Sarah Brady, *A Good Fight* (2002), 92–115.

56. On "lying and buying," see Brady Center to Prevent Gun Violence, *The NRA: A Criminal's Best Friend* (2006), 13.

57. On the old NRA's support of waiting periods, including Frank C. Daniel's statement of support, see Alan Webber, "Where the NRA Stands on Gun Legislation," *American Rifleman*, March 1968, pp. 22–23; Davidson, *Under Fire*, 194.

58. On the new NRA's opposition to the Brady bill, see Spitzer, *Politics of Gun Control*, 136–40; Dennis Henigan, *Lethal Logic: Exploding the Myths that Paralyze American Gun Policy* (2009), 75.

59. On the NRA's killer amendment, see Spitzer, *Politics of Gun Control*, 136–37; Brady Center, *NRA*, 14.

60. On the Republican presidents' support of the Brady bill, see Spitzer, *Politics of Gun Control*, 141. Reagan's statement was reported in Davidson, *Under Fire*, 248. On the NRA's support of Reagan, see Davidson, *Under Fire*, 37–42.

61. On the NICS, see Brady Center, *NRA*, 15. The waiting period was five working days, so weekends and holidays made the actual time longer in some cases.

62. The quotation can be found in Brady Center, *NRA*, 12, and Spitzer, *Politics of Gun Control*, 140.

63. On the NRA's effort to overturn the Brady bill in its entirety, see Brady Center, *NRA*, 12 (2006); Spitzer, *Politics of Gun Control*, 140. The Supreme Court's *Printz* decision can be found at 521 U.S. 898 (1997).

64. On the flaws in the NICS reporting and the Virginia Tech massacre, see Allen Rostron, "Incrementalism, Comprehensive Rationality, and the Future of Gun Control," *Maryland Law Review* 67 (2008): 551–54

65. The NRA lawyer's words and the data on background check denials were reported in Henigan, *Lethal Logic*, 14–15.

66. On the Columbine massacre, see Henigan, *Lethal Logic*, 33–34; Brady Center, *NRA*, 11. See also Brooks Brown and Rob Merritt, *No Easy Answers: The Truth behind Death at Columbine* (2002); Dave Cullen, *Columbine* (2009).

67. For a critique of the idea that there's a "gun show loophole," see David B. Kopel, "The Facts about Gun Shows," *Cato Institute*, Jan. 10, 2000, available at http://www.cato.org/pub_display.php?pub_id=4835. On the real problem being the "secondary market" loophole, see Rostron, "Incrementalism," 556–57; Spitzer, *Politics of Gun Control*, 140; Henigan, *Lethal Logic*, 57; Abigail

Kohn et al., "Straight Shooting on Gun Control: A Reason Debate," *Reason*, May 2005, available at http://www.reason.com/news/show/32181.html.

68. On the percentage of gun sales that go through the secondary market, see Spitzer, *Politics of Gun Control*, 140.

69. The gun show study was detailed at www.gunshowundercover.org.

70. On Anderson's purchase of guns for Harris and Klebold, see Brown and Abel, *Outgunned*, 100–101.

71. On the ATF assessment of the private sale loophole and discussion of the gun control Catch-22, see Henigan, *Lethal Logic*, 56, 150; Rostron, "Incremental-ism," 557.

72. Anderson's remarks were recounted in Henigan, *Lethal Logic*, 33; Brown and Abel, *Outgunned*, 100–101.

73. For Lott's argument, see John R. Lott Jr., *More Guns, Less Crime: Under-standing Crime and Gun-Control Laws* (1998). On the controversy over Lott's claims about relying on national surveys, see Jon Weiner, *Historians in Trouble: Plagiarism, Fraud, and Politics in the Ivory Tower* (2005), 136–48; Mark V. Tushnet, *Out of Range: Why the Constitution Can't End the Battle over Guns* (2007), 95–97.

74. See Tushnet, *Out of Range*, 96.

75. See Weiner, *Historians in Trouble*, 136–48.

76. On Kennesaw's gun mandate, see Davidson, *Under Fire*, 136. On Harrold's guns in schools law, see Andrew Clark, "Weapons: The American School Where Teachers Carry a Pen, a Ruler, and a Gun," *Guardian*, Aug. 18, 2008, p. 3.

77. On the longstanding NRA-law enforcement alliance, see Spitzer, *Politics of Gun Control*, 96–97; Davidson, *Under Fire*, 89; Burbick, *Gun Show Nation*, 47. On the divide between law enforcement and the NRA over recent gun control laws, see Davidson, *Under Fire*, 85–114, 258–59; Brady Center, *NRA*, 4.

78. On the controversy over "cop-killer" bullets, see Davidson, *Under Fire*, 85–95.

79. See ibid., 92.

80. Ibid., 90.

81. On the split between major police groups and the NRA, see Spitzer, *Politics of Gun Control*, 97, 209 n. 67.

82. LaPierre's statements were reported in Henigan, *Lethal Logic*, 140–42.

83. Casey's view is quoted at http://www.saneguns.org/gunlobby/nra_cops.html.

84. On Abrams, see Brady Center, *NRA*, 5, 28; Henigan, *Lethal Logic*, 148.

85. See Larry Pratt, "Gun Control: Unconstitutional and Harmful," March 1997, available at http://gunowners.org/op9701.htm.

86. See Vin Suprynowicz, "Second Amendment: Changing of the Guard," Feb. 18, 1998, available at http://gunowners.org/op9802.htm; Larry Pratt, "Repeal of Semi-Auto Ban Is Only the First Step," March 1996, available at http://gunowners.org/op9607.htm; Larry Pratt, "All Guns Are Machine Guns, Right?," July 2003, available at http://gunowners.org/op0333.htm; Kathryn A. Graham, "Felons and Guns Revisited," Dec. 13, 2003, available at http://gunowners.org/op0368.htm.

87. Zelman's views and the Blueprint can be found on the organization's website, www.jpfo.org.

88. See Joshua Horwitz and Casey Anderson, *Guns, Democracy, and the Insurrectionist Idea* (2009).

89. See "No Compromise against Gun Control," interview of Aaron Zelman, available at http://jpfo.org/articles-assd/no-compromise.htm.

90. See Larry Pratt, "Strange Priorities," Oct. 2001, available at http://gunown ers.org/op0136.htm; Larry Pratt, "Did Gun Control Lead to 9/11?," Jan. 2004, available at http://gunowners.org/op0401.htm.

91. Paul's statements were found in a video interview available at http://youtube .com/watch?v=xdxTg9x3Mbg.

92. For examinations of the militias and their Second Amendment inspiration, Robert L. Snow, *Terrorists Among Us: The Militia Threat* (2002), 111, 151; David Helvarg, "The Anti-Enviro Connection," in *Guns in America*, ed. Jan E. Dizard et al. (1999), 445.

93. On Waco, Ruby Ridge, and the Brady bill as sparks for the militia movement, see Snow, *Terrorists Among Us*, 22; Daniel Levitas, *The Terrorist Next Door* (2002), 301. On the number of militias, see Joe Mandak, "Militias: Is It All Talk or a Real Danger?: Waning Memberships in the Groups in Pennsylvania and Other States Not Seen as a Death Knell," *Pittsburgh Post-Gazette*, May 31, 2004, p. B14.

94. Wayne LaPierre, *The Global War on Your Guns: Inside the U.N. Plan to Destroy the Bill of Rights* (2006), xvii, 45–46, 59, 91, 221.

95. Burbick's assessment can be found in Burbick, *Gun Show Nation*, 170. On Koernke, see Dees, *Gathering Storm*, 87.

96. On the Oklahoma City bombing, see Lou Michael and Dan Herbeck, *American Terrorist: Timothy McVeigh and the Oklahoma City Bombing* (2001). See also Snow, *Terrorists Among Us*, 94–104; Joel Dyer, *Harvest of Rage: Why Oklahoma City Is Only the Beginning* (1998), 214–35; Brady Center, *NRA*, 23. On McVeigh's relationship with the NRA, see Davidson, *Under Fire*, 296. On the militia that asked McVeigh to leave, see David B. Kopel, "The Militias Are Coming," *Reason*, Aug./Sept. 1996, available at http://reason.com/ archives/1996/08/01/the-militias-are-coming.

97. On the NRA's disavowing of the militias, see "Policy Statement of the National Rifle Association on Extremist Organizations and Militia Groups," June 7, 1995. See also Feldman, *Ricochet*, 239. On T. J. Johnston and Richard Mack, see Leonard Zeskind, "Armed and Dangerous: The NRA, Militias and White Supremacists Are Fostering a Network of Right Wing Warriors," *Rolling Stone*, Nov. 2, 1995.

98. Abigail Kohn's informed view of gun owners was reported in Kohn et al., "Straight Shooting on Gun Control." The polling data come from Tom W. Smith, *2001 National Gun Policy Survey of the National Opinion Research Center: Research Findings* (Dec. 2001), esp. table 11. For further evidence of the support for gun control among gun owners, see the poll discussed in E. J. Dionne Jr., "Beyond the NRA's Absolutism," *Washington Post*, Dec. 10, 2009.

99. The departure of the initial D.C. lawyer in the case, the missed deadlines, and Gura's words were reported in Doherty, *Gun Control on Trial*, 56–57, 63.

100. This meeting was described to me by Gura, interview with Alan Gura, March

17, 2009. A similar account is provided in Doherty, *Gun Control on Trial*, 63–64.

101. Gura's characterization of Halbrook's theory as "crazy" was told to me in interview with Alan Gura, March 17, 2009. For the Ashcroft memorandum, see Ashcroft, "Memorandum to All United States' Attorneys re: United States v. Emerson."

102. On the DOJ's raising of the standing issue, see Doherty, *Gun Control on Trial*, 64. The D.C. Circuit Court ruling throwing out the *Seegars* case can be found at 396 F.3d 1248 (D.C. Cir. 2005).

103. On the recruitment of plaintiffs, see Levy, "Anatomy of a Lawsuit," 27–29; Paul Duggan, "Lawyer Who Wiped Out D.C. Ban Says It's about Liberties, Not Guns," *Washington Post*, March 18, 2007, p. A1; Taranto, "Alan Gura," A7; Doherty, *Gun Control on Trial*, 27–40; John Gibeaut, "A Shot at the Second Amendment," *American Bar Association Journal*, Nov. 2007, available at http://abajournal.com/magazine/a_shot_at_the_second_amendment/.

104. On the influence of the NAACP on the libertarian lawyers, see Levy, "Anatomy of a Lawsuit," 29.

105. On the six plaintiffs, see Doherty, *Gun Control on Trial*, 28–40. Gura's statement was reported in Elissa Silverman and Allison Klein, "Plaintiffs Reflect on Gun Ruling," *Washington Post*, March 11, 2007, p. C1. A few of the plaintiffs were featured in Harry Jaffe, "DC Gun Rights: Do You Want This Next to Your Bed," *Washingtonian*, March 1, 2008, available at http://www.washingtonian.com/articles/people/6732.html.

106. On Heller's attempt to register a handgun, see Doherty, *Gun Control on Trial*, 40–41, 67; Levy, "Anatomy of a Lawsuit," 27.

107. The D.C. Circuit Court ruling on the standing of Gura's plaintiffs was *Parker v. District of Columbia*, 478 F.3d 370 (D.C. Cir. 2007).

108. On Heller, see Doherty, *Gun Control on Trial*, 39–40; Brian Doherty, "How the Second Amendment Was Restored: The Inside Story of How a Gang of Libertarian Lawyers Made Constitutional History," *Reason*, Dec. 2008.

109. Levy's remark was found in Levy, "Anatomy of a Lawsuit," 31.

Chapter 4: GUNS OF OUR FATHERS

1. For a comprehensive study of law review articles on the Second Amendment, see Robert J. Spitzer, "Lost and Found: Researching the Second Amendment," *Chicago-Kent Law Review* 76 (2000): 349.

2. On the "standard model" label, see Carl T. Bogus, "The History and Politics of Second Amendment Scholarship: A Primer," *Chicago-Kent Law Review* 76 (2000): 22. The terminology was coined in Glenn Harlan Reynolds, "A Critical Guide to the Second Amendment," *Tennessee Law Review* 62 (1995): 463.

3. See Robert A. Sprecher, "The Lost Amendment," *American Bar Association Journal* 51 (1965): 699. On Sprecher's article, see Bogus, "History and Politics of Second Amendment Scholarship," 5–8.

4. See Reynolds, "Critical Guide to the Second Amendment," 461.

5. On the NRA funding of pro-individual-rights scholarship, see Bogus, "History and Politics of Second Amendment Scholarship," 22.

6. On the emergence of the New Right and its ties to the Second Amendment, see Reva B. Siegel, "Dead or Alive: Originalism as Popular Constitutionalism in Heller," *Harvard Law Review* 122 (2008): 191. Richard A. Viguerie, one of the leaders of the movement, described it in his book *New Right: We're Ready to Lead* (1981).

7. On the need for "counterrights," see Steven Teles, *The Rise of the Conservative Legal Movement* (2008), 87. On the establishment of conservative think tanks, see Bruce J. Schulman and Julian E. Zelizer, *Rightward Bound: Making America Conservative in the 1970s* (2008): 152–68. On the establishment of the Second Amendment Foundation, see Siegel, "Dead or Alive," 209–10.

8. On the birth of originalism, see Teles, *Rise of the Conservative Legal Movement*; Siegel, "Dead or Alive," 191. Jackson's remark comes from his concurring opinion in the landmark Supreme Court decision *Youngstown Sheet & Tube Co. v. Sawyer*, 343 U.S. 579 (1952). For discussion about the founders' intention to give courts the power of judicial review, see Gordon S. Wood, *The Creation of the American Republic, 1776–1787* (1969): 291–305; Sylvia Snowiss, *Judicial Review and the Law of the Constitution* (1990).

9. On Scalia's role in the Ford Administration, see Joan Biskupic, *American Original: The Life and Constitution of Supreme Court Justice Antonin Scalia* (2009): 38–43.

10. On Scalia's role with the early Federalist Society, see Teles, *Rise of the Conservative Legal Movement*, 141; Biskupic, *American Original*, 76–78.

11. On the conservative public interest firms, see Teles, *Rise of the Conservative Legal Movement*, 58–89, 220–64.

12. On Meese and the Reagan administration's impact on conservative legal change, see Teles, *Rise of the Conservative Legal Movement*, 141–45, 157–60.

13. The story of the Glorious Revolution told here was cobbled together from a number of sources. Among the most helpful are G. M. Trevelyan, *The English Revolution, 1688–1689* (1938); John Miller, *The Glorious Revolution*, 2d ed. (1997); Maurice Ashley, *The Glorious Revolution of 1688* (1966); Edward Vallance, *The Glorious Revolution: 1688—Britain's Fight for Liberty* (2009).

14. On the Magna Carta, see James Clark Holt, *Magna Carta*, rev. ed. (1992).

15. On James's abuse of the Militia and Game Acts, see Joyce Lee Malcolm, *To Keep and Bear Arms: The Origins of an Anglo-American Right* (1996), 103–5; Joyce Lee Malcolm, "The Right of the People to Keep and Bear Arms: The Common Law Tradition," *Hastings Constitutional Law Quarterly* 10 (1983): 303–4; Joyce Lee Malcolm, "The Role of the Militia in the Development of the Englishman's Right to be Armed—Clarifying the Legacy," *Journal of Firearms and Public Policy* 5 (1993): 143; Robert Hardaway et al., "The Inconvenient Militia Clause of the Second Amendment: Why the Supreme Court Declines to Resolve the Debate over the Right to Bear Arms," *St. John's Journal of Legal Commentary* 16 (2002): 67. On the repressive dynamics of game laws generally, see Stephen P. Halbrook, *That Every Man Be Armed: The Evolution of a Constitutional Right* (1994): 41–43, 51. On 98 percent of Englishmen being Protestant, see Don B. Kates Jr., "Handgun Prohi-

bition and the Original Meaning of the Second Amendment," *Michigan Law Review* 82 (1983): 237.

16. Blackstone's account of the right to bear arms and the English cases from the 1700s can be found in Halbrook, *That Every Man Be Armed*, 49–54.

17. On disarmament in the colonies, see Halbrook, *That Every Man Be Armed*, 58–65; Stephen P. Halbrook, "Encroachments of the Crown on the Liberty of the Subject: Pre-Revolutionary Origins of the Second Amendment," *University of Dayton Law Review* 15 (1989): 103–18.

18. On George Washington's guns, see Ashley Halsey Jr., "George Washington's Favorite Guns," *American Rifleman*, Feb. 1968, p. 23.

19. On Jefferson's guns, see Ashley Halsey Jr. and John M. Snyder, "Jefferson's Beloved Guns," *American Rifleman*, Nov. 1968, p. 17. The quotation comes from a letter Jefferson wrote to Peter Carr on Aug. 19, 1785, which is reprinted in *The Papers of Thomas Jefferson*, ed. Julian P. Boyd et al., vol. 8 (1953), 405, 407.

20. On Paul Revere's ride and the incidents at Concord and Lexington, see Brendan Morrissey, *Boston 1775: The Shot Heard Around the World* (1995), 35–48; David Hackett Fischer, *Paul Revere's Ride* (1994). The famous line about the first shot fired in Concord comes from Ralph Waldo Emerson, "Concord Hymn" (1837).

21. Kates shared this story with me in interview with Don Kates, Oct. 9, 2009, and in an email exchange on Nov. 18, 2009.

22. Kates told me the details of his background in interview with Don Kates, Oct. 9, 2009. For additional information, see Frank Rossi, "Taking Both Sides of a Heated Issue," *Philadelphia Inquirer*, July 8, 1988; Victor S. Navasky, "The Yales vs. the Harvards (Legal Division)," *New York Times*, Sept. 11, 1966; Tracie L. Thompson, "Unconventional Lawyer on the Cutting Edge," *Los Angeles Daily Journal*, Nov. 19, 1992, p. 5.

23. Kates's first article on guns was Don B. Kates Jr., "Why a Civil Libertarian Opposes Gun Control," *Civil Liberties Review* 3 (June/July and Aug./Sept. 1976). The Michigan article was Don B. Kates Jr., "Handgun Prohibition and the Original Meaning of the Second Amendment," *Michigan Law Review* 82 (1983): 204.

24. On the Revolutionary-era declarations, see Halbrook, *That Every Man Be Armed*, 64.

25. On the failure of the Articles of Confederation, see Jack N. Rakove, "The Collapse of the Articles of Confederation," in *The American Founding: Essays on the Formation of the Constitution*, ed. J. Jackson Barlow et al. (1988), 225. On the Anti-Federalists, see Saul Cornell, *The Other Founders: Anti-Federalism and the Dissenting Tradition in America, 1788–1828* (1999).

26. On the fear of a standing army at the command of the president, see Clayton E. Cramer, *Armed America: The Remarkable Story of How and Why Guns Became as American as Apple Pie* (2006), 183.

27. See Kates, "Handgun Prohibition," 222. On the Pennsylvania minority report, see Robert H. Churchill, "Gun Regulation, the Police Power and the Right to Keep Arms in Early America: The Legal Context of the Second Amendment," *Law and History Review* 25 (2007): 168–69.

28. See Kates, "Handgun Prohibition," 222–23.

29. On Madison's original twelve amendments, see Richard E. Labunski, *James Madison and the Struggle for the Bill of Rights* (2006), 237–51, 278–80.

30. See Kates, "Handgun Prohibition," 213–18.

31. See ibid., 215–17. On George Mason's view of the militia, see Halbrook, *That Every Man Be Armed*; Reynolds, "Critical Guide to the Second Amendment," 473.

32. Kates, "Handgun Prohibition," 215, 219. See also Churchill, "Gun Regulation," 171; Thomas Y. Davies, "Recovering the Original Fourth Amendment," *Michigan Law Review* 98 (1999): 622. On arming police departments, see Alexander DeConde, *Gun Violence in America: The Struggle for Control* (2001), 93–94.

33. See Stephen P. Halbrook, *The Founders' Second Amendment: Origins of the Right to Bear Arms* (2008), 166.

34. See Kates, "Handgun Prohibition," 213, 220–21.

35. Neily's characterization comes from Clark Neily, "District of Columbia v. Heller: The Second Amendment Is Back, Baby," *Cato Supreme Court Review, 2007–2008* (2008), 127, 131. On the initial reception of Kates's work by mainstream constitutional scholars, see Don B. Kates, "A Modern Historiography of the Second Amendment," *U.C.L.A. Law Review* 56 (2009): 1216.

36. See Sanford Levinson, "The Embarrassing Second Amendment," *Yale Law Journal* 99 (1989): 637.

37. On the reaction to Levinson, see Bogus, "History and Politics of Second Amendment Scholarship," 12–15; Kates, "Modern Historiography," 1216–17; Saul Cornell, "'Don't Know Much about History': The Current Crisis in Second Amendment Scholarship," *Northern Kentucky Law Review* 29 (2002): 657–58. Tribe's view was recounted in Tony Mauro, "Scholar's Shift in Thinking Angers Liberals," *USA Today*, Aug. 27, 1999.

38. For an analysis of the effect of gun control on the 1988 election, see Dave Kopel, "Gun Control and the 1988 Election," available at http://www.davekopel.com/2A/Mags/1988elec.htm.

39. See Saul Cornell, *A Well-Regulated Militia: The Founding Fathers and the Origins of Gun Control in America* (2006); David Konig, "The Second Amendment: A Missing Transatlantic Context for 'the Right of the People to Keep and Bear Arms,'" *Law and History Review* 22 (2004): 119; David Konig, "The Persistence of Resistance: Civic Rights, Natural Rights, and Property Rights in the Historical Debate over 'the Right of the People to Keep and Bear Arms,'" *Fordham Law Review* 73 (2004): 539.

40. See Neily, "District of Columbia v. Heller," 132.

41. On colonial and Revolutionary-era militia laws, see Churchill, "Gun Regulation," 141–65; Robert H. Churchill, "Gun Ownership in Early America: A Survey of Manuscript Militia Returns," *William and Mary Quarterly*, 3d ser., 60 (2003): 615–42; Saul Cornell and Nathan DeDino, "A Well Regulated Militia: The Early American Origins of Gun Control," *Fordham Law Review* 73 (2004): 508–10; Cramer, *Armed America*, 181.

42. On Berthold Schwarz, see John Read, *Explosives* (2008): 70–71. On the reports of gunpowder dating back to the third century, see W. W. Greener, *The Gun and Its Development*, 9th ed. (2002), 13–15. On the Chinese arrow shooter,

see Will Fowler et al., *The History of Pistols, Revolvers and Submachine Guns* (2008), 11. On the Statute of Northampton, see Earl R. Kruschke, *Gun Control: A Reference Handbook* (1995): 63.

43. On the disarmament of Catholics, see Alexander DeConde, *Gun Violence in America: The Struggle for Control* (2001), 14.

44. On the early colonial gun laws, see Lee Kennett and James Laverne Anderson, *The Gun in America: The Origins of a National Dilemma* (1975), 37–46. On da Vinci's wheel lock, see DeConde, *Gun Violence in America*, 7.

45. On the disarmament of slaves, see Robert J. Cottrol and Raymond T. Diamond, "The Second Amendment: Toward an Afro-Americanist Reconsideration," *Georgetown Law Journal* 80 (1991): 323–34; Clayton E. Cramer, "The Racist Roots of Gun Control," *Kansas Journal of Law and Public Policy* 4 (1995): 17–18. On restrictions on free blacks and people of mixed race, see Cramer, *Armed America*, 30–38. On gun licensing for free blacks, see Cornell and DeDino, "Well Regulated Right," 517.

46. On the disarmament of whites in the colonial and Revolutionary eras, see Churchill, "Gun Regulation," 155–56; DeConde, *Gun Violence in America*, 22; Cramer, *Armed America*, 102, 114, 133–34, 143–44 (2006); Cornell, "'Don't Know Much about History,'" 670; Cornell and DeDino, "Well Regulated Right," 506–8.

47. On the proportion of Loyalists potentially subject to disarmament, see Churchill, "Gun Regulation," 160.

48. On these gun control laws, see Cramer, *Armed America*, 63, 187–90; Cornell and DeDino, "Well Regulated Right," 512; DeConde, *Gun Violence in America*, 21.

49. The Boston law was the act of March 1, 1783, ch. 13, 1783 Mass. Acts, p. 218.

50. See Kates, "Handgun Prohibition," 259–67. The Halbrook article was Stephen P. Halbrook, "To Bear Arms for Self-Defense: Our Second Amendment Heritage," *American Rifleman*, Nov. 1984, p. 28.

51. On Henderson, see Saundra Torry, "Favorites Seen for Appeals Court Posts," *Washington Post*, Feb. 17, 1990, p. B3; "Court Deflates Campaign Finance Law," *USA Today*, May 2, 2003. Bob Levy shared his view of Henderson with me in interview with Robert Levy, Sept. 22, 2009. On Griffith, see Carol D. Leonnig, "Appeals Court Nominee Let His Bar Dues Lapse," *Washington Post*, June 4, 2004, p. A21.

52. On Silberman, see Michelle Goldberg, "The Partisan 'Mastermind' in Charge of Bush's Intel Probe," *Salon.com*, available at http://dir.salon.com/story/news/feature/2004/02/10/silberman/index.html. On his awards from the Federalist Society, see the entry on Laurence H. Silberman on wikipedia.org. On Silberman's originalism, see Peter Robinson, "As It Is Written," *National Review Online*, March 13, 2009, available at http://www.forbes.com/2009/03/12/constitution-originalism-supreme-court-opinions-columnists-justice-scalia.html; "Uncommon Knowledge: Interview with Laurence Silberman," available at http://fora.tv/2009/08/05/Uncommon_Knowledge_Judge_Laurence_Silberman.

53. On Kim's background, see "Todd Kim Named Solicitor General," available at http://www.dcwatch.com/govern/occ060322.htm. Kim's stint on the game

show can be seen at http://www.youtube.com/watch?v=38H2QllyRi4. His stepping in at the last minute to argue the D.C. gun cases was described to me by Alan Morrison in interview with Alan Morrison, Sept. 26, 2009, and by others involved in the litigation.

54. The oral argument in the D.C. circuit court was described to me by Robert Levy, Clark Neily, and Alan Gura. See interview with Robert Levy, Sept. 22, 2009; interview with Clark Neily, Sept. 25, 2009; interview with Alan Gura, Jan. 24, 2009. A website that has an "informal transcript" of the oral argument can be found at http://k-romulus.blogspot.com/2006/12/parker-v-dc-oral-argument-transcript.html.

55. See interview with Robert Levy, Sept. 22, 2009.

56. The D.C. Circuit Court opinion can be found at *Parker v. District of Columbia*, 478 F.3d 370 (D.C. Cir. 2007).

Chapter 5: CIVIL WAR

1. Morrison recounted to me the details about his background and hiring by the District of Columbia. Interview with Alan Morrison, Sept. 25, 2009. See also David Nakamura, "Attorney for D.C. in Gun Ban Case Fired," *Washington Post*, Jan. 3, 2008, p. B1; Tony Mauro, "Moving On: A Nader Protégé with Friends in High Places," *Legal Times*, May 24, 2004.

2. Interview with Alan Morrison, Sept. 25, 2009.

3. On the opposition of gun control groups to the District's appealing to the Supreme Court, see David Nakamura, "D.C. Wants High Court to Hear Gun Case," *Washington Post*, July 17, 2007, p. A1; James Oliphant, "D.C. Gun Case May Hit Chicago," *Chicago Tribune*, Sept. 5, 2007.

4. On Alito's and Roberts's ties to the Federalist Society, see Charles Lane, "Roberts Listed in Federalist Society '97-98 Directory,'" *Washington Post*, July 25, 2005; "Federalist Society," *Right Web*, Nov. 29, 2006, available at http://right web.irc-online.org/profile/Federalist_Society.

5. On Roberts's confirmation hearings, see "Text of John Roberts' Opening Statement," *USA Today*, Sept. 12, 2009, available at http://www.usatoday.com/news/washington/2005-09-12-roberts-fulltext_x.htm; "Profile: John G. Roberts Jr.," *New York Times*, July 1, 2009, available at http://topics.nytimes.com/top/refer ence/timestopics/people/r/john_g_jr_roberts/index.html. Among the notable cases were *Gonzales v. Carhart*, 550 U.S. 124 (2007) (abortion); *Parents Involved in Community Schools v. Seattle School District*, 551 U.S. 701 (2007) (school integration); and *Ledbetter v. Goodyear Tire and Rubber Co., Inc.*, 550 U.S. 618 (2007) (workplace discrimination). Justice Breyer's lament was in his dissenting opinion in *Parents Involved in Community Schools v. Seattle School District*, 551 U.S. 701 (2007) (Breyer, J., dissenting).

6. Sunstein's prediction was announced in Cass R. Sunstein, "Staring Down the Barrel," *Boston Globe*, Dec. 2, 2007. Henigan's view was reported in Oliphant, "D.C. Gun Case May Hit Chicago."

7. Kim would not discuss his position with me, but his view was confirmed by other reliable sources, who wish to remain anonymous.

8. Interview with Alan Morrison, Sept. 25, 2009; interview with Walter Del-linger, Sept. 24, 2009; Nakamura, "D.C. Wants High Court to Hear Gun Case," A1; Adrian M. Fenty and Linda Singer, "Fighting for Our Handgun Ban," *Washington Post*, Sept. 4, 2007, p. A17.

9. On the Supreme Court's interest in "circuit splits," see Stefanie A. Lindquist and David E. Klein, "The Influence of Jurisprudential Considerations on Supreme Court Decisionmaking: A Study of Conflict Cases," *Law and Society Review* 40 (2006): 136.

10. On the outrage of the Gura team, see Brian Doherty, *Gun Control on Trial* (2008), 83. Levy reported his arrangement of the meeting in interview with Robert Levy, Sept. 22, 2009. The date and the participants of the NRA meet-ing were relayed to me in interview with Clark Neily, Sept. 25, 2009. The quo-tations came from Doherty, *Gun Control on Trial*, 83; Robert A. Levy, "Should Congress or the Courts Decide D.C. Gun Ban's Fate?," *Examiner*, April 3, 2007, available at http://www.examiner.com/a-653443~Robert_A__Levy__ Should_Congress_or_the_courts_decide_D_C__gun_ban_s_fate_.html.

11. Neily's reaction was reported to me in interview with Clark Neily, Sept. 25, 2009.

12. This incident was reported to me in interview with Robert Levy, Sept. 22, 2009.

13. Interview with Alan Morrison, Sept. 24, 2009.

14. *Printz v. United States*, 521 U.S. 898 (1997).

15. Ibid. (Thomas, J., concurring).

16. Maxine Burkett, "Much Ado about . . . Something Else: D.C. v. Heller, the Racialized Mythology of the Second Amendment, and Gun Policy Reform" (unpublished manuscript) (2008), available at http://papers.ssrn.com/sol3/ papers.cfm?abstract_id=1111768.

17. On the Klan's raid on Williams's home, see Lou Falkner Williams, *The Great South Carolina Ku Klux Klan Trials, 1871–1872* (1996), 76–80; Jerry L. West, *The Reconstruction Ku Klux Klan in York County, South Carolina, 1865–1877* (2002), 123–24; Stephen P. Halbrook, *Freedmen, the Fourteenth Amendment, and the Right to Bear Arms, 1866–1876* (1998), 141–44; Louis F. Post, "A 'Car-petbagger' in South Carolina," *Journal of Negro History* 10 (1925): 10. On the uniforms of the early Klan, see Allen W. Trelease, *White Terror: The Ku Klux Klan Conspiracy and Southern Reconstruction* (1971), 4–5, 53; James Michael Martinez, *Carpetbaggers, Cavalry, and the Ku Klux Klan: Exposing the Invis-ible Empire during Reconstruction* (2007), 1–6.

18. On the southern fear of blacks with guns, see West, *Reconstruction Ku Klux Klan in York County*, 58; Trelease, *White Terror*, xxii, xlii. On the Louisiana slave revolt of 1811, see Robert L. Paquette, "'A Horde of Brigands?' The Great Louisiana Slave Revolt of 1811 Reconsidered," *Historical Reflections* 35 (2009): 72; Harvey Wish, "American Slave Insurrections before 1861," *Journal of Negro History* 22 (1937): 299. On Turner's slave revolt, see Stephen B. Oates, *The Fires of Jubilee: Nat Turner's Fierce Rebellion* (1975).

19. On the disarmament of free blacks in the early 1800s, see Burkett, "Much Ado about . . . Something Else"; Clayton Cramer, "The Racist Roots of Gun Con-

trol," *Kansas Journal of Law and Public Policy* 42 (1995): 17. The North Carolina case was *State v. Newsom*, 27 N.C. 250 (1844).

20. On the militias in the War of 1812, see Carl Edward Skeen, *Citizen Soldiers in the War of 1812* (1999); DeConde, *Gun Violence in America*, 42–43.

21. On the repurposing of militias into slave patrols, see Clayton E. Cramer, *Armed America: The Remarkable Story of How and Why Guns Became as American as Apple Pie* (2006), 185; Robert J. Cottrol and Raymond T. Diamond, "The Second Amendment: Toward an Afro-Americanist Reconsideration," *Georgetown Law Journal* 80 (1991): 337–38; Burkett, "Much Ado about . . . Something Else."

22. On the state constitutional guarantees of the right to bear arms in the early 1800s, see Saul Cornell, *A Well-Regulated Militia: The Founding Fathers and the Origins of Gun Control in America* (2006), 142.

23. See Timothy S. Huebner, "Roger B. Taney and the Slavery Issues," *Journal of American History* 97 (2010): 17; Don E. Fehrenbacher, "Rober B. Taney and the Sectional Crisis," *Journal of Southern History* 43 (1977): 555.

24. On the Palmetto Guard, see Cornell, *Well-Regulated Militia*, 167.

25. On the Union soldiers buying their guns, see Noah Andre Trudeau, *Out of the Storm: The End of the Civil War, April–June 1865* (1995), 379. On the advice to black soldiers, see Alexander DeConde, *Gun Violence in America: The Struggle for Control* (2001), 73.

26. On the Black Codes, see Eric Foner, *Reconstruction: America's Unfinished Revolution, 1863–1877* (2002), 199–202. On the disarmament provisions of the Black Codes, see Cottrol and Diamond, "Second Amendment," 345; David B. Kopel, "The Klan's Favorite Law," *Reason*, Feb. 15, 2005, available at http://reason.com/archives/2005/02/15/the-klans-favorite-law; Cornell, *Well-Regulated Militia*, 168–69.

27. On the post–Civil War posses, see Trelease, *White Terror*, xlv–xlvi, 51; Cornell, *Well-Regulated Militia*, 169.

28. On the origin of the KKK, see Trelease, *White Terror*, 3–12.

29. On the origin of the name Ku Klux Klan, see ibid., 4, 61.

30. On the many commercial items with the Klan name, see ibid., 60.

31. On the spread of the Klan name, see ibid., 10–12.

32. On Carroll, see West, *Reconstruction Ku Klux Klan in York County*, 35. On the Klan goal of white supremacy and strategy of disarmament, see Trelease, *White Terror*, 29; Kopel, "Klan's Favorite Law."

33. On Spooner and Tiffany, see Cornell, *Well-Regulated Militia*, 153–54; Akhil Reed Amar, *The Bill of Rights: Creation and Reconstruction* (1998), 262. On Beecher, see Debby Applegate, *The Most Famous Man in America: The Biography of Henry Ward Beecher* (2006), 280–83; Cornell, *Well-Regulated Militia*, 155.

34. On the events surrounding the beating of Sumner, see William Cullen Bryant II, *Power for Sanity: Selected Editorials of William Cullen Bryant, 1829–1861* (1994), 289–90; Daniel Wait Howe, *Political History of Secession to the Beginning of the American Civil War* (1914), 271–72; Cornell, *Well-Regulated Militia*, 155–56 (2006).

35. Sickles's order is discussed in Cornell, *Well-Regulated Militia*, 170.

36. On the Freedmen's Bureau and the Civil Rights Act of 1866—and their focus on the right of freedmen to have guns for self-defense—see Halbrook, *Freedmen*, 1–32.

37. On John Bingham, see Garrett Epps, *Democracy Reborn: The Fourteenth Amendment and the Fight for Equal Rights in Post-Civil War America* (2007), 95–98, 168–71.

38. These statements were recounted in Amar, *Bill of Rights*, 183, 187.

39. See ibid., 266.

40. Doolittle's statement was reported in *Congressional Globe*, 40th Cong., 2d sess., 1867, p. 1644.

41. On the history of lynching, see Sherrilyn A. Ifill, *On the Courthouse Lawn: Confronting the Legacy of Lynching in the Twenty-first Century* (2007); "Lynching," in Cyndi Banks, *Punishment in America: A Reference Handbook* (2005), 90–91.

42. On the Klan's seizure of black militia weapons, see DeConde, *Gun Violence*, 74.

43. On the Colfax Massacre of 1873, see Charles Lane, *The Day Freedom Died* (2009); LeeAnna Keith, *The Colfax Massacre: The Untold Story of Black Power, White Terror, and the Death of Reconstruction* (2008).

44. See Leonard Williams Levy, "United States v. Cruikshank," *Encyclopedia of the American Constitution*, ed. Leonard Williams Levy et al., vol. 2 (1986), 527.

45. Alan Morrison, himself a runner, recounted the history of Nickles's relationships with Fenty and Singer. Interview with Alan Morrison, Sept. 25, 2009.

46. On Nickles and the Bank of America lawsuit, see Carol D. Leonnig, "Fenty General Counsel Halted Action against Bank in Tax Fraud Case," *Washington Post*, Jan. 28, 2008, p. B1. The District did eventually file suit against Bank of America.

47. See David Nakamura and Carol D. Leonnig, "Attorney General Quits; Clash with Fenty Aide Cited; Top Lawyer Felt Sidelined," *Washington Post*, Dec. 18, 2007, p. B1.

48. On the objection to Nickles's appointment, see Michael Neibauer, "D.C. Council Panel Rejects Peter Nickles as Attorney General," *Washington Examiner*, Nov. 18, 2008.

49. Interview with Alan Morrison, Sept. 25, 2009.

50. On Morrison's firing, see Tony Mauro, "Alan Morrison Is Benched," *BLT: Blog of the Legal Times*, Jan. 2, 2008, available at http://legaltimes.typepad.com/blt/2008/01/alan-morrison-i.html.

51. For Nickles's defense of Morrison's firing, see Nakamura, "Attorney for D.C. in Gun Ban Case Fired," B1. Vladeck's reaction to the Morrison firing was reported ibid.

52. On Mendelson's reaction to the Morrison firing, see ibid.

53. Details of the Montana threat to secede over the *Heller* case can be found at http://gunowners.org/op0820.htm.

Chapter 6: THE WILD WEST

1. All quotations from the Supreme Court oral argument come from the transcript available at http://www.supremecourtus.gov/oral_arguments/argu

ment_transcripts/07-290.pdf. For purposes of clarity, I have cleaned up the transcript to eliminate stutters or repetitions. On the friezes in the Supreme Court, see http://www.supremecourtus.gov/about/north&southwalls.pdf.

2. On the Supreme Court spittoons, see Joan Biskupic, "Supreme Court Holds to Tradition," *USA Today*, March 19, 2007. On Minton, see Kim Isaac Eisler, *A Justice for All: William J. Brennan, Jr. and the Decisions That Transformed America* (1993), 96; Bernard Schwartz, *Inside the Warren Court* (1983), 66.

3. On the Supreme Court Building, see http://www.supremecourtus.gov/about/courtbuilding.pdf.

4. On Dellinger, see David Nakamura, "An Old Hand at Court Gears Up for Battle," *Washington Post*, March 18, 2008, p. B1. On Dellinger's graciousness to Gura, see David Kopel, "Oral Argument in DC v. Heller: The View from the Counsel Table," March 31, 2008, available at http://www.davekopel.com/Corner/2008-January-to-March.htm.

5. On Dellinger, see Nakamura, "Old Hand," B1.

6. Interview with Walter Dellinger, Sept. 24, 2009.

7. On Dellinger's other Supreme Court cases, see Nakamura, "Old Hand," B1; interview with Walter Dellinger, Sept. 24, 2009.

8. On Kennedy's upbringing and education at the London School of Economics, see Jeffrey Toobin, "Swing Shift," *The New Yorker*, Sept. 12, 2005.

9. On Ted Kennedy's famous "Robert Bork's America" speech, see John Vile et al., "Robert H. Bork," in *Great American Judges* (2003), 111, 115. On Bork's confirmation hearings and the role of privacy in that battle, see Robert F. Nagel, *Judicial Power and American Character* (1996), 28.

10. On Ginsburg's failed nomination, see Stephen L. Carter, *The Confirmation Mess* (1995), 6–7; Michael J. Gerhardt, *The Federal Appointments Process* (2003), 196.

11. On Kennedy's confirmation hearings, see Linda Greenhouse, *Becoming Justice Blackmun: Harry Blackmun's Supreme Court Journey* (2006), 189.

12. On the privacy of the Supreme Court Justices' conference, see "How the Court Works," available at http://www.supremecourthistory.org/03_how/subs_how/03_a09.html.

13. On Kennedy's abortion flip-flop, see Nina Totenberg, "Documents Reveal Battle to Preserve 'Roe,'" National Public Radio, available at http://www.npr.org/templates/story/story.php?storyId=1745254; Jan Crawford Greenburg, *Supreme Conflict: The Inside Story of the Struggle for Control of the United States Supreme Court* (2007), 155–56.

14. The Colorado case was *Romer v. Evans*, 517 U.S. 620 (1996). *Lawrence v. Texas* can be found at 539 U.S. 558 (2003). For an example of a constitutional scholar who believes Kennedy's decisions might lead to same-sex marriage protection, see David M. Wagner, "Beyond 'Strange New Respect,'" *Weekly Standard*, March 14, 2005.

15. On conservatives' denouncements of Kennedy, see Wagner, "Beyond 'Strange New Respect'"; Rich Lowry, "America's Worst Justice," *National Review Online*, July 1, 2008; Toobin, "Swing Shift."

16. Interview with Walter Dellinger, Sept. 24, 2009.

17. Gura's view of Kennedy was shared with me in interview with Alan Gura, Jan. 24, 2009. The quotation comes from James Taranto, "Alan Gura: How a Young

Lawyer Saved the Second Amendment," *Wall Street Journal*, July 19, 2008, p. A7. On Gura's libertarianism, see "Alan Gura: The High Stakes of the DC Gun Ban Case," available at http://youtube.com/watch?v=hFDlVgIgr8E.

18. No two accounts of the Shootout at the O.K. Corral are exactly alike. My own was based on these sources: Paula Mitchell Marks, *And Die in the West: The Story of the O.K. Corral Gunfight* (1996); Bill O'Neal, *Encyclopedia of Western Gunfighters* (1991); Joseph G. Rosa, *The Gunfighter: Man or Myth?* (1980); and Steven Lubet, *Murder in Tombstone: The Forgotten Trial of Wyatt Earp* (2006).

19. On the cultural legacy of the Shootout at the O.K. Corral, see Allen Barra, *Inventing Wyatt Earp: His Life and Many Legends* (2009), 6.

20. On the immigrants to the western frontier, see R. W. Mondy, "Analysis of Frontier Social Instability," *Southwestern Social Science Quarterly* 24 (1943): 167; Joe B. Frantz, "The Frontier Tradition: An Invitation to Violence," in *The History of Violence in America* (1969). On the increasing popularity of handguns after the Civil War, see Don Kates, "Toward a History of Handgun Prohibition," in *Restricting Handguns* (1989); Carl P. Russell, *Guns on the Early Frontier* (1962). On Colt, see William Hosley, "Guns, Gun Culture, and the Peddling of Dreams," in *Guns in America: A Reader*, ed. Jan E. Dizard et al. (1999), 47–85.

21. Turner's landmark paper is reprinted in Frederick Jackson Turner, *The Frontier in American History* (1920), 1–38.

22. See John Mack Faragher, *Rereading Frederick Jackson Turner: "The Significance of the Frontier in American History" and Other Essays* (1994).

23. James Truslow Adams, "Our Lawless Heritage," *Atlantic Monthly*, Dec. 1928, p. 732. The quotation about law on one's hip is from Henry Sinclair Drago, *The Great Range Wars: Violence on the Grasslands* (1970), 93. On today's violence as a legacy of the frontier, see Robert Weisberg, "Values, Violence, and the Second Amendment: American Character, Constitutionalism, and Crime," *Houston Law Review* 39 (2002): 1; Adams, "Our Lawless Heritage"; Frantz, "Frontier Tradition."

24. W. Eugene Hollon, *Frontier Violence: Another Look* (1974), 195; Ray Allen Billington, *Westward Expansion: A History of the American Frontier*, 3d ed. (1967), 678.

25. Robert R. Dykstra, *The Cattle Towns* (1968).

26. On homicide in Tombstone and Deadwood, see Richard Shenkman, *Legends, Lies, and Cherished Myths of American History* (1988), 112.

27. On visitors to Virginia City, see Robert Athearn, *Westward the Briton* (1953), 59–60. Shenkman's view was expressed in Shenkman, *Legends, Lies, and Cherished Myths*, 112.

28. On crime on the frontier, see Michael N. Canlis, "The Evolution of Law Enforcement in California," *Far-Westerner* 1 (1961): 1; Harry H. Anderson, "Deadwood, South Dakota: An Effort at Stability," *Montana: The Magazine of Western History*, Jan. 1970. On the paucity of locks, see Hollon, *Frontier Violence*, 209–11; Holden, "Law and Lawlessness on the Texas Frontier, 1875–1890," *Southwestern Historical Quarterly* 44 (1940): 188. For a view of the Wild West that suggests violence was more common, see Roger D. McGrath, *Gunfighters, Highwaymen, and Vigilantes: Violence on the Frontier* (1987).

29. Dykstra's words are from his *Cattle Towns*, 112. On Buffalo Bill, see David Courtwright, *Violent Land* (1996); David B. Kopel, "America's Only Realistic Option: Promoting Responsible Gun Ownership," in *Guns in America*, 459. Hollon's words are from his *Frontier Violence*, 29.

30. See, e.g., Richard Poe, *The Seven Myths of Gun Control: Reclaiming the Truth about Guns, Crime, and the Second Amendment* (2001), 27–29.

31. Dykstra, *Cattle Towns*, 121.

32. Ibid., 121–22. See also Courtwright, *Violent Land*.

33. On Dodge, see Dykstra, *Cattle Towns*, 117.

34. See Clayton Cramer, *Concealed Weapon Laws of the Early Republic: Dueling, Southern Violence, and Moral Reform* (1999); Clayton Cramer, *For the Defense of Themselves and the State: The Original Intent and Judicial Interpretation of the Right to Bear Arms* (1994), 141–64.

35. Cramer, *Concealed Weapon Laws*, 7, available at http://www.claytoncramer .com/popular/duelinganddeliverance.pdf. On James Stephen Hogg's view of concealed weapons, see Alexander DeConde, *Gun Violence in America: The Struggle for Control* (2001), 98.

36. John Potter, *Archaeologia Graeca, or The Antiquities of Greece* (1818), 453; William Blackstone, *Commentaries on the Laws of England*, ed. John Taylor Coleridge, vol. 4 (1825), 149.

37. For early state cases on the constitutionality of concealed carry bans, see *State v. Reid*, 1 Ala. 612 (1840); *State v. Mitchell*, 3 Blackf. 229 (Indiana 1833); *Aymette v. State*, 21 Tenn. 154 (1840); *State v. Buzzard*, 4 Ark. 18 (1842); *State v. Chandler*, 5 La. Ann. 489 (1850). The Kentucky case was *Bliss v. Commonwealth*, 12 Ky. 90 (1822). On the amending of the Kentucky Constitution, see DeConde, *Gun Violence in America*, 52.

38. On Texas, see the act of April 12, 1871, General Laws of Texas, Chapter XXXIV. On Florida, see sec. 7202 of the General Laws of Florida, referred to in *Watson v. Stone*, 4 S.E. 2d 700 (Fla. 1941); *Carlton v. State*, 58 So. 486, 488 (Fla. 1912). On Oklahoma, see 21 Okla. St. Ann. § 1271 (1890) (repealed 1971). Idaho also had a ban on open carry, but it was declared unconstitutional in *In re Brickey*, 70 P. 609 (Ida. 1902).

39. *Mont. Code Ann.*, sec. 45-8-316(1) (amended); 21 Okla. St. Ann., sec. 1271 (1890) (repealed 1971); *State v. Gohl*, 90 P. 259 (Wash. 1907). See also N.Y. Penal Law, sec. 1897 (banning concealed carry of firearms without a license).

40. On Deringer, see Charles G. Worman, *Gunsmoke and Saddle Leather: Firearms in the Nineteenth Century American West* (2005), 262–67. On Lincoln's assassination with a Deringer, see Mike Cumpston and Johny Bates, *Percussion Pistols and Revolvers: History, Performance and Practical Uses* (2005), 25–26.

41. See John Lott Jr. and David Mustard, "Crime, Deterrence, and Right-to-Carry Concealed Handguns," *Journal of Legal Studies* 26 (1997): 19.

42. See Ian Ayres and John J. Donahue, "Shooting Down the 'More Guns, Less Crime' Hypothesis," *Stanford Law Review* 55 (2003): 1272; David Olson and Michael Maltz, "Right-to-Carry Concealed Weapon Laws and Homicide in Large U.S. Counties: The Effect on Weapon Types, Victim Characteristics, and Victim-Offender Relationships," *Journal of Law and Economics* 44 (2001):

762; Dan Black and Daniel Nagin, "Do Right-to-Carry Laws Deter Violent Crime?," *Journal of Legal Studies* 27 (1998): 214.

43. See Ayres and Donahue, "Shooting Down the 'More Guns, Less Crime' Hypothesis," 1202; Lott and Mustard, "Crime, Deterrence, and Right-to-Carry Concealed Handguns," 24.

44. Dykstra, *Cattle Towns*, 137.

45. On the entrepreneurial motives of frontier communities to quell violence, see ibid., 114–15, which includes the quotation from the Caldwell editor.

46. On Ordinance No. 9, see http://www.pr.state.az.us/text/featurestories/tcsh phist/shootout.html.

47. On Thomas's views of oral argument, see Paul Bedard, "This Is Not Perry Mason," *U.S. News & World Report*, Nov. 29, 2007. On Thomas's four-year (and counting) silence, see Tony Mauro, "Does Justice Thomas' Silence Thwart Advocacy?," *National Law Journal*, Feb. 22, 2010, available at http://www.law.com/jsp/article.jsp?id=1202443920475&rss=newswire.

48. On the right to bear arms in state constitutional law and the allowance of reasonable regulation, see Adam Winkler, "Scrutinizing the Second Amendment," *Michigan Law Review* 105 (2007): 683. On Dellinger's sense that he might get Kennedy's vote, see interview with Walter Dellinger, Sept. 24, 2009.

49. Gura recounted his reaction to Kennedy in interview with Alan Gura, Nov. 21, 2008.

Chapter 7: GUNS, GANGSTERS, AND G-MEN

1. On the solicitor general and his influence generally on the Court, see Lincoln Caplan, *The Tenth Justice: The Solicitor General and the Rule of Law* (1987); Rebecca Mae Salokar, *The Solicitor General: The Politics of Law* (1994). For an illustrative study of the SG's influence, see Ryan J. Owens and Ryan C. Black, "Solicitor General Seduction: Influencing Supreme Court Justices to Overcome Their Preferences," available at http://papers.ssrn.com/sol3/papers.cfm?abstract_id=1432822.

2. On Clement's being the youngest SG in half a century, see Greg Stohr, "Clement Will Take Over for Gonzales with Reputation 'Unscathed,'" *Bloomberg News*, Aug. 28, 2007, available at http://www.bloomberg.com/apps/news?pid=washingtonstory&sid=a.oCtftUK.So.

3. On Clement, see Vanessa Blum, "Point Man," *Legal Times*, Jan. 16, 2004; Ameet Sachdev, "Ex-Kirkland Lawyer Named Acting U.S. Attorney General," *Chicago Tribune*, Aug. 28, 2007; Robert Barnes and Amy Goldstein, "A Conservative Insider More at Home in the Law Than in Policy," *Washington Post*, Aug. 28, 2007. On Clement's torture statement, see Stohr, "Clement Will Take Over for Gonzales."

4. On Clement's skills as a SG, see Blum, "Point Man"; Barnes and Goldstein, "Conservative Insider."

5. On the many amicus briefs filed in the D.C. gun case, see Robert Barnes, "D.C. Gun Case Draws Crowd of High Court 'Friends,'" *Washington Post*, March 9, 2008, p. A7.

6. The case referred to here is *Grutter v. Bollinger*, 539 U.S. 306 (2003).

7. For Clement's brief, see Brief for the United States as Amicus Curiae in District of Columbia v. Heller, No. 07-290; Barnes, "D.C. Gun Case Draws Crowd," A7. I've joined two amicus briefs in major Second Amendment cases at the Supreme Court. In *Heller*, my brief argued that the Court should follow the longstanding and uniform approach of state courts interpreting constitutional protections for the right to bear arms and adopt a standard of review permitting the government leeway to enact effective gun control laws. Two years later, in *McDonald v. City of Chicago*, 130 S. Ct. 3020 (2010), the brief I signed on to argued that the Court should read the Constitution to make the individual right to bear arms guaranteed by the Second Amendment applicable to state and local governments, for many of the reasons identified in chapter 5.

8. On Gura's reaction to Clement's brief, see Robert Barnes, "Cheney Joins Congress in Opposing D.C. Gun Ban," *Washington Post*, Feb. 9, 2008, p. A1; interview with Alan Gura on Youtube.com, available at http://youtube.com/watch?v=T86vvEPr3Vw&feature=related.

9. On the hostile response by gun rights advocates to Clement's amicus brief in the gun case, see "Behold a Traitor to the Constitution," *Liberty Zone* (blog), Jan. 14, 2008, available at http://libertyzone.blogspot.com/2008/01/behold-traitor-to-constitution.html; Eric Cantor, "Sign the Petition and Help Protect Our Second Amendment Rights," *Red State* (blog), Jan. 13, 2008, available at http://archive.redstate.com/blogs/rep_eric_cantor/2008/jan/13/sign_the_petition_and_help_protect_our_second_amendment_rights; Jim Shepard, "Hanging Together in the District," *Shooting Wire*, Jan. 14, 2008, available at http://www.shootingwire.com/archives/2008-01-14; Barnes, "D.C. Gun Case Draws Crowd," p. A7; Jonathan Adler, "Fred Hits DoJ for 'Overlawyering Gun Rights Case,'" *Corner* (blog), *National Review Online*, Jan. 16, 2006, available at http://corner.nationalreview.com/post/?q=ZDhjN2M5YzZjM2IwN2IwNm U1ZjRlZjEyYzgwNGRjYTM=; "Misfire at Justice," *Wall Street Journal*, Jan. 22, 2008, p. A18; Barnes, "Cheney Joins Congress," A1.

10. On the White House's being stunned, see Robert D. Novak, "Gun Battle at the White House?," *Washington Post*, March 13, 2008, p. A17. On the credulousness of the White House's being stunned, see Marty Lederman, "Novak, Clement, Cheney, and the Gun Case," *SCOTUSblog*, March 13, 2008, available at http://www.scotusblog.com/wp/novak-clement-cheney-and-the-gun-case/print/.

11. See John Ashcroft, "Memorandum to All United States' Attorneys re: United States v. Emerson," Nov. 9, 2001, available at http://www.ccrkba.org/pub/rkba/Legal/AshcroftMemo.pdf.

12. On Cheney's brief, see Linda Greenhouse, "Gun Case Causes Bush Administration Rift," *New York Times*, March 17, 2008; Barnes, "Cheney Joins Congress," A1.

13. On the possibility of Clement's reversing course at oral argument, see Novak, "Gun Battle at the White House?," A17; Lederman, "Novak, Clement, Cheney, and the Gun Case." Ken Starr's assessment of Clement's sense of institutional integrity was reported in Barnes and Goldstein, "Conservative Insider."

14. Two twentieth-century federal laws regulated guns prior to the 1930s. In 1919, Congress imposed a 10 percent tax on manufacturers as a revenue-raising measure. In 1927 Congress outlawed the sending of concealable firearms through the U.S. Postal Service. The 1927 law did not prohibit shipping of concealable firearms by other methods, like private postal services. See Franklin E. Zimring, "Firearms and Federal Law: The Gun Control Act of 1968," *Journal of Legal Studies* 4 (1975): 135–36.

15. On the tradition of state and local criminal law enforcement, see Mary M. Stolberg, "Policing the Twilight Zone: Federalizing Crime Fighting during the New Deal," *Journal of Policy History* 7 (1995): 393. See also Kenneth O' Reilly, "A New Deal for the FBI: The Roosevelt Administration, Crime Control, and National Security," *Journal of American History* 69 (1982): 638. On Attorney General Bonaparte's proposal, see Stolberg, "Policing the Twilight Zone," 395.

16. U.S. Constitution, amendment XVIII (1919). On the rationale behind the Eighteenth Amendment, see Richard F. Hamm, *Shaping the Eighteenth Amendment: Temperance Reform, Legal Culture, and the Polity, 1880–1920* (1995).

17. On Capone's life and times, see John Kobler, *Capone: The Life and World of Al Capone* (2003); Luciano J. Iorizzo, *Al Capone: A Biography* (2003); Laurence Bergreen, *Capone: The Man and His Era* (1996). These books provide most of the material on Capone referred to in this chapter.

18. On the North Side Gang, see the books on Capone cited earlier, in addition to Rose Keefe, *Guns and Roses: The Untold Story of Dean O'Banion, Chicago's Big Shot before Al Capone* (2003); T. J. English, *Paddy Whacked: The Untold History of the Irish American Gangster* (2005), 150–51 n. 2.

19. On the Tommy Gun, see William J. Helmer, *The Gun That Made the Twenties Roar* (1969); Jack Lewis et al., *The Gun Digest Book of Assault Weapons* (2007), 194; Frank Iannamico, *American Thunder: The Military Thompson Submachine Guns* (2000).

20. On the Gatling gun, see Barton C. Hacker and Margaret Vining, *American Military Technology: The Life Story of a Technology* (2006), 41–43; Joseph Berk, *The Gatling Gun: 19th Century Machine Gun to 21st Century Vulcan* (1991). On Maxim, see Malcolm Brown, "100 Years of 'Maxim's Killing Machine,'" *New York Times*, Nov. 26, 1985; John Ellis, *The Social History of the Machine Gun* (1981), 33–38; Edwin J. C. Sobey, *A Field Guide to Household Technology* (2007), 147.

21. See Helmer, *Gun That Made the Twenties Roar*.

22. On the St. Valentine's Day Massacre, see the Capone sources cited above, in addition to William J. Helmer and Arthur J. Bilek, *The St. Valentine's Day Massacre: The Untold Story of the Gangland Bloodbath That Brought Down Al Capone* (2003). The quotation comes from Ellis, *Social History of the Machine Gun*, 154.

23. On Berardi's photos of the massacre, see Tim Kirby, "Photojournalism: Diana Is Not Its Greatest Victim," *Independent*, Sept. 29, 1997, available at http://www.independent.co.uk/news/media/media-photojournalism-diana-is-not-its-greatest-victim-1241830.html. On the new technologies of the Prohibition era and their frequent use of crime stories, see Claire Bond Potter, *War on Crime: Bandits, G-Men, and the Politics of Mass Culture* (1998), 77.

24. On the Chicago Police Department's paucity of machine guns, see Ellis, *Social History of the Machine Gun*, 155.

25. On the Federal Aid Road Act of 1916 and the growth in automobile sales, see William Kaszynski, *The American Highway: The History and Culture of Roads in the United States* (2000), 52–54; Christopher Finch, *Highways to Heaven: The AUTObiography of America* (1992); Potter, *War on Crime*, 84, which also discusses the Rand McNally road atlas of 1924.

26. On Bonnie and Clyde, see John Treherne, *The Strange History of Bonnie and Clyde* (1984); Nate Hendley, *Bonnie and Clyde: A Biography* (2007), 60; Jeff Guinn, *Go Down Together: The True, Untold Story of Bonnie and Clyde* (2009). See also Potter, *War on Crime*, 75–105.

27. On Dillinger, see Potter, *War on Crime*, 146–50; Kenneth O'Reilly, "A New Deal for the FBI: The Roosevelt Administration, Crime Control, and National Security," *Journal of American History* 69 (1982): 642–44. On the other notorious criminals of the era who used Tommy Guns and cars, see Ellis, *Social History of the Machine Gun*, 157; Potter, *War on Crime*, 62.

28. See Potter, *War on Crime*, 76. Potter also discusses how Bonnie's sex and Clyde's viciousness were essential aspects of their fame. See ibid., 76–77.

29. On Clyde's theft of the National Guard Armory and the photos of Bonnie, see Hendley, *Bonnie and Clyde*, xvi, 60; Potter, *War on Crime*, 93.

30. On bystanders soaking up Bonnie's blood and cutting off Clyde's ear, see Potter, *War on Crime*, 104.

31. On the rise of pressure for federal action to combat the likes of Bonnie and Clyde and Capone, see Potter, *War on Crime*, 2, 8, 66. On Cummings, see ibid., 103; Stolberg, "Policing the Twilight Zone," 393, 394.

32. On the Great Depression and the crash of 1929, see John Kenneth Galbraith, *The Great Crash of 1929* (1997); Amity Shlaes, *The Forgotten Man: A New History of the Great Depression* (2008); Robert S. McElvaine, *The Great Depression: America 1929–1941* (1993).

33. On the New Deal, see Sidney M. Milkis and Jerome M. Mileur, eds., *The New Deal and the Triumph of Liberalism* (2002); Arthur M. Schlesinger, *The Coming of the New Deal, 1933–1935* (2003); Robert F. Himmelberg, *The Great Depression and the New Deal* (2001); William E. Leuchtenburg, *Franklin D. Roosevelt and the New Deal, 1932–1940* (2009).

34. FDR's speech is quoted in Stolberg, "Policing the Twilight Zone," 407. See also Potter, *War on Crime*, 105–9.

35. The quoted Roosevelt words come from his address at the National Parole Conference, April 17, 1939, available at http://www.presidency.ucsb.edu/ws/index.php?pid=15744. See also Stolberg, "Policing the Twilight Zone," 398.

36. On Cummings, see John R. Vile, *Great American Lawyers: An Encyclopedia* (2002), 150–52; Stolberg, "Policing the Twilight Zone," 400.

37. On the case in which Cummings refused to prosecute, see Vile, *Great American Lawyers*, 152.

38. On the ineffectiveness of harsher penalties during the Prohibition era, see Sasha Abramsky, *Hard Time Blues* (2002), 144. Cummings's "war on organized crime" speech is recounted in Potter, *War on Crime*, 110.

39. On Prohibition's failure and Liggett's testimony, see Potter, *War on Crime*, 11,

22. Rockefeller's letter is recounted in Daniel Okrent, *Great Fortune: The Epic of Rockefeller Center* (2003), 246–47.

40. Roosevelt's quip was recounted in Charles W. Bamforth, *Grape v. Grain: A Historical, Technological, and Social Comparison of Wine and Beer* 54 (2008).

41. On the old Bureau of Investigation, see O'Reilly, "New Deal for the FBI," 641; Potter, *War on Crime*, 40–42. See generally Richard Gid Powers, *Broken: The Troubled Past and Uncertain Future of the FBI* (2004).

42. On the growth of the Bureau of Investigation, see Stolberg, "Policing the Twilight Zone," 404–5. On Kelly's famous line, see Potter, *War on Crime*, 109.

43. The description of G-men as symbols of national generation is from Potter, *War on Crime*, 2. On G-men culture promotion, see O'Reilly, "New Deal for the FBI," 645; Powers, *G-Men*. On Hoover's rhetorical question about machine guns, see Rhodri Jeffreys-Jones, *The FBI: A History* (2007), 86.

44. On the National Crime Commission, see Stolberg, "Policing the Twilight Zone," 398–99; Alfred B. Rollins Jr., *Roosevelt and Howe* (2001), 201–2. On the attempt on Roosevelt's life, see Alexander DeConde, *Gun Violence in America: The Struggle for Control* (2001), 135.

45. On the 1919 and 1927 federal gun laws, see Zimring, "Firearms and Federal Law," 135–36.

46. On the Lochner era, see Howard Gillman, *The Constitution Besieged: The Rise and Demise of Lochner Era Police Powers Jurisprudence* (1993); G. Edward White, *The Constitution and the New Deal* (2002); Barry Cushman, *Rethinking the New Deal Court: The Structure of a Constitutional Revolution* (1998).

47. On the court-packing plan, see William E. Leuchtenburg, *The Supreme Court Reborn: The Constitutional Revolution in the Age of Roosevelt* (1996), 82–84; Burt Solomon, *FDR v. The Constitution: The Court-Packing Fight and the Triumph of Democracy* (2009).

48. On Cummings's decision to rely on the taxing power for gun control, see Brian L. Frye, "The Peculiar Story of United States v. Miller," *New York University Journal of Law and Liberty* 3 (2008): 62; Stephen P. Halbrook, "Congress Interprets the Second Amendment: Declarations by a Co-equal Branch on the Individual Right to Keep and Bear Arms," *Tennessee Law Review* 62 (1995): 606–7. Chief Justice John Marshall's words come from his famous opinion in *McCulloch v. Maryland*, 17 U.S. 316 (1819).

49. On Dillinger's spree and its effect on Congress's deliberations on Cummings's crime bills, see Stolberg, "Policing the Twilight Zone," 404; O'Reilly, "New Deal for the FBI," 642–44.

50. On the National Firearms Act of 1934, see Frye, "Peculiar Story," 60–63; Harry Henderson, *Gun Control* (2000), 16; DeConde, *Gun Violence in America*, 145.

51. On the belief that criminals would not comply with the law, see Frye, "Peculiar Story," 60–61.

52. On Capone, see the sources cites above. On Alcatraz and Homer Cummings, see Stolberg, "Policing the Twilight Zone," 406.

53. On FDR's statement about law enforcement facing machine-gun fire, see O'Reilly, "New Deal for the FBI," 643. On the effectiveness of the National Firearms Act, see Frye, "Peculiar Story," 62. On the Federal Firearms Act of

1938, see David T. Hardy, "The Firearms' Owners Protection Act: A Historical and Legal Perspective," *Cumberland Law Review* 17 (1988): 594.

54. On Cummings's pursuit and killing of Dillinger (and the rumor about the ear), see O'Reilly, "New Deal for the FBI," 644.

55. On the Sullivan Act, see Glenn H. Utter, "Sullivan Law," in *Encyclopedia of Gun Control and Gun Rights* (2000), 292–94. On Sullivan, see Daniel Czitrom, "Underworlds and Underdogs: Big Tim Sullivan and Metropolitan Politics in New York, 1889–1913," *Journal of American History* 78 (1991): 536. On the draft riots, see Paul Gilje, *Rioting in America* (1996), 92–94. On the growing concern with handguns, see DeConde, *Gun Violence in America*, 105–8.

56. On Marcus Loew, see Robert Sobel, *The Entrepreneurs: Explorations within the American Business Tradition* (2000), 247.

57. On the Sullivan law, see DeConde, *Gun Violence in America*, 108–9.

58. On the racism partially behind the Sullivan Act, see Robert J. Cottrol and Raymond T. Diamond, "Never Intended to Be Applied to the White Population: Firearms Regulation and Racial Disparity—The Redeemed South's Legacy to a National Jurisprudence?," *Chicago Kent Law Review* 70 (1995): 1307. On the ban on aliens owning pistols in states other than New York, see "The Uniform Firearms Act," *Virginia Law Review* 18 (1932): 907 n. 20 (listing California, Connecticut, North Dakota, Nevada, and West Virginia). On the discriminatory application of New York's gun laws, see DeConde, *Gun Violence in America*, 107.

59. On McKinley's assassination, see H. Wayne Morgan, *William McKinley and His America*, rev. ed. (2004). On the assassination attempt on Gaynor, see Edward Robb Ellis and Jeanyee Wong, *The Epic of New York City: A Narrative History* (2004), 481–83. The famous photo of Gaynor, with Lincoln rushing to his side, is available at http://iconicphotos.wordpress.com/2009/05/30/shooting-of-mayor-gaynor/.

60. On the murder rate spike in New York and the recommendation of the medical examiner for handgun regulation, see "Editorial," *New York Tribune*, Jan. 30, 1911, p. 3. On the *American Bar Association Journal*, see J. P. Chamberlain, "Legislatures and the Pistol Problem," *American Bar Association Journal* 11 (1925): 597. On the push in New York for reform, see DeConde, *Gun Violence in America*, 108.

61. On the Revolver Act, see National Conference of Commissioners on Uniform State Laws, *Handbook of Proceedings* (1924), 711–48; Charles V. Imlay, "The Uniform Firearms Act," *American Bar Association Journal* 12 (1926): 767.

62. A concise history of the National Conference of Commissioners can be found on the organization's website, at www.nccusl.org. When the conference first met in 1892, its title was the Conference of State Boards of Commissioners on Promoting Uniformity of Law in the U.S. A history of the National Conference of Commissioners, and by extension the uniform law movement, is Richard E. Coulson, "The National Conference of Commissions of Uniform State Laws and the Control of Law-Making—A Historical Essay," *Oklahoma City University Law Review* 16 (1991): 295. See also Rudolf H. Heimanson, "Federalism and the Uniform Law Movement," *New York Law School Law Review* 6 (1960): 161.

63. See Imlay, "Uniform Firearms Act," 767.

64. See ibid.

65. On the adoption of the Uniform Firearms Act, see Edward H. Sheppard, "Note, Control of Firearms," *Missouri Law Review* 34 (1969): 384 n. 184; "The Uniform Firearms Act," *Virginia Law Review* 18 (1932): 904 n. 1.

66. On the Uniform Firearms Act in New York, see "Uniform Firearms Act," 904 n. 1.

67. For an example of Frederick's being called "the best shot in America," see the testimony reported in U.S. Congress, *Hearings before the Committee on Ways and Means of the House of Representatives*, 73d Cong., 2d sess. (1934). That hearing transcript also provides some details about his background and his gun collection, and includes his testimony relating to the National Firearms Act of 1934. On his Olympic medals, see Jay V. Bavishi, *Ivies in Athens: The Deep Bond between Two Great Sporting Traditions: The Olympic Games and the Ivy League* (2006), 74. On the Campfire Club, see Stephen May, *Maverick Heart: The Further Adventures of Zane Grey* (2000), 19; U.S. Congress, *Hearings before the Committee on Expenditures in the Department of Commerce and Labor*, 62d Cong., 1st sess. (1911) (describing the Campfire Club's role in the protection of seals). On the North Dakota wildlife management area named after Frederick, see North Dakota Wildlife Management Area Guide, available at http://gf.nd.gov/hunting/wildlife.html.

68. On Imlay and Frederick on the National Conference of Commissioners, see U.S. Congress, *Hearings before the Committee on Ways and Means of the House of Representatives*, 73d Cong., 2d sess. (1934), 38; Alan C. Weber, "Where the NRA Stands on Gun Legislation," *American Rifleman*, March 1968, p. 22. On the NRA's promoting of model firearms legislation, see the congressional hearings cited above and Don B. Kates, "Handgun Prohibition and the Original Meaning of the Second Amendment," *Michigan Law Review* 82 (1983): 209–10.

69. On the NRA's support of the 1934 and 1938 federal gun control laws, see Weber, "Where the NRA Stands on Gun Legislation," 22. See also DeConde, *Gun Violence in America*, 141–43.

70. Frederick's quoted words come from Karl T. Frederick, "Pistol Regulation: Its Principles and History," a series of articles originally published in the *American Rifleman* and subsequently republished in three parts in the now defunct *American Journal of Police Science*. The articles can be found in *Journal of Criminal Law and Criminology* 22 (1931): 440; ibid., 22 (1932): 72; and ibid., 23 (1933): 531. The NRA's comment on the Sullivan law can be found in Osha Gray Davidson, *Under Fire: The NRA and the Battle for Gun Control* (1998), 29.

71. On the earlier, broader proposals to restrict handguns in federal law and the NRA's opposition, see Constance Emerson Crooker, *Gun Control and Gun Rights* (2003), 87; Lee Kennett and James LaVerne Anderson, *The Gun in America: The Origins of a National Dilemma* (1975), 208–11. The House Report on the National Firearms Act is quoted in Frye, "Peculiar Story," 62.

72. On Frederick's view of the Second Amendment, see Frederick, "Pistol Regulation," 531; U.S. Congress, *Hearings before the Committee on Ways and Means of the House of Representatives*, 73d Cong., 2d sess. (1934), 38.

73. On the history of *United States v. Miller*, see Frye, "Peculiar Story," 48.
74. On Jackson, see Eugene C. Gerhart, *America's Advocate: Robert H. Jackson* (1958); G. Edward White, "Personal versus Impersonal Judging: The Dilemmas of Robert Jackson," in *The American Judicial Tradition: Profile of Leading American Judges*, 2d ed. (1988), 230–50. See also Brief of the United States in *United States v. Miller*, 307 U.S. 174 (1939).
75. See *United States v. Miller*, 307 U.S. 174 (1939). On Taft's view of McReynolds, see Alpheus Thomas Mason, *William Howard Taft: Chief Justice* (1964), 215. On McReynolds's anti-Semitism, see Leonard Baker, *Brandeis and Frankfurter: A Dual Biography* (1984), 370.
76. See Frye, "Peculiar Story," 48. Frye argues that Judge Ragon was an ardent gun control advocate and possibly conspired with the Justice Department to free Layton and Miller to ensure that the case was appealed. If true, it is hard to understand why Ragon would have given Miller such lenient treatment for his gun crime once the Supreme Court had issued its ruling.
77. The quotations come from *Hickman v. Block*, 81 F.3d 98 (9th Cir. 1996) (internal quotations omitted).
78. All quotations from the Supreme Court oral argument come from the transcript available at http://www.supremecourtus.gov/oral_arguments/argument_transcripts/07-290.pdf. For purposes of clarity, I have cleaned up the transcript to eliminate stutters and repetitions.
79. The quotation comes from Gerald Gunther, "The Supreme Court, 1971 Term—Foreword: In Search of Evolving Doctrine on a Changing Court: A Model for a Newer Equal Protection," *Harvard Law Review* 86 (1972): 8. A few years back, I conducted an empirical study that showed that strict scrutiny was often, but definitely not always, fatal. See Adam Winkler, "Fatal in Theory and Strict in Fact: An Empirical Analysis of Strict Scrutiny in the Federal Courts," *Vanderbilt Law Review* 59 (2006): 793.
80. Joan Biskupic, "Rehnquist Left Supreme Court with Conservative Legacy," *USA Today*, Sept. 4, 2005.
81. On Webster, see Irving H. Bartlett, *Daniel Webster* (1978); Robert V. Remini, *Daniel Webster* (1997). On the *Dartmouth College* case, see Maurice G. Baxter, *Daniel Webster and the Supreme Court* (1966); Francis N. Stites, *Private Interest and Public Gain: the Dartmouth College Case, 1819* (1972). On Webster's speech in the Senate, see Allan Nevins, *Ordeal of the Union*, vol. 1, *Fruits of Manifest Destiny, 1847–1852* (1947), 288.
82. On Webster's oral argument in the *Dartmouth College* case and Joseph Story's reaction to it, see Leonard Baker, "Daniel Webster and the Dartmouth Case," *Litigation* 3 (1976): 35.

Chapter 8: BY ANY MEANS NECESSARY

1. Interview with Alan Gura, Jan. 24, 2009.
2. Levy's remark is recounted in Paul Duggan, "For Young Area Lawyer, the Supreme Compliment," *Washington Post*, March 18, 2008, p. B1.
3. The quotation comes from Duggan, ibid.

4. Ibid.; Interview with Alan Gura, Jan. 24, 2009.

5. All quotations from the Supreme Court oral argument come from the transcript available at http://www.supremecourtus.gov/oral_arguments/argument_transcripts/07-290.pdf. For purposes of clarity, I have cleaned up the transcript to eliminate stutters or repetitions.

6. Suprynowicz's complaints can be found in Vin Suprynowicz, "'And Every Other Terrible Instrument,'" *Las Vegas Review-Journal*, March 23, 2008, available at http://www.lvrj.com/opinion/16936861.html. Gura told me about the hate mail he received in interview with Alan Gura, Jan. 24, 2009.

7. Interview with Alan Gura, Jan. 24, 2009.

8. Larry Pratt, "The Uncompromisable Right to Keep and Bear Arms: Preparing Now for the Battles That Are Sure to Come," posted on the Gun Owners of America website in June 2008, available at http://gunowners.org/by-larry-pratt/. On the NRA's comments, see Brian Lyman, "Alabama Gung-ho for Guns," *Mobile Register*, July 20, 2008, p. A1. In 1990, the NRA asked a federal court to overturn the federal law banning the sale of new machine guns to civilians. See Michael Isikoff, "NRA Pushes Machine Gun Ownership," *Washington Post*, Dec. 28, 1990, p. A17.

9. See Richard Poe, *The Seven Myths of Gun Control: Reclaiming the Truth about Guns, Crime, and the Second Amendment* (2001), 175–83; Ted Nugent, "A 'Supreme' Court? I Can Do Better," available at http://www.rollingstone.com/rockdaily/index.php/2008/06/27/ted-nugent-takes-aim-at-supreme-court-obama-in-gun-crazy-rant/.

10. Gura's statements in this paragraph come from interview with Alan Gura, Jan. 24, 2009; Brian Doherty, "How the Second Amendment Was Restored: The Inside Story of How a Gang of Libertarian Lawyers Made Constitutional History," *Reason*, Dec. 2008, available at http://www.reason.com/news/show/129991.html.

11. My account of the Black Panthers was informed by Bobby Seale, *Seize the Time: The Story of the Black Panther Party and Huey P. Newton* (1991); Huey P. Newton, *Revolutionary Suicide* (1973); David Hilliard and Kent Zimmerman, *Huey* (2006); Curtis J. Austin, *Up Against the Wall: Violence in the Making and Unmaking of the Black Panther Party* (2006); Charles Earl Jones, *The Black Panther Party* (1998); Huey P. Newton et al., *The Black Panther Leaders Speak* (1976); Cynthia Deitle Leonardatos, "California's Attempt to Disarm the Black Panthers," *San Diego Law Review* 36 (1999): 947; Jane Rhodes, "Fanning the Flames of Racial Discord: The National Press and the Black Panther Party," *International Journal of Press/Politics* 4 (1999): 95; Donna Murch, "The Campus and the Street: Race, Migration, and the Origins of the Black Panther Party in Oakland, CA," *Souls* 9 (2007): 333.

12. On the freedom riders, see Raymond Arsenault, *Freedom Riders* (2006). On the bombing of the Sixteenth Street Baptist Church, see David J. Garrow, *Bearing the Cross: Martin Luther King, Jr., and the Southern Christian Leadership Conference* (1986). On freedom summer, see Doug McAdam, *Freedom Summer* (1990).

13. On the Watts riot, see Liza N. Burby, *The Watts Riot* (1997).

14. On police hostility to the civil rights movement, see John R. Salter Jr., "Social

Justice Community Organizing and the Necessity for Protective Firearms," in *The Gun Culture and Its Enemies*, ed. William R. Tonso (1989), 19; Leonardatos, "California's Attempt to Disarm the Black Panthers," 951.

15. On the police problems in Oakland in the early 1960s, see Murch, "Campus and the Street," 334–37. On the police killings of 1966 and the Panthers' belief that the police were trying to keep the black community down, see Austin, *Up Against the Wall*, 43, 53, 59–60.

16. Seale's words are recounted in Seale, *Seize the Time*, 85. On Malcolm X, see Peter Louis Goldman, *The Death and Life of Malcolm X* (1979). For Malcolm X's statement, see Austin, *Up Against the Wall*, 31. Sartre's use of the "by any means necessary" idea can be found in *Dirty Hands*, act 5, scene 3 (1948), reprinted in Jean-Paul Sartre, *No Exit and Three Other Plays* (1955).

17. For Newton's and Seale's statements, see Austin, *Up Against the Wall*, 32, 164. On Malcolm X and the Second Amendment, see Alexander DeConde, *Gun Violence in America: The Struggle for Control* (2001), 173.

18. On the black panther of the Lowndes County Freedom Organization and Newton's Black Panther Party of Self-Defense, see Austin, *Up Against the Wall*, 34.

19. See ibid., 92–94. On Newton and Seale's sales of Mao's book, see Seale, *Seize the Time*, 79–81.

20. See Austin, *Up Against the Wall*, 49, 61, 156.

21. On Martin Luther King and guns, see Garrow, *Bearing the Cross*, 62, 69; Austin, *Up Against the Wall*, 159. On the possession of firearms for self-defense among civil rights activists generally, see John Salter and Don B. Kates Jr., "The Necessity of Access to Firearms by Dissenters and Minorities When Government Is Unwilling or Unable to Protect," in *Restricting Handguns: The Politics of Liberation in America*, ed. Don B. Kates Jr. (1979), 185, 186.

22. Newton's statement is from Austin, *Up Against the Wall*, 54.

23. My account of the Panthers' visit to the state Capitol in Sacramento was informed by the sources listed in n. 11 above, in addition to these contemporaneous newspaper accounts: Jerry Rankin, "Heavily Armed Negro Group Walks into Assembly Chamber," *Los Angeles Times*, May 3, 1967, p. A3; Martin Smith, "Capitol Gun-Toters Draw Solon's Fury," *Sacramento Bee*, May 3, 1967, p. A1.

24. Information on California's Capitol Building can be found on the website of the California State Capitol Museum, http://capitolmuseum.ca.gov.

25. On the Dowell protests, see Seale, *Seize the Time*, 146–48.

26. On Mulford's bill to fight the free-speech agitators at Berkeley, see David B. Frohnmayer, "Comment: The University and the Public: The Right of Access by Nonstudents to University Property," *California Law Review* 54 (1966): 132.

27. On Mulford's calling into the radio program, see Newton, *Revolutionary Suicide*, 150–51; Hilliard and Zimmerman, *Huey*, 62.

28. On Newton's suggestion to Seale that the Panthers visit the state Capitol, see Seale, *Seize the Time*, 148–49.

29. See Rankin, "Heavily Armed Negro Group Walks into Assembly Chamber," A3.

30. The headline, which referred to the Panthers' carrying guns, appeared in the *San Francisco Sunday Examiner and Chronicle*, April 30, 1967. The Newton statement is from Austin, *Up Against the Wall*, 78.

31. On California's gun control laws before the Mulford Act, see Leonardatos, "California's Attempt to Disarm the Black Panthers," 969.

32. On Mulford's racial focus, see ibid., 973.

33. Ibid., 980.

34. On Reagan's remark upon signing the Mulford Act, see "Reagan Signs Loaded Gun Bill into Law," *Los Angeles Times*, July 29, 1967, p. A2.

35. On the Mulford Act's putting a stop to the Panthers' armed police patrols but some members still carrying guns, see Austin, *Up Against the Wall*, 119, 166. On Newton's shootout with the police, see ibid., 88. On other Panther shootouts with police, see Leonardatos, "California's Attempt to Disarm the Black Panthers," 966.

36. On Cleaver's leadership of the Panthers, see Austin, *Up Against the Wall*, 74f.

37. On COINTELPRO, see Cartha "Deke" DeLoach, *Hoover's FBI* (1995), 291; Nelson Blackstock, *COINTELPRO* (1988), 14.

38. On guns in the postwar era, see DeConde, *Gun Violence in America*, 155–56.

39. On JFK and Oswald, see William J. Vizzard, *Shots in the Dark: The Policy, Politics, and Symbolism of Gun Control* (2000), 93; Mark Fuhrman, *A Simple Act of Murder* (2006), 68–70.

40. On Dodd's effort to secure new federal gun control, see Vizzard, *Shots in the Dark*, 93–97.

41. The description of Dodd comes from Robert T. Mann, *Legacy to Power* (2003), 260. On Colt revolvers, see Herbert G. Houze et al., *Samuel Colt: Arms, Art, and Invention* (2006). On Winchester rifles, see Harold Francis Williamson, *Winchester: The Gun That Won the West* (1952).

42. On Dodd's background, see Mann, *Legacy to Power*, 260–64; Jay Robert Nash, *Citizen Hoover* (1972), 234. On the Little Bohemia raid, see John Fox, "FBI Raid at Little Bohemia," available at http://www.fbi.gov/multimedia/bohemia042309/transcript.htm.

43. On Johnson's legislative success generally and his push for gun control, see Spitzer, *The Politics of Gun Control* (1995), 112, 121.

44. See Harvard Sitkoff, *The Struggle for Black Equality, 1954–1992*, rev. ed. (1993), 187. On the Newark and Detroit riots, see ibid., 188–89; Austin, *Up Against the Wall*, 81–84. On the man whose Molotov cocktail burned down his own home, see the *Kerner Commission Report*, available at http://www.eisenhowerfoundation.org/docs/kerner.pdf.

45. On Brown's incitement to riot, see Sitkoff, *Struggle for Black Equality*, 203.

46. On the Stanford Research Institute's report on the 1967 riots, entitled "Firearms, Violence, and Civil Disorders," see *Federal Firearms Legislation: Hearings before the Subcomm. to Investigate Juvenile Delinquency of the Comm. on the Judiciary*, U.S. Senate, 90th Cong., 2d sess. (1968), 295–300.

47. On the rise in gun sales, especially handguns, between 1958 and 1968, see Peter Squires, *Gun Culture or Gun Control?* (2000), 62–63. On Dodd's reliance on FBI statistics, see *Federal Firearms Legislation* (statement of Senator Dodd). On the growth of imported firearms, see Franklin E. Zimring, "Firearms and Federal Law: The Gun Control Act of 1968," *Journal of Legal Studies* 4 (1975): 144.

48. On Dodd's ethics scandal, see Mann, *Legacy to Power*, 261–64.

49. On how the King and Kennedy assassinations changed the dynamics of gun control legislation, see Vizzard, *Shots in the Dark*, 95–97.

50. See Robert Sherrill, *The Saturday Night Special* (1973), 52.

51. Dingell's remarks about the Nazis can be found in *Federal Firearms Legislation* (statement of Representative Dingell). On Dodd's translation of Nazi guns laws, see ibid., 489 (Exhibit no. 62).

52. Spitzer's view was expressed in Spitzer, *Politics of Gun Control*, 125. Johnson's disappointment is recounted in Samuel C. Patterson and Keith R. Eakins, "Congress and Gun Control," in *The Changing Politics of Gun Control*, ed. John M. Bruce and Clyde Wilcox (1998), 45, 52.

53. Orth's testimony in Congress is recounted in Osha Gray Davidson, *Under Fire: The NRA and the Battle for Gun Control* (1998), 30. On Orth's moderate support of the final Gun Control Act, see "Congress Threshes Out Gun Law Issue," *American Rifleman*, Nov. 1968, pp. 22–25; Alan C. Webber, "Where the NRA Stands on Gun Legislation," ibid., March 1968, p. 22.

54. On the vigorous opposition of some in the NRA, see Patterson and Eakins, "Congress and Gun Control," 45, 50. On the anti-gun control positions of the specialized gun press, see Vizzard, *Shots in the Dark*, 94. For the quotations regarding the paper targets and ducks and discussion of the effort to fire Orth, see Davidson, *Under Fire*, 30–31.

55. On the view of gun enthusiasts that gun control of the 1960s was designed to harass gun owners, see Allen Rostron, "Incrementalism, Comprehensive Rationality, and the Future of Gun Control," *Maryland Law Review* 67 (2008): 563. On the dissatisfaction of gun owners generally with the Gun Control Act, see Davidson, *Under Fire*, 53–59.

56. On ATF's history, see its website, at http://www.atf.gov/about/atfhistory.htm; Jim Moore, *Very Special Agents: The Inside Story of America's Most Controversial Law Enforcement Agency—The Bureau of Alcohol, Tobacco, and Firearms* (2001). On ATF's being ill prepared to oversee licensing of gun dealers, see Vizzard, *Shots in the Dark*, 106–25.

57. On ATF's problems with gun owners over licensing, see Davidson, *Under Fire*, 49–51; Vizzard, *Shots in the Dark*, 124. For examples of hard-liners' complaints, see ibid., 123–26.

58. On the Ballew controversy, see *Ballew v. United States*, 389 F. Supp. 47 (D. Maryland 1975); Moore, *Very Special Agents*, 144–46. For an example of the continuing misrepresentation of the incident, see James R. Lewis, *From the Ashes: Making Sense of Waco* (1994), 89–90. On William Loeb's characterization of ATF, see Joan Burbick, *Gun Show Nation: Gun Culture and American Democracy* (2006), 81.

59. On Scott's call for repeal of the Gun Control Act, see Woodson D. Scott, "A Statement," *American Rifleman*, March 1980, p. 16. On Dingell's advice to the NRA about lobbying, see Richard Feldman, *Ricochet: Confessions of a Gun Lobbyist* (2008), 42.

60. On Scalia's use of oral argument to persuade other justices, see Joan Biskupic, *American Original: The Life and Constitution of Supreme Court Justice Antonin Scalia* (2009), 214.

61. The empirical study determining that Scalia was the funniest justice is Jay Wexler, "Laugh Track," *Green Bag*, 2d ser., 9 (2005): 59.

62. On Breyer's lengthy questions, see Jess Bravin, "Judging the Justices: Some Statistics from 2009–2010 Oral Arguments," *Law Blog, Wall Street Journal*, available at http://blogs.wsj.com/law/2010/07/19/judging-the-justices-some-statistics-from-2009-10-oral-arguments.

Chapter 9: DECISION

1. On the conference, see Del Dickson, *The Supreme Court in Conference, 1940–1985* (2001), 3–21.

2. On the role of the junior justice in the conference, see ibid., 5–6.

3. On the rituals of the conference, see ibid., 4–11.

4. The Madeira story is recounted ibid., 36.

5. For media accounts of the oral argument, see Robert Barnes, "Justices Appear Skeptical of D.C.'s Handgun Ban," *Washington Post*, March 19, 2008, p. A1; Linda Greenhouse, "Court Weighs Right to Guns, and Its Limits," *New York Times*, March 19, 2008, p. A1. Dellinger's view was shared with me in interview with Walter Dellinger, Sept. 24, 2009.

6. See Tom Goldstein, "Wild Opinion Speculation," *SCOTUSblog*, June 23, 2008, available at http://www.scotusblog.com/2008/06/wild-opinion-speculation/.

7. A transcript of Scalia's speech at the Waldorf-Astoria is available at http://www.manhattan-institute.org/html/wl1997.htm.

8. See Margaret Talbot, "Supreme Confidence: The Jurisprudence of Antonin Scalia," *The New Yorker*, March 28, 2005, p. 40; Joan Biskupic, *American Original: The Life and Constitution of Supreme Court Justice Antonin Scalia* (2009), 4, 17, 95. Scalia's comment comes from a radio program on which he was a guest. See "Supreme Court Justice Antonin Scalia: Transcript," *Mad about Music*, available at http://www.wqxr.org/programs/mam/2010/jan/03/transcript/.

9. Scalia's description comes from Lesley Stahl, "Justice Scalia on the Record," *60 Minutes*, Sept. 14, 2008, available at http://www.cbsnews.com/stories/2008/04/24/60minutes/main4040290.shtml.

10. See http://www.manhattan-institute.org/html/wl1997.htm.

11. See Dennis J. Goldford, *The American Constitution and the Debate over Originalism* (2005), 28.

12. See Biskupic, *American Original*, 8.

13. See ibid., 283.

14. See, e.g., "Fox News/Opinion Dynamics Poll," May 18–19, 2010, available at http://www.pollingreport.com/court.htm. On the growing support for originalism among Americans and its causes, see generally Jamal Greene, "Selling Originalism," *Georgetown Law Journal* 97 (2009): 695.

15. See Jeffrey Toobin, *The Nine: Inside the Secret World of the Supreme Court* (2007), 65, 368–69; Adam Winkler, "Justice Scalia and the Coarsening of American Culture," *Huffington Post*, July 1, 2006, available at http://www.huffingtonpost.com/adam-winkler/justice-scalia-the-coarse_b_24203.html; Biskupic, *American Original*, 131.

16. On Scalia and Ginsburg, see Biskupic, *American Original*, 277–78.

17. On Brennan and his clerks, see Stephen J. Wermiel, "William Joseph Brennan, Jr.," in *The Supreme Court Justices: A Biographical Dictionary*, ed. Melvin I. Urofsky (1994), 49, 53. See Biskupic, *American Original*, 132.

18. On Scalia's chambers, see Toobin, *The Nine*, 234. On his speech about hunting, see Biskupic, *American Original*, 346.

19. Interview with Alan Gura, Jan. 24, 2009.

20. On the libertarian lawyers' encounters with Suter, see interview with Clark Neily, Sept. 25, 2009.

21. Interview with Alan Gura, Jan. 24, 2009.

22. Interview with Clark Neily, Sept. 25, 2009.

23. See *District of Columbia v. Heller*, 554 U.S. 570 (2008).

24. See James Taranto, "Alan Gura: How a Young Lawyer Saved the Second Amendment," *Wall Street Journal*, July 19, 2008, p. A7.

25. Interview with Alan Gura, Jan. 24, 2009.

26. See Linda Greenhouse, "Three Defining Opinions," *New York Times*, July 13, 2008, p. WK4; Bret Boyce, "Heller, McDonald and Originalism," *2010 Cardozo Law Review De Novo* 2, available at http://www.cardozolawreview .com/index.php?option=com_content&view=article&id=131:boyce20102& catid=20:firearmsinc&Itemid=20; Eric Posner, "Will Heller Implode?," *Slate*, June 29, 2008, available at http://www.slate.com/blogs/blogs/convictions/ archive/2008/06/29/will-heller-implode.aspx.

27. See Greenhouse, "Three Defining Opinions," WK4; Tony Mauro, "Supreme Court Strikes Down D.C. Gun Ban," *Legal Times*, June 27, 2008, available at http://www.law.com/jsp/article.jsp?id=1202422582170 (quoting McGinnis).

28. See Elaine McArdle, "In Inaugural Vaughan Lecture, Scalia Defends the 'Methodology of Originalism,'" *Harvard Law School News*, Oct. 3, 2008, available at http://www.law.harvard.edu/news/spotlight/constitutional-law/ scalia-vaughan-lecture.html.

29. Debra Cassens Weiss, "Second Amendment Ruling Is Justice Scalia's Originalism 'Legacy,'" *ABA Journal Weblog*, June 27, 2008, available at http://www .abajournal.com/news/article/second_amendment_ruling_is_justice_scal ias_originalism_legacy/.

30. On the Mayflower, see Keith McClinsey, *Washington D.C.'s Mayflower Hotel* (2005). I attended this convention.

31. See Adam Liptak, "Ruling on Guns Elicits Rebuke from the Right," *New York Times*, Oct. 21, 2008.

32. On Posner, see Robert F. Blomquist, "Introduction: Renaissance Judge," in *The Quotable Judge Posner: Selections From Twenty-five Years of Judicial Opinions* (2010).

33. Richard Posner, "In Defense of Looseness: The Supreme Court and Gun Control," *New Republic*, Aug. 27, 2008.

34. J. Harvie Wilkinson III, "Of Guns, Abortion, and the Unraveling Rule of Law," *Virginia Law Review* 95 (2009): 253.

35. For a transcript of Lund's speech, see "Civil Rights: The Heller Case— Minutes from a Convention of the Federalist Society," *New York University Journal of Law and Liberty* 4 (2009): 293. For Lund's disagreement

with Wilkinson's criticism of *Heller,* see Nelson Lund and David B. Kopel, "Unraveling Judicial Restraint: Guns, Abortion, and the Faux Conservatism of J. Harvie Wilkinson, III," *Journal of Law and Politics* 25 (2009): 1.

36. See also Adam Winkler, "Heller's Catch-22," *UCLA Law Review* 56 (2009): 1551.

37. See The Uniform Militia Act of 1792, 1 U.S. Stat. 271, passed May 8, 1792. See also Robert J. Spitzer, *Gun Control: A Documentary and Reference Guide* (2009), 48.

38. See Winkler, "Heller's Catch-22," 1551.

39. See ibid.

40. See ibid.

41. *McDonald v. City of Chicago,* 130 S. Ct. 3020 (2010).

42. See Liptak, "Ruling on Guns."

43. Interview with Dennis Henigan, Dec. 2, 2009.

44. On the Little Rock Nine, the famous photograph, and the relationship between Eckford and Bryan, see David Margolick, "Through a Lens, Darkly," *Vanity Fair,* Sept. 24, 2007, available at http://www.vanityfair.com/politics/features/2007/09/littlerock200709?printable=true&currentPage=all#ixzz0zt ZmqkGn; Elizabeth Jacoway, *Turn Away Thy Son: Little Rock, the Crisis That Shocked the Nation* (2007).

45. On Bates, see her memoir, Daisy Bates, *The Long Shadow of Little Rock: A Memoir* (1987).

46. Wilkinson, "Of Guns, Abortion, and the Unraveling Rule of Law," 253.

47. See Mark Greenberg and Harry Litman, "Rethinking Gun Violence," working paper available at http://papers.ssrn.com/sol3/papers.cfm?abstract_id=1531371.

48. Dennis A. Henigan, "The Heller Paradox: A Response to Robert Levy," *Cato Unbound CATO,* July 16, 2008, available at http://www.cato-unbound.org/2008/07/16/dennis-henigan/the-heller-paradox-a-response-to-robert-levy/; Jacob Sullum, "Second Sight," *Reason,* Oct. 23, 2001, available at http://www.reason.com/news/show/35880.html; Glenn Harlan Reynolds, "Letter to the Editor," *Reason,* June 1996, p. 10, available at http://www.reason.com/news/show/29954.html.

49. See Tom W. Smith, *2001 National Gun Policy Survey of the National Opinion Research Center* (2001) 34, available at http://www.mindchanging.com/politics/guncontrolsurvey.pdf.

50. See Cass A. Sunstein, "Second Amendment Minimalism: *Heller* as *Griswold,*" *Harvard Law Review* 122 (2008): 246; Jane S. Schacter, "Courts and the Politics of Backlash: Marriage Equality Litigation, Then and Now," *Southern California Law Review* 82 (2009): 1153; Michael J. Klarman, "*Brown* and *Lawrence* (and *Goodridge*)," *Michigan Law Review* 104 (2005): 431.

EPILOGUE

1. Interview with Alan Gura, Jan. 24, 2009.

2. Interview with Clark Neily, Sept. 25, 2009.

3. Ibid.

INDEX

ABOUT THE AUTHOR

ADAM WINKLER is a professor at UCLA School of Law, where he specializes in constitutional law. He lives in Los Angeles with his wife and daughter.